Florida's Gubernatorial Politics
in the Twentieth Century

For Coby,
Beth Ann, Eric and
Daniel,

who saw the birth of the book, and
in hopes that the contents well
make some sense to you.

Love,

Richard

April, 1981

Florida's Gubernatorial Politics
in the Twentieth Century

David R. Colburn

and

Richard K. Scher

A Florida State University Book
University Presses of Florida
Tallahassee

Library of Congress Cataloging in Publication Data

Colburn, David R.
   "Florida's gubernatorial politics in the twentieth
century.

   Bibliography: p.
   Includes index.
   1. Florida—Governors. 2. Florida—Politics
and government. I. Scher, Richard K., joint
author. II. Title.
JK4451.C64   353.975903'1   80–10277
ISBN 0–8130–0644–9

University Presses of Florida is the central agency for scholarly publishing of the State of
Florida's university system. Its offices are located at 15 NW 15th Street, Gainesville, FL
32603. Works published by University Presses of Florida are evaluated and selected for
publication by a faculty editorial committee of any one of Florida's nine public universities:
Florida A&M University (Tallahassee), Florida Atlantic University (Boca Raton), Florida
International University (Miami), Florida State University (Tallahassee), University of
Central Florida (Orlando), University of Florida (Gainesville), University of North Florida
(Jacksonville), University of South Florida (Tampa), University of West Florida (Pensacola).

Typography by American Graphics Corporation
Fort Lauderdale, Florida

PRINTED IN U.S.A.

Acknowledgments

ONE of the most enjoyable aspects of any project of this sort comes at the end when you can pause and express your thanks to all those who have provided assistance. We would like to express our appreciation to the library staffs at Florida State University, the Florida State Division of Archives and Records Management, Florida State Library, and the University of South Florida for their friendly cooperation. We would like to note a special debt to Elizabeth Alexander and Ellen Hodges of the P. K. Yonge Library of Florida History, University of Florida, who were unfailing in their assistance for four years. We appreciate the help of Joan Morris of the State Photographic Archives, Strozier Library, Florida State University, Tallahassee, and Steve Kerber, P. K. Yonge Library of Florida History, University of Florida, Gainesville, for help in selecting illustrations.

We also owe a special debt to our students who took time away from their studies and recreation to run down books, examine newspapers, and assist us with interviews: Edward Kallal, Bonnie Fleming Wilson, Patricia Willis, Adele Setnor Stone, and Karen Davis Rosenberg.

Our colleagues who read and reread this manuscript when they had more pressing things to do—James Button, Earl Black, Manning Dauer, Herbert Doherty, Marian Irish, William Kelso, George Pozzetta, and Samuel Proctor—we thank for their support, patience, and friendship. In particular we are grateful to George Pozzetta, who shared with us many of his notes and ideas on immigrant groups in Florida, and to Marian Irish, who spent many hours reading and critiquing the manuscript. We are especially indebted to Manning Dauer, who helped us develop a framework for this study and who assisted us in the preparation of our introductory and concluding chapters. His many stories of Florida governors also kept us entertained when the project was getting tedious. We also wish to thank the Institute for Support of American Culture for its critical support.

We would also like to acknowledge our debt to our typists, Adrienne Turner and Karen Griggs, who insisted on doing a professional job, despite our best efforts to the contrary.

Our research was greatly aided by grants from the Division of Sponsored Research and the Social Sciences Research Council at the University of Florida. Parts of this book have appeared in article form: "Florida Gubernatorial Politics: The Fuller Warren Years," *The Florida Historical Quarterly* 53 (April 1975): 389–408; "Race Relations and Florida Gubernatorial Politics since the *Brown* Decision," *The Florida Historical Quarterly* 55 (October 1976): 153–69; and "Aftermath of the *Brown* Decision: The Politics of Interposition," *Tequesta* 37 (1977): 62-81. We thank these journals for giving us permission to reprint these materials.

We also thank Malcolm Johnson, former editor of the *Tallahassee Democrat,* for the corrections he helped us to make in a late stage of proofs of this book. For errors of fact or interpretation that may remain, the authors are alone responsible.

We both owe a special debt of thanks to our families: to wife Marion Colburn for her constant encouragement, and children—Margaret, David, and Katherine Colburn—for those long wrestling matches that kept their father sore but also relaxed, and to Gregory Scher, whose faith in his father helped enormously during some bleak times, a very special "thank you." We dedicate this book to them.

Contents

Introduction   1

PART I: Demographic Setting

1. Florida in the Twentieth Century: An Overview
   of Its Development   11
2. Origins and Backgrounds of Florida's Governors   33
3. Gubernatorial Campaigning in Florida   59

PART II: The Structure and Processes of
the Governor's Office

4. Constitutional Setting and Structure of the
   Governor's Office   101
5. The Executive Office in Florida   115
6. The Governor and the Legislature   155

PART III: Gubernatorial Initiatives

7. Economic Development   187
8. Race Relations   220
9. Education   237
10. Criminal Justice   259

PART IV: Appraisal

11. Florida's Governors: A Critical Evaluation 275

Notes 297

Bibliographic Essay 321

Index 331

To
Marion, Margaret, David, and
Katherine Colburn
and
Gregory Scher

Introduction

UNTIL quite recently there were relatively few full-length scholarly studies of gubernatorial politics. Presidential and mayoral politics have been examined with much greater frequency. Even those studies which focused on state politics tended to ignore gubernatorial leadership. The historical literature on state governors has also been quite limited and has usually been confined to biographies of particular executives. Further, the general historical surveys, such as Louisiana State University's *History of the South* series, have dealt only peripherally with the executive office.

This situation seems to be changing, and prospects for such gubernatorial studies in the future appear quite promising. There is a growing realization that the role of the governor is becoming more important in the political life not only of the states but of the nation as well. The emergence on the national scene of many prominent governors—Nelson Rockefeller of New York, Ronald Reagan of California, John Connally of Texas, George Wallace of Alabama, Jerry Brown of California, Jimmy Carter of Georgia, and Reubin Askew of Florida—underscores how far this development has progressed. Moreover, the impact of governors on their states is being reexamined, and their importance as leaders and problem solvers is being looked at with a fresh eye. The governor's significance has been accentuated by the realization that the nation's problems cannot be solved by Washington alone.

Although there has not been any deluge of new works on gubernatorial politics, governors' increased visibility has led to Thad Beyle and J. Oliver Williams' study, *The American Governor in Behavioral Perspective* (New York, 1972) and to Earl Black's *Southern Governors and Civil Rights* (Cambridge, 1976) and has also nurtured this study.

We have written this book with the view that the governor is primarily a problem solver. It is our assumption that his principal function is to define the

1

problems of his state and to establish programs to alleviate them. In doing this, he does not operate in a vacuum; he must work closely with other political figures, including legislators, interest groups, local and federal officials, party functionaries, and other members of the executive branch. It is this interaction between the governor and other political groups and individuals that creates the flesh and blood of gubernatorial politics. The extent to which the governor can persuade the public and its representatives to follow his direction and implement his programs is the most important measure of his leadership.

On the basis of this perspective, our study of Florida gubernatorial politics has proved most intriguing. Throughout the twentieth century Florida has had the most fragmented political structure in the South. Democratic gubernatorial primaries with six or more candidates have been the rule rather than the exception. This atomized system has seriously undermined the independence of the governor by forcing him to make promises to various political factions before he can be nominated. The governor's independence has also been impaired by an outdated constitution, which created a collegial executive branch (the cabinet), strengthened the legislature at the expense of the governor, and, until recently, made him ineligible to succeed himself. Limited in these many ways, the Florida chief executive has usually found it difficult to govern effectively.

Our aim in this book is to demonstrate how Florida's governors have functioned in such a political environment in the twentieth century. We try to show not just how gubernatorial politics "work" but how individual men governed the state during their terms of office. One of our assumptions is that individuals do make a difference in politics. While institutional and aggregate studies are useful, we feel it would be a serious mistake to ignore the contribution of individuals to their political environment. Finally, since we examined the politics of the Florida governor over three-quarters of a century, we are in a position to judge, historically, his impact on the state, the trends of gubernatorial leadership, and the changes occurring in the office itself.

We believe it essential to make explicit at the outset the framework of our study. Scholars use theoretical models and paradigms for a variety of purposes, including the generation of hypotheses and the development of general theory. Our framework, shown in chart 1, has a more limited purpose but, we hope, a more specific and immediately useful one. We provide a broad view of the Florida governorship and place it in the context of the state's twentieth-century social, political, and economic fabric. We also examine interrelationships among the governor's personal background, state politics, the executive office, and policy issues, thereby allowing a thorough consideration of these parts without losing sight of their relationship to the whole. Thus, this framework is not to be regarded as a rigorous systems model, as it has been developed in social science,[1] but as a logical guide through the tangle of Florida gubernatorial politics. Most important, our schema permits a qualitatively systematic gathering and analysis of data, thus aiding in making judgments about the relative effectiveness of the office and those who have occupied it.[2]

The first part of our analysis comprises those factors which have helped shape Florida as a political entity and which have influenced the personal and political development of its governors. These conditions are not immutable. Indeed, they change periodically as the state undergoes socioeconomic and political metamorphoses and as individual governors bring new ideas and forms of leadership to the office.

In this section we examine the demographic setting as it relates to Florida's economic, social, and political development in this century. We believe demographic factors are often crucial in determining the opportunities available to a particular governor. If, for example, the state is in the throes of economic recession or depression, the chances for gubernatorial initiatives are severely impaired, no matter what the governor's disposition. We discuss population patterns (especially migration and urbanization), economic development and changes in the economic condition of the state, and party politics and political traditions. We also briefly assess some of Florida's traditional problem areas which have touched on gubernatorial politics: economic issues, race, and education. Making these explicit enables us later on to appraise how effectively governors have responded to state needs.

The second part of the demographic setting in our analysis of the backgrounds of Florida's governors deals with their early lives and political experiences and shows the "ladder of success" they had to climb toward the governorship. We are especially concerned with investigating possible patterns to be discerned from this material.

In the third chapter in the section we examine campaigning. The principal question explored is how candidates for the office mobilize voters and assemble winning coalitions. It is our contention that the type of campaign a governor conducts, the promises he makes, and the alliances he builds provide a framework for his entire administration.

The second section is an investigation of the major features of the Florida governorship. Through structural/functional analysis we seek to determine the major functions of the office, its inherent strengths and weaknesses, and, most important, how governors have dealt with the requirements, assets, and liabilities of the Florida governorship. We seek to avoid a purely institutional or static analysis by examining, over time, the actual dynamics of the office, its operations and processes.

We deal with the constitutional setting of the office, with emphasis on the legal context which helps shape the behavior of governors, and with its administrative and legislative functions. These two are perhaps the most

CHART 1. An Analysis of Gubernatorial Leadership

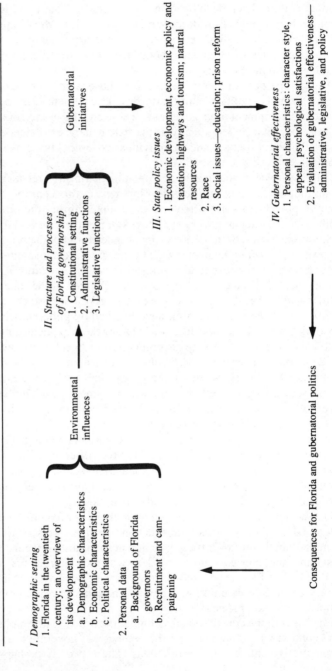

I. Demographic setting
1. Florida in the twentieth century: an overview of its development
   a. Demographic characteristics
   b. Economic characteristics
   c. Political characteristics
2. Personal data
   a. Background of Florida governors
   b. Recruitment and campaigning

Environmental influences

II. Structure and processes of Florida governorship
1. Constitutional setting
2. Administrative functions
3. Legislative functions

Gubernatorial initiatives

III. State policy issues
1. Economic development, economic policy and taxation; highways and tourism; natural resources
2. Race
3. Social issues—education; prison reform

IV. Gubernatorial effectiveness
1. Personal characteristics: character style, appeal, psychological satisfactions
2. Evaluation of gubernatorial effectiveness—administrative, legislative, and policy

Consequences for Florida and gubernatorial politics

critical of all functions the governor must perform, and they must be examined in order to gain an understanding of the "flesh and blood" of the governorship.

The last major part of our analysis consists of an investigation of gubernatorial initiative. It should be noted that not all such initiatives involve public policy. There are, for example, symbolic and psychological initiatives that can be extremely important.[3] While we allude to some of them occasionally, they do not form a central part of our analysis. Rather, we are concerned with the substantive, even tangible, aspects of gubernatorial behavior. Again, it is our argument that governors must respond to the problems that confront them and which to some degree they define. In our view, policy is the principal instrument which governors have for coping with state issues. We want to determine how Florida governors have responded to the perennial, pressing problems of the state, in particular those over which they might exercise some control. This focus allows us to evaluate carefully the performances of governors as they seek solutions to urgent, but long-term, problems.

We have divided these gubernatorial initiatives into three major categories. These divisions are not arbitrarily chosen; they represent recurring issues in the state, and they are issues which directly concern the governor. Agriculture, for example, is traditionally important in Florida, but we do not discuss it at any length because it is an area in which governors have not been directly involved. The Commissioner of Agriculture and his department, and important farm and other agricultural interests in the state, have largely determined agricultural policy in this century. Thus, our choice of policy areas is necessarily limited and selective, but we hope it is indicative of the kind of issues with which governors have actively dealt in solving state problems.

First we discuss economic development; we treat economic policy and taxation, tourism and highways, and development and conservation of natural resources. We then assess race relations in the state and, last, social issues, indicators of which are education and prison reform.[4]

Included in the consideration of gubernatorial initiatives are analyses of the ideological preferences of the governors on these issues. Strictly speaking, ideological preferences should be listed in Chapter 2 ("Origins and Backgrounds of Florida Governors"). However, we include them here because the historical record of the ideological perspective of Florida governors prior to their assuming office is extremely sketchy. In some cases, especially of the early governors, it is essentially an unknown quality, since few of their pronouncements have come down to us. Nevertheless, we include a discussion of ideological preferences because they do influence behavior. While our principal concern is with the actual performances of governors in dealing with problems, we also want to try to learn what motivates their responses.

Our categories of ideological preference are as follows:

A. Economic ideology
   1. Conservative: an economic policy that emphasizes a free enterprise system with few government regulations.
   2. Moderate: an emphasis on some government regulation to insure protection for workers and consumers.
   3. Liberal: an emphasis on government regulations and responsibility. It can include some government ownership.
B. Race
   This dimension has varied somewhat depending on the period. For the time prior to World War II we have given a moderate rating to those governors who supported legal rights for blacks and an end to mob violence; after World War II the rating refers to a governor's position on integration.
   1. Conservative: maintenance of segregation; following the *Brown* decision in 1954, open opposition to integration.
   2. Moderate: paternalistic attitude towards blacks, with some protection of black rights; following 1954, gradual acceptance of integration because of the weight of legal authority.
   3. Liberal: active endorsement of school desegregation, black voting rights, and racial integration.
C. Social issues
   Here again the time period has been crucial. In general, recognition of labor and support of schools and prison reform are key indicators. Again we have provided a set of three categories:
   1. Conservative: little emphasis on expansion of state social services; primarily concerned with "holding the line" on state expenditures.
   2. Moderate: some expansion of state social services, largely in response to population growth.
   3. Liberal: expansion of state social services and improvement in quality to approach national norms.

In the final section of our analysis gubernatorial effectiveness is discussed. This represents an explicit attempt to rate the capabilities of the twenty-one men who have governed Florida during this century. First we have established a set of categories concerning the personal characteristics of the governor.

A. Personal appeal (alternatives)
   1. Charismatic: the governor has the ability to generate widespread emotional support. Franklin D. Roosevelt or John Kennedy are examples at the presidential level.

2. Gregarious: the governor creates a feeling of warmth and rallies support on a personal level. Warren Harding and Gerald Ford are examples.

3. Reserved: the governor's appeal consists of formality in office with a sense of reticence in his relationship to the public. An intellectual appeal is also included in this category. Adlai Stevenson and Calvin Coolidge are examples.

B. Character

1. Active: the individual is dynamic in work habits and proposes solutions to problems. He seeks to mold public opinion. Lyndon Johnson and Harry Truman are examples.

2. Passive: the leader is heavily influenced by public opinion. Warren Harding, William Howard Taft, and Calvin Coolidge are examples.

C. Psychological satisfactions from office

1. Positive: the individual derives psychological satisfaction from the office and generates feelings of confidence. Franklin Roosevelt is an example.

2. Negative: the leader derives little psychological satisfaction from the office and frequently generates hostile feelings. Herbert Hoover is an example.

D. Style

1. Demagogue: the individual deliberately appeals to fear and hate. He plays on the emotions of the public to produce support based on racial hatred or other elements. George Wallace is an example.

2. Neopopulist and populist: the leader appeals to the "common man" as opposed to the elite. Jimmy Carter is an example.

3. Businesslike: the executive attracts support as a manager and competent administrator. Calvin Coolidge and Herbert Hoover are examples.

We have also attempted to rank Florida governors on their administrative, legislative, and policy effectiveness. For each of these areas, governors are rated "effective," "ineffective," or "mixed." In order to achieve a standing of "effective" in the category of administrative and legislative functions, a governor has to have shown evidence of understanding his administrative and legislative duties, and an ability to carry them out in a way which demonstrates forceful, positive, constructive leadership. Thus ideological concerns are irrelevant here: conservative, moderate, and liberal governors have equal opportunity for effective administrative and legislative leadership. Under the "policy" category, however, governors must demonstrate both an ability to create new programs, or to move the state forward in new areas, and an understanding of state problem areas and the ability to relate policy proposals to those areas. Thus in our judgment it is not enough for a governor to create new policies; to be effective he must also use policy as an instrument for problem solving.

Finally, we offer some discussion of the governors' public ethics. It is our contention that any evaluation of gubernatorial effectiveness must include a consideration of the moral behavior of the governor while he is in office. His moral leadership not only sets a tone for his administration, but indeed influences the public's perception of politicians and the extent to which it will have faith in, and be supportive of, the government.

Strictly speaking, the last chapter is an addendum to our analysis. Nonetheless, we believe an evaluation of the governors should be included. More specifically, on the basis of our information, we suggest what it takes to be an effective governor in Florida and which governors seem to us to have been the most effective, and why. The last part of the book is an assessment of the overall development of the Florida governorship during this century and a commentary on what is likely to happen in the future.

Part I

Demographic Setting

PART I of this study examines the political, social, and economic developments in Florida and the personal and political background of the state's twenty-one governors in this century. The first chapter discusses Florida's southern characteristics and the dramatic demographic changes that have occurred since World War II. The last two chapters of this section address the questions who are the Florida governors, and how did they reach the office? The second chapter looks specifically at recruitment patterns, and studies both the socioeconomic and political backgrounds of state governors. The third chapter assesses gubernatorial campaigns and focuses on the relationship between issues, personalities, campaign techniques, and strategies as they have unfolded during this century.

1

Florida in the Twentieth Century:
An Overview of Its Development

FLORIDA has undergone remarkable socioeconomic and demographic changes in the twentieth century. At the start of the century it was a rural, southern state with many frontier characteristics. Nearly half the state was unsettled, and the majority of the population was engaged in agricultural or related activities. Less than sixty years later Florida was an urban state and had taken on many of the characteristics of the rapidly growing Sunbelt states such as California, Arizona, New Mexico, and Texas. Tourism had replaced agriculture as the principal source of income, and the state had become remarkably diverse in its social and ethnic composition. Not surprisingly, the nature and breadth of these changes have profoundly affected the state's politics in the twentieth century.

FLORIDA IN THE SOUTH

Observers of Florida have long noted that the Sunshine State is different from most of its southern neighbors. Thirty years ago V. O. Key, Jr., showed that although the South could not be considered a homogeneous political region, Florida, even then, was different in its politics from other southern states. Other contemporary analysts have largely confirmed this view.[1]

Even if Florida is "The Different State," it also has many features in common with other southern states during this century. Inescapable, for example, is its geographical setting. It is the most southern of all the states, and in any regional classification it must be considered along with its southern neighbors. Throughout most of its history Florida's economy has been primarily agricultural, like that of most of its neighbors. Since the end of World War II industry has moved to the South, and into Florida, but agriculture, and the rural agrarian heritage, remain influential in its politics.

11

Moreover, while Florida's economy has diversified along with the economies of other southern states, its base remains relatively narrow, resting fundamentally on tourism and related services, agriculture, mining, and a small but growing manufacturing sector.[2]

Most important in tying Florida to other southern states is its heritage. Florida was part of the Confederacy, and if it did not suffer as much as other states from the Civil War and Reconstruction, it nevertheless carried the scars from these two periods far into the twentieth century. In particular, through law and custom a caste system was established which permeated the entire society. Although racial hatred did not exist in as virulent a form as in some of its neighboring states, there has been considerable racial prejudice, and Florida has had more than its share of ugly racial incidents.[3]

Another important aspect of Florida's shared southern heritage, and one which has dramatically shaped the state's politics in the twentieth century, has been the traditional party structure. Since the end of Reconstruction (1877) Florida has been primarily a Democratic state; the Republican party emerged as a significant second party only in the 1960s. Indeed, it is this history of one-party (or, perhaps, no-party) politics which most closely ties Florida to other southern states. Politics in Florida throughout much of this century can be seen largely as an effort by the white population to use the Democratic party to maintain white supremacy and to prevent the rise of a Republican party. The state's politics must also be viewed as a struggle within the Democratic party between traditional, rural (particularly northern) Florida and the growing, more urban, more progressive, generally southern regions. With a range of variation, all of this is characteristic of the style of politics found throughout the South during most of this century.[4]

FLORIDA IN THE TWENTIETH CENTURY

Five major historical periods characterize the state's development over the past eight decades: populist-progressivism, 1900–1916; demogogic populism and postwar economic boom, 1916–25; Florida's depression and national depression, 1926–40; postdepression and explosive growth, 1940–74; contemporary Florida, 1974 to date.

In 1900 Florida was a sparsely populated, frontier-like state. Despite a large land area, it had the smallest population in the South (528,542). Most of the people lived in the counties within fifty miles of the Georgia and Alabama borders. The rest of the state had a few small cities—Daytona Beach, Orlando, Tampa, Palm Beach and Miami; the remainder was wilderness punctuated by small towns like Sanford, Palatka, and Chiefland. In fact, until 1940 Florida had more open acreage and more frontier characteristics than any other eastern or southern state. Most Floridians believed that development was necessary, that the future of the state required opening up areas for settlement. A corollary of this sparse settlement was the small role played by manufacturing (cigar making in Tampa was an exception). Over half the population was engaged in agriculture; predominant crops were cotton, tobacco, vegetables, and citrus. Considerable extractive industry existed, specifically: lumbering, naval stores (resin and turpentine), and mining of limerock and phosphates. The small cities had commercial enterprises, some shipping, and the beginnings of a tourist industry. Thus, in 1900, a low-income economy prevailed with an estimated annual per capita income of $112 compared with an estimated national average of $202.[5]

Racial tensions carried over from the Civil War and were an important influence in Florida during the latter part of the nineteenth century. Throughout the South, Reconstruction had freed and enfranchised the former slaves. Military occupation and Republican domination marked the period 1865–76. After 1877 Floridians, like their southern neighbors, attempted to return their institutions to pre-1860 conditions. In the process they gradually repressed the freedoms of black Floridians and rejected the Republican party. The political effect of this development augmented the Democratic party and reduced the Republican party to minority status in the state. In particular, the office of governor became inaccessible to Republicans after 1876. This was the Bourbon or "silk hat" era in Florida politics.

At the end of this period, a populist-progressive movement developed throughout the country. A peculiarity of this political era in the South and in Florida after 1900 was the disenfranchisement of blacks. The state's politics became one-party, Democratic, and white. A largely white, Democratic primary system was introduced and it became essentially a contest between two factions—lower middle class labor (progressive-populist or "wool hat") and conservative or Bourbon ("silk hat") candidates.

Racism permeated this era, heightening the conflict between the concept of white supremacy and the democratic concept of equal opportunity. As Gunnar Myrdahl observed in *An American Dilemma,* this ideological dichotomy created a reservoir of racial tension that stood ready to erupt into violence.[6] In the United States, from 1882 to 1936 there were 4,717 lynchings; 3,421 involved blacks. There were 281 lynchings in Florida during this period; 256 involved blacks.[7] From 1900 to 1930, a period for which figures have been compiled for black lynchings per 10,000 blacks in the population, Florida led the country with 4.5 per 10,000 blacks, twice as high as the figures for Mississippi, Georgia, and Louisiana, three times the Alabama rate, and six times the South Carolina rate.[8] In addition to racism, Florida's frontierlike environment contributed to the lawless nature of the society.

The fourth important variable in Florida early in the century was the conservative economic attitude created by the desire for growth. Even among the reformers of the populist-progressive period, the idea of draining the Everglades to permit settlement of the southern part of the state was a cardinal tenet. Led by governors William Jennings and Napoleon Broward, the movement to drain and reclaim millions of acres of glades in South Florida became the state's dominant program from 1900 until the start of World War I.

The period 1916–25 was a time of turmoil and growth in Florida. Sidney J. Catts, elected governor in 1916, was swept into office on a wave of prohibitionist, anti-Catholic, racist sentiment. A man of enormous energy, he quickly polarized the entire state, and his tenure marked a period of extreme conflict between his demagogic efforts to establish certain populist reforms and the conservative Bourbons who tried to stop him and his programs.

The 1900 Florida Democratic Party Convention in Jacksonville. William Sherman Jennings was the frontrunner, but a badly fragmented party cast an exhausting 44 ballots before he won the nomination for governor. It was the last such nominating convention in Florida; in 1904 began the use of the direct primary system. P. K. Yonge Library of Florida History.

During the early 1920s, after Catts' term, Florida experienced a period of rapid growth, the most significant development of which was the land boom, when millions of dollars poured into the state (in most instances on a purely speculative basis), and the population increased dramatically. Resting on a shaky economic base, the land boom had begun to collapse by the mid-1920s. The economy of the entire state suffered tremendously, and Florida entered a period of prolonged economic decline. The severity of the Florida depression can be measured by the sharp decline in all aspects of business. The assessed value of real estate property dropped from $623 million in 1926 to $441 million in 1930. From 1925 to 1926 Florida's bank holdings declined by $300 million. There were forty bank failures. The Seaboard and Florida East Coast Railroads' incomes were cut in half by 1936, and both railroads went into receivership.[9] Florida's economic collapse in 1926 merged into the national business collapse of 1929–40. This economic crisis spanned the administrations of four Florida governors—Doyle Carlton, David Sholtz, Fred Cone, and Spessard Holland—and severely restricted their financial maneuverability.

The postdepression period witnessed a substantial economic recovery, but the years 1940–45 permitted no chance for state spending because of World War II economic shortages. After the war rapid growth began quickly, and it accelerated through the 1950s and 1960s; from 1940 to 1970 the population expanded from 1,897,414 to 6,789,443. This era also marked the end of Florida's resemblance to other southern states. It now assumed the social and economic characteristics of rapid-growth states such as Arizona, Nevada, and California.[10] This period was characterized by virtually unregulated growth, with per capita income rising to approach the national average. Florida emerged in 1970 as the ninth most populous state. In social terms, this period also marked the decline of overt forms of segregation and discrimination in the state.

The current period, 1974 to date, began with continued economic expansion, but in the nationwide recession during the middle of the decade the state's growth slowed once again. A modest form of neopopulism emerged in the person of Governor Reubin Askew, who sought a number of governmental, economic, and social reforms. The extremely rapid growth of the state caused concern among many Floridians, and for the first time attention was given to planning and even limiting future development. Ranking high on the list of these new concerns was the preservation of the environment.

DEMOGRAPHY

What perhaps distinguishes Florida most from its southern neighbors is the physical size and the relative heterogeneity of and rapid changes in its population. Florida is a very large state, the largest in the Southeast. The road

TABLE 1.1. Population of Florida, Other Southeastern States, and the U.S., Census Years 1880–1970

Year	Florida	Alabama	Arkansas	Georgia	Kentucky	Louisiana	Mississippi
1880	269,493	1,262,505	802,525	1,542,180	1,648,690	939,946	1,131,597
1890	391,422	1,513,401	1,128,211	1,837,353	1,858,635	1,118,588	1,289,600
1900	528,542	1,828,697	1,311,564	2,216,331	2,147,174	1,381,625	1,551,270
1910	752,619	2,138,093	1,574,449	2,609,121	2,289,905	1,656,388	1,797,114
1920	968,470	2,348,174	1,752,204	2,895,832	2,416,630	1,798,509	1,790,618
1930	1,468,211	2,646,248	1,854,482	2,908,506	2,614,589	2,101,593	2,009,821
1940	1,897,414	2,832,961	1,949,387	3,123,723	2,845,627	2,363,880	2,183,796
1950	2,771,305	3,061,743	1,909,511	3,444,578	2,944,806	2,683,516	2,178,914
1960	4,951,560	3,266,740	1,786,272	3,943,116	3,038,156	3,257,022	2,178,141
1970	6,789,443	3,444,165	1,923,295	4,589,575	3,218,706	3,641,306	2,216,912

Year	North Carolina	South Carolina	Tennessee	Virginia	West Virginia	U.S.
1880	1,399,750	995,577	1,542,359	1,512,565	618,457	50,189,209
1890	1,617,949	1,151,149	1,767,518	1,655,980	762,794	62,979,766
1900	1,893,810	1,340,316	2,020,616	1,854,184	958,800	76,212,168
1910	2,206,287	1,515,400	2,184,789	2,061,612	1,221,119	92,228,496
1920	2,559,123	1,683,724	2,337,885	2,309,187	1,463,701	106,021,537
1930	3,170,276	1,738,765	2,616,556	2,421,851	1,729,205	123,202,624
1940	3,571,623	1,899,804	2,915,841	2,677,773	1,901,974	132,164,569
1950	4,061,929	2,117,027	3,291,718	3,318,680	2,005,552	151,325,798
1960	4,556,155	2,382,594	3,567,089	3,966,949	1,860,421	179,323,175
1970	5,082,059	2,590,516	3,923,687	4,648,494	1,744,237	203,184,772

SOURCES: U.S. Department of Commerce, Bureau of the Census, *Census of Population 1960*, vol. 1, pt. 2; *1970 Census of Population: General Population Characteristics*, advance report for each state.

distance from Key West to Pensacola is greater than that from Pensacola to Chicago. Not surprisingly, the sheer distance helps account for many of the socioeconomic and political differences. Like its neighbors, Florida has a large white Anglo-Saxon Protestant population, especially in the northern and western parts of the state, and a large black population, but it has also received throughout the century substantial immigrations of such diverse ethnic and religious groups as Greeks, Italians, Poles, Orientals, Jews, Cubans in the 1960s, and Vietnamese in the 1970s. There are more than 400,000 Cubans in the Miami area.[11] This ethnic diversity suggests the possibility of a wide range of interests in the state and a more fluid politics than would likely be found in other, more demographically homogeneous, southern states.

Equally significant in the state's politics has been the heavy rate of immigration from the North. In every decade of this century Florida's population growth has far exceeded the national average, and it remains the second fastest growing state in the country. Several Florida counties continue to lead the nation in rate of growth. Table 1.1 shows the rapid increase in Florida's population between 1880 and 1970. Especially noticeable is the change in the post–World War II period, when Florida easily outstripped its neighbors in population growth. In 1950 the state had nearly 3 million people and ranked twentieth in population. In 1960, the population had increased to nearly 5 million. By 1970, Florida had 6.8 million people, ranking ninth nationally, and projections for 1980 were for a population of over 9 million and a national ranking of eighth. The cumulative growth rate over the previous thirty years had been on the order of 175 percent, rivaled only by the population growth in Arizona and Nevada (both states started with much smaller populations, however).[12]

Table 1.2 is revealing in its comparison of birthrates in Florida and the United States for selected years between 1930 and 1974. For the total and white populations the Florida birthrate has been consistently lower than the national average; the nonwhite birthrate has been higher since 1960. The rapid increase in Florida's population, therefore, has not been simply or even primarily a result of fertility among Florida's residents. The change has resulted from arrivals of newcomers in massive numbers. The vast majority of Floridians have not been native born but have come from other parts of the country, especially the South, the Midwest, and urban Northeast. "The consequence is a rapidly changing politics, with voters having little background in local politics and few local ties," writes political scientist Manning Dauer.[13]

Shifts in Florida's population have not been uniform; most of the change has been concentrated in the urban areas. Throughout this century Florida has had a higher percentage of its population living in urban centers than has

any other southern state.[14] Presently 80.5 percent of the people live in urban
areas. This figure is slightly higher than the national average (see Table 1.3).
As Key observed, urban populations are not immune to demagogic appeals,
but the rusticity of other southern states has been less apparent in Florida
because of the need for politicians to appeal to at least a reasonably substantial urban and ethnic population. Indeed, it is probably the presence of
significant urban centers that has prevented racial issues from playing as
prominent a role in Florida as in other southern states.[15]

The growth of urban Florida has caused the emergence of what one
long-time observer of the state's politics calls a "giant suburbia," a continuous belt of cities and towns running up the west coast from Fort Myers to
Tampa, across central Florida through Orlando and Daytona Beach, and
south through Fort Lauderdale and Miami. This region is not monolithic,

TABLE 1.2. Resident Live Birthrates—Total, White, and Nonwhite Birthrates per 1,000
Population in Florida and the U.S.

Year	Total		White		Nonwhite	
	Florida	U.S.[a]	Florida	U.S.[a]	Florida	U.S.[a]
1930[b]	18.3	21.3	17.9	20.6	19.3	27.5
1940	17.6	19.4	17.0	18.6	19.1	26.7
1950	22.8	24.1	20.7	23.0	30.5	33.3
1960	23.1	23.7	20.5	22.7	34.9	32.1
1970	16.8	18.4	15.0	17.4	26.2	25.1
1974	13.4	(NA)	11.6	(NA)	24.4	(NA)

SOURCES: U.S. Department of Commerce, Bureau of the Census, *Statistical Abstract of the
United States,* annual editions; State of Florida, Department of Health and Rehabilitative
Services, Division of Health, *Florida Vital Statistics,* 1973, and 1974 preliminary release.
a. Data for 1930, 1940, and 1950 are adjusted for underregistration.
b. Recorded data.
NA, not available.

and, in fact, includes some socially and politically diverse areas. It has, for
example, been the spawning ground of a growing Republican party. (With
the exception of Hillsborough County/Tampa, and Dade County/Miami, the
urban/surburban ring tends to be politically conservative.) This suburban
horseshoe has also been the area of the state which has attracted both
Florida's growing retirement population (more than 17 percent of the state's
population is over age sixty-five, compared to about 10 percent nationally)
and most of its new manufacturing industry. Florida's northern urban areas
have also increased in size during this period of rapid growth. Fifteen of
Florida's sixty-seven counties account for nearly 80 percent of the state's
population.[16]

ECONOMICS AND FLORIDA

Accompanying this population explosion in the twentieth century has been Florida's transformation from a primarily agrarian economy to a mixed one that relies heavily on tourism and services. Agriculture is still important, especially citrus, sugarcane, dairy products, greenhouse and nursery ornamentals, vegetable crops, and livestock.[17] Agricultural employment, however, has declined in absolute numbers and in percentage of the work force throughout the century. In 1920 agricultural workers numbered 279,370 in Florida and comprised 28.8 percent of the population. By 1960 the number had declined to 105,419 and the percentage to 2.1; both figures were the lowest in the Southeast. The number of farms shows no steady

TABLE 1.3. Urban and Rural Populations of Florida and the U.S., 1890–1970

| | Florida | | | | U.S. | |
| | Urban | | Rural | | Percent | Percent |
Year	Number	Percent	Number	Percent	Urban	Rural
1890	77,359	20	314,065	80	35	65
1900	107,031	20	421,511	80	40	60
1910	219,080	29	533,539	71	46	54
1920	353,575	37	614,955	63	51	49
1930	759,778	52	708,433	48	56	44
1940	1,045,791	55	851,623	45	57	43
1950	1,813,890	65.5	954,415	34.5	64	36
1960	3,661,383	73.9	1,290,177	26.1	69.9	31.1
1970	5,468,737	80.5	1,321,306	19.5	80	20

SOURCES: U.S. Department of Commerce, Bureau of Census, *1970 Census of Population,* vol. 1; *Characteristics of the Population,* pt. 1, United States Summary, sec. 1, pp. 42, 60–61.

change over time. In 1920 Florida had 54,005 farms and in 1935 a maximum of 72,857. By 1954 the number was again nearly at the 1920 level, but by 1974 it had shrunk to 34,000.[18] As the state's population continued to soar, farming land became too valuable to farm, and many farmers sold out to developers for large profits. In addition, citrus growing and beef cattle farming are being increasingly taken over by corporations. Despite these developments the number of acres being farmed has increased since 1960.

Perhaps the most important indicators of the state's changing economy are per capita income and nonagricultural employment. Between 1948 and 1974 Florida's per capita income approached that for the United States as a whole, although it still lagged behind. In 1948, Florida's per capita income was $1,180 compared to $1,430 for the U.S.; in percentage terms, Florida's figure was 82.5 percent of the national figure. By 1974, the figures for Florida and the U.S. were, respectively, $5,235 and $5,434, the state figure representing 96.3 percent of the national average.[19] (In 1900, the estimated Florida per capita income had been $112 compared to a national average of $202.) While the state has consistently ranked ahead of other southeastern states in per capita income, a fairly steady gap remained between the Florida and the national figures. In 1900 the gap was $90; in 1948 it was $250; in 1974 it was $199. It should also be noted that Floridians' income on a per capita basis has not been evenly distributed. The figures are very much skewed because of a concentration of wealth in the upper income categories. Specifically, the income for the top 15 percent has been very high, while the remainder of the state's population has a rather low income. Due to the concentration of wealth at the top, the Florida figures seem to compare favorably with the national ones.[20]

Relatively little of the state's available wealth is taxed. State and local taxes have traditionally been low, and in a recent survey the Florida tax effort (expressed as a share of personal income) was only 10.0 percent compared to a national average of 12.5 percent, ranking Florida forty-seventh among the states.[21] While Florida's aggregate wealth is high by southern standards, it is highly concentrated among a small minority of residents and little taxed. Indeed, proponents of development argue regularly against raising tax rates on the grounds that the low rates attract corporations and persons of wealth to the state.

Changes in Florida's nonagricultural sector since 1939 are detailed in Table 1.4. Particular attention should be paid to changes in employment patterns in construction, finance, insurance and real estate, and services. In construction, employment rose from 26,800 in 1939 to 203,900 in 1972. In the category of finance, insurance, and real estate, the figures increased from 15,200 to 153,800. In services the figures grew from 53,500 to 460,300. In 1939, these sectors accounted for 24.5 percent of Florida's nonagricultural work force, by 1972 for 34 percent. From 1939 to 1970 nonagricultural employment rose by 452 percent, the third largest state increase and well above the national average of 130.6 percent.

In 1975 manufacturing represented approximately 16 percent of Florida's total revenue, compared to agriculture's 5 percent, construction's 9 percent, and service trades' 19 percent. In comparison to other states, especially heavily populated ones, Florida's manufacturing component is quite small. What this means, as a recent observer noted, is that the state's economy is peculiar: "high per-farm income, few farms; low manufacturing income; high proportion of wage earners in service trades; and high earnings in hotels and motels."[22] The relative growth of Florida's economy can be further illustrated by data from several other important sectors. The increase in the value of Florida's mineral production has been dramatic from 1930 to 1972, from 2,766 percent compared to 525 percent for the entire United States.[23] Florida's recent wealth has thus been highly dependent on tourism, agriculture, and mineral production.

Finally, the increase in government receipts and expenditures served to stimulate economic growth in the private sector. Tax revenues in this period rose from $205 million in 1951 to $2.9 billion in 1974 (see Table 1.5). Expenditures and disbursements rose from $290 million to $8.2 billion. Total state revenues went from $294 million in 1951 to $8.4 billion in 1973–74.

TABLE 1.4. Nonagricultural Employment—Employment by Industrial Classification in Florida, 1939–72 (in thousands)

Year	Total	Mining	Construc-tion	Manufac-turing	Transpor-tation & public utilities
1939	390.8	3.3	26.8	71.4	49.9
1940	424.4	3.7	38.9	75.9	53.0
1950	704.4	6.2	66.8	102.3	66.7
1960	1,320.6	8.5	121.8	206.7	101.1
1970	2,152.1	8.6	171.8	321.6	156.0
1972	2,407.5	9.3	203.9	334.7	170.9

Year	Wholesale and retail trade	Finance, insurance, and real estate	Services	Govern-ment
1939	110.9	15.2	53.8	59.5
1940	118.4	16.2	55.8	62.5
1950	204.2	31.9	107.1	119.2
1960	360.9	82.5	218.6	220.5
1970	564.0	132.1	400.2	397.8
1972	634.1	153.8	460.3	440.5

SOURCE: U.S. Department of Labor, Bureau of Labor Statistics, *Employment and Earnings: States and Areas, 1939–72* (1974).

The biggest change, of course, has been in federal grants to the state and local governments (Table 1.6). In 1937 total federal aid to Florida was $2.8 million; by 1974 the figure was $1.2 billion. During approximately this same period, government employment rose very rapidly, as shown in Table 1.4, a development whose significance was not lost on the state's conservatives. In 1939 there were 59,500 government employees in Florida; by 1972 there were 440,500. What this shows is not simply the growth of big government (with public employment climbing rapidly) but the impact which federal dollars have had on the enormous increase in size of Florida's government.

These data demonstrate that Florida's growth has been dramatic and that it has brought numerous problems and difficulties to which government generally, and governors in particular, have had to respond. The Florida economy, while growing very rapidly, has not been particularly well balanced or stable during this century. As a result it has been especially prone to suffer from economic dislocations such as the depression of the 1920s and 1930s and the recession and Arab oil embargo of the mid-1970s. The heavy service emphasis makes the Florida economy strongly dependent on what happens in other parts of the country. Finally, its failure to tax its considerable available wealth limits government's ability to deal with pressing social issues.

TABLE 1.5. Total Revenue, Expenditures, and Tax Revenue of the State Government of Florida, 1951–74 (in $ thousands)

Year ending June 30	Total revenue	Tax revenues	Total expenditures
1951	293,922	205,000	289,894
1960	1,286,965	584,719	1,270,241
1966	2,020,978	901,888	2,011,881
1971	3,994,289	1,717,277	3,989,555
1974	8,375,294	2,907,113	8,223,719

SOURCES: U.S. Department of Commerce, Bureau of the Census, *Compendium of State Government Finances* (annual); Comptroller of Florida, *Annual Report of the Comptroller,* fiscal year 1973–74.

FLORIDA POLITICS

Not only has the economy heightened differences between Florida and its southern neighbors, but the one-party political system traditionally found in Florida has helped to mark it off from other southern states. If Democratic party politics in the South during the twentieth century is viewed along a continuum ranging from stable to unstable, Florida occupies the extreme position at the unstable end. Writing in 1949, Key characterized Florida politics in this century as "every man for himself"; it was a state in which "anything can happen in elections, and does."[24] Permanent alliances and a stable party structure were nonexistent. Individual candidates built their own factions and their own organizations; there was virtually no alliance-building among candidates. Once in office politicians favored only the loosest attachments with one another, and these tended to be of a temporary, *ad hoc* sort. On election day contestants of widely differing political persuasions might be chosen, and they would be forced to deal with each other as best they could upon assuming office. Moreover, unlike other southern states, there was neither a hierarchy within the system of factions nor sharp lines (especially of an ideological nature) separating them.

Throughout most of the century, Florida has literally had an atomized system of factional politics. Why this should have been the case was, and remains, a topic of endless speculation for observers of Florida politics. The large size and geographical diversity of the state have been important: not only are population centers widely separated, but their dissimilar economics and ethnic groupings have helped give rise to different kinds of political cultures. Tremendous intrastate distances, the lack of rapid communication and transportation systems for most of the century, and the dispersion and differentiation among populations nurtured localism, which in turn promoted political fragmentation and factionalism. Rare has been the Florida

TABLE 1.6. Aid Received by Government of Florida from the Federal Government, 1937–74 (in $ thousands)

Year Ending June 30	Total
1937	2,761
1940	7,089
1950	42,579
1960	171,371
1965	230,312
1970	509,409
1974	1,160,863

SOURCES: U.S. Department of Commerce, Bureau of the Census, *Financial Statistics of States,* changed to *State Finances* in 1942 and to *Compendium of State Government Finances* in 1947 (annual); U.S. Department of the Treasury, Division of Government Accounts and Reports, *Federal Aid to States,* annual reports.

candidate who could attract a large statewide following. Indeed, it has not been unusual in gubernatorial primaries for a candidate to win a convincing majority in his home county and those immediately adjacent to it but less than 20 percent of the vote in other parts of the state. This tendency has contributed enormously to the endless shifting of factions within the state.[25]

The heavy immigration into the state has also contributed to the political fragmentation. This flood of newcomers has brought about a system of politics which is "without form and without issue." Loyalties have not been established, and there has not been time for traditional habits in political behavior to develop for much of this recently arrived population. It was not unreasonable, V. O. Key, Jr., argued, to expect "a diverse, recently transplanted population" to lead to "an unstable politics."[26] Significantly, immigration has accelerated fragmentation along regional lines. Immigrants from the Northeast have tended to settle in the southeastern section of the state around Miami; midwesterners have generally located near St. Petersburg and Tampa on the midwest coast and in central Florida near Orlando; immigrants from the South have preferred the northern, Panhandle area.[27]

Urban-rural and sectional cleavages have been especially important in Florida politics. Not always clear-cut or easy to identify, they have, nevertheless, been recurrent. It has been possible, as Key noted, to see differences in voting patterns between cities and rural areas. It has also been possible to observe this cleavage in legislative actions prior to legislative reapportionment in 1967.[28] A friends-and-neighbors kind of localism in which rural legislators sought to reward their sections of the state often at the expense of urban Florida prevailed in Tallahassee. Nonetheless, this cleavage has been blurred in Florida because of the lack of any unifying ties among the cities. Frequently legislators from northern urban areas have allied themselves with rural North Floridians against representatives from South Florida, especially on issues of roads and public services.

The urban-rural cleavage has been blurred further by the failure of cities to vote as a bloc in gubernatorial elections. While cities form an important part of any gubernatorial candidate's support, prior to 1956 no faction in Florida was ever constructed that included all of the state's cities, nor was any faction up to that time built which relied exclusively on urban, as opposed to rural, bases of support, in spite of the large percentage of the population living in urban centers. Typically cities have voted sectionally in statewide elections.[29] Only in recent years have gubernatorial candidates such as LeRoy Collins, Reubin Askew, and Robert Graham put together factions which included significant blocs of urban voters in all parts of the state. The elections of Askew and Graham may well represent the emergence of a true "urban vote" which seeks specific programs in such areas as schools, roads, and health care from its candidates.

Sectionalism has been much easier to identify in Florida's politics. As will be shown, splits between the northern and southern parts of the state have been crucial in gubernatorial elections and subsequent administrations. Sectional support for gubernatorial candidates, and for particular issues, can be seen clearly by comparing the locations of those counties which voted for particular candidates. A marked clustering effect, which reflects both local and sectional tendencies, is invariably observed. The traditional north-south sectional division, moreover, has been fraught with subsectional cleavages. Northern Florida, for example, has not been politically homogeneous in this century (although in the early decades it was far more so than in recent years), and the western or Panhandle section of the state frequently has been at odds with the eastern part. In addition, the southeastern section, including the so-called Gold Coast (Palm Beach to Miami) has often voted differently from either the west coast urban areas or the urbanized central region. Some

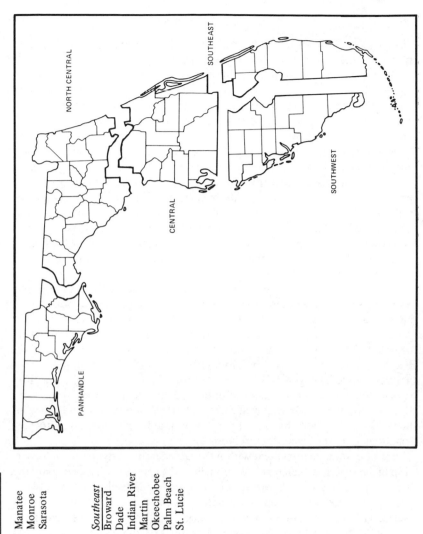

Political Regions of Florida

Panhandle
Bay
Calhoun
Escambia
Franklin
Gadsden
Gulf
Holmes
Jackson
Liberty
Okaloosa
Santa Rosa
Walton
Washington

North Central
Alachua
Baker
Bradford
Clay
Columbia
Dixie
Duval
Flagler
Gilchrist
Hamilton
Jefferson
Lafayette
Leon
Levy
Madison
Nassau
Putnam

St. Johns
Suwannee
Taylor
Union
Wakulla

Central
Brevard
Citrus
Hernando
Hillsborough
Lake
Marion
Orange
Osceola
Pasco
Pinellas
Polk
Seminole
Sumter
Volusia

Southwest
Charlotte
Collier
De Soto
Glades
Hardee
Hendry
Highlands
Lee

Manatee
Monroe
Sarasota

Southeast
Broward
Dade
Indian River
Martin
Okeechobee
Palm Beach
St. Lucie

observers of Florida politics consider the central area to be a separate political section altogether (see Figure 1.1).[30]

During this century, Florida politics have been generally nonideological and even relatively issue-free. Liberal-conservative splits have been few (when they occur, it is usually in the form of populist/Bourbon or wool hat/silk hat cleavages discussed earlier). In many gubernatorial contests it has been hard to tell which of the candidates have been more "liberal" or "conservative" than the others. Often they have said much the same thing, and voters have had to differentiate on the basis of tone, style, personality, and county of origin rather than on ideology or substance. Ideologues have occasionally been prominent—Sidney Catts and Sumter Lowry, gubernatorial candidate in 1956, were perhaps the most notable examples—but generally they have not been well received by the voting population. Governors and other politicians in the state who appeared to have been most successful during much of the century have occupied a relatively limited ideological range from conservative to moderately progressive.

Issues, too, have not played consistently significant roles in the state's politics. Although the remark of a North Florida judge that issues "don't have a damn thing to do" with Florida's politics is something of an overstatement, it is true that state politics here have not been especially issue oriented. The structure of factional politics seems to account for this. Factions have been based fundamentally on personality. Campaigns for political office have generally taken the form of contests among competing personalities rather than clashes of either ideologies or positions on issues. Even during those gubernatorial elections in which issues seem to play an important role, there has usually been as much attention given to personalities as to the issues themselves.[31]

Because of the factionalism within the Democratic party, political leadership in the state has been seriously impaired. The governor has been only the head of a winning faction, and his claim to statewide leadership usually has had to rest precariously on such factors as his personality, his stand on particular issues, his ability to use patronage, and his winning percentage in the Democratic primary. Moreover, before 1968 the governor could not succeed himself, further limiting his ability to control the party. Finally, he has been surrounded by a cabinet that comprises a group of competing political executives. These men also have had statewide constituencies, independent of his, usually more stable and permanent than his own, which serve to diffuse executive leadership.(This point will be expanded in later chapters.)

The continual turmoil within the Democratic party has jeopardized its control of state politics as the Republican party has grown in influence since the mid-1950s. In 1954 there were about 115,000 registered Republicans in the state, which was about three times the number in 1938. By 1964 there were approximately 500,000 Republicans registered in Florida. Ten years later the figure had doubled, and Republican registration has now passed the one million mark. Although on a national basis Republican registration seems to be declining slightly, in Florida it has grown dramatically (see Table 1.7). In the mid-1970s Republicans comprised about 30 percent of the state's total number of registered voters.[32]

Most of the state's Republicans live in fairly new urban and suburban areas in central and southern Florida (see Table 1.8). They are concentrated in the coastal regions on both sides of the state: 58.6 percent of the state's Republicans live in these areas. Another 40.2 percent live in the central Florida urban areas surrounding Orlando. Only 1.2 percent of the Republicans in Florida reside in northern and western rural areas. Further evidence of the causal relationship between migration patterns and the increase in the

TABLE 1.7. Florida Voter Registration, 1938–70

Year	Republicans	Independent and no party	Democrats	Total registered voters
1938	35,377	—	593,048	628,425
1950	60,665	—	1,006,580	1,067,245
1960	338,390	22,223	1,656,023	2,016,636
1970	711,090	61,523	2,024,387	2,797,000

SOURCE: Dauer, "Florida: The Different State," p. 111.

number of Republicans can be found in the fact that over 75 percent of them were born outside the South (see Table 1.9). Only about one-third of the state's population is native born, but it would appear that the number of Republican residents has been disproportionately increased by immigration.[33]

The Republicans, however, are by no means all alike. In fact, the two predominantly Republican regions are remarkably distinct in terms of certain social and economic characteristics (see Table 1.9). Republicans living in the central area are on the average about ten years younger than their coastal counterparts. More than 80 percent of those on the coasts were originally from outside the South, and many have apparently moved to Florida to retire. In contrast, nearly half of those in the central region are native southerners who appear to have migrated to Florida at a relatively young age. Perhaps the greatest contrast is in income. Nearly 60 percent of Republicans in the central region earn more than $13,000 per year; fewer than half of those living in the coastal regions are in this income bracket.[34]

The political implications of this diverse Republican population are clear. Socioeconomic differences between the two groups of Republicans suggest that candidates must face the problem of appealing to two Republican constituencies with differing political interests and priorities. "For the candidates, success in Florida depends upon their ability to devise a campaign strategy to force a majority out of the state's diverse Republican electorate," according to pollster Paul Cohen. As if this process is not difficult enough, to attain statewide office the party must also attract a large bloc of Democratic voters. Registered Democrats still outnumber Republican registrants in Florida 2.5 to 1.[35]

Another important change in Florida politics since the end of World War II has been a substantial increase in the number of black voters. Throughout most of this century the number (and percentage) of blacks in Florida has been less than that in other southern states (Table 1.10). Key, as well as others, has noted that this relatively low percentage has prevented the issue of race from being as important in the state's politics as it is in other southern states. Virtually disenfranchised before 1940, blacks now constitute about 15

TABLE 1.8. Democratic and Republican Registration in Selected Florida Counties, 1970

County	Republican	Democratic	Other	Total
Counties with over 100,000 population				
Alachua	4,212	31,177	898	36,287
Brevard	28,718	55,546	2,543	86,807
Broward	91,515	144,952	8,402	244,869
Dade	69,843	389,070	7,060	465,973
Duval	20,484	182,980	4,214	207,678
Escambia	6,517	73,867	1,209	81,593
Hillsborough	26,736	179,381	2,700	208,817
Leon	3,462	34,865	525	38,852
Orange	36,535	86,031	2,902	125,468
Palm Beach	50,466	96,748	4,818	152,032
Pinellas	118,928	129,390	6,436	254,754
Polk	14,248	79,791	1,015	95,054
Sarasota	29,719	23,578	1,682	54,979
Volusia	19,849	59,877	1,809	81,535
Lee	12,313	29,984	621	42,918
Smaller counties with Republican registration higher than 30 percent of Democratic registration				
Charlotte	5,234	8,424	379	14,037
Collier	3,834	8,290	348	12,472
Indian River	4,045	10,608	425	15,078
Lake	2,451	7,312	601	10,364
Lee	12,313	29,984	621	42,918
Manatee	14,407	26,453	1,277	42,137
Martin	3,283	9,101	167	12,551
Osceola	3,086	9,323	141	12,550
Pasco	9,575	22,148	665	32,388
Seminole	7,047	20,817	620	28,484

SOURCE: Dauer, "Florida: The Different State," p. 112.

TABLE 1.9. Registered Republicans in Florida

	Statewide (%)	Coastal (over 33.3% GOP)	Central (10–33% GOP)
Age			
18–34	19.1	16.2	30.2
35–49	16.8	14.9	23.8
50–64	26.6	27.7	23.0
65 and over	37.4	41.2	23.0
Average age, years	56	58	49
Place of Origin			
South	23.1	17.6	42.9
Non-South	76.9	82.4	57.1
Employment Status			
Employed	36.1	33.5	47.6
Retired	38.1	41.6	23.4
Keeping house	16.2	15.7	17.7
Other	9.7	9.2	11.3
Marital Status			
Married	69.4	67.4	77.0
Widowed	18.4	20.5	10.3
Other	12.3	12.4	12.7
Income			
Under $7,000	24.2	25.7	18.6
$7,000–12,000	26.0	26.7	23.0
$13,000–20,000	31.1	29.7	35.4
Over $20,000	18.7	17.9	23.0
Education			
0–11 years	9.4	9.1	9.6
High school graduate	60.1	61.3	55.2
College graduate	30.5	29.6	35.2

SOURCE: Paul M. Cohen, "The Florida Poll," *Gainesville Sun,* January 18, 1976.

percent of the voting age population and about 11.3 percent of those who are eligible to vote (Table 1.11). Despite the increase in the number of black voters, their percentage has remained rather constant in the last twenty years due to the growth of the white population. Nonetheless, the emergence of the black voter has profoundly affected Florida gubernatorial politics. As the chapters on campaigning (3) and race relations (8) will show, since 1965 a number of candidates have openly courted the black voter.[36] The vast majority of the state's black voters are Democrats; only about 2 percent of the state's Republicans are black. Their support in an election, especially in a crowded primary, can spell the difference between victory and defeat. Blacks have also begun to seek public office in Florida. While there were only two in the state legislature (both in the house of representatives) and none in the Florida congressional delegation before 1980, blacks are increasingly found on city councils and in other local governmental offices.[37]

Demographic Setting

TABLE 1.10. Population, by Race, for Florida, Other Specified
Southeastern States, and the U.S., 1930–70

Year and state	White	Negro
1930		
Florida	1,035,390	431,828
Georgia	1,837,021	1,071,125
Alabama	1,700,844	944,834
Mississippi	998,077	1,009,718
Louisiana	1,322,712	776,326
South Carolina	994,049	793,681
U.S.[a]	110,286,740	11,891,143
1940		
Florida	1,381,986	514,198
Georgia	2,038,278	1,084,927
Alabama	1,849,097	983,290
Mississippi	1,106,327	1,074,578
Louisiana	1,511,739	849,303
South Carolina	1,084,308	814,164
U.S.[a]	118,214,870	12,865,518
1950		
Florida	2,166,051	603,101
Georgia	2,380,577	1,062,762
Alabama	2,079,591	979,617
Mississippi	1,188,632	986,494
Louisiana	1,796,683	882,428
South Carolina	1,293,405	822,077
U.S.[a]	134,942,028	15,042,286
1960		
Florida	4,063,881	880,186
Georgia	2,817,223	1,122,596
Alabama	2,283,609	980,271
Mississippi	1,257,546	915,743
Louisiana	2,211,715	1,039,207
South Carolina	1,551,022	829,291
U.S.[a]	158,454,956	18,860,117
1970		
Florida	5,711,411	1,049,578
Georgia	3,387,516	1,190,779
Alabama	2,528,983	908,247
Mississippi	1,393,283	815,770
Louisiana	2,539,547	1,088,734
South Carolina	1,794,430	789,041
U.S.[a]	177,612,309	22,672,570

SOURCES: Figures for 1930 and 1940 are from *Florida Statistical
Abstract, 1967*, p. 16. Figures for 1950–70 are from *Florida Statistical
Abstract, 1971*, p. 20.
a. Conterminous.

Reapportionment has also brought about a significant alteration in the state's politics.[38] Prior to 1967, the Florida legislature was one of the worst apportioned in the nation. For example, in 1961, 12.3 percent of the state's population could elect a majority of the senate, and 14.7 percent a majority of the house. Although the 1885 constitution required that reapportionment be effected every ten years, only minor changes had been implemented during the first sixty years of the twentieth century. Most governors did not even try to force the issue. The absence of reapportionment in the years following World War II meant that the state legislature came to be controlled by the so-called Pork Chop Gang. The porkchoppers (the name was coined by James Clendinen, an editor of the *Tampa Tribune*) were a group of north

TABLE 1.11. Voter Registration by Race in Florida, 1950–70

Year	No. blacks registered	Percent registered of black voting age population	No. whites registered	Percent registered of white voting age population
1950	116,215	NA	951,030	NA
1960	183,080	39.4	1,819,667	69.3
1970	302,000	55.3	2,495,000	65.5

SOURCE: *Florida Statistical Abstract,* 1972, p. 515; Register of Voters, Report of Secretary of State, 1950, copy in files of Political Science Department, University of Florida, Gainesville.

Florida legislators, most visible in the senate, who prominently displayed their rural backgrounds and orientation. They were remarkably unsympathetic to the needs of Florida's growing urban population.

In 1967 the United States Supreme Court ruled in *Swann* v. *Adams,* 385 U.S. 440, that the malapportionment of the Florida legislature was unconstitutional and ordered apportionment based on legislative districts of equal population. The reapportionment which was mandated by the Court's decision brought about the end of the stranglehold of the porkchoppers. The balance of power in the legislature was shifted to South Florida, and urban and especially suburban interests began to be prominently reflected in both the senate and the house. From an ideological point of view, however, the change has not been as dramatic as some may have expected. As noted earlier, Florida has been, and remains, primarily a conservative state. Most of the new legislators have come from the emerging, largely suburban areas of the state, and although by no means uniformly conservative, they tend to lean in this direction, particularly with regard to taxation and spending programs.[39]

While wrestling with the reapportionment question, Floridians realized that the state constitution was as outmoded as their legislature. Written in

1885 but amended more than 150 times, it was criticized because it contained inconsistencies, contradictory material, and detailed provisions which might better be found in statutes than in the constitution. In 1966 a Citizens Constitutional Revision Commission met and prepared a new document which was presented to the legislature in 1967. After that body changed several of its provisions, the voters overwhelmingly ratified the new constitution in November 1968.[40]

Specific provisions of the new constitution which dealt with the executive and which served to strengthen this branch overall will be considered in detail in a separate chapter. Briefly, the new constitution has strengthened the governor's office by permitting him to succeed himself for a second term and by increasing his administrative authority over state agencies and departments. While the constitutional revisions increased the powers of the governor, they did not do so at the expense of the legislature. The legislature has been modernized by means of the 1969 Legislative Reorganization Act, which established a large professional staff to act as a legislative reference bureau and to advise legislative committees; an ongoing, year-round system of committee meetings; presession meetings to deal with prefiled bills; and a computerized tracking system for bills.

The magnitude and diversity of these social, economic, and political changes have profoundly affected Florida politics in this century. The sheer breadth of these developments has confronted the state with a host of problems requiring governmental leadership and direction if chaos is to be avoided. Because the executive branch of government can act more readily and efficiently than the legislative branch, Florida governors have been the focus of efforts to deal with the problems of the twentieth century.

2

Origins and Backgrounds of Florida's Governors

HOW does a person become governor of Florida? What are the backgrounds of Florida governors? Has there been any pattern to their political careers? What happens to ex-governors of Florida? The answers to these questions can provide an understanding of the men who have held the office. They can also help determine whether there is a particular path to the executive mansion.

In an effort to find recruitment patterns for the office of governor in Florida, data of two different kinds have been examined. First demographic and socioeconomic analyses of the backgrounds of Florida governors are presented and discussed. These include the following variables: father's occupation; birthplace and early life; place of residence; religion; education; occupation; military service; membership in organizations; and age upon assuming office.

A second set of data on recruitment patterns consists of the political offices which future Florida governors have held on the way to the chief executive's chair. Examining these variables provides answers to two important questions, and some related ones: Do any public offices in Florida seem to act as springboards for future governors? And, how long is the "apprenticeship" period; that is, how much time must be spent in lesser offices before a successful campaign for the governorship can be launched?[1]

Finally, in this chapter we examine the careers of Florida's ex-governors. Prior to 1968 Florida governors could not succeed themselves and could expect to spend only four years in office (LeRoy Collins was the only exception). Therefore, the state has had a number of relatively young ex-governors. Did they remain politically active, or did they return to law practice or business, never to be heard from again?

There have been numerous reasons why men have sought the governorship. In many cases these reasons have been as varied as the men holding the office. Generally, Florida governors felt they could provide the state with good, honest leadership. Specifically, however, the reasons have ranged from ideological differences with other gubernatorial candidates to a long-standing ambition to be governor to a feeling that one could do better than his predecessors. Millard Caldwell commented that he had been persuaded to run by prominent businessmen who opposed the New Deal philosophy of candidate Lex Green. LeRoy Collins became a candidate in 1954 because he had been a close friend of former governor Dan McCarty and felt Charley Johns would not continue McCarty's programs. Fuller Warren and Farris Bryant were apparently interested in the office from childhood. According to Warren's sister, he "always wanted to be governor."[2] Bryant remarked that his mother wanted him to be governor and he talked about the office throughout his early years. Reubin Askew said he sought the governorship because he wanted to return the office to the stature it achieved under Governor Collins, and he was convinced that Earl Faircloth would have been unable to do so.[3]

FATHERS' OCCUPATIONS AND FUTURE GOVERNORS' EARLY LIVES

Of the twenty-one governors who have held office since 1900, fourteen, or 67 percent, were born into families whose principal source of income was agriculture (Table 2.1).[4] This reflected the predominantly rural, agricultural nature of Florida, and of the South generally, throughout most of the twentieth century. A substantial number of the governors were actually born and reared on farms, and the families of most of them appear to have been in modest economic circumstances. While none was of the classic, poverty-stricken, "dirt farmer" type often found in the South, very few of the families could be considered well-to-do. Albert Gilchrist's father owned a 200,000 acre plantation in South Carolina and hundreds of slaves. And yet as a young boy Gilchrist knew poverty when his father died and the family's holdings were lost during the Civil War. Napoleon Broward's grandfather and father had extensive property holdings in Duval County but lost them also during the War between the States. Sidney Catts' family was at one time wealthy and socially prestigious in Alabama. But when their wealth was depleted during the postwar economic slump in the South, young Catts worked as an itinerant minister and salesman of patent medicines.

Five of the fourteen farming families were involved in Florida's emerging citrus industry. Weather conditions, however, made citrus growing a very speculative enterprise in the late nineteenth and early twentieth centuries.

TABLE 2.1. Early Background of Florida Governors

Governor	Religion	Rural-Agricultural	Non-rural	Father's occupation and governor's place of birth
Jennings, 1901–1905	Baptist		X	Judge Walnut Hill, Illinois
Broward, 1905–9	Presbyterian	X		Landowner, cattle owner Duval County, Florida
Gilchrist, 1909–13	Episcopalian	X		Landowner, planter Greenwood, South Carolina
Trammell, 1913–17	Baptist	X		Citrus grower, farmer Lakeland, Florida
Catts, 1917–21	Baptist	X		Planter Alabama
Hardee, 1921–25	Baptist	X		Farmer Taylor County, Florida
Martin, 1925–29	Baptist	X		Farmer, citrus grower Plainfield, Florida
Carlton, 1929–33	Baptist	X		Citrus grower Wauchula, Florida
Sholtz, 1933-37	Congregationalist		X	Business, real estate Brooklyn, New York
Cone, 1937–41	Baptist	X		Farmer Benton, Florida
Holland, 1941–45	Methodist	X		Citrus grower, abstractor Bartow, Florida
Caldwell, 1945–49	Protestant non-denominational	X		Lawyer, farmer Beverly, Tennessee
Warren, 1949–53	Baptist	X		Farmer Blountstown, Florida
McCarty, 1953	Episcopalian	X		Land developer, citrus grower Ft. Pierce, Florida
Johns, 1953–55	Baptist	X		Sheriff Starke, Florida
Collins, 1955–61	Episcopalian		X	Grocer Tallahassee, Florida
Bryant, 1961–65	Methodist		X	Farmer, accountant Marion County, Florida
Burns, 1965–67	Methodist		X	Politician, businessman Chicago, Illinois
Kirk, 1967 71	Episcopalian		X	Businessman San Bernadino, California
Askew, 1971–79	Presbyterian		X	Carpenter Muskogee, Oklahoma
Graham, 1979–	Church of Christ	X		Farmer, politician Coral Gables, Florida

John Martin's father lost his entire grove in the freeze of 1896, and Park Trammell's, Spessard Holland's, and Dan McCarty's families were all hit hard by that freeze and those in the first decade of the twentieth century. However, Holland's father's groves recovered sufficiently to enable him to become one of the first Florida producers to ship citrus to northern markets. Dan McCarty's family farmed very successfully, despite the freezes. With the exception of these two men, however, the twentieth-century governors who came from agricultural backgrounds had relatively modest and humble economic origins.

A comparison of the pre-1940 with the post-1940 governors reveals a significant socioeconomic difference in their backgrounds. Eight of the governors prior to 1940 were reared on farms in the rural South. After 1940 only six of eleven governors were raised on farms, and only one of the six most recent governors, Robert Graham, had an agricultural background. This development parallels the decline of agriculture in relation to the growth of other sectors of the economy since World War II. It also suggests that the postwar governors should have developed programs and goals different from those of the men who held office prior to 1940.

The governors who came from nonagricultural backgrounds also came from families that lacked wealth. William Sherman Jennings was a cousin of William Jennings Bryan, and the two remained close during their lives, but Jennings' family was never well-to-do. The father of Charley Johns, who served as acting governor after Dan McCarty died in office, was for a time sheriff of Bradford County. LeRoy Collins' father owned a small grocery store in Tallahassee. Reubin Askew's father left the family when the boy was very young, and his mother supported six children as a maid and seamstress.

The early life of twentieth-century Florida governors gives added support to the conclusion that few of them grew up with any economic advantages. Napoleon Broward was orphaned at twelve; at fourteen he began work in a log camp and later was employed as a farmhand, a steamboat roustabout, a cod fisherman in Newfoundland, and a pilot on the St. Johns River. Soon after his father died, Albert Gilchrist, at the age of nine, was forced to take a job hauling wood to market. Although Park Trammell spent his early years living and working on a farm near Lakeland, at age sixteen he moved to Tampa, where he was employed at various times as a newspaperman, carpenter, orange picker, and clerk. Trammell studied at night, and in some respects personifies the "self-made" man image so popular in American folklore. Cary Hardee began teaching school at age seventeen although he had no formal education. Despite his lack of training, he read law and was admitted to the bar at age twenty-two. John Martin began working as a store clerk when he was fifteen.

Spessard Holland's background was rather different from that of most of the other governors. Although his father was a successful citrus farmer, he did suffer considerable financial loss in the freeze of the winter of 1894–95 and was often faced with considerable monetary difficulties after that. Holland was offered a contract to play baseball with the Philadelphia Athletics. He decided, however, to attend Emory University in Georgia, and he eventually became a college professor.

Even several of the more recent Florida governors of the post-1940 period had to begin work at an early age. Fuller Warren came from a relatively poor farming family and held a series of jobs as a young boy. Claude Kirk joined the Marines at age seventeen and served in both the second World War and Korea before attending law school. During his youth Reubin Askew held jobs as a paperboy, shoe shiner, and clerk. Bob Graham was personally responsible for twenty registered Angus cattle at the age of sixteen.

In spite of the modest financial origins of many of Florida's twentieth-century governors, several of them came from families with rather distinctive backgrounds. Gilchrist was a descendant of the grandfathers of both George Washington and James Madison. John Martin's maternal grandfather was a member of the Secessionist Convention, and was one of seven men who drew up the Confederate Constitution. Both of Spessard Holland's grandfathers served in the Confederate armed forces. His father was president of the school board, and his mother was president of the Carnegie Library Association, in Bartow. He also had relatives in both the Virginia and Georgia legislatures. Charley Johns' older brother Mackley, a member of the Florida Senate, was president-designate of the 1933 senate but died before he could begin his term. Bryant's uncle Ion Farris was twice Speaker of the Florida House of Representatives. Graham's father served eight years in the state senate and finished third in the 1944 Democratic gubernatorial campaign.

This overview of the economic backgrounds of the Florida governors makes clear that their origins were not in the propertied, monied class. Indeed, most of them came from modest backgrounds and overcame numerous disadvantages. Only Albert Gilchrist could claim an aristocratic heritage, although his social position had been eroded by the Civil War. In many respects (and this point will be amplified below) Florida's governors exemplify the upwardly mobile, ambitious young men in the tradition of American "Horatio Alger" success stories. It should also be noted that while most of the governors had no economic advantages as young men, in a considerable number of cases there was a family precedent of public service or service-mindedness.[5]

BIRTHPLACE

An examination of the birthplaces of Florida governors indicates that they do not, as a group, come from aristocratic, patrician families with deep roots in the state. These men seem to reflect what is true for the state's population as a whole: many of its citizens were born elsewhere in the country.

Of the governors since 1900, only twelve, or 57 percent, were native born. Of the other nine, four were born in the South (Gilchrist in Greenwood, South Carolina, although his mother was a Floridian; Trammell in Macon County, Alabama; Catts in Pleasant Hill, Alabama; and Caldwell, near Knoxville, Tennessee). Two were born in the West (Kirk in San Francisco, California; and Askew in Muskogee, Oklahoma). And three were born in the North or Midwest (Jennings in Walnut Hill, Illinois; Sholtz in Brooklyn, New York; and Burns in Chicago, Illinois, although he always considered himself a native of Louisville, Kentucky, where his parents had their home).

As implied earlier, the native-born Florida governors came mostly from northern or rural parts of the state: Broward from Duval County; Hardee from Perry in Taylor County; Martin from Marion County; Carlton from Wauchula in Hardee County; Cone from Columbia County; Holland from Bartow in Polk County; Warren from Blountstown in Calhoun County; McCarty from Fort Pierce in St. Lucie County; Johns from Starke in Bradford County; Collins from Tallahassee in Leon County; and Bryant from near Ocala in Marion County. Of these governors, only McCarty and Graham came from southern Florida. Both men's origins were distinctly rural in character, and each was closely identified with agricultural interests in the state.

If the birthplaces of the ten pre-1940 governors are compared to those of the eleven post-1940 governors, there is very little difference, and no pattern can be found. Of the earlier group, five were native Floridians and five were not; three were born in the South and two in the North or Midwest. Seven of the post-1940 governors were natives, one came from the South, two from the West, and one from the Midwest. What this suggests is that even in the "modern" period Florida's population remains heavily composed of immigrants from the North, and more importantly the pool of recruitment for Florida governors has still not become limited to citizens with deep roots in the state. Indeed, three of Florida's four most recent governors, Haydon Burns, Claude Kirk, and Reubin Askew, were all born out-of-state.[6]

PLACE OF RESIDENCE

Very few Florida governors have resided in, or been identified with, the state's big cities. Indeed, their heavily rural, agricultural backgrounds have already been noted. Of those not residing on farms, most lived in towns or small cities, mainly in North and Central Florida.

Napoleon Broward was the first governor to live in a large city, Jacksonville. This northern Florida city was the residence of four later governors too: John Martin; Fuller Warren, who moved there from Blountstown in 1929, served on the Jacksonville City Council, and later represented it in the legislature; Haydon Burns, who settled there in 1922; and Claude Kirk, who moved to the city in the early 1950s. Millard Caldwell and LeRoy Collins both lived in Tallahassee, but Caldwell much preferred rural life to that of the small capital city. Although he was from the northern part of Florida, Collins was one of the few governors who was actually identified with its southern, urban interests, and it was this section of the state that insured his election in 1954 and reelection in 1956. Askew lived in Pensacola, a medium-sized city in the Florida Panhandle, after age nine. Graham was the first man elected governor who resided in one of the major urban centers in the southwestern, central, or southeastern parts of the state.

RELIGION

While the patterns of birthplaces and places of residence have not changed very much during the twentieth century, the same cannot be said of the religious affiliations of the governors. Of the twenty-one, nine were Baptists, four were Episcopalians, three were Methodists, two were Presbyterians, one was Congregationalist, one was Church of Christ, and one was Protestant nondenominational. Gilchrist, although christened an Episcopalian and in this study considered as such, was also active in the Baptist church. Sholtz, a Congregationalist, was a converted Jew. Unquestionably the heavy percentage of Baptists among Florida governors has been a function of their rural or small town, North Florida origins. Northern Florida lies at the southern edge of the Bible Belt.

There is a significant pattern to the religious preferences of the governors in the pre- and post-1940 groups. In the early period, seven of the ten governors were Baptists, two were Episcopalians, and one was Presbyterian. In the post-1940 period, there have been only two Baptists, while there have been three Episcopalians, one Presbyterian, three Methodists, one Church of Christ, and one Protestant nondenominational. This marked change in the religious preferences of the governors paralleled the changing religious composition of the state as ever greater numbers of urban nonfundamentalists from northern and midwestern states moved into Florida.[7]

EDUCATION

Education has been an important factor in the lives of Florida's governors (see Table 2.2); eighteen of the twenty-one attended college and thirteen attended law school. This constitutes a remarkable record since only a very small minority of the general population ever attended college in the pre-1940 period and even fewer attended advanced professional schools. Florida's future governors thus used higher education to overcome their

TABLE 2.2. Education of Florida Governors

Governor	No higher ed.	Undergraduate	Law degree	UF Law	Other Law School
Jennings		Southern Illinois Normal	X		Union Law School, Chicago
Broward	X				
Gilchrist		U.S. Military Academy (no degree)			
Trammell		Vanderbilt & Fla. Ag. Col. (no degree)	X		Cumberland University, Cumberland, Tenn.
Catts		Auburn and Howard (no degree)	X		Cumberland University, Cumberland, Tenn.
Hardee	X				
Martin	X				
Carlton		Stetson	X		Columbia University
Sholtz		Yale	X		Stetson University
Cone		Florida Agriculture College[a]			
Holland		Emory	X	X	
Caldwell		University of Mississippi	X		University of Virginia
Warren		University of Florida	X		Cumberland University Cumberland, Tenn.
McCarty		University of Florida			
Johns		University of Florida			
Collins		Eastman School of Business	X		Cumberland University, Cumberland, Tenn.
Bryant		University of Florida	X		Harvard
Burns		Babson College (no degree)			
Kirk		Emory	X		University of Alabama
Askew		Florida State University	X	X	
Graham		University of Florida	X		Harvard

a. Florida Agriculture College was the predecessor of the University of Florida.

modest backgrounds and to facilitate their economic and social progress in society. Only three of the early governors—Napoleon Broward, Cary Hardee, and John Martin—received no formal higher education. Significantly, fifteen Florida governors attended at least one university outside the state. This again points out the mobile nature of Florida's population.[8]

While their academic records are rather mixed, many of Florida's governors evidenced leadership potential during their high school and college days. Dan McCarty was president of the junior class at the University of Florida and vice-president of the student body. Millard Caldwell was a star athlete with letters in four major sports. Doyle Carlton won a college scholarship to Stetson for his rhetorical ability. Fuller Warren was president of the sophomore class, a writer for the campus student newspaper, *The Alligator,* and a member of the varsity debating team at the University of Florida. Spessard Holland was an outstanding baseball player and was recruited by Connie Mack to play with the Philadelphia Athletics. Reubin Askew not only had an outstanding academic record at Florida State and the University of Florida but was also elected president of the student body at both schools and served in several honor societies. Robert Graham was Phi Beta Kappa and chancellor of the Honor Court as well as president of Sigma Nu and Phi Eta Sigma at the University of Florida. Many governors obviously developed strong leadership traits and political skills during their student careers.[9]

OCCUPATION

Not surprisingly, all but five Florida governors—Broward, Gilchrist, McCarty, Johns, and Burns—or 76 percent, have been attorneys. Hardee, Martin, and Cone, moreover, were admitted to the bar without ever having attended law school. As lawyers these men represented the business interests of this developing state, which helped shape their own business or "Chamber of Commerce" orientations.

Law is by far the most dominant profession among politicians. What is especially noteworthy, however, is the number of Florida governors who were engaged in other occupational pursuits before they became chief executive (Table 2.3). While sixteen governors were attorneys, nine were also businessmen, five were landowners, ranchers, or citrus growers, two were bankers, three were insurance men, and two were in other professions.

TABLE 2.3. Occupation of Florida Governors

Governor	Lawyer	Busi- nessman	Rancher, citrus, ag.	Banker	Insurance	Other
Jennings	X					
Broward		X				
Gilchrist			X			X
Trammell	X	X	X			
Catts	X	X			X	X
Hardee	X			X		
Martin	X					
Carlton	X	X				
Sholtz	X					
Cone	X			X		
Holland	X					
Caldwell	X		X			
Warren	X					
McCarty		X	X			
Johns		X			X	
Collins	X					
Bryant	X					
Burns		X				
Kirk	X	X			X	
Askew	X					
Graham	X	X	X			

In this last category are Gilchrist, who was a surveyor and a civil engineer in addition to being a citrus grower, and Catts, who was an ordained minister, and who held pulpits between 1886 and 1914. Several of the governors who were attorneys achieved considerable prominence in their other occupations. Hardee, who organized the First National Bank of Live Oak, became president of the Florida Bankers Association in 1910. Martin in the 1940s became coreceiver and later trustee of the Florida East Coast Railroad. Carlton was president of the Florida State Chamber of Commerce in 1951 and 1952. Cone also served as president of the Florida State Bankers Association. Thus the governors were prominently involved in the business development of the state whether they were lawyers or not.

As a group these men were generally successful in their particular occupations. A few even became affluent before achieving the governorship (Claude Kirk and Robert Graham for example), and several became comfortable, if not rich, after leaving office. Trammell, an attorney, was also a prominent citrus grower and newspaper editor and publisher. McCarty was a well-to-do cattleman and citrus grower who organized the Indian River Citrus Association, a growers' cooperative. Johns, who had to leave the University of Florida before graduating because of a lack of funds, later became a prominent businessman in Starke. Burns was a successful businessman in Jacksonville before entering politics. The Florida governor with the most unconventional sequence of occupations prior to pursuing a political career was undoubtedly Napoleon Bonaparte Broward. He owned and operated several boats, including a mail and passenger steamer and a tugboat. He ran a lumberyard and worked as a developer of phosphate mines. Most fascinating, though, was his occupation during the Spanish-American War of 1898. Broward made eight voyages on his tugboat through the Spanish blockade of Cuba while running guns to Cuban revolutionaries.[10]

MILITARY SERVICE

Broward's military activity was not atypical. Twelve, or 57 percent of Florida's governors in the twentieth century served in the armed forces, some with considerable distinction. Four were in the army (Gilchrist, Trammell, Caldwell, and McCarty); five served in the navy (Sholtz, Warren, Collins, Bryant, and Burns); two were in the Air Force (Holland and Askew); and one was a Marine (Kirk). Many future governors were mustered out of service as officers. The available data indicate that at least nine held officer rank by the time they left the service. This figure includes Dave Sholtz, who served during World War I as a naval ensign and left the naval reserves as a lieutenant-commander. This high incidence of officers among Florida governors may have resulted from leadership capabilities which they demonstrated during their military service. Certainly, their military activity helped them develop leadership abilities.

Several Florida governors had unusual or noteworthy military careers. Broward was never in the service, but as already noted he served as a gunrunner during the Spanish-American War. Gilchrist was a brigadier general in the Florida militia, but in 1898, at the outbreak of the Spanish-American War, he resigned his position to enlist as a private in the infantry. He was eventually mustered out as a captain. During World War I Holland was a volunteer serving in the coastal artillery, but later, as a lieutenant, he requested to be transferred to France, where he served as a flyer. He was awarded the Distinguished Service Cross for his exploits in several important battles. McCarty was in the field artillery during World War II. He landed at Normandy on D-Day, and received such decorations as the Legion of Merit, the Bronze Star, the Purple Heart, and the Croix de Guerre. Claude Kirk volunteered for the Marines at age seventeen, and by nineteen he was commissioned as a lieutenant; he served three years in World War II and again in the Korean conflict. Askew was a paratroop sergeant in World War II and like Kirk served as an officer in Korea.[11]

ORGANIZATIONS

Whether active in the military service or not, twentieth-century governors have been enthusiastic participants in civic organizations. Indeed, virtually every Florida governor has been a member of several different groups, clubs, societies, and lodges. Some, such as Martin, Sholtz, Holland, Warren, McCarty, Burns, Askew, and Graham, belonged to more than ten different voluntary organizations. Civic and service organizations seem to be most preferred by the governors, and they have consistently belonged to such groups as the Masons, Elks, Moose, Shriners, Rotary, Kiwanis, Chamber of Commerce, American Legion, Veterans of Foreign Wars, and Odd Fellows. It should be noted that many of these associations are distinctly business-oriented and afforded these men the contacts with which to further their political ambitions.[12]

AGE UPON ASSUMING OFFICE

Florida's governors have been comparatively young men (Table 2.4). The youngest, Trammell, was thirty-six years old upon assuming office. The oldest, Cone, was sixty-five. Eleven, or 53 percent, were forty-four or younger when they were inaugurated; sixteen, or 76 percent, were less than fifty; twenty, or 95 percent, were under fifty-four years of age. The mean age of Florida governors is 45 years; by excluding Fred Cone, who was 12 years older than the next oldest governor (Catts, who was 53), the mean drops to 44 years. There is relatively little difference in mean ages between the pre- and post-1940 governors. For the early years it is 45.5 years (43.3 excluding Cone); for the modern period, it is 45.4 years.[13]

Two conclusions can be drawn from this information. First, relatively young men have been elected governor in Florida. More important, the relatively low ages suggest that the recruitment time span for Florida governors is fairly short. They have generally risen rapidly through the levels of lower offices which they have held. Indeed, as we will show in the next

TABLE 2.4. Age of Florida Governors Upon Assuming Office

Governor	Age at Inauguration
Jennings	37
Broward	47
Gilchrist	51
Trammell	36
Catts	53
Hardee	44
Martin	40
Carlton	41
Sholtz	41
Cone	65
Holland	48
Caldwell	47
Warren	43
McCarty	41
Johns	47
Collins	45
Bryant	50
Burns	52
Kirk	41
Askew	43
Graham	42

section, Florida public officials with ambitions for the governorship have begun their pursuit of the office rather early in their political careers and have not been content to dally, biding their time, at the lower echelons. Unquestionably the state's traditionally tumultuous, fragmented, decentralized form of politics helps account for the relatively brief "apprenticeship" period of Florida governors and the young age at which most have been elected. In the case of post-1940 governors, World War II, and to some extent the Korean War, actually delayed the ascendancy of a number of future governors to the office. Fuller Warren finished third in the 1940 gubernatorial primary at age thirty-five and would have been a strong contender in 1944 had he not entered the Navy. Thus he had to wait until 1948 before renewing his pursuit of the governorship. Much the same might also be said about the political careers of

Dan McCarty, Claude Kirk, and Reubin Askew; their ambitions were all interrupted or delayed by wartime service.

POLITICAL CAREER PRIOR TO GOVERNORSHIP

Florida governors spent an average (mean) of 11.5 years in public service before becoming chief executive[14] (Table 2.5). However, the figure is somewhat misleading because of the variation in the length of the governors' political careers. Two, Catts and Kirk, had no prior public service. One, Cone, had thirty years of previous experience.[15]

The public service positions held by Florida governors early in their political careers included a range of offices at all levels of government (although only one held a federal post). Four—Trammell, Martin, Cone, and Burns—were mayors. Burns was mayor of Jacksonville for five terms, while Trammell served two terms in Lakeland, Martin three in Jacksonville, and Cone two in Lake City. Jennings, Broward, and Warren served on the city councils of their respective cities of residence; their mean service was 3.3 years. Five governors—Jennings, Broward, Holland, Burns, and Askew—held county offices, including county commission seats but excluding county judgeships; the mean county service was 1.6 years. Jennings sat one year as county judge, and Holland served eight years in that capacity. Thus, nine Florida governors, or 43 percent, held political positions at the local level during their public service careers prior to reaching the chief executive's office.

Fourteen of the governors, or 67 percent, were members of the state house of representatives. The mean number of terms served is 2; one term in the Florida house is two years, and thus the mean figure represents some 4.0 years of service. Bryant served the longest, six terms. Contrary to popular belief, most of those who served in the house did not hold the position of Speaker. Only five did: Jennings, Gilchrist, Hardee (who twice was Speaker), McCarty (who was the youngest at age 29), and Bryant (who followed in his Uncle Ion Farris' footsteps).

Eight of the governors, or 38 percent, served in the state senate. Johns served the longest; he was continuously in the Senate between 1935 and 1966. His case is something of an anomaly, because his nearest competitor in terms of length of service was Collins, who served four terms. Because he was only acting governor, Johns retained his seat in the senate, and also his presidency of that body. The mean number of terms served by Florida governors in the senate is three, or if Johns is omitted, two (one term is four years). Three governors, Trammell, Cone, and Johns, served as president of the senate, and two, Johns and Askew, served as president pro tem. Interestingly, only five governors, Trammell, Johns, Collins, Askew, and Graham, served in both the state house and the senate. Trammell served one

TABLE 2.5. Political Career of Florida Governors Prior to Inauguration

Governor	Years in prior political career	Mayor	City council	County commissioner or other county office	County judge	State house	Speaker	State senate	Senate president or pro tem	U.S. Congress	Other
Jennings	8		X	Circuit Court Commissioner X	X	X	X				Presidential Elector; Chairman, Democratic State Convention
Broward	9		X	Sheriff X		X					State Board of Health
Gilchrist	5					X	X				Board of Visitors, U.S. Military Academy
Trammell	13	X				X		X	X		State Attorney General
Catts	0										
Hardee	12					X	X				State's Attorney
Martin	6	X									Customs Inspector
Carlton	N.A.							X			City Attorney for Tampa
Sholtz	16					X					State's Attorney; City Judge

Cone	30	X						X	X		Three-time Delegate to Democratic Convention; once Chairman; State Democratic Chairman
Holland	18			X County Prosecutor	X			X			
Caldwell	13					X				X U.S. House	City Attorney; County and School Board Attorney
Warren	10		X			X					Delegate, Democratic National Convention
McCarty	6					X	X				
Johns	18					X		X	X		
Collins	16					X		X			
Bryant	11					X	X				Charter Director, Citizens Constitutional Committee
Burns	15	X		X							
Kirk	0										
Askew	14			X Assistant County Solicitor		X		X	X		
Graham	10					X		X			

N.A. Not available.

term in each; Johns one in the house and nine in the senate; Collins three in the house and four in the senate; Askew two in each; and Graham two in each. Thus a total of seventeen governors, or 81 percent, spent at least a brief period in the Florida state legislature. Johns, of course, served the longest; Collins the next longest. LeRoy Collins spent a total of seven terms in the legislature, beginning his career at age twenty-five and, except for a period during World War II, serving continuously until 1954, when he was elected governor. Only Millard Caldwell served in the United States Congress (four terms in the House of Representatives) prior to becoming governor.

Florida governors have held a variety of other public service positions prior to becoming chief executive. Some of these posts were of short duration (e.g., Cone was a delegate to the Democratic National Conventions in 1924 and 1928 and was chairman of the Florida delegation at the convention in 1932). Others have encompassed several years (e.g., Hardee was state's attorney for eight years). Thirteen of the governors, or 63 percent, have held one or more of these political positions; the mean is 1.5 positions. They range from relatively modest posts at the local level (Carlton was city attorney in Tampa during the 1920s; Sholtz served as city judge in Daytona Beach) to more prominent state positions (Trammell was the state attorney general from 1908 to 1912).

With the exception of service in the state legislature, no clear pattern emerges from the prior political careers of Florida governors. Examining the data in another way underscores the difficulty in finding any patterns. A key variable in analyzing the recruitment of Florida governors is not just which offices were held previously, but which office was the last one occupied before the governorship was reached (Table 2.6).[16]

Ten of the governors, or 48 percent, held an office in the legislature just prior to becoming chief executive. Yet it is not possible to say whether the house or the senate has been more important in serving as a springboard to the office. Five governors came from the house (Gilchrist, Hardee, Warren, McCarty, and Bryant), and five came from the senate (Holland, Johns, Collins, Askew, and Graham). Two, Martin and Burns, were mayors before becoming governor. None held a nonjudicial county position, and only one, Caldwell, was in Congress. Seven governors, or 33 percent, held "other" kinds of public service positions. These include service on the State Board of Health (Broward); as state attorney general (Trammell); as municipal officials (Carlton and Sholtz); and as a party official (Cone). Only Claude Kirk held no public service position, although he had run for office and lost and had headed the state Democrats for Nixon in 1960. Clearly it is difficult to find any pattern among the governors' springboard offices.

If, however, the data are gathered into pre- and post-1940 categories, a modest pattern does emerge. In the pre-1940 group, only two, Gilchrist and Hardee, used the legislature, specifically the house of representatives, as a springboard. None used the senate. One, Jennings, was on the city council and Martin was mayor of Jacksonville. The other six governors held "other" offices. In the post-1940 group, however, eight governors were in the state legislature just prior to becoming chief executive. Three were in the house (Warren, McCarty, and Bryant) and five were in the senate (Holland, Johns, Collins, Askew, and Graham). One was a mayor (Burns) and one (Kirk) held no office.

While inferences from this data must be made carefully, it would appear that in the post-1940 period the state legislature, and particularly the senate,

TABLE 2.6. Springboard Positions for Florida Governors

Governor	Mayor	City council	County commissioner or other county office	County judge	State house	State senate	U.S. Congress	Other
Jennings		X						
Broward								State Board of Health
Gilchrist					X			
Trammell								State Attorney General
Catts								None
Hardee					X			
Martin	X							
Carlton								Tampa City Attorney
Sholtz								Daytona Beach City Judge
Cone								State Chairman, Democratic Party
Holland						X		
Caldwell							X	
Warren					X			
McCarty					X			
Johns						X		
Collins						X		
Bryant					X			
Burns	X							
Kirk								None
Askew						X		
Graham						X		

has served as the most important springboard to the governorship. It is here that the major pool of future Florida governors is to be found. The senate is the senior legislative body and seems to be regarded as such by Florida citizens and the press. Its members receive more publicity than members of the house and are usually looked to for leadership on important state issues. This finding becomes especially noteworthy in view of the almost complete absence of Florida cabinet positions as springboards to the governorship. Only one governor (Trammell) even held a cabinet post. It thus appears that the members of the cabinet do not form a significant pool of potential governors. In light of the long service of most cabinet members, this is not surprising; many have decided to stay in their positions and have not even sought the gubernatorial nomination. The same can be said about Florida's delegation to the United States Congress. Caldwell is the only governor with prior service in Congress, and he had been retired from that office for some four years before running for the governorship. Clearly the governor's single four-year term did not offer any attraction to Florida's congressional delegation.

A possible exception to the importance of the state legislature as a springboard to the governorship may well be the office of lieutenant governor, established by the 1968 constitution. Under the 1885 constitution Florida had no such office. Yet, as political scientist Joseph Schlesinger has found, in those states which have a lieutenant governor, the office has often been a very important springboard to the governorship.[17] There is an important structural difference, however, between Florida's lieutenant governorship and the office which Schlesinger found to be a significant recruitment pool for the governorship. In Florida the lieutenant governor is not elected separately from the governor as is often the case in other states. Thus he cannot build his own constituency independently of the governor.

How much this will affect the chances of the Florida lieutenant governor's advancing to the chief executive's office remains to be seen. It seems likely, however, that the continued fragmentation of Florida's political parties, the lieutenant governor's close ties and associations with the incumbent governor, and the traditional antipathy of Florida voters to anything resembling a political machine or dynasty may well prevent the office from emerging as the most important springboard to the governorship. Askew's lieutenant governor, Jim Williams, ran a poor third in the Democratic gubernatorial campaign of 1978. It is even possible that the emergence of lieutenant governors as candidates for the governorship will increase party fragmentation as they vie with other candidates, especially from the senate, for the gubernatorial nomination in the primaries.

Another important source of information concerning the previous political careers of governors is the amount of time they have served in state offices. There are several reasons why this measure is important. State offices provide the most public visibility (other than national offices) for potential governors, and this can be useful in building a statewide constituency. A number of governors, in addition, did not occupy state office directly before attaining the governorship, and it is important to note whether or not they had state experience at all prior to their successful campaigns. Finally, in several cases there was a hiatus between the governorship and the position previous to it. Length of state service gives at least an indirect indication of "residual" statewide visibility which could be used to build a constituency for a successful gubernatorial campaign.

TABLE 2.7. State Elected Offices Held by Florida Governors Prior to Inauguration

Governor	Years in state office	Years in house	Years in senate	Years in cabinet
Jennings	4	4		
Broward	1	1		
Gilchrist	4	4		
Trammell	6	2		4 Attorney General
Catts	0			
Hardee	4	4		
Martin	0			
Carlton	4		4	
Sholtz	2	2		
Cone	6		6	
Holland	8		8	
Caldwell	4	4		
Warren	4	4		
McCarty	6	6		
Johns	19	2	17	
Collins	16	6	10	
Bryant	11	11		
Burns	0			
Kirk	0			
Askew	12	4	8	
Graham	10	4	6	

Seventeen governors, or 85 percent (see Table 2.7), held state offices during their ascent to the governorship.[18] Four did not: Catts, Martin, Burns, and Kirk. Thirteen, or 62 percent, used a state office as their springboard position. All but three of these positions were legislative. Those which were not included Broward's service on the State Board of Health, Trammell's position as attorney general, and Cone's activity in the Democratic party. These seventeen governors served an average of 5.3 years in prior state offices; if Cone and Johns are excluded as anomalies, the figure drops to 5.0 years. What this suggests is that the period of prior state service is relatively short. While governors have had 11.5 years of previous political experience (10.5 without Cone), only about five of those years were spent in a state office. Considering that only one governor (Trammell) spent any time in a state executive office, and also considering the relatively short period of exposure which most Florida governors have had at the state level, it must be inferred that most of them did not have a very detailed knowledge of state government and politics before becoming governor.

It is sometimes said that to be a successful gubernatorial candidate in Florida, a person must run at least twice for the office: once to become known throughout the state and once to be elected. This is true in only a few cases. Only five governors, or 24 percent, have run twice or more before winning. All the others were successful on the first try.[19] Interestingly, those who have employed this electioneering device have done so since 1940. With the tremendous socioeconomic changes occurring since that time, a first campaign has been particularly helpful in gaining recognition and building a constituency. In the cases of Warren and McCarty, their relative youth, inexperience, and the presence of more well-known candidates in their first races undoubtedly hurt them very much; by the second race each was well known. Bryant was the front-runner in 1956 until the popular incumbent, LeRoy Collins, was declared eligible to run again; Bryant's campaign promptly went into eclipse, although his campaign experience greatly facilitated his effort four years later. In 1960 Burns was faced with a host of well-known candidates, including Bryant. However, the Jacksonville mayor's statewide exposure in that campaign unquestionably helped him win the race four years later. Finally, it should be noted that Kirk, who only ran once for the governorship, in 1966, had campaigned in 1964 for the Senate against Spessard Holland. While he failed to unseat the popular senior senator, he did succeed in making his name well known. Given a highly fragmented Democratic party in 1966, Kirk was able to capitalize on this recognition factor and translate it into a gubernatorial victory.

POSTGUBERNATORIAL CAREER

According to conventional wisdom Florida's ex-governors fade away when they leave office: they are finished as political figures and are neither seen nor heard from again. However, in view of the relatively young age of most of these men and their fairly brief prior political careers, it might be expected that they would remain politically active following their tenure in office, and seek additional public service. Both of these statements are partially correct. Florida ex-governors have overwhelmingly sought subsequent public office, but usually they have been unsuccessful in their attempts. After leaving the governorship, their political careers are generally over.

Florida governors were divided into two groups for purposes of analyzing their postgubernatorial careers. The first consists of ex-governors who ran for public office at least once (not necessarily successfully), who were appointed to a governmental or political position at national, state, or local levels, or who were politically active in some other capacity. The other group is comprised of those who retired to practice law, to enter business, or to do something else without ever again entering active political life; these ex-governors are considered politically inactive.

Seventeen governors, or 85 percent, remained politically active after leaving office (Table 2.8). That is, they sought or held some additional elective office. Table 2.8 shows that the office most commonly pursued has been that of United States senator. This is completely understandable in view of senatorial prestige and the apparent similarities in the constituencies of governors and senators. Ten governors have sought the nomination for U.S. senator (Napoleon Broward, it should be noted, made two attempts; he failed to secure the nomination in 1908 but succeeded in 1910, only to die before assuming office). Of these ten, however, only three have been successful: Broward, Park Trammell (who served in the Senate from 1916 to 1936), and Spessard Holland (who was in the Senate from 1946 to 1971). The others— Broward (in 1908), Catts, Martin, Carlton, Sholtz, Cone (who actually ran in 1940 while he was still governor), Collins, and Bryant—were all defeated.[20]

Five ex-governors sought the gubernatorial nomination again: Catts, Hardee, Martin, Warren, and Kirk. Not one of them succeeded. Catts and Martin, in fact, attempted without success to gain the nominations for both senator and governor. The former tried for the Senate in 1920 and for the governorship in 1928; the latter for senator in 1928 and for governor in 1932. The 1932 Democratic primary, moreover, was noteworthy for having two ex-governors, Hardee and Martin, in the field. Neither succeeded in gaining the nomination.

There are several reasons why Florida governors seem to be unable to transfer their constituencies to another office or to hold them together for another successful election. The fluid, transient nature of the state's politics undoubtedly is most important. There has been little permanence or stability in the alignment of electoral factions within the state. At each election candidates must attempt to assemble a winning coalition. That this was done once in no way means it can be done again, at another time and for another office. This is particularly true after the governor has been out of office for a few years, and the public has had time either to forget him or through selective remembrance to recall only the negative aspects of his administration.

Florida citizens have also resisted the establishment of anything resembling a political dynasty or machine. Power, in Florida's political culture, remains decentralized.[21] To give an individual repeated access to power through a variety of important offices is, of course, antithetical to this set of beliefs. As a result, Floridians have felt that after an individual has held the governor's office, he should retire, and should not have an opportunity to

TABLE 2.8. Postgubernatorial Career: Politically Active or Inactive Governors

Governor	Politically Active				Politically Inactive	
	U.S. Senate	Governor	Appointive office	Other	Law	Other
Jennings			State Improvement Fund Council			
Broward	1908—Defeated 1910—Nominated					Died in NYC
Gilchrist						
Trammell	1916-36					
Catts	Defeated in 1920	Defeated in 1928				
Hardee	Defeated in 1928	Defeated in 1932				
Martin	Defeated in 1936	Defeated in 1932				
Carlton			Special attorney for state 1947			
Sholtz	Defeated in 1938					
Cone	Defeated in 1940					
Holland	Served 1946-71					
Caldwell			Administrator, civil defense	Chairman, Southern Regional Education; state supreme court		
Warren		Defeated in 1956				
McCarty						Died in office
Johns				State senate		
Collins	Defeated in 1968	Reelected in 1956	2 appointments			
Bryant	Defeated in 1970		2 appointments			
Burns				Defeated in 1971 for mayor of Jacksonville		
Kirk		Defeated in 1978				
Askew		Reelected in 1974	U.S. ambassador for trade negotiations.		Lawyer, Miami	

mold the state's political system according to his own wishes. He certainly must not be allowed to dominate it through the establishment of a machine. The only exceptions to this seem to have been Trammell and Holland, neither of whom really tried to establish a machine (although Holland was a political ally of his successor, Millard Caldwell), and both of whom seemed to be genuinely admired by the citizens of Florida.

Finally, governors make enemies while they are in office; they cannot please all the people all of the time. Moreover, what captures the imagination of the public in one election may very well prove unacceptable in another. This is especially true in campaigns in which personality is more important than issues. Florida's highly fragmented political system and its cultural bias against political dynasties, coupled with the ex-governor's lack of appeal, make it very difficult for him to reassemble what was once a winning coalition. Perhaps the public is simply tired of him and his rhetoric.

Five politically active ex-governors have been appointed to political office. Jennings was appointed by Broward, his successor and political ally, as counsel to the State Improvement Fund. In 1947 Carlton was appointed by the cabinet as a special attorney to help with the negotiations for Florida's acquisition of the Ringling Museum. Caldwell himself held several appointed positions. From 1950 to 1952 he was President Truman's administrator in charge of federal civil defense. In February of 1962 he was appointed to the Florida Supreme Court to complete an unexpired term; later that same year he was reelected to the court without opposition. In 1967 Caldwell was elected chief justice, and two years later he retired. After serving as president of the National Association of Broadcasters, LeRoy Collins held two federal appointive positions. He was named by President Johnson as the first director of the Community Relations Service because of his reputation for handling race relations problems, and later Johnson appointed him under secretary of commerce, a position Collins resigned in 1966. He was defeated in 1968 by Edward Gurney in the general election for the U.S. Senate. Farris Bryant also held a number of appointive positions. After leaving office he practiced law and headed several insurance firms in Jacksonville, but in 1966 President Johnson appointed him director of the Office of Emergency Planning and a member of the National Security Council. In 1967 Johnson named him to the U.S. Advisory Commission on Intergovernmental Relations, on which he served for two years as chairman. In 1970 Bryant was defeated in a runoff for the Democratic nomination for the U.S. Senate.

Three ex-governors have sought other kinds of political positions. Caldwell was chairman of the Board of Control, Southern Regional Education Board, from 1948 to 1951; he was extremely interested in the coordination of higher education in the South. His tenure on the state supreme court has already been noted. Charley Johns returned to the state senate, which he never officially left, and served until 1966. Finally, Haydon Burns sought a sixth term as Jacksonville's mayor in 1971, but was defeated.

Seven governors, or 35 percent, were politically active on more than one occasion after leaving office. Broward, Catts, and Martin each ran twice for public office. Carlton sought the senate nomination in 1936 (he lost), and in 1947 he became a special attorney for the state. The various positions held by Caldwell, Collins, and Bryant have already been mentioned.

Only two Florida ex-governors were politically inactive (McCarty died in office while still a young man and is not included in these data). Gilchrist lived some thirteen years after leaving office but apparently never sought or held public office again.

SUMMARY

Joseph Schlesinger pointed out that in most states there is no well-defined pattern which future governors follow en route to the office.[22] Florida certainly fits this description. Well-defined patterns of recruitment seem to correlate with stable political systems in which there is a marked degree of party cohesion and interplay of competition. Florida politics for most of the twentieth century has been exactly the opposite.

But this is not to say that no patterns at all can be discerned in the backgrounds of Florida governors. The demographic data suggest that while these men are members of a political elite, they do not share many of the advantages common to the early lives of members of other governing elites. In general, their backgrounds have been middle or lower class. A few seem to have overcome a subsistence existence and economic deprivation on the way up. Virtually all have been college educated and most have attended law school. Most were in the armed forces, where they early showed leadership ability. Most have been successful in their careers as attorneys or businessmen (sometimes both). All have been Protestants, with Episcopalian replacing Baptist in the modern period as the most frequent religious affiliation. Most have been relatively young men.

The information presented also makes clear that Florida governors have been an upwardly mobile group. Many have overcome disadvantaged backgrounds to become members of the middle class (some went beyond it) by the time they came into office (and certainly when they left office they retained, at a minimum, middle-class status). In Florida there is no class of "patricians" which sends its sons into the governor's office. Quite the opposite seems to be the case. Indeed, it may well be that this group of upwardly mobile, ambitious, well-educated men (few of whose roots go beyond one generation as Florida residents) perceived politics generally and the governor's office in particular as mechanisms for increasing their rate of ascent on the socioeconomic ladder. For at least some, politics was a way out of a working class occupation and into a white-collar profession. The fact that most Florida governors were self-made men probably accounts, in part, for the conservative economic ideology expounded during their administrations. Certainly, the open, fluid, discontinuous style of Florida politics provided numerous entry points for those individuals who wished to use the political system to enhance their social status.

Patterns in the prior political careers of Florida governors are more difficult to find. Most assumed the governorship at a relatively young age. This lends credence to the conclusion that politics has been an important instrument of social mobility for Florida governors. The brevity of the apprenticeship period is especially noticeable in the case of state offices; most Florida governors who held state office occupied their positions for less than five years, and a few held no state posts at all. The governors have served in a variety of public offices in their march to the chief executive's chair. Service in the legislature seems to be an important prerequisite in the modern period for a successful campaign for the governorship. Whether this situation will change as a result of the development of a lieutenant governor's office remains to be seen.

Finally, it appears that Florida ex-governors do not retire on leaving office. Seventeen, or 85 percent, entered some kind of political campaign after leaving the governorship. Most have been unsuccessful in their attempts. It is of interest that with three exceptions, all who sought additional office tried to become either U.S. senators or, again, governors of Florida (the exceptions were Caldwell's unopposed campaign for the Supreme Court, Johns' continuous service in the state senate, and Burns' unsuccessful try for the office of mayor of Jacksonville). Completely missing from this roster are any attempts to be elected to the state legislature (except for Johns, whose case is clearly anomalous) or the U.S. House of Representatives. Evidently these offices were not seen as an upward or lateral step by Florida governors. A number of Florida ex-governors accepted appointive posts of considerable prestige and importance at the federal level. Thus, they have tended to remain on the political scene after leaving office. In general, however, those who pursued additional public office met only discouragement and defeat. Changes in demographic circumstances following his term in office, coupled with the traditional antipathy of Floridians for electing governors to other offices, make it very difficult for a former chief executive to transfer (or even maintain) his constituency.

One final note about ex-governors. Virtually none of them has been called upon by incumbent governors for advice or support. It is common for incumbent presidents to call upon former presidents, regardless of their party, for "counsel" or "advice." Most of this is undoubtedly for political, rather than substantive, purposes; it suggests to the population a willingness by the incumbent to take advantage of the expertise, experience, and "wisdom" of former presidents. In the case of Florida governors, however, exactly the opposite is true. Few governors have called upon predecessors for advice, even though there may have been four or five or even more former governors alive at the time. It was most unusual for Caldwell to have appointed Carlton a special attorney for the state, and for Bryant to have appointed Caldwell to the supreme court. Every governor interviewed for this study unequivocally stated that he felt no obligation to consult former governors. Indeed, LeRoy Collins indicated that it was the responsibility of ex-governors to stay out of the way of the incumbent.

The reasons are not hard to find. They lie mainly in the fragmented nature of the state's politics. With a highly factionalized one-party system, each governor must form his own organization and his own administration. This rarely, if ever, includes the faction of the incumbent governor due to cultural bias against political dynasties. In addition, any effort by the incumbent to form close alliances with former governors would probably not be well received by other public officials and the general population. It would look too much like a power play. Finally, no governor wants to incur the political debts of one of his predecessors, or be identified with his mistakes. As a result, a Florida governor can generally expect to be ignored by those who come after him.

3

Gubernatorial Campaigning in Florida

RECONSTRUCTION was over and nearly all white Floridians breathed a deep sigh of relief. It had officially ended in 1877 and in celebration of the event, the politics of Republicanism was virtually abandoned. The party represented an era Floridians wanted to put behind them. The Civil War and the military occupation that followed severely dislocated the state's economy, society, and politics.[1] After 1877, Floridians, like their southern neighbors, were determined to return their institutions to pre-1860 status as best they remembered it. That meant the repression of freed black Floridians and the rejection of the Republican party.

The effects of these developments was to reduce the Republican party to the position of a minority party in Florida politics. In particular, it made the office of governor inaccessible to a Republican after 1876. From that date until 1966, the party's gubernatorial nominees were decisively beaten in the November elections. Beginning in 1900 and continuing through the gubernatorial election of 1956 the Republican nominee received more than 30 percent of the vote on only three occasions. Generally, he received less than 25 percent of the vote. In 1940 the Democratic nominee, Spessard Holland, ran without Republican opposition. While the Republican nominees made more respectable showings in the 1960 and 1964 general elections, they did not pose a serious threat to the Democratic candidates. It was not until 1966 and the pro-civil rights stance of the state and national Democratic leadership that the Republican party successfully challenged Democratic supremacy at the gubernatorial level.

As a result of the demise of the Republican party after 1876, Florida's governor was selected not in the November election but in the spring Democratic primary. The meaning of the party's nomination was quite clear by the turn of the century. In November 1904, Napoleon Broward, the

Democratic nominee, received a cable from a supporter: "There is no use for me to extend congratulations for your victory was assured before the voting commenced." Democratic confidence was unbridled thereafter. During the summer of 1944, Millard Caldwell, after securing the Democratic nomination but before winning the November general election, selected several prominent Floridians to make a thorough study of education and prepare a revision of the state educational codes that he could submit to the legislature. As recently as 1964, the Democratic nominee was assumed by nearly all Floridians to be the state's next governor. In that year Governor Farris Bryant invited Haydon Burns, victor in the spring primary, to attend the National Governors Conference in June as his representative.[2]

By the beginning of the twentieth century the November election was generally ignored by the Democratic gubernatorial nominee. A typical November campaign might see the party's nominee touring the state at a leisurely pace, talking to the people about the programs he intended to pursue once he assumed office in January. LeRoy Collins, for example, spent $292,000 seeking the Democratic gubernatorial nomination in 1956 but only $174 campaigning against his Republican opponent in the fall.[3] Several Democratic candidates did not bother to campaign at all. Millard Caldwell said he "ignored [the] race" in November and, instead, prepared for his accession to the governorship in January.[4]

The Republican candidate was a sacrificial lamb and, generally, he knew it. Few of the Republican nominees between 1876 and 1960 bothered to campaign vigorously. It just was not worth the effort and expense. Most candidates stayed at home, visited a few major cities, and bought some newspaper advertisement space. Prior to 1960 the Republicans were seriously handicapped by a shortage of funds. In 1952 Harry Swan campaigned for the governor's office with a budget of less than $5,000. By way of contrast, the Democratic candidates spent nearly $500,000 in the 1952 primary. The party's nominee, Dan McCarty, spent nearly $230,000 on the primary alone.[5] Most Republicans accepted the nomination as a necessary sacrifice to retain the party's visibility and integrity. In addition, the party's continued viability enabled it to receive federal patronage during Republican administrations which would not have been forthcoming otherwise.

Because of the weakness of the Republican party, factionalism developed quickly within Democratic ranks. Personal ambitions could not be assuaged by pleas for party loyalty since the party's nomination meant certain victory in the fall. In 1901 the party members voted to eliminate the nominating convention and party platform. Party politics quickly dissolved into groupings around particular individuals or issues. By 1931 Governor Doyle Carlton was moved to observe that "the state-wide primary with no party platform has destroyed organized democracy and party leadership, and has made every candidate for office the democratic party within himself."[6] The collapse of party loyalties also provided a small outlet for Republican ambitions. Governor Broward commented in 1904 that several members of the Republican party were now masquerading within the ranks of the Democratic party.[7]

The Democratic gubernatorial primary in the spring thus became the battleground where personalities were attacked, issues debated, promises made, deals arranged, and the next governor determined. As a result, the primary was a wide open donnybrook with as many as fourteen candidates running for the state's highest office. The state constitution of 1885 encouraged such political chaos by making the incumbent governor ineligible for reelection. V. O. Key, Jr., noted in 1949 that Florida politics had deteriorated to the point where it was literally every candidate for himself.[8] This description was particularly true of the state's gubernatorial politics.

While the eclipse of the Republican party was a central factor in the development of Democratic factionalism, it alone does not explain the political confusion that came to characterize Florida's Democratic gubernatorial primaries. The party's factionalism has been facilitated and compounded by the state's social and economic instability and its geographical configuration. Throughout the twentieth century but particularly since World War II, Florida has experienced significant changes in such important areas as population, urbanization, education, industrialization, per capita income, and race relations. This observation is not new. Key was aware of the importance of most of these issues thirty years ago. What he failed to note at that time, however, was that the changes in these areas had interacted throughout most of the past seventy-five years, and these changes had been accelerated by the state's tremendous growth since World War II. Because of these developments, Florida has experienced significant socioeconomic change since 1900 and especially since 1945. Factionalism within the Democratic party has only been exacerbated by these conditions.

DEMOCRATIC FACTIONALISM, 1900–1956

Party factionalism had clearly emerged by 1900 even though the Democratic gubernatorial nominee was selected by party convention. William Sherman Jennings, an ex-Yankee from Illinois and cousin of the nation's most prominent Democrat, William Jennings Bryan, was the preconvention favorite. He had served the state party faithfully in the past as speaker of the house of representatives and chairman of the state Democratic convention. In several speeches prior to the convention Jennings had endorsed various progressive reforms including free textbooks for children, corporate and railroad controls, and state leasing of convicts.[9] He had also written hundreds of letters to politicians around the state in an effort to line up support for the convention. His leading opponents at the opening of the convention in

June were Dannitte H. Mays of Jefferson County, William Hall Milton, Jr.,
of Jackson County, Frederick Myers of Leon County, and Judge James D.
Beggs of Orange County. Each candidate attempted to build a coalition at the
convention by using his home county as a base of support. This electioneering device also proved quite popular after the adoption of the primary
system.

During the first day of the convention in Jacksonville, Jennings' opponents tried to sabotage his candidacy by drawing attention to his northern
origins and alleging he was named for the hated Yankee general William
Tecumseh Sherman. Jennings was also accused of engaging in "south-hating
antics" although his opponents declined to specify what these "antics"
were.[10] The "bloody shirt" of the Civil War and Reconstruction was still
being waved by Democrats in Florida, and it was not without considerable
influence even in 1900 as events of the convention would prove.

When the voting for a gubernatorial nominee commenced on the third day
of the convention, Jennings assumed the lead at the end of the first ballot with
78.5 votes. However, he was far short of the 188 votes needed for the
nomination. Seven ballots later the votes were largely unchanged; the
convention then adjourned with little hope for an early settlement. The
deadlock continued well into the afternoon of the following day with
Jennings stubbornly refusing to withdraw although he was still well short of
the 188 votes. Finally, Jennings' two major opponents, Frederick Myers and
Dannitte Mays, withdrew on the thirty-fifth and forty-first ballot, respectively. On the forty-fourth ballot Jennings was awarded the nomination as
much for his perseverance and because of party fatigue as for his popularity.[11]

The 1900 convention was significant because it pointed out how difficult it
had become to keep factionalism within the bounds of the convention
system. The proceedings made it quite clear that party leaders were strongly
divided over Jennings' candidacy. A number of Democrats clearly felt that
he was too progressive and too much a Yankee to be their gubernatorial
candidate. The forty-four ballots had established a convention record, and
reporters described the nomination as the hardest political fight they had ever
observed.[12] With the virtual demise of the Republican party by 1900 and the
emergence of progressivism, the Democratic party in Florida had become so
factionalized that the possibility of a more harmonious convention in the
future appeared extremely doubtful.

Not surprisingly, the party members endorsed a proposal to use a direct
primary system to decide the Democratic gubernatorial nomination in 1904.
Party leaders argued that such a primary was a more democratic process
although many members no doubt felt that it would be less divisive than the

internecine warfare of the convention system. In 1901 the legislature formally approved the convention's recommendation.[13]

The adoption of the direct primary made politics more open and democratic and, consequently, brought about several changes in gubernatorial campaigning. For instance, in 1904, Napoleon Broward and his aides prepared a pamphlet which contained an autobiographical sketch, his platform, and his experiences as captain of his own boat. This brochure played upon the popular appeal of Horatio Alger by emphasizing Broward's poor youth and his successful struggle to overcome various social and economic hardships. Broward mailed this biographical sketch "to every registered white voter in the State" to enhance his public identity.[14]

Broward and his opponents, Congressman Robert W. Davis, C. M. Brown, and Dannitte H. Mays, were forced by the primary system to go out on the hustings and meet with the citizens of each town. Florida was a very rural state in 1904 and the candidates had to journey into isolated areas if they hoped to gain popular favor. By announcing his candidacy in October 1903, over seven months before the primary, Broward was able to visit each section of the state and enhance his public visibility. Historian Samuel Proctor noted in his biography of Broward that the candidate spent several months "in dusty day coaches and rickety buggies [and] . . . on horseback" touring Florida.[15]

Broward's campaign was aided substantially by the endorsement of Governor William Jennings. Broward had gained Jennings' support by campaigning for him in 1900 and by warmly encouraging his gubernatorial programs. Enlisting support of the outgoing governor became especially important to the candidates in the first primary. It gave the endorsed candidate publicity and helped him build a coalition between his followers and those of the outgoing governor. Jennings' secretary, Charles H. Dickinson, for example, campaigned actively in Broward's behalf apparently hoping to be chosen as his secretary if he were elected governor.[16] Such support virtually assured a candidate of a spot in the second primary. The governor's backing, however, could also hurt a candidate's chances as history would show, particularly in the second primary. Floridians have been rather proud of their political independence and have resented any hint of machine politics. On occasion, such as in the 1948 campaign, the governor's endorsement has alienated a substantial number of voters who felt he was trying to handpick his successor.

The ties between Jennings and Broward did not end with Jennings' endorsement. Broward's campaign adopted and built upon many of the progressive issues raised during Jennings' administration. For example, throughout his campaign Broward denounced the railroad and corporate interests in Florida. He appealed to the small, independent retailer, contending that "a hundred stores are better than one. If trusts are permitted to control we shall become a country of paupers and beggars."[17] He also made the issue of drainage of the Everglades a major plank in his platform. Indeed, Broward's campaign literally became a referendum on the drainage issue — should the lands be left to the business interests and railroads to exploit, or should they be left to the state for the benefit of all the people?

While the issues raised by Broward were not new, the gubernatorial primary served to popularize them. These topics received additional publicity during the stormy years of Broward's governorship. As a result, the drainage question and other progressive matters Broward discussed in 1904 and which he pursued vigorously throughout his four years in office remained important campaign issues in 1908 and 1912.

Broward's opponents represented different interests in the state and campaigned on issues that would also remain prominent in the next two campaigns. Congressman Davis, supported by the Bourbon and railroad interests of Florida, called for a businesslike government and belittled the Broward drainage plan.[18] Although Davis failed to be elected in 1904 his conservative, businesslike approach to government had tremendous influence as a campaign issue in Florida. This plank was a part of most gubernatorial platforms in the twentieth century and no pronouncement was heard more frequently. It was one of the issues which crossed rural-urban lines and which could be depended upon not to alienate any significant bloc of voters. Florida was a poor state throughout much of the twentieth century and desperately needed business investments to achieve full employment and a measure of prosperity. Many politicians saw this campaign stance as an effective way to attract northern business interests.

Davis' campaign attacked Broward as an opponent of conservation and responsible government and a man of little real ability. Davis tried to damage Broward's credibility in the runoff by presenting a notarized statement which alleged that Broward while sheriff of Jacksonville had appointed a Negro deputy sheriff.[19] The charge had little effect on the outcome of the campaign, however, since Broward's racial views were known to mirror the racial attitudes of white Floridians.

Broward meanwhile derided Davis' connections with the railroad interests and the free passes he received from these corporations while in Congress. He also noted wryly that Davis had resigned from Congress in 1904 complaining about the financial expense (the salary was $5,000 and a congressman received ten cents per mile for travel) and now he was running for governor at a flat salary of $3,500.[20] In a very close runoff Broward defeated Davis by a mere 714 votes.

C. M. Brown, the third candidate, emphasized his Confederate War record under the command of General Robert E. Lee. A Civil War record was still an important asset in state politics during the early twentieth century; however, it did not guarantee victory in the first or second primary. A Democratic candidate had to have some political experience or, at least, the political wisdom to know how to run a campaign. Brown lacked both the experience and expertise. He merely reiterated the promise of Broward to help the common man. His campaign generated little public enthusiasm.[21]

The campaign of 1908 saw John Stockton of Jacksonville running on a platform endorsing the policies of Governor Broward. Stockton and Broward were close personal friends and Broward worked diligently for Stockton's election.[22] His chief opponent, Albert Waller Gilchrist, campaigned on his military record and his political moderation. Gilchrist's campaign was launched in an interesting manner, one which was widely copied by subsequent candidates. He had his friends publicly call on him to run for governor; shortly thereafter he announced his candidacy.[23] This campaign device had the effect of making him appear to be a statesman responding to the pleas of the citizenry rather than an ambitious politician. Gilchrist sounded like Congressman Robert Davis in 1904 when he promised a businesslike administration and refused to attack the corporate interests. But Gilchrist added a new and important feature to Davis' appeal: "When I went into this campaign, I made up my mind that I would not array masses against classes, or vice versa."[24] It was this promise to avoid playing upon class hatred, a pledge made frequently by the redeemers or "Bourbon" politicians in neighboring southern states, that softened and made more palatable to the Florida voters the conservative, businesslike appeal. Gilchrist added that he had no faction or machine. He would accept anyone and everyone's support including that "of the corporations, of the anticorporations, the prohibitionists, the antiprohibitionists, of the local optionists, the Christians and the Jews, and of the Gentiles, the 'Publicans and sinners.' He would even accept the support of the Pharisees."[25] Gilchrist also introduced a unique element into the campaign; it was a postcard with a picture of three monkeys in different poses followed by the caption "Hear no evil, see no evil, speak no evil."[26] Although the postcard seems rather amateurish by today's political standards, it received wide circulation and gave Gilchrist greater voter visibility than his opponents.

Stockton tried to undermine Gilchrist's growing support by accusing him of receiving $360,000 in campaign contributions from liquor interests around the country. The size of the account made most people skeptical of Stockton's charge, and Gilchrist's offer of $1,000 to anyone who could prove the allegation seemed to allay the fears of the remaining doubters.[27]

In 1912 Park Trammell, attorney general of Florida, campaigned largely on his record as a "legislator and Attorney General." He also placed considerable emphasis on his humble beginnings and his eventual success in life by means of thriftiness and hard work. He expanded this appeal to the common man by endorsing such progressive principles of the day as "the rule of many instead of the rule of the few," and the protection of "the people more firmly in their rights." However, Trammell, like Gilchrist, offered a little something to all Floridians when he promised to conduct his administration on a businesslike basis. This platform coupled with Trammell's attractive, youthful personality assisted his victory in the first primary.[28]

The 1916 Democratic campaign was unique in Florida's history. It was, perhaps, the state's most emotional and highly charged campaign, and it was the first in which blatant demogoguery was interjected. It also saw the emergence of a man who was to influence Florida gubernatorial politics for a decade and who was the first (and last) to be elected governor as a third party candidate.

Initially, the campaign appeared to be little different from those that preceded it. The Democratic party had decided in 1913 to eliminate the second primary because of its expense and to replace it with a one-primary system of first and second choices. But this change did not appear to portend any serious problems since the party had been discussing the idea on and off since 1904.[29] William V. Knott, state treasurer, was the precampaign favorite. He was closely allied with the conservative forces in Florida politics and, like Gilchrist and Trammell before him, called for a businessman's administration. His leading opponent seemed to be former speaker of the house Ion Farris of Jacksonville who represented the more progressive segment of the Democratic party and whose support came largely from the workers and the city reformers. One of the four other candidates was Sidney J. Catts, a former Alabama Baptist preacher and an insurance salesman of small means. Catts was initially given little chance of receiving the nomination until anti-Catholicism reared its ugly head and he quickly capitalized upon it.

The activities of the Guardians of Liberty clubs and the writings of Thomas E. Watson in his *Jeffersonian* magazine helped spread religious hatred and fear. Each took advantage of the growth of nativism in the country as a whole and the latent anti-Catholicism in rural, Baptist Florida. Guardians of Liberty clubs were active throughout Florida as opponents of parochial schools and liquor. Watson's journal was vehemently anti-Catholic and seemed to have had a large number of readers in the state.[30] In 1916 there were just enough Roman Catholics in Florida to convince Protestants that the "Catholic menace" was real.

Religious animosities were exacerbated with the adoption of the Sturkie Resolution by the state Democratic committee. The resolution sought to prevent from voting in the Democratic primary any person who opposed a candidate because of his religious views or who belonged to any secret organization which attempted to influence political action.[31] The resolution was clearly aimed at the Guardians of Liberty and Tom Watson.

Catts was able to exploit the unpopularity of the resolution to his immediate advantage. Campaigning from town to town in a Model T Ford equipped with a loudspeaker, he claimed Cardinal James Gibbons had sent Catholic money into Florida to secure passage of the Sturkie Resolution. He also contended that as much as $180,000 had been spent by the Catholic Church to bring about his defeat.[32] Catts played upon the religious fears he aroused by sending his aide, Jerry Carter, dressed as a priest, into rural, Protestant Florida where he made violently anti-Catts speeches. Catts also wore guns on both hips because he claimed Apalachicola Catholics had threatened his life.[33]

As with so many demagogues, Catts' appeal to the common man was largely negative. He offered few programs which would improve the economic or social condition of the poor. (He did talk in general terms of lower taxes and better schools for the poor.) Instead, he attacked Catholics, corporations, and blacks, and, generally, in that order. He opposed a liberal arts education for blacks, arguing that it was a waste of time and taxpayers' dollars.[34] In his scheme of things, blacks would be restricted to menial, hard labor.

The returns from the first primary were very close but were also very slow in arriving, leading to charges of fraud by both Knott's and Catts' factions. The State Canvassing Board composed of the secretary of state, attorney general, and treasurer initially awarded the certification of nomination to Catts with a 263 vote majority. But the state supreme court on an appeal from Knott ordered another recount and ruled, less than thirty days before the general election, that Knott had won by 23 votes. In commenting on the tremendous confusion caused by the close vote and the two different findings, the *Ocala Weekly Banner* reflected the sentiment of many when it announced "we will support the Democratic nominee whoever it is."[35]

During the period between the June 2 runoff and the court's ruling on October 7, Knott had suspended his campaign activities. Catts meanwhile had taken a short breather and then resumed his travels in a truck equipped with a calliope to signal his arrival. During the course of the campaign Catts made seven trips across Florida. In response to the court-ordered recount, Catts declared at several stops: "I could have opened the ballot boxes the same way as was done in behalf of Mr. Knott and could have had them stuffed in my favor, but I would rather not be elected than be elected dishonestly."[36]

After the supreme court's decision was announced, the Prohibition party in Florida nominated Catts. He now sounded a new call which had widespread popular appeal — he was the "people's nominee" opposed by Knott, "The Court's nominee." Indeed, many Democratic politicians as well as ordinary citizens felt that the party's nomination had been stolen from Catts. Several prominent Democrats, including James B. Hodges of Lake City, campaigned for Catts in the general election.[37]

Knott tried to draw attention to his experience as a politician and his record as a state treasurer, but the public was not listening. They had been stirred into a virtual frenzy by Catts' rhetoric and the emotional appeals of Tom Watson and the Guardians of Liberty. As a result, Knott's low-key, issue-oriented campaign was largely ignored. Catts won the election decisively,

Governor Sidney J. Catts riding in his inaugural parade in January 1917. An electrifying personality, Catts initiated several campaign techniques that were widely used by subsequent governors, including the use of automobiles to reach as many voters as possible, megaphones to broadcast campaign speeches, and advance men to prepare crowds for his arrival in remote hamlets. State Photographic Archives.

capturing thirty-eight of the state's fifty-two counties with 31,349 votes to Knott's 24,623.[38]

The intraparty strife and the emotionalism that had been generated by Catts' campaign alienated many party stalwarts. While they had come to accept the factionalism that existed in the party primary, few had envisioned the divisions created by Catts' candidacy. For most Democrats it was one thing to have a general bloodletting during a thirty-day period every four years but it was quite another to have a five-month party bloodletting. In addition, it appeared that most party regulars, excluding the Catts faction, generally abhorred the appeal to the masses made by the candidate. These traditionalists believed that a campaign should be conducted with some decorum and that it was not a completely unbridled affair. As a result, a number of party leaders moved to heal the wounds and to prevent a reemergence of the tactics of the 1916 campaign. Their progress was necessarily slow because of the strength of the Catts forces, but by 1932 the party had returned to the second primary system and had also barred from the general election anyone defeated for the same position in the primary election.[39]

In 1920 the gubernatorial campaign returned to the more traditional issues established prior to Catts' candidacy. The leading candidate and eventual nominee Cary Hardee called for "an economical administration," and a return to good business principles in government. Catts' influence had not completely disappeared in 1920. Van Swearingen, attorney general during Catts' governorship, was believed by many to be the Catts candidate. However, the former governor was held in such disfavor after his four years in office that Swearingen frequently denied having any ties with the Catts people except when he was in Catts country. Swearingen was also handicapped by his ineffectiveness as a campaigner; he lacked the personal magnetism and dynamism of Sidney Catts. Hardee, who had been a prominent member of the legislature, easily defeated his two opponents on a conservative, anti-Catts platform.[40] In many respects, the anti-Catts members of the Democratic party seemed to have coalesced around Hardee's candidacy. "Catts-ism" had been effectively killed off by this coalition and Hardee's victory in 1920, although Catts himself would remain prominent in party affairs for another eight years.

From 1920 to 1932, it was very difficult to discern differences between the platforms of the candidates despite the collapse of the economic boom in 1926. During these three gubernatorial campaigns the issues were largely those of conservative, economical government. Several candidates also emphasized the need to attract more money into Florida, and they supported programs to increase tourism, bring in new industry, aid agriculture, and build better roads. These particular issues have remained very popular in the state up to the present time.

Although issues were not particularly decisive during this period, personalities and campaign styles were. John W. Martin, the party's nominee in 1924, was an able campaigner. He entered the race barely known outside of his native Jacksonville, where he had been mayor for three terms. Catts, Worth W. Trammell, brother of United States Senator Park Trammell, and Frank E. Jennings, former speaker of the house, were generally better known than Martin. More than any of the other candidates, however, Martin was able to capitalize on the mood of Floridians in the early 1920s. Campaigning throughout the state as diligently and as effectively as Catts, Martin promised a sane, businesslike administration and a road construction program which, he announced, would attract tourists and industry. His commitment to the state's growth at, as he described it, a small price, plus his aggressive campaign style secured him the nomination.[41] Catts continued to demonstrate his personal strength among the rural voters by running a strong second to Martin. Well aware of the importance of rhetoric in gubernatorial campaigning, Catts told the farmers that they had only three real friends in the world, "Jesus Christ, Sears, Roebuck, and Company, and Sidney J. Catts." He also referred to himself as "Uncle Catts" and promised to represent the common people against the rich and the corporations.[42]

Despite the post-1926 economic slump in Florida, the campaign issues in 1928 did not appear dramatically different from those raised in 1924. The candidates were still talking about "a sane, economical and constructive administration." Catts was still on the scene and running for governor again. On this occasion he tried to ride the anti–Al Smith sentiment to victory. Perhaps the only major difference between the 1924 and 1928 campaigns was the staid, somber nature of the candidates, their emphasis on retrenchment in government, and the public's concern with Smith's presidential candidacy. Even then, however, Doyle Carlton, a former member of the legislature and the preprimary favorite, sounded very much like Martin when he advocated good government, good schools, and good roads. In the last analysis, Carlton's record as a sensible, pragmatic politician and his well-organized campaign assured him an easy victory in the primary over three rather weak opponents.[43]

By 1932 Florida was deeply mired in the national depression. The hurricanes of 1926 and 1928, the failure of the land boom, and the fruit fly pestilence had devastated the state's economy well before the onset of the depression. The financial collapse of the nation merely added the final coup de grace to Florida's economic trials. Floridians, therefore, were anxious for change, for someone to lead them out of the depression.

The principal gubernatorial candidates in 1931 were both former governors—Cary Hardee and John W. Martin. Although both promised to restore economic stability, they spent most of the time belittling one another's leadership. Martin, in particular, referred repeatedly to Hardee's four years in office as "the vacant chair term."[44] These two men and the other six candidates promised retrenchment in government, fiscal conservatism, and little else. Once again the race boiled down to personalities rather than issues. This determinant and the depression proved to be the keys to David Sholtz' surprising victory.

Sholtz had little political experience, having served but one term in the state legislature. He had been active in civic affairs in Daytona Beach as organizer and president of the Chamber of Commerce. He served subsequently as president of the Florida Chamber of Commerce. In planning his election strategy, Sholtz opted for a statewide barnstorming campaign to overcome his lack of recognition by the voters. He proved to be a new and refreshing personality, and to many he was the man Florida needed in this time of crisis. Sholtz capitalized on this pyschological need: he criticized both former governors as unsuitable for the demands of the depression and offered himself as "new blood."[45]

Narrowly making the runoff against Martin, Sholtz continued his barnstorming tactics throughout the state. He lashed out at Martin for his political connections and accused him of trying to establish a political machine. He promised to rid the state of "political racketeers" and to "make politics fit for decent men and women to participate in." Sholtz' criticism of Martin's political ties and his effort to seek a second term proved very effective in the runoff. Only one governor had been reelected in Florida since it had become a state and most Floridians apparently agreed that one term as governor was enough for any man. Sholtz' campaign also benefited by Martin's contention that Sholtz was a Jew. Sholtz quickly proved he was not Jewish. As one of his campaign workers put it, Sholtz was in fact an Episcopalian and that was "something midway between a Methodist and a Baptist."[46] Martin's personal attack on Sholtz was a last-ditch effort to undermine Sholtz' growing popularity; it failed. Sholtz defeated the former governor with nearly 63 percent of the vote.

In many ways the 1936 campaign closely paralleled that of 1932. Once again there were an inordinate number of candidates (fourteen) trying to capitalize on the public's frustration with the depression. Each sought to build upon his support in his home county and qualify for the runoff. Of the fourteen candidates, only William C. Hodges, president of the senate, and Peter Tomasello, Jr., speaker of the house, were prominent figures in Florida politics. All fourteen candidates called for adequate school funding and each opposed new taxes. Fred Cone of Lake City, former president of the state senate, but out of the legislature since 1913, had the most unique slogan; he promised to lower "the budget to balance taxes instead of raising taxes to balance the budget."[47] Like Sholtz before him, Cone was regarded as an independent with no particular political ties. He ran a strong grass roots campaign, particularly in rural North Florida which he called home and where he had been a farmer, lawyer, and banker. It was principally these two factors which enabled him to defeat Judge Raleigh Petteway of Tampa in the runoff.

Petteway's campaign was hurt by charges that he was a "reformer" and that he would try to "reform" the state in the manner of President Franklin Roosevelt. He also had to defend himself against the allegation that David Sholtz' administration was backing his campaign. His greatest handicap, however, was his straight-laced image and the widespread belief that he would reenact prohibition and end gambling. Cone captured the attention of Floridians through his campaign rhetoric and held it; Petteway did not.[48]

By 1940 the Democratic party in Florida was still feeling the economic effects of the depression. Eleven candidates campaigned for the nomination in that year, hoping to build upon the economic frustrations of Floridians and to become the state's next governor. But, interestingly enough, forces were at work in 1940 which promised to restore a measure of stability to Florida politics. For the first time since 1928 a figure of some statewide reputation, Spessard Holland, had announced as a candidate. Holland had been a well-known county judge in Polk County and a prominent member of the state senate. In addition, his campaign received substantial support from the business community headed by Ed Ball of the Du Pont interests. Holland's chances were aided by the state's economic condition. With the depression almost behind them, Floridians were searching for a measure of stability and Holland, an undramatic but honest and solid appearing fellow, seemed to promise just that.

Holland's leading opponent in the eleven-man field was Francis Whitehair of DeLand. Whitehair was generally recognized as the political leader of Volusia County. The Volusia machine was one of the very few long-lasting political organizations in Florida.[49] While the support of this well-organized, tightly knit machine helped Whitehair secure a spot in the runoff, it greatly weakened his candidacy in the second primary. His affiliation with this organization was regarded with considerable distrust by the voters outside his home county. Holland successfully exploited this issue in the runoff, arguing that "Democracy is on trial in Florida as it is elsewhere in the world" and the choice was "that of machine government or independent government."[50] Whitehair retaliated in kind, promising that if Holland was elected governor, Florida would have "an invisible government of chain stores, the Du Ponts, . . . the road contractors and the fertilizer octopus."[51] Whitehair also tried to divert public attention from his political ties by running on a platform that promised a little something for everyone. In particular, he endorsed old age pensions, better educational facilities, aid for dependent children, equal rights for women, more aid to agriculture, a better highway program, and a more workable health department.[52] Whitehair's ties with the Volusia machine, however, proved his undoing and Holland, who refused to let the public forget this fact, won very decisively with 57 percent of the vote. An interesting footnote to the primary was Fuller Warren's candidacy. A politically ambitious young man from Jacksonville, but relatively unknown outside that city, Warren ran a campaign very much like David Sholtz had in 1932. However, by 1940, with World War II imminent, it was clear that Floridians were looking more for experience and stability than for a fresh personality.

Millard Caldwell, the party's nominee in 1944, was backed by the same business leaders that had supported Holland in 1940. Caldwell, a lawyer-businessman, promised "just a sensible, businesslike administration if I am elected governor of the State." He also declared that Florida's resources must stay committed to the war effort. Caldwell decided early in the campaign that "[Lex] Green was the man I'd have to run it off with and I fashioned my campaign to that end."[53] Green, a member of the house of representatives, was the best known of the seven candidates, but he had earned a reputation as a "liberal" in state political circles for his support of Franklin D. Roosevelt and his domestic and foreign policies. Throughout the first and second primary, Caldwell concentrated his attack on Green's alleged liberalism. In particular, Caldwell berated Green's free-spending approach to government. This campaign charge has been one of the most successful in Florida gubernatorial politics. Floridians have shown a persistent dislike of liberal, free-spending candidates at the state level. Caldwell defeated Green by over 40,000 votes.

Shortly before Caldwell's victory in the Democratic primary, the Supreme Court ruled in *Smith* v. *Allwright* (321 U.S. 649) that Texas' all white Democratic primary was unconstitutional. While the decision boded ill for Florida's lily-white primary, blacks would not begin to influence gubernatorial politics until the decade following the Voting Rights Act of 1965.[54]

Florida's postwar population and economy grew dramatically, entering what might be described as a "take-off" phase. Fuller Warren, who had gained statewide attention by his impressive third-place finish in 1940, had been campaigning for the party's nomination since his return from the Pacific in 1945. However, his campaign barely took notice of the dramatic changes that Florida was experiencing. His platform called for increased tourism, removal of cattle from the highways, citrus reform, and centralized state purchasing.[55]

Dan McCarty, Warren's chief opponent, and three other candidates ran on platforms almost identical to Warren's. When his opponents announced their platforms, Warren and his aides pointed out, to his advantage, that he was the first candidate to bring these matters before the public.

During the campaign Warren captured the interest of many voters with his dynamic speaking delivery, colorful personality, and handsome features. In fact, Warren was one of Florida's ablest campaigners. He exploited his physical assets by conducting a statewide speaking tour, meeting personally with local political leaders, and advertising extensively in state newspapers. This approach proved very effective in the primary and runoff against Dan

On the eve of World War II, gubernatorial leadership in Florida passed from Fred Cone to Spessard Holland. Holland's entire administration was to be engulfed in the conflagration as Floridians prepared for war, especially to defend the state's vast coastline from German intrusion. Left to right: Mrs. Cone, Mrs. Holland, Governor Cone, Governor-elect Holland. State Photographic Archives.

McCarty who had strong political backing but little popular support. McCarty had the support of some of Caldwell's staff which helped him secure a place in the second primary. However, the support ultimately proved a liability to McCarty's campaign. Warren used it to his advantage in the runoff by accusing Caldwell of trying to build a political dynasty.[56]

The 1948 primary introduced a new era in campaign fund raising in the state's gubernatorial politics. Over $1 million was apparently contributed to the five candidates. Warren alone received as much as $450,000 to $500,000 although he signed a statement alleging he received only $12,241.[57] The contributions permitted Warren much greater latitude than his opponents, particularly in advertising. Without television and with only modest use of radio, advertising and a statewide personal appearance campaign were the most effective ways to reach the voting public in Florida. Warren's campaign was sufficiently financed to permit him to do both and do them well.

The runoff between Warren and McCarty presented Floridians with a unique political contest: Warren, the candidate of rural North Florida, opposed by McCarty, the wealthy citrus grower from South Florida. Conditions in the state favored Warren. The tremendous growth of South Florida in the previous five years had kept that region more fragmented than North Florida, which had also grown in population but largely through immigration from Alabama, Mississippi, South Carolina, and Georgia. These new residents generally shared the rural political views of northern Floridians.[58] This development in conjunction with Warren's campaign style and financial support ensured his victory in 1948.

Although unsuccessful in his first gubernatorial bid, McCarty had favorably impressed a number of Floridians by his common sense and honesty. In 1952 he ran again and won rather easily. In retrospect, his election was facilitated by Warren's difficulties as governor and a realization by many Floridians that McCarty had probably been the abler man in 1948.[59] Despite Dwight Eisenhower's victory over Adlai Stevenson in the presidential campaign in Florida, McCarty easily defeated his Republican opponent, Harry Swan, in the fall. While the Dixiecrat bolt from the Democratic party in 1948 and Stevenson's liberalism caused Floridians to question their loyalty to the national Democratic party, they showed no inclination as yet to support the Republican party in state elections.

Shortly after McCarty had taken office he suffered a heart attack and died in September. According to the constitution, the president of the senate (Charley Johns) became acting governor. The state supreme court subsequently ruled that a new election would be held in 1954 to choose McCarty's successor. During the one year he was acting governor, Johns alienated a number of McCarty's supporters by removing from office several of his political appointees who, Johns claimed, were trying to discredit him. When Johns declared his intention to seek the governorship the McCarty people turned to state Senator LeRoy Collins as their candidate. Collins had been a close personal friend of McCarty and had helped him shape his legislative program. The campaign dwelt almost exclusively on Johns' suspension of the McCarty officials, with the third candidate, Brailey Odham, trying unsuccessfully to get the two leaders to discuss substantive issues.

The turning point in the campaign occurred during a television debate between Collins and Johns in Miami. Johns' aides had taken out an advertisement in the early edition of the *Miami Herald* on the same day of the debate. The advertisement contended that Collins had been roundly beaten in the debate by Johns. Collins managed to secure a copy of the ad shortly before the debate was to be aired that evening. As the cameras focused in on Collins, he displayed the *Miami Herald* ad and asked Johns to explain its meaning. Flabbergasted, Johns replied weakly, "I do not have anything to do with advertising. I didn't know about it." However, his lack of poise throughout the remainder of the debate suggested that he knew more than he had admitted. As the television program came to a close, Collins further unnerved Johns when he asked him why he had voted against a bill to unmask the Klan. Clearly embarrassed by the question, Johns said, "I made a mistake." During the remaining days of the primary, Collins pointed to both episodes as examples of Johns' lack of responsibility. Collins was also able to capitalize on one of the more humorous episodes in an otherwise rough campaign. Henry Trafficante, an alleged mobster in Tampa, was arrested by police for gambling, and, while being put in a police van, was heard by reporters to shout: "Johns is our man." Johns denied ever knowing Trafficante but Collins refused to let the matter drop, declaring that organized crime was backing Johns.[60] The voters appeared to be swayed by Collins' hard-hitting campaign and selected him as the party's nominee with a 55 percent plurality.

RACE, REPUBLICANISM, AND CONTINUED DEMOCRATIC FACTIONALISM

Just prior to the 1956 primary, the state supreme court ruled that Collins was eligible for reelection since he had served only two years as governor. In retrospect, the decision paled in significance next to the campaign of that year. The 1956 campaign marked the emergence of race as an important campaign issue, the advent of the modern gubernatorial campaign, and the resurgence of Republicanism. When the United States Supreme Court rendered the *Brown* v. *Board of Education of Topeka, Kansas,* (347 U.S. 483) decision in 1954, which called for an end to *de jure* segregated schools, Floridians had reacted initially in a mild fashion. In the gubernatorial election held that year Collins and Johns declared their support for segregation and let the matter drop. Each seemed unsure of the effect of the decision and, instead, concentrated on more traditional issues.[61]

By the 1956 campaign, however, public opinion had sufficiently polarized over the *Brown* decision so that candidates were no longer uncertain about its impact. Three of the four major candidates in 1956 promised repeatedly to retain segregation. The platform of Sumter Lowry, a wealthy Tampa businessman, consisted of a single plank: 100 percent maintenance of segregation. He denounced "integration as part of a communist conspiracy to destroy the moral fibre of the nation by creating a 'mongrel' race incapable of preventing a red take-over." He and Farris Bryant, state representative from Ocala, supported an interposition resolution to block federal government enforcement of the *Brown* decision. The first plank in the platform of former governor Fuller Warren pledged him to "do everything in my power to maintain segregation." One veteran observer noted early in the campaign that the outcome of the election was likely to be determined by who could defend his racial position most vigorously and "out-seg" the other candidates.[62]

LeRoy Collins, who was running for reelection after serving out the last two years of McCarty's term, campaigned largely on his record as governor and his ability as a problem solver. Because of the racial appeal being made by his opponents, Collins also found it necessary to address himself to the issue of segregation. He promised to retain segregation, but he pledged to do so only by peaceful and lawful means. He refused to endorse an interposition resolution.[63] As he told his audience on a number of occasions, "If you want a governor who will get the white people to hate the Negroes and incite the Negroes to hate the white people then you don't want LeRoy Collins to be your governor." Collins' moderate racial stance and his position as governor made him the popular target of his segregationist opponents. Sumter Lowry frequently referred to him as the NAACP candidate, contending that he "has used every conceivable means to line up the Negro bloc vote controlled by the NAACP."[64]

Unlike his opponents, however, Collins believed that with Florida's rapidly expanding population and urban growth a gubernatorial candidate could not win solely on a racial appeal. In this respect and in the campaign techniques he employed, Collins significantly affected the nature of gubernatorial campaigning in Florida. He and his aides were cognizant of the public's needs, particularly in the areas of education and employment, as a result of this urban expansion. His promise to improve schools and attract more industry had great appeal in the state's urban centers.[65] Even more important, however, Collins' promise to continue his fight to reapportion the legislature gained him the plaudits and the votes of urban Floridians. The state legislature was one of the most malapportioned in the nation, and Collins' long struggle with the pork-chop legislature in 1955 and 1956 to remedy this inequity had secured him the urban support he would need in the 1956 Democratic primary. Collins made sure this point was not lost on the public by calling a special legislative session in June, one week after the election, to reconsider his reapportionment plan.

In concentrating his campaign in urban areas, he broke away from traditional campaign strategies which emphasized numerous local public addresses and travel into each of the state's communities. Collins and his aides felt that the nature of his platform and the racist appeal of his opponents severely limited his chances in the rural areas of Florida. On this basis, his campaign relied on the urban vote for victory. To reach as many of these people as possible Collins made extensive use of radio and television. He was the first candidate to exploit successfully both media. A handsome, well-groomed man, who quickly charmed even the most unfriendly audience, Collins was eminently successful at employing such techniques. He also utilized the airplane rather than the automobile to barnstorm around the state. Florida's geographical configuration, particularly with regard to its urban centers, mandated this change in transportation. The wisdom of Collins' campaign was reflected in his unprecedented first-primary nomination; he carried the ten leading metropolitan counties with 72 percent of the vote.[66]

The state Republican party, which had made substantial electoral advances in 1952 due to the national leadership of presidential candidate Dwight David Eisenhower, who carried Florida, and the state leadership of gubernatorial candidate Harry Swan, continued to build upon these recent gains. Despite a poor showing in 1954 and a shortage of campaign funds in 1956, William Washburne, the party's nominee, received 266,980 votes or 56,000 more than Swan had received in 1952. Nevertheless, the Republican candidate posed no threat to the Democratic nominee; Collins received 747,753 votes although he chose not to campaign against Washburne.

Collins' victory on a racially moderate platform did not bring an end to such appeals. His last four years in office were turbulent ones racially for Florida, and, as a result, segregation was still an emotional issue in 1960. Farris Bryant, the leading candidate in that year, reiterated his firm belief in segregation. He also pledged that if elected governor he would "maintain segregation by every honorable and constitutional means." Eight of the other nine candidates denounced what state senator Fred Dickinson called "creeping integration."[67]

Collins broke an established precedent by openly endorsing and campaigning for Doyle Carlton, Jr., a moderate on racial issues. Collins dismissed Bryant as an apostle of "reaction, retreat and regret"; he argued that Florida could not afford four more years of racial confrontation. In breaking with this precedent Collins gained few new supporters for Carlton. Floridians in general resented the governor's moderate racial posture and felt that he was trying to saddle them with four more years of his leadership.[68]

Bryant and Carlton, who met in the runoff, agreed on the need for more funding for public schools and universities. Bryant also endorsed a more ambitious highway construction program and the creation of a cabinet position on tourism. In addition, he promised to pare $50 million from state appropriations, a pledge that seemed impossible to fulfill in light of his other statements.[69]

Heavily financed by the state's major business leaders, Bryant's campaign was better able to reach the people than were those of his opponents. One device he employed was a television show entitled "Breakfast with the Bryants." Full of pabulum and sweetness, it was quickly canceled for lack of viewers. His aides also put together a small booklet which described

Governor-elect Farris Bryant and wife Julia met supporters for breakfast on the morning of his inauguration, January 3, 1961. In his campaign Bryant relied heavily on television to reach Florida's large and widely scattered population. LeRoy Collins in 1956 and Bryant in 1960 ran the first media-oriented gubernatorial campaigns. State Photographic Archives.

Bryant's poor youth, his financial struggles through college and law school, his honesty, and his support of education and commitment to segregation. Several of his opponents belittled what they characterized as the Bryant "comic books." Nevertheless, the pamphlets enjoyed a wide circulation and seemed to enhance his visibility with the voters. In the last analysis, however, his victory over Carlton occurred largely because of the racial frustrations of white Floridians and their resentment toward Governor Collins for his policy of racial moderation. Bryant emphasized his belief in "firm segregation" as opposed to Carlton's moderate approach. He also maintained that Carlton's success in the first primary was attributable to the "Negro bloc vote."[70]

Racial issues remained very influential in the 1964 campaign. Haydon Burns, a surprising third-place finisher in 1960, alternately denounced the Civil Rights Act of 1964 and attacked the NAACP as a band of troublemakers. During his sixteen years as mayor of Jacksonville, Burns had gained a reputation as a hardliner on civil rights for his standing order to arrest sit-in demonstrators. During the 1964 gubernatorial campaign, Burns reiterated his opposition to civil rights demonstrations in Jacksonville. He declared that no one had the right to "force their presence at certain hotels, restaurants and other businesses...." He dramatically deputized 496 city firemen as a "special police force" to deal with such a demonstration in March 1964.[71] His strong-arm tactics appeared to meet the approval of most Floridians and, when combined with his powerful showing in 1960, placed him in the forefront of the 1964 campaign.

Racial issues were of such importance during the three post-*Brown* gubernatorial campaigns that even moderates in Florida felt compelled to express support for segregation. LeRoy Collins declared during the 1956 campaign that he stood "firmly and squarely with the people of Florida who ... overwhelmingly desire a continuation of our long established traditions of segregation." Doyle Carlton, who lost to Bryant in 1960 while campaigning as a racial moderate, promised the voting public that he would "preserve segregation in a lawful manner." Only Robert King High, the 1964 opponent of Haydon Burns, managed to avoid such commitments. High had blunted racial violence in Miami by personally meeting with black and white leaders of the community and directing the integration of the city's school system. However, in his desperation to overcome Burns' lead in the runoff, High disclosed an invitation which, he claimed, had been sent by Burns to the president of the NAACP in Jacksonville inviting him to attend a dance in Burns' honor.[72]

Despite such statements and allegations, the role played by moderates in stemming racial appeals was one of the important features of Florida gubernatorial campaigning during this period. LeRoy Collins, who defeated his militant segregationist opponents in 1956, argued repeatedly that Florida could not grow and develop in an atmosphere of racial turmoil. He chastised his opponents for agitating the race issue. He also accused them of "irresponsibility" in their attacks on his administration. Carlton endorsed Collins' racial policies in the 1960 campaign. He also promised to uphold federal and state laws and oppose an interposition resolution. In 1964 Robert King High campaigned for the black vote and pledged his support to the public accommodations section of the 1964 Civil Rights Act. He called the equal treatment of all Americans the "most sensible issue of our times." He promised to promote "racial tranquility," adding that no governor could allow racial problems to "be settled in the street with brickbats and axe handles."[73]

The influence exercised by these candidates made it very difficult for racial extremists to win the Democratic nomination. No such candidate won a Democratic or Republican primary during this period and only Sumter Lowry ran a particularly strong campaign. Yet he failed to push Collins into a runoff. Bill Hendrix, a Ku Klux Klan leader from Oldsmar, made segregation his only issue in 1960 as Lowry had in 1956. Hendrix finished a dismal eighth in a ten-man field. In addition to the key role played by moderates, Florida's population diversity with many people from the Northeast settling on the state's southeast coast and many from the Midwest settling on the west coast has significantly affected the results achieved by racial extremists.[74] Collins, Carlton, and High offered these recent inhabitants and other moderate Floridians a serious alternative to racial extremism.

Because race was the predominant issue during this period, the campaigns tended to be emotional; personalities were emphasized often at the expense of issues. After easily winning the 1956 nomination, Collins remarked that he was very pleased that no runoff was needed. He felt that the personal bitterness stirred up among the candidates and the general population during the regular campaign would have been intensified still further in a second primary. The Democratic runoff in 1960 between Bryant and Carlton was a bitter contest in which each accused the other of being a "demagogue" and "race baiter." Bryant also attacked Carlton as a "moderate integrationist" and supporter of the *Brown* decision. Carlton retaliated in kind, contending that he had witnesses who saw Bryant "eating dinner" with blacks in a Jacksonville restaurant.[75]

In 1964 and 1966, Democratic gubernatorial campaigns saw the gradual decline of racial issues. Robert King High's campaign in 1964 during which he openly endorsed integration and the public accommodations section of the 1964 civil rights bill was an important development. Although he was decisively beaten in that campaign by Burns, High still managed to win 465,500 of the 1,013,600 votes cast.[76] His impressive vote total was a warning to other gubernatorial aspirants that a substantial minority of Floridians had modified their views on race. In addition, the passage of the Civil Rights Act of 1964 and the Voting Rights Act of 1965 diminished the viability of a purely racial appeal. The passage of the voting act increased the size of Florida's black electorate to nearly 17 percent which discouraged racist appeals by gubernatorial candidates. Further, court-ordered school desegregation and federally directed public accommodation use had resulted in tacit acceptance of desegregation by Florida politicians.[77]

The 1966 Democratic gubernatorial primary also helped defuse the issue of race. Haydon Burns, whose reelection chances had been seriously impaired by an inept and severely criticized administration, actively solicited the black vote in Florida. Burns made repeated reference to his appointment of Clifton Dyson, a West Palm Beach black, to the Board of Regents and several blacks to other state positions.[78] High, meanwhile, had once again wooed and won the NAACP endorsement. For the first time in its history, Florida had two Democrats in a runoff who sought and claimed black voter support.

While this development was certainly unique, in the last analysis, the Democratic nomination was decided on other issues. Facilitating High's triumph was the support of Scott Kelly, who had finished a close third in the first primary, and the inability of Haydon Burns to convince Floridians that his two-year administration was not as incompetent as the newspapers portrayed it.

High's victory over Burns by no means guaranteed his election in the fall. The Republican party had made significant strides in the 1960 and 1964 gubernatorial elections and appeared to be on the verge of capturing the office. Its inability to come up with candidates who had sufficient political experience and the reluctance of most Democrats to turn the state over to Republican leadership accounted in large measure for the party's lack of success prior to 1966.[79] The Republicans had been out of power for so long that there were very few who had any political experience.

The inability of Republican gubernatorial candidates to capture the office was particularly evident in 1964. In that year opposition to the administration of President Lyndon Johnson was so widespread in Florida that many Democrats felt that Haydon Burns' candidacy was in jeopardy, especially since Johnson was running for election in 1964. But the Republican nominee, Charles Holley, proved to be a poor campaigner and was unable to exploit voter discontent with the Democratic party in Florida. Indeed, Holley alienated numerous citizens by his slanderous attacks against Burns; he charged Burns with maintaining a $1,200,000 secret account in the Bank of Nova Scotia in Nassau and presented a bank ledger to prove his assertion. Burns subsequently refuted Holley's allegation but he was forced to journey to Nassau to do so, thus absenting himself temporarily from the campaign. Within a matter of days Holley alleged that Burns was under investigation by the United States Department of Justice on charges of tax fraud. During the course of the campaign Holley also stated that during Burns' mayoralty "vice [was] running rampant in the city of Jacksonville under police protection."[80] It was Holley's unfounded accusations and his obvious political naivete that proved his undoing and resulted in Burns' decisive victory—he captured 58 percent of the vote.

Republican Claude Kirk's campaign in 1966 was managed with considerably more sophistication. The Republicans were two years older and much wiser after the 1964 debacle. In addition, the party benefited from the continued public dissatisfaction with Lyndon Johnson and his Great Society, and the division within the Democratic party over the nomination of Robert King High. High had alienated many conservative Democrats in the state with his progressive racial views and his political ties with the Kennedys of Massachusetts. Political scientists Donald R. Matthews and James W. Prothro in their study *Negroes and the New Southern Politics* observed that a southerner's party identification no longer "tells us how he evaluates the parties. . . ." Party images were "changing within the white electorate of the South—and changing toward a more favorable view of the GOP." Indeed, Governor Burns refused to support High's candidacy because of these views, and several cabinet members actively campaigned for Kirk.[81]

Realizing the discord within the Democratic party, Kirk played up the differences in political views between himself and High. In particular he criticized High's racial attitudes. During a speech at DeLand for example, Kirk spotted a man wearing a High campaign button; he asked the man whether he knew High's position on open housing. When the man replied that he did not, Kirk called on High to explain his position. High, of course, had made no statement on open housing and did not want to.[82] Kirk's ruse, however, made it appear that High had endorsed open housing and it served to accentuate Kirk's charge that High was an extreme liberal. Kirk also exploited public dissatisfaction with the race riots in the cities, Vietnam, and inflation. In fact, he spent most of the campaign addressing these issues and attacking Johnson's domestic and foreign policies. It was difficult to tell at times whether Kirk was running against Johnson or High, which, of course, was exactly his campaign strategy, given the public's frustration with the Great Society.[83] One seventy-year-old Florida woman commented, "The name [Republican] offends my sensibilities but actually in some ways it is more like the old Democratic party I once believed in."[84]

Kirk's advantage was that he was a very able campaigner. Friendly, flamboyant, and a fine speaker, he quickly charmed those who might have had some hesitancy about voting for a Republican. Robert Erwin Lee, who had revitalized Republicanism in Colorado, directed Kirk's campaign, which emphasized the candidate's personal magnetism. He seldom talked about issues other than to mention "The American Dream." When reporters asked him to describe this American dream or to discuss various issues, Kirk replied that he and his aides were preparing a series of White Papers on these matters. Kirk finally released these papers (on water pollution, highways, and schools) shortly before the general election. Thereafter, he referred all reporters' questions on issues to the White Papers and otherwise refused to answer them.[85] Kirk's lack of political experience never became a real factor in the campaign. High was constantly on the defensive and unable to exploit this issue. As a result, Kirk was able to hide his political weaknesses during the campaign, something he would be unable to do once he became governor.

Kirk's four years in office brought demands for change even within the Republican party. Jack Eckerd, a drugstore chain tycoon and a prominent figure in the Republican party, and Skip Bafalis, a legislator from West Palm Beach, challenged Kirk for the party's nomination. Bafalis alleged that Florida had become the laughing stock of the nation under Kirk while Eckerd declared it was "sad that the President didn't invite Florida to his meeting in New Orleans, but with a governor like we've got, I can't blame him."[86] Kirk did very little campaigning in the first primary, apparently convinced he would win the nomination easily; his confidence proved unfounded. Running what appeared to be a millionaire's race and employing Robert Ailes, a television adviser to President Nixon, and Floyd Glisson, a corporation vice president, to manage his campaign, Eckerd forced Kirk into a second primary.

Kirk continued to run essentially a low profile campaign against Eckerd. Apparently his aides had convinced him that his flamboyant, publicity-seeking image was a definite liability. Kirk did accuse Eckerd of fragmenting the party and of trying to "buy the governor's office."[87] Eckerd kept up a steady attack on Kirk's irresponsibility in office but was unable to convince the Republican constituency that he could do a better job or that he could defeat the Democratic candidate in the fall election. His rather drab, uninspiring personality coupled with his inability to debate with Kirk undermined the success of his attack upon Kirk's personal qualifications.

The Democratic party had remained factionalized despite Kirk's victory in 1966 and the growing strength of the Republican party in Florida. Four candidates sought the nomination in that year: Earl Faircloth, former attorney general of Florida, Chuck Hall, mayor of Miami, Jack Mathews, state senator from Jacksonville, and Reubin Askew, state senator from Pensacola. Earl Faircloth was the clear favorite because of his statewide recognition and his strong support from the business community. He ran a traditional, business-oriented campaign, promising to make Florida "the world center of the future," but never specifically saying how he planned to accomplish this goal. During the first primary it often seemed that Faircloth was campaigning against Kirk rather than against the three other Democrats; he frequently berated Kirk's administration and called for a return to responsible government.[88] Faircloth's campaign aides appeared quite confident that their candidate would be paired off against Kirk in the general election.

Mathews ran essentially the same campaign as Faircloth. He did address himself more frequently to the problems facing Florida, but he was unable to inspire voter support in what many reporters considered a rather lackluster campaign.[89] Chuck Hall's campaign was in sharp contrast to Mathews'. Tall, handsome, he cut an interesting figure campaigning in his own DC-3 and a white Rolls Royce. Hall, a teetotaler and nonsmoker, sounded like a latter day version of Billy Sunday urging a moral reformation of society as he called for an abolition of pornography, stiff drug penalties, and stricter discipline on college campuses. Hall's campaign made for an interesting sideshow but few people took him seriously, especially his opponents who seldom mentioned him.[90]

Reubin Askew was hardly known outside his native Escambia County when he announced his candidacy. Indeed, the man running as his lieutenant governor, Tom Adams, was much better known throughout the state. Nevertheless, Askew's campaign style made a quick and, ultimately, long-lasting imprint on the public mind. His personality was not particularly colorful nor his rhetoric very dramatic, but he did appear to be honest and sincere, qualities which seemed in short supply during the Kirk years.

Tall, angular, with rather handsome, clean-cut features, Askew was especially impressive on television where his sermonesque speeches attracted a large following. Incorporating many of LeRoy Collins' campaign techniques, Askew made extensive use of television, and developed strong organizational support in urban areas. His platform broke away from traditional, noncontroversial issues, urging instead a corporate income tax to modify a "grossly unfair" tax structure, severe penalties for businesses that polluted the environment (including removal from the state if necessary), greater participation by young people in government, and a drug program emphasizing stricter law enforcement, public education, and rehabilitation. The uniqueness of an issue-oriented campaign was made even more remarkable by the candidate's subsequent statements. When asked why he made pledges on such controversial issues, Askew replied that he wanted the governorship but "not so bad that I would spend four years of frustration with my hands tied." Askew referred to Faircloth's no new tax promise as "essentially a phony pledge because I think it means that those who are getting preferential treatment now would continue to get it."[91]

Despite finishing over 20,000 votes behind Faircloth in the first primary and Hall's and Mathews' endorsements of Faircloth, Askew continued to attract considerable attention for his openness and frankness. As one official noted: "I'm just glad to see a candidate have the guts to say what he thinks."[92] Faircloth, who promised little more than standpattism in government, found it very difficult to mobilize his forces to stem the tide for Askew. Askew's faction complicated any effort in this regard by keeping up a constant attack on Faircloth's nonplatform and promising that Askew's election would get Florida moving again. The success of Askew's campaign was borne out by the results; he carried the majority of the counties in the northeast, central, and southern parts of the state, winning by over 120,000 votes.

The endorsement of Faircloth and the widespread criticism of Kirk, even in his own party, virtually assured Askew's election. Kirk could not win without significant Democratic support but his four years in office had alienated so many Democrats that such support was simply not forthcoming. That, however, did not stop Kirk from trying. Calling Askew a "momma's boy" and a "patsy powderpuff for polluters," Kirk campaigned vigorously throughout the state, questioning Askew's ability to be governor. He also accused his opponent of being antibusiness, prolabor, and in favor of pornography. Utilizing his powers as governor, he attempted to advance his candidacy by announcing a new low-cost housing project for the elderly in Pinellas County and holding an emergency legislative session to regulate insurance rates.[93]

Kirk's efforts were all in vain, however. Askew kept most Democrats within the party by promising to restore honesty and respectability to state government. In addition, his reputation remained untarnished despite Kirk's attempts to belittle him. The final election results had Askew the victor with 57 percent of the vote. He also carried all the urban counties except Orange and Sarasota.

After four years during which he established himself as one of the state's most popular governors, despite his endorsement of busing to achieve racial equality, Askew was renominated in the first primary over the minor opposition of his former lieutenant governor Tom Adams. Askew's most effective campaign device was the $100 limitation he placed on all campaign contributions to minimize, as he put it, the potential influence of big corporations on his governorship.[94] This proved to be an excellent campaign tactic in 1974. The news of the large contributions made to President Nixon's reelection treasury and the favors these corporate officials subsequently received were still in the headlines. Askew's announcement was well received by the press and the public and served to heighten his popularity.

The Republicans selected Jerry Thomas to oppose Askew. The nomination underscored the party's instability and inexperience; Thomas had been a Democrat and had been serving as president of the state senate when he broke with Askew. Thomas was apparently quite ambitious and unwilling to wait another four years to be governor. He attributed his abandonment of the party to ideological problems; for him the party had become too liberal under Askew's leadership. Thomas campaigned largely on this issue; he argued that the governor did not truly represent the political attitudes of Floridians—he was liberal, antibusiness, probusing, and a radical environmentalist. Thomas' attack made some dent in the Askew image but not enough to concern the governor and his campaign aides. In fact, Askew virtually ignored Thomas during the campaign except to chide him for failing to publish his income tax returns.[95] Askew won reelection quite easily with 61 percent of the vote and captured every urban county in the state, defeating Thomas by over 400,000 votes.

The 1978 gubernatorial election followed in the tradition of Florida politics, with a few modern touches. Initially more than a dozen candidates sought the Democratic nomination, but only seven eventually filed for it. Six of these were viable candidates: Robert Shevin, state attorney general from Miami; Robert Graham, state senator and wealthy lawyer-farmer from Miami Lakes; Bruce Smathers, youthful secretary of state from Jacksonville and son of former U.S. Senator George Smathers; Jim Williams, Reubin Askew's lieutenant governor; Hans Tanzler, mayor of Jacksonville; and former governor Claude Kirk, who switched party affiliation. Two candidates campaigned for the Republican nomination: Lou Frey, U.S. congressman from the Orlando area, and Jack Eckerd, drugstore magnate and former head of the General Services Administration from Pinellas County. Interestingly, and undoubtedly in an attempt to appeal to women voters, three candidates (Williams, Kirk, and Eckerd) selected women running mates.

In the Democratic race, Shevin was the front-runner from the outset. A popular attorney general who managed to appeal to both urban South Florida and conservative rural elements, he had spent four years building an organization and masterminding a winning strategy. Even as late as a month before the first primary in September, Shevin was far ahead in the polls, although Graham received more newspaper endorsements. Graham adopted a unique strategy reminiscent of Senator Lawton Chiles' walk through the state in 1970. A boyish, energetic, highly intelligent man, Graham's main problem was lack of name recognition. To counter this, Robert Squier, former campaign aide to President Jimmy Carter, portrayed Graham in hard hat and denims; the candidate took on 100 different jobs in 100 days during the campaign, including such positions as bellhop, waiter, hospital orderly, stable boy, and steelworker. It was a gimmicky plan, designed for its public relations and media appeal, but it worked: Graham received enormous coverage by the media, and apparently many Floridians regarded his attempt to discover more about the state and its people as genuine and sincere.[96]

None of the other candidates could match the enormous expenditures and organizational capabilities of Shevin and Graham. Both ran thoroughly professional campaigns. Both relied heavily on the media; each spent more than $1 million in the first primary alone (as did Jack Eckerd). This was probably the most media-oriented, and expensive, gubernatorial campaign in Florida history (total expenditures for the three elections apparently exceeded $12 million). Shevin won the first primary with 35 percent of the vote; Graham was second with 25 percent. Shevin led in twenty-three of the state's sixty-seven counties, mostly in the coastal and southern regions; Graham led in thirty counties, including those in northern and Panhandle areas; his strength there was partially a result of the appeal of his running mate, Wayne Mixson, a popular businessman-agriculturalist from Marianna.[97]

Issues were not very important in the first primary, since all candidates generally agreed on a tough, law-and-order approach to crime; economic development of the state; and budget restraint. Only Graham, who favored tax reform, and Kirk, who advocated approval of a constitutional provision permitting casino gambling in Miami (the other candidates were all adamantly opposed to this), put forward unique policy positions.[98]

There was even less emphasis on issues in the second primary in which greater significance was placed on personality and style instead. Political writer Robert Rothman described the runoff as a "grudge match" and "slugfest." Shevin tried to characterize Graham as a free spending, Harvard-educated liberal, and cast himself as the true moderate-conservative. His campaign, however, took on a tone of negativism and stridency. His television and radio advertisements, in fact, became so vitriolic in their portrayal of Graham that some stations eventually refused to broadcast one of them. Graham became so incensed by one Shevin newspaper advertisement that he burst into a Miami radio studio while Shevin was being interviewed on a talk show and demanded an immediate explanation.[99]

The negativism of Shevin's campaign eventually cost him the nomination. He appeared desperate, even though he was the front-runner, and spent more time (and money) criticizing Graham than advocating his own candidacy. Graham exploited these attacks by not replying in kind, remaining cool, defending his record, and talking about tax reform. Graham won the runoff easily with 54 percent of the vote, 470,202 to Shevin's 408,226. Graham did well everywhere, maintaining his strength in Central and North Florida and cutting into Shevin's support in the southern, coastal, and other urban parts of the state.[100]

The Republican primary was not as vigorous as the Democratic but paralleled it in media emphasis. Eckerd, the winner, contributed over $1 million of his own money, and eventually spent about $2.3 million in the primary and general election. More important, the election illustrated the fundamental, ongoing division in the Republican party discussed in Chapter 1. Frey was the central Florida candidate; his support came from the old Kirk-Gurney faction. Eckerd's base of support initially came from Cramer-coastal Republicans. Rather quickly, however, Eckerd developed a commanding lead. In spite of scandals which came to light in the General Services Administration, he himself remained untarnished. This, combined

Gubernatorial candidate Bob Graham worked at 100 different jobs during his campaign in an effort to gain the support of "everyday" people. While the strategy was contrived and designed for publicity, it helped him to overcome lack of recognition and to develop a statewide constituency. His strategy also emphasized the importance of personality rather than issues in gubernatorial campaigning. Photo courtesy *West Palm Beach Post-Times,* Russell Bronson, photographer.

with Eckerd's vastly superior resources and the excellence of his media campaign, gave him the Republican nomination with 64 percent of the vote.[101]

To win the general election, Eckerd would have had to attract many disaffected Democrats, and hope additionally that the nasty runoff had split the Democratic party. Unfortunately for Eckerd, it did not happen in 1978. The Democratic party quickly drew together, with Shevin endorsing and even campaigning for Graham. It was the Republicans who were split; Frey refused to help Eckerd, which suggests that Republican fragmentation had still not been overcome. The general election was low-key, with more attention paid to the gambling referendum than to the gubernatorial contest. The overwhelming numerical advantage of state Democrats, coupled with a slick, smooth media campaign, enabled Graham to win with 56 percent of the vote, 1,373,263 to 1,091,670 for Eckerd.[102]

CONCLUSIONS

Graham's election in 1978 brought to an end the twenty-second gubernatorial election in this century. If any one campaign style has predominated during this period, it has been what political scientists William Havard and Loren Beth termed "the Chamber of Commerce" candidate. Such a politician has based his campaign on conservative, businesslike principles, and a promise to build more roads, improve agricultural conditions, and bring in more tourists. Because Florida's prosperity has been built, in large measure, on such a tenuous, nonmanufacturing economic base, this campaign pledge has generally been well received in all sections of the state. The conservatism of Florida's gubernatorial candidates has also existed "because the unstructured nature of the region's politics favors the status quo, [and] because the bulk of the region's working class have black skins and do not vote."[103] A candidate who has espoused this Chamber of Commerce philosphy has won nearly every election in this century.

The "Chamber of Commerce" candidate did not have to be a well-known politician although it helped; it was also very beneficial to have the support of the business community. Candidates who enjoyed both assets included such governors as Spessard Holland, Doyle Carlton, Fuller Warren, Cary Hardee, Farris Bryant, and Haydon Burns. Since personalities have decided more gubernatorial campaigns than have issues, however, an inexperienced candidate with little public exposure could win on such a platform. To do so he had to barnstorm the state in an exciting manner. He also had to seek the nomination at a propitious moment. John Martin, for example, was able to sense the temper of the times in Florida during the 1920s and exploited this to his advantage with an aggressive, promise-the-people-more-prosperity campaign. Similarly, David Sholtz utilized the depression to enhance his candidacy by offering himself as a fresh new face with new ideas to over-come the state's economic woes.

In the first two decades of the twentieth century a Democratic candidate could readily secure the nomination without campaigning south of Ocala. Miami had a small population during this period and the areas around it were virtually uninhabited. Hillsborough and Pinellas counties had fairly sub-stantial voting populations in the cities of Tampa and St. Petersburg, but the communities around them were very small. After 1920 but before 1956 it was essential for a Democratic candidate to expand his base of support into another geographic area of the state. Thus, if a candidate had strong support in rural, North Florida (the Panhandle and the North-Central part of the state), he had to gain the endorsement of voters in Central or South Florida. No candidate from 1920 to 1956 won the Democratic nomination without significant voter support in another geographical section of the state, because none of these sections housed a majority of the eligible voters. In addition, the state's urban centers did not contain a majority of the population and even when they did after 1960 a candidate could not rely on these communities to vote as a bloc (they have done so only in the 1956 and 1974 Democratic primaries).

Nevertheless, during the course of the twentieth century certain political trends have emerged in Florida gubernatorial politics, particularly during the second primary. The Panhandle area in northwest Florida has tended to vote as a cohesive unit since 1920. In five gubernatorial elections the region has unanimously endorsed one candidate. In nine of the other eleven elections at least twelve of the fifteen counties have supported the same candidate. The north central region of the state, encompassing eighteen counties, has also voted with a great deal of unanimity since 1920. In four elections this section has supported one Democratic candidate. In seven of the remaining eleven elections at least fourteen of the eighteen counties have voted for the same man. In addition, these two largely rural sections have tended to vote with a degree of commonality. In nine of sixteen elections both regions supported the same candidate. A Democratic politician from one of these two sections of the state (e.g., Fuller Warren) has traditionally had an advantage over an opponent from another geographic section (such as Dan McCarty) because of these voting patterns. However, a candidate from the Panhandle or the north central area still needed voter support from one of the other regions—central or South Florida—if he hoped to secure the party's nomination. The central and southern sections of the state have not exhibited any clear, identifiable voting patterns either within their respective regions or in coalition.

Historically, there has been no clear-cut way for a candidate to appeal to another section of the state for support other than through promises for new roads, new schools, more tourists, or agricultural improvements. Historian

Herbert J. Doherty has suggested that the rural, Panhandle region of the state could be appealed to with a neo-populist platform. In particular, he mentions the liberal candidacy of Fuller Warren as being attractive to voters from this section of Florida.[104] While such an appeal may have assisted his candidacy, Warren's birth in this section of the state, his rhetorical ability, and his flamboyant campaign style were emphasized to a much larger degree when he campaigned than his liberalism, and, in the last analysis, it appears that the personality issues won him the support of this region. With the selection of a lieutenant governor in 1974, it now appears possible to win the support of another region in the state by choosing a running mate for strategic reasons as Robert Graham appears to have done.

The year 1956 marked a turning point in gubernatorial campaigning for three important reasons, and in this sense it can be called a watershed period for Florida gubernatorial politics. It saw the emergence of race as a hotly debated issue, the initial stages in the revitalization of the Republican party, and the introduction of LeRoy Collins and a new style of gubernatorial campaigning. Race had always been an issue in Florida gubernatorial politics even if it smoldered below the surface. However, it took the announcement of the *Brown* decision in 1954 to thrust it into the open once again. Although Collins endorsed the concept of segregation in the 1954 and 1956 Democratic primaries, he urged voters on both occasions to obey the law and he denounced racial extremism.

The decline of racism as a factor in Florida gubernatorial campaigning has been a result of the efforts of such candidates as Collins, Doyle Carlton, Jr., Robert King High, and Reubin Askew and of the social and political changes effected by the federal government. It does not appear to have been in response to an expanding black electorate. Blacks constitute only 11 percent of the electorate in Florida, and less than a majority of these voters exercise their franchise. Even though the presence of black voters has prevented racial appeals from reemerging in gubernatorial campaigns, their influence has been relatively small otherwise. No gubernatorial candidates, for example, have espoused programs to assist the poor, the vast majority of whom are black. Until black Floridians register and vote in greater numbers, they will have a relatively modest impact on gubernatorial candidates and their platforms in the Democratic primary and general election.

Collins was also the first candidate to utilize modern campaign techniques, particularly television, in seeking voter approval. More important, however, he was the first (and only) candidate to appeal to one constituency—the urban voters of Florida—and be victorious in doing so. His campaign strategy was copied, for the most part, by Doyle Carlton, Jr., and Robert King High; each unsuccessfully tried to corral the same constituency. High did succeed in securing the party nomination in 1966 with such a campaign strategy but it backfired in his election bid against Kirk. Although Collins' campaign techniques were successful, the problems encountered by Carlton and High pointed out the difficulty of placing so much reliance on such a strategy. Because of the population make-up of the state, the urban areas could not be depended on to vote as a bloc (they have done so only in the 1956 and 1974 campaigns). Generally, these population centers have tended to reflect the voting patterns of the geographic areas in which they are located. Reubin Askew pursued the Collins' strategy in 1970 and 1974, but he was working from a base of political support in the northwest-Panhandle region of Florida.

The emergence of the Republican party has yet to bring an end to factionalism in the state Democratic party. The growth of Republicanism has been restricted by the party's own internal bickering, especially among professional Republicans and Confederate Democrats. Many Republicans have resented and have been reluctant to support former Democrats for the party's nomination and in the general election. The party has also been hurt by the flamboyance and incompetence of Governor Kirk. Moreover, his break with state Republican party chairman and U.S. senatorial candidate William Cramer and his support of G. Harrold Carswell, former federal judge, whose 1970 nomination to the U.S. Supreme Court by President Richard Nixon was rejected by the Senate, for the 1970 Senate Republican nomination resulted in a deep division within the Republican party from which it has still not completely recovered. Former United States Senator Edward Gurney, too, has caused considerable damage to the state Republican party by both his close ties to former President Richard Nixon's administration and his alleged involvement in political corruption during the 1970s. As long as Democrats are fairly well assured of victory in the November elections and as long as the state continues to experience chaotic growth in several socioeconomic areas, the party will remain fragmented despite the leadership of men such as Reubin Askew. Continued growth of the Republican party, which seems certain in this conservative state, however, will do much to reduce Democratic factionalism if not end it altogether. The Democratic party cannot permit such divisiveness in September and hope to defeat a strong Republican organization in November.

Once a Democratic candidate had overcome the chaos and frustration of the party primary and defeated his Republican opponent in November, his problems were by no means all behind him. First and foremost, he had to come to grips with the state constitution (which meant the 1885 constitution until it was rewritten in 1968) and the limitations and opportunities it made legally available to his administration.

TABLE 3.1. Total Vote and Percentage of Total Vote for Governors in General Elections

1900	William S. Jennings (Democrat)	29,251	81.0
	Matthew B. Macfarlane (Republican)	6,238	17.3
	A. M. Morton (People's)	631	1.7
1904	Napoleon B. Broward (Democrat)	28,971	79.2
	Matthew B. Macfarlane (Republican)	6,357	17.4
	W. R. Healey	1,270	3.4
1908	Albert W. Gilchrist (Democrat)	33,036	78.8
	John M. Cheney (Republican)	6,453	15.4
	A. J. Pettigrew (Socialist)	2,427	5.8
1912	Park Trammell (Democrat)	38,977	80.4
	William R. O'Neal (Republican)	2,646	5.5
	Thomas W. Cox (Socialist)	3,467	7.2
	J. W. Bingham (Prohibition)	1,061	2.2
	William C. Hodges (Progressive)	2,314	4.7
1916	Sidney J. Catts (Democrat)	39,546	47.7
	William V. Knott (Democrat)	30,343	36.6
	George W. Allen (Republican)	10,333	12.5
	C. C. Allen (Socialist)	2,470	3.0
	Noel A. Mitchell	193	.2
1920	Cary A. Hardee (Democrat)	103,407	77.9
	George E. Gay (Republican)	23,788	17.9
	W. L. VanDuzer (Republican, White)	2,654	2.0
	F. C. Whitaker (Socialist)	2,823	2.2
1924	John W. Martin (Democrat)	84,181	82.8
	William R. O'Neal (Republican)	17,499	17.2
1928	Doyle E. Carlton (Democrat)	148,455	61.0
	W. J. Howey (Republican)	95,018	39.0
1932	David Sholtz (Democrat)	186,270	66.6
	W. J. Howey (Republican)	93,323	33.4
1936	Fred P. Cone (Democrat)	253,638	80.9
	E. E. Callaway (Republican)	59,832	19.1
1940	Spessard L. Holland (Democrat)	334,152	100.0
	(No Opponent)		
1944	Millard F. Caldwell (Democrat)	361,007	78.9
	Bert L. Acker (Republican)	96,321	21.1
1948	Fuller Warren (Democrat)	381,459	83.4
	Bert L. Acker (Republican)	76,153	16.6
1952	Dan McCarty (Democrat)	624,463	74.8
	Harry S. Swan (Republican)	210,009	25.2
1954	LeRoy Collins (Democrat)	287,769	80.5
	J. Tom Watson (Republican)	69,852	19.5
	(Watson died before election.)		
1956	LeRoy Collins (Democrat)	747,753	73.7
	William A. Washburne, Jr.		
	(Republican)	266,980	26.3

(*continued*)

TABLE 3.1—*Continued*

1960	Farris Bryant (Democrat)	849,407	59.8
	George C. Petersen (Republican)	569,936	40.2
1964	Haydon Burns (Democrat)	933,554	56.1
	Charles R. Holley (Republican)	686,297	41.3
	Write-in votes for others	43,630	2.6
1966	Robert King High (Democrat)	668,233	44.9
	Claude R. Kirk, Jr. (Republican)	821,190	55.1
1970	Claude R. Kirk, Jr., and		
	Ray C. Osborne (Republican)	746,243	43.1
	Reubin Askew and		
	Tom Adams (Democrat)	984,305	56.9
1974	Reubin O'D. Askew and		
	J. H. "Jim" Williams (Democrat)	1,118,954	61.2
	Jerry Thomas and		
	Mike Thompson (Republican)	709,438	38.8

SOURCE: Allen Morris, *The Florida Handbook, 1979–1980,* 17th ed. (Tallahassee: The Peninsular Publishing Company, 1979), pp. 491–92.
NOTE: Figures taken from official canvass of returns.

TABLE 3.2. Vote for Governor, Democratic Primaries

		1st primary	2nd primary
1904	Napoleon B. Broward, Jacksonville	13,247	22,979
	Robert W. Davis, Green Cove Springs	13,020	22,265
	C. M. Brown, Ocala	9,312	
	Dannitte H. Mays, Monticello	8,562	
1908	Albert W. Gilchrist, Punta Gorda	23,248	32,465
	John C. Stockton, Jacksonville	20,968	23,291
	Jefferson B. Brown, Key West	8,986	
1912	Park Trammell, Lakeland	27,111	
	W. H. Milton, Marianna	12,406	
	John W. Watson, Miami	10,760	
	Cromwell Gibbons, Jacksonville	10,406	
	Edward M. Semple, Key West	868	

		1st choice votes	2nd choice votes
1916	William V. Knott, Tallahassee	24,765	8,674
	Sidney J. Catts, DeFuniak Springs	30,067	3,351
	Ion L. Farris, Jacksonville	13,609	
	F. M. Hudson, Miami	7,418	
	F. A. Wood, St. Petersburg	7,674	
1920	Cary A. Hardee, Live Oak	52,591	1,559
	Lincoln Hulley, DeLand	5,591	
	Van C. Swearingen, Jacksonville	30,240	1,459

(continued)

TABLE 3.2—*Continued*

		1st choice votes	2nd choice votes
1924	John W. Martin, Jacksonville	55,715	17,339
	Sidney J. Catts, DeFuniak Springs	43,230	6,067
	Frank E. Jennings, Jacksonville	37,962	
	Charles H. Spencer, Tampa	1,408	
	Worth W. Trammell, Miami	8,381	
1928	Doyle E. Carlton, Tampa	77,569	28,471
	J. M. Carson, Miami	3,271	
	Sidney J. Catts, DeFuniak Springs	68,984	9,066
	Fons A. Hathaway, Jacksonville	67,849	
	John S. Taylor, Largo	37,304	

		1st primary	2nd primary
1932	David Sholtz, Daytona Beach	55,406	173,540
	Stafford Caldwell, Miami	44,938	
	Charles M. Durrance, Jacksonville	36,291	
	Arthur Gomez, Key West	9,244	
	Cary A. Hardee, Live Oak	50,427	
	Thomas S. Hart, Tampa	9,525	
	John W. Martin, Jacksonville	66,940	102,805
	J. Tom Watson, Tampa	3,949	
1936	Fred P. Cone, Lake City	46,842	184,540
	Grady Burton, Wauchula	24,985	
	Stafford Caldwell, Jasper	19,789	
	Jerry W. Carter, Tallahassee	35,578	
	Dan Chappell, Miami	29,494	
	R. B. Gautier, Miami	1,607	
	William C. Hodges, Tallahassee	46,471	
	Amos Lewis, Marianna	8,068	
	Carl Maples, Wakulla	2,389	
	Mallie Martin, Crestview	4,264	
	B. F. Paty, West Palm Beach	34,153	
	W. Raleigh Petteway, Tampa	51,705	129,150
	Peter Tomasello, Jr., Okeechobee	22,355	
	J. R. Yearwood, Winter Haven	1,049	
1940	Spessard L. Holland, Bartow	118,862	272,718
	James Barbee, Jacksonville	33,699	
	J. H. Clancy, Panama City	2,703	
	Walter B. Fraser, St. Augustine	36,855	
	Carl Maples, Wakulla	2,426	
	B. F. Paty, West Palm Beach	75,608	
	Burton Schoepf, Tampa	8,055	
	Frederick Van Roy, Crystal River	2,716	
	Fuller Warren, Jacksonville	83,316	
	Hans Walker, Ocala	21,666	
	Francis P. Whitehair, DeLand	95,431	206,158

(continued)

TABLE 3.2—*Continued*

		1st primary	2nd primary
1944	Millard F. Caldwell, Tallahassee	116,111	215,485
	J. Edwin Baker, Umatilla	27,028	
	Ernest R. Graham, Pennsuco	91,174	
	R. A. (Lex) Green, Starke	113,300	174,100
	Raymond Sheldon, Tampa	27,940	
	Frank D. Upchurch, St. Augustine	30,524	
1948	F. D. Akin, Miami	2,792	
	Richard H. Cooper, DeLand	8,152	
	Colin English, Fort Myers	89,158	
	Bernarr Macfadden, Miami Beach	4,540	
	Dan McCarty, Fort Pierce	161,788	276,425
	Basil H. Pollitt, Miami	1,261	
	W. A. Shands, Gainesville	62,358	
	Fuller Warren, Jacksonville	183,326	299,641
	J. Tom Watson, Tampa	51,505	
1952	Alto Adams, Fort Pierce	126,426	
	Bill Hendrix, Oldsmar	11,208	
	Dan McCarty, Fort Pierce	361,427	384,200
	Brailey Odham, Sanford	232,565	336,716
	Dale E. Spencer, Kissimmee	6,871	
1954	LeRoy Collins, Tallahassee	222,791	380,323
	Charley E. Johns, Starke	255,787	314,198
	Brailey Odham, Sanford	187,782	
1956	Farris Bryant, Ocala	110,469	
	LeRoy Collins, Tallahassee	434,274	
	Sumter L. Lowry, Tampa	179,019	
	W. B. (Bill) Price, Jacksonville	3,245	
	Peaslee Streets, Lake Park	5,086	
	Fuller Warren, Miami Beach	107,990	
1960	Harvie J. Belser, Bonifay	30,736	
	Farris Bryant, Ocala	193,507	512,757
	Haydon Burns, Jacksonville	166,352	
	Doyle E. Carlton, Jr., Wauchula	186,228	416,052
	Thomas E. (Ted) David, Hollywood	80,057	
	Fred O. Dickinson, West Palm Beach	115,520	
	George Downs, Winter Park	6,320	
	Bill Hendrix, Oldsmar	8,517	
	John M. McCarty, Fort Pierce	144,750	
	Jim McCorvey, Hialeah	5,080	
1964	Haydon Burns, Jacksonville	312,453	648,093
	Fred (Bud) Dickinson, West Palm Beach	184,865	
	Robert King High, Miami	207,280	465,547
	Frederick B. Karl, Daytona Beach	85,953	
	Scott Kelly, Lakeland	205,078	
	John E. (Jack) Mathews, Jacksonville	140,210	

(*continued*)

Demographic Setting

TABLE 3.2—*Continued*

		1st primary	2nd primary
1966	Haydon Burns, Jacksonville	372,451	509,271
	Sam Foor, Tallahassee	11,343	
	Robert King High, Miami	338,281	596,471
	Scott Kelly, Lakeland	331,580	
1970	Reubin Askew, Pensacola, and		
	Tom Adams, Orange Park	206,333	447,025
	Earl Faircloth, Miami, and		
	George G. Tapper, Port St. Joe	227,413	328,038
	Chuck Hall, Miami, and		
	Pat Thomas, Quincy	139,384	
	John E. Mathews, Jacksonville,		
	and Elton J. Gissendanner,		
	North Miami	186,053	
1974	Tom Adams, Tallahassee, and		
	Burl McCormick, Hialeah	85,557	
	Reubin O'D. Askew, Pensacola,		
	and J. H. "Jim" Williams, Ocala	579,137	
	Norman Bie, Clearwater, and		
	Florence S. Keen, Palm Beach	39,758	
	Ben Hill Griffin, Jr., and		
	Eleanor F. Griffin, Frostproof	137,008	

SOURCE: Allen Morris, *The Florida Handbook, 1979–1980*, 17th ed. (Tallahassee: The Peninsular Publishing Company, 1979), pp. 493–95.

Note: Commencing in 1970, candidates for governor and lieutenant governor ran in tandem. First named is the candidate for governor.

Note: Between 1913 and 1931, Florida used a one-primary system intended to serve the same purpose as the present double primary in selecting party nominees. It also was the hope that the elimination of the second primary would reduce the expense of campaigns. Each voter had the opportunity of marking the ballot for both a first and a second choice when there were more than two candidates. The two candidates receiving the most first-choice votes were then awarded additionally the second-choice votes marked for them by first-choice supporters of only the eliminated candidates. The total of these first- and second-choice votes determined the winner. It was not mandatory for the voter to mark two choices and many did not.

Part II

The Structure and Processes
of the Governor's Office

PART II consists of three chapters dealing with legal, structural, and functional bases of the Florida governorship, thus defining the potentialities and strengths, the liabilities and weaknesses of the office. After an examination of the constitutional development of the governor's office, the two succeeding chapters analyze the governor's principal duties as chief administrator and chief legislator. While not his only functions, they are probably the most important and most varied. They are also the ones for which the public will hold the governor most accountable and responsible, and therefore are crucial in determining the effectiveness of the governor as leader of the state.

4

Constitutional Setting and Structure of the Governor's Office

AN examination of the constitutional basis and governmental structure of the Florida executive cannot provide a complete picture, or total understanding, of how the governor and other members of the executive branch actually behave in office. The governor's office is, after all, an intensely individual and political one. And yet the state's constitutional setting provides a framework within which executive politics must operate, and thus it strongly influences the behavior of the governor and his executive colleagues.

More specifically, an examination of the constitutional framework can provide considerable insight into the following three areas, each of which forms an important basis of executive politics. First, the constitution defines the structure of state government. That is, it indicates what form government takes, and more importantly suggests how each part of the government stands in relation to all others. The constitution also prescribes in a general way the distribution of powers within the government. Thus, in addition to creating the structure of government, the constitution suggests where formal arenas of decision-making exist, and which members of the government have authority and responsibility for particular decisions and actions. Finally, the constitution provides an insight into the rules under which the processes of state politics generally, and gubernatorial politics in particular, are carried out. Rules are never neutral in politics; some branches of government receive advantages, while others are disadvantaged, under the framework provided by the rules. Thus, while the constitutional setting of the executive branch does not solely define state politics, the framework it establishes strongly influences those politics. The state constitution is also a changing, evolving document. Over time not only do particular provisions (or even whole articles) within the constitution change, but individual words, phrases, and clauses take on new meanings. Hence, to gain an accurate picture of the constitutional setting of the governor's office in Florida requires a historical examination of the changes and developments that have occurred since its inception.

The constitution of 1885 is the document which provided the framework for gubernatorial and executive politics throughout most of the twentieth century.[1] Although it followed the Reconstruction Era, the hostilities and cleavages this period engendered in the state's politics remained strong in the memory of Floridians. Moreover, between 1877 (generally regarded as the end of Reconstruction) and 1885 additional conflicts developed in the state's politics. In particular, those years witnessed a growing socioeconomic clash between two groups. One was the so-called Bourbons, the ruling elite of Florida who favored minimal government and encouraged economic development. The other group comprised agrarians, independents, early populists, and others generally disenchanted by or disillusioned with the Bourbons. The times seemed right for a new constitution; indeed, one historian has written that by 1884 "Emotionally, the carpetbag constitution of 1868 was a wrong to be righted."[2]

Thus, the new constitution that was written in 1885 must be seen as a reaction against Reconstruction as well as the Bourbon period which followed it. But if it was a reaction, it took a decidedly conservative, not radical, form. In terms of the provisions written for the executive, the document deliberately sought to dismantle many of the powers which had been granted to the governor in the Reconstruction constitution. The office of lieutenant governor was abolished; the governor's enormous appointment powers for local officials were taken from him (in order to allow greater county level home rule for white political dissidents unhappy with Bourbonism); the governor was no longer permitted to succeed himself; and a unique system was established which would deliberately fragment executive power. Indeed, the 1885 constitution (which was ratified by the voters in 1887 and took effect in 1888) was typical of many late nineteenth-century constitutions, especially in its mistrust of a strong state executive. One student of Florida constitutional history wrote in 1959 that as a result of provisions for the executive in the constitution of 1885, "the office of governor of Florida is, institutionally, a weak one."[3]

Under Article IV of the 1885 constitution, the governor was to be popularly elected and was vested with the executive power of the state.[4] His term was four years, and he could not succeed himself. This latter provision made it difficult for twentieth-century Florida governors to carry out some of their administrative and legislative duties. The chief executive was to ensure that the laws were faithfully executed; he was granted supervisory veto power and an item veto in the case of appropriations bills; he could call special legislative sessions; he had power to grant reprieves and suspend fines for a limited period, to make certain appointments, and to suspend public officials not subject to impeachment. He was commander-in-chief of the militia. Finally, the governor had a mandate to inform the legislature about conditions within the state and to recommend to it any measures he felt necessary or desirable.

These provisions are not unusual in state constitutions of this period.[5] But it is the other sections of Article IV (as well as parts of other articles which concern the executive branch), along with statutory law and custom, which have given Florida an executive structure unique in American politics.

The 1885 constitution provided for six other executive officers, each of whom was to be elected separately from the governor: the secretary of state, attorney general, comptroller, treasurer, superintendent of public instruction, and commissioner of agriculture. Each officer served a four-year term, and there was no prohibition against consecutive succession. Sections 21 through 27 of Article IV of the constitution defined the responsibilities of these officials and also gave to each "such other duties as shall be prescribed by law." This latter clause gave rise to some anomalies which served to fragment the executive branch. For example, until recently state prisons were under the direction of the commissioner of agriculture, while road camps for prisoners were under the aegis of the State Road Department, directed by the State Road Board, which was appointed by the governor.

The presence of elected officials, other than the governor, in the executive branch is, of course, very common in American states. The uniqueness of Florida, however, stems from the manner in which these six officials operate. Collectively they and the governor have become known as the "cabinet," although the 1885 constitution did not provide it with any official status (later amendments, custom, and legislation did).

While the cabinet system reduced the authority of the governor, proponents argued that it kept the chief executive from becoming an independent and autocratic figure. During the course of the twentieth century the cabinet has met on a regular, usually weekly basis in order to discuss state problems and consider policy alternatives which encompass the activities of more than one state department. Through custom as well as statute, the governor chaired meetings of the cabinet, but he had no other special privileges. His was simply one voice among seven.[6]

Two other aspects of Florida's executive structure caused administrative difficulties for the governor. The 1885 constitution, as well as subsequent legislation, established numerous ex-officio administrative boards and commissions which were composed either of the entire cabinet or several members of it. Most of the agencies added since 1885 have been placed directly under the governor's aegis; the State Road Department is such an example. The result of this development has been that the newer administrative functions of government fell under the governor's control, while the older functions were controlled by the members of the cabinet, who, as already noted, were not responsible to him. To avoid having the executive office working at cross-purposes and thus causing a breakdown in government, ex-officio boards were established to provide for a certain unity of policy.[7] Some of these boards have been in extremely critical positions regarding the creation of public policy; for example, members of the cabinet have constituted the Budget Commission (whose responsibility was to draw up a biennial budget), the State Board of Conservation, the Board of Commissioners of State Institutions, the State Board of Education, and the State Pardon and Parole Board. Originally there were twenty-two boards or commissions; by the 1940s the number had grown to thirty. Moreover, there

A formal portrait of Governor Park Trammell (center, seated) and his cabinet. The others shown are (seated, left to right) Secretary of State H. Clay Crawford and Treasurer John Christian Luning; (standing, left to right) Superintendent of Public Instruction William Sheats, Comptroller Thomas West, Attorney General William V. Knott, Commissioner of Agriculture William A. McRae. P. K. Yonge Library of Florida History.

were considerable disparities among cabinet members regarding the number of boards or commissions on which each sat. During the 1940s the governor sat on nineteen; the secretary of state, ten; comptroller, thirteen; treasurer, seventeen; attorney general, seventeen; superintendent of public instruction, seven; and the commissioner of agriculture, ten. The governor, obviously, was not a member of each of these commissions or boards, and clearly could not influence, except perhaps indirectly, the policy decisions they made. This constitutional-structural arrangement served to diffuse and decentralize administrative authority in the executive branch.[8]

This diffusion, and even disintegration, of the governor's executive authority was further compounded by the creation, largely in haphazard fashion, of a vast array of state agencies and bureaus. By the mid-1960s the number of state agencies had reached some 150, but there was little, if any, organizational principle tying them together. Rather, agencies were simply created to deal with a specific problem and placed under some board, commission, or department, often without reference to how they fit in with other bureaus. As a result, different agencies sometimes worked at cross-purposes, and almost always operated without knowledge of how other governmental units, engaged in similar or related activities, were functioning. By the 1960s, and even before, the Florida executive branch had become a sticky morass in which lines of authority, responsibility, and accountability were blurred.

Governors, however, were not completely without resources to overcome at least some of their administrative weaknesses. Alliances with cabinet members, even on an ad hoc basis, could help secure departmental (and often agency) cooperation. Patronage, especially in the form of appointments, could be used to strengthen a governor's position. Finally, through his control of the so-called little cabinet, a group of agencies and administrative boards the heads and members of which he could appoint, the governor could exert a considerable amount of leverage throughout the administrative branch. Moreover, as we discuss in Chapter 5, there were often areas of cooperation and agreement between governors and their cabinets.

But all this notwithstanding, the unique, even idiosyncratic, structure and constitutional framework of the Florida executive has had serious consequences for gubernatorial leadership. Even when he received the cooperation of individual cabinet members, from a constitutional standpoint the governor had no direct control over some parts of the executive branch. Administrative authority was dispersed; the governor had no direct authority over key departments, and many state boards and bureaus were beyond his reach. Yet, as political scientists Manning Dauer and William Havard point out, the governor's "political position [made] him accountable in the eyes of the public for the complete operation of the executive branch."[9] Constitutionally, then, governors often had difficulty imposing their priorities on other executive officials and institutions. However, in practice this formal dispersion of authority could be overcome. By relying on prestige, personality, patronage, and other available political resources, and through other means of persuasion, at least some governors were able to convince other cabinet members, executive boards and commissions, and many state agencies to follow their leadership.

The difficulties governors incurred by this dispersion of authority and chaotic arrangement of administrative agencies have been compounded further by additional characteristics of the cabinet system. Members of the cabinet have been able to succeed themselves, and once they have reached office they have been very difficult to displace. Between 1885 and 1959 only four cabinet members seeking reelection were defeated; between 1901 and 1970, discounting two brief temporary cabinet appointments, the members of the cabinet served an average of nearly twelve years. R. H. Gray was secretary of state for thirty years; Nathan Mayo was commissioner of agriculture for thirty-seven years. Because of their length of service, their vast experience in their respective departments, and the political ties they had developed over the years, these two men administered their agencies with almost no interference or input from the governor's office. In addition, their opinions carried great weight in cabinet meetings, sometimes even superseding the opinion of a weak governor. Between 1900 and 1959 the commissionership of agriculture was held by only four men; three men had been secretary of state; six had been comptroller; four had been treasurer; and five, superintendent of public instruction.[10]

Cabinet members, then, saw governors come and go, and while instances of overt gubernatorial-cabinet conflicts are rare, members have had wide latitude to operate independently of the chief executive. This has been particularly true during the long period prior to 1967 when the Florida legislature was dominated by rural, largely North Florida representatives and senators. Members of the cabinet often developed close working relationships with these legislators, many of whom also served for lengthy periods. Cabinet members also developed close ties with local county officials, traditionally among the most powerful political figures in the state. In addition, each member of the cabinet quickly formed his own constituency composed largely of the clientele groups for his department. For example, the state treasurer has been closely associated with insurance companies; the comptroller with banks; the superintendent of public instruction with local school boards and professional education associations; and the agriculture commissioner with powerful farming interests such as the Farm Bureau. Members of the cabinet could depend on the support of their clientele groups quite independently of who happened to be governor, or what campaign promises gubernatorial candidates were making. Governor Reubin Askew pointed to a related problem: cabinet members were in some measure restricted by their respective departments and often tried to play the role of department head in cabinet meetings. The effect was to inject a parochial, limited view in policymaking. Finally, many of the boards and commissions on which members of the cabinet sat operated by an "authority" system in which deference was paid to that member who supposedly had expertise on a particular issue. Thus the governor was not always the most influential member even of the boards on which he sat. All of this served further to weaken the Florida governor's policy and administrative options.[11]

The cabinet system and the array of administrative agencies it engendered has, of course, had its defenders as well as detractors. The former generally have argued that the system provided "stability" and "continuity" for Florida's government. Reflecting the bias of Floridians against concentrated power in the hands of the chief executive, they argued that the cabinet system provided insurance against a demogogic and dictatorial governor, and served to prevent the establishment of statewide political machines or dynasties (the latter point seems ironic in view of the long tenure many cabinet members have held). Governors themselves have often publicly defended the existence of the cabinet system. David Sholtz, for example, noted that "I look upon Florida not from a political standpoint, but from the standpoint of a big business. I happen to be, by the mandate of the people, the president of the largest corporation in Florida. I was put here by the stockholders of the state. The cabinet represents the executive council. [The] . . . Legislature [is] the board of directors." Sholtz was simply restating a theme that has been common in Florida politics. For instance, four years earlier, Governor Doyle Carlton stated at his inauguration: "The governor and his cabinet should act as a board of directors of a corporation in which every citizen of the state is a stockholder, and exercises the most rigid business supervision without political fear or favor over the various activities of the state government."[12] The cabinet system thus fit the corporate model many governors desired for state government.

One has the feeling, though, that in some cases the governors defended the cabinet system more for political fence-building or -mending than from personal conviction. Not to endorse the cabinet system would have been politically damaging, since it was so firmly entrenched in Florida's political history and culture. Thus, LeRoy Collins, who on occasion criticized the cabinet system, and later proposed to change it, also praised it for the "safeguards" and "balance" it brought to Florida.[13] Republican Claude Kirk was even more critical of the cabinet system than was Collins. He publicly assailed its Democratic members for their "partisanship" and "obstructionism." Yet Kirk, too, had to retreat from his attacks on the cabinet when a Republican poll showed that Floridians overwhelmingly favored it.[14]

Florida governors, whether they liked it or not, were thus forced to deal with the executive framework established by the 1885 constitution, and they did so with varying degrees of success. By the end of World War II, though, it became increasingly clear to many Floridians that the old document was an unsatisfactory instrument for dealing with the state's burgeoning problems. Indeed, by 1945 the constitution had been amended nearly 100 times and had not only become excessively long, detailed, and rigid but contained inconsistencies and even contradictions.

In the early 1940s the Florida Bar Association, the state League of Women Voters, and a number of legislators and interested private citizens began efforts to write a modern, flexible constitution. Under the provisions of the 1885 document, however, whole articles of the constitution could be changed only by calling a constitutional convention; this could only be achieved by a two-thirds vote of all members of both houses of the legislature and approval in a popular referendum. In 1941, 1945, and 1947 the legislature failed to pass bills calling for a convention. On November 2, 1948, Florida voters approved an amendment that made it much easier to make substantial changes in the constitution: thereafter it was possible for the legislature to propose revisions of constitutional articles without the necessity of calling a convention. These proposals would then be submitted to the citizens for ratification or rejection.[15]

After 1948, various interest groups, sometimes united under the aegis of the Citizen Constitution Committee of Florida, submitted suggestions for constitutional change to each legislative session. Some of the proposals would have had far-reaching consequences for the state executive. For example, in 1949 a proposal was advanced which would have permitted the governor to consolidate or abolish boards, commissions, and bureaus which had conflicting or overlapping jurisdictions. It would also have created a whole new system of departments to streamline those existing under the cabinet system. The force of the state's constitutional tradition, however, and the dominance of the Florida legislature by rural, conservative, status-quo-oriented politicians prevented any significant changes in the constitution from being made during the late 1940s and early 1950s. The political situation in the state was such that neither public opinion nor legislative support could be mobilized for a thorough review of the constitution.

But in 1955 intensive efforts to write a whole new constitution for Florida began because of the confluence of two separate but related forces. In September 1953, Governor Dan McCarty died, and under the terms of the constitution the president of the senate, Charley Johns of Starke, was to assume the duties of the office. No one was quite certain, however, exactly what Johns' status was because of the vagueness of the constitutional language. Article IV, Section 19, merely stated: "In case of the impeachment of the Governor, his removal from office, death, resignation or the inability to discharge his official duties, the powers and duties of Governor shall devolve upon the President of the Senate for the residue of the term. ...."

Three different court cases, each requiring a decision of the Florida Supreme Court, were needed before it was determined that Johns was acting governor only, and that a special election would have to be held in 1954 to fill the remaining years of the McCarty term. The ambiguity of the situation resulted in calls by numerous private groups, citizens, and public officials to clarify the language to prevent similar confusion should such circumstances arise again.

The second force pushing for constitutional reform was LeRoy Collins, then state senator from Leon County. Collins was a close friend of McCarty's, and he was elected governor in the special 1954 election, defeating Johns and Brailey Odham of Sanford. High on Collins' list of priorities was constitutional revision. He was concerned with clarifying the line of succession in the event of a governor's death or disability (one of his proposals was to create an office of lieutenant governor), as well as with reorganizing the cabinet and entire executive branch. It was this latter suggestion that provoked sharp opposition from cabinet members. Collins noted that a reexamination of the cabinet was needed, and he proposed a new

Governor Dan McCarty (seated) signing papers; his brother John (standing, left) and Earl Powers, chairman of the State Turnpike Authority, look on. McCarty was in office for only nine months, but his administration was notable for its high moral standards, the quality of its appointees, and its forward-looking plans for highway and other state construction. State Photographic Archives.

method of selecting members. He observed that the legislature regarded the cabinet as something of a "dumping ground" for added state responsibilities, and this made administrative control even more difficult. Part of his plan for constitutional reform in 1955 included streamlining the cabinet system; he even went so far as to suggest that the governor be allowed to appoint members of the cabinet, and thereby promote efficiency in state government. He did not, however, recommend abolishing the cabinet, although in its new form it would advise the governor on policy matters rather than establish policies in consultation with the governor. Because of his numerous conflicts with the rural-dominated legislature over his legislative proposals and reapportionment, Collins felt he needed a loyal, cooperative cabinet. Nevertheless, Secretary of State R. A. Gray reacted very negatively to Collins' idea, even asking publicly whether the governor was not, in fact, seeking some sort of "dictatorship" for his office. Attorney General Richard Ervin echoed Gray's criticism of Collins.[16]

Collins was interested in revising more than just the executive article of the constitution. He wanted a complete overhauling of the document. Between 1885 and 1955, 158 amendments had been proposed and 106 adopted, leaving the old constitution looking like a patchwork quilt. The proposals he submitted to the 1955 legislature included: clarification of the line of succession to the governorship, creation of the office of lieutenant governor, reorganization of state agencies and bureaus, and revision of budgeting and auditing procedures. The legislature, however, opposed Collins' plan. The governor had alienated many of its members by supporting legislative reapportionment. The legislature instead established a thirty-seven-member Florida Constitutional Advisory Commission, on which a majority of the members were rural-oriented and not sympathetic to constitutional reform.

The commission prepared recommendations for the 1957 legislative session. While it did provide for a lieutenant governorship and clarified the line of succession, "Nothing was done about the disintegration of executive authority and the proliferation of constitutional boards and agencies."[17] In modifying the commission's work, the legislature further weakened the governorship by reducing his appointment powers and formally recognizing the cabinet, thereby dispersing more widely his administrative authority.

Although he was not completely satisfied with the proposed constitution, Collins felt it was the best he could get, and he spent over a year campaigning on its behalf. The voters, however, never had a chance to pass judgment on it. In late July the Florida Supreme Court removed the proposed constitution from the ballot. The legislature had attached several other matters to the constitution (including a reapportionment amendment) and had stipulated that a rejection of any of these issues would mean the defeat of the entire package. The court ruled that this "daisy-chain" stipulation was unconstitutional.[18] Efforts toward constitutional reform during the Collins administration ceased at this point. A minor, although not insignificant, alteration was made to the constitution in 1964. It provided for a change in the cycle of state elections, moving them from those years in which national elections were held to alternate years. The expressed purpose was to separate state from national issues since the former were generally overwhelmed by the presidential campaign. Of particular concern to state Democrats, however, was the trend by Floridians to vote for the Republican national ticket. Florida had not voted for the Democratic presidential candidate since 1952, with the exception of 1964, and state party leaders feared that the continuation of this practice would jeopardize the state Democratic ticket.[19]

Serious attempts at constitutional revision did not begin until 1965. By then, demands for legislative reapportionment were increasing throughout the state, particularly in South Florida, and the legislature itself needed institutional reform. It became increasingly clear that constitutional revision would be needed in order to accomplish these goals. In 1965 the legislature established a Constitutional Revision Commission to prepare a draft document for future legislative consideration. The commission was to be appointed by the governor, the speaker of the house, president of the senate, and the chief justice of the state supreme court.

The commission met during 1966 and prepared a document which was to be submitted to the 1967 legislature. However, in January 1967, the United States Supreme Court declared in *Swann* v. *Adams* (385 U.S. 440) that the legislature was illegal because of the imbalance in apportionment, and it ordered new elections to be held based on a new reapportionment formula. The newly elected legislature which met in April, then, had a remarkably different membership from earlier legislatures; it was the first one to reflect the tremendous growth in Florida's metropolitan areas.[20]

Unquestionably the new composition of the legislature greatly facilitated the overhauling of Florida's outdated constitution. The regular session of the 1967 legislature was unable to consider the draft document prepared by the commission. However, Governor Claude Kirk firmly believed that constitutional change was needed. His commitment was largely based on budgetary considerations and party interests. Pledged to "give the greatest service to the greatest number [of citizens] at the lowest cost ...," Kirk stated "Until we have a new state constitution, we are imprisoned in the strait jacket of a nineteenth century tax structure."[21] More important, however, he felt the Republican party, still a weak second party in Florida, stood to gain from any changes made in the old constitution. As a result, he called three special sessions of the legislature, and finally, in a very brief session, meeting from June 24 to July 3, 1968, it adopted a document which was submitted for approval to the voters in November of that year. It was overwhelmingly ratified, and went into effect in January 1969.

Governor Reubin Askew presides over a session of the Florida cabinet. During his eight years as governor, Askew pushed the state in new directions on race relations, environmental protection, industrial development, and corporate responsibility. An extraordinarily dynamic and hardworking governor, Askew was rumored to be a possible presidential candidate in 1976. Left to right: Commissioner of Agriculture Doyle Conner; Governor Askew; Comptroller Fred O. Dickinson, Jr.; Secretary of State Richard Stone. P. K. Yonge Library of Florida History.

With the exception of Article V on the judiciary, the new constitution was a complete revision of the old 1885 document.[22] Modification of Article IV on the executive was not extensive, but the changes were significant, and overall they served to increase the power of the governor. Section 4 specifically created the "cabinet" as a constitutional body of the six statewide-elected administrative officers. Cabinet members were to be elected with no tenure limitations. Minimum age requirements for governor and cabinet were established; candidates must be at least thirty, and state citizenship and residency requirements for the governor were increased from five to ten years. Most important, Section 3 provided that the governor may succeed himself for a second four-year term unless he has previously served six years. This provision will undoubtedly allow a certain continuity and stability which had previously been lacking in the governor's office and in gubernatorial politics. In addition, the governor's potential for longer tenure will increase his leverage with the legislature. This is especially true since the legislature now meets annually, rather than biennially; formerly the governor's only real opportunity to secure passage of his legislative program was during his first year in office; by the third year he was already a lame duck, and legislators were less inclined to follow his leadership.

Sections 2 and 3 of the new Article IV created the office of lieutenant governor and established the line of succession to the governor's office. The candidates for lieutenant governor were to run on the same ticket as their respective gubernatorial candidates. Also, no specific duties or powers were assigned to the lieutenant governor. The governor designates the lieutenant governor's duties. Should the governor's office become vacant, the lieutenant governor succeeds to the position.

The new constitution originally limited the number of executive departments to thirty, exclusive of those provided for in the constitution, but this was subsequently changed to twenty-five. Thus the constitution actually mandated the reorganization of the 150-odd state agencies into a more cohesive, functionally aligned structure. However, the constitution mitigated some of the potential benefits of this reorganization by providing that some of the departments were to be placed under the direct control of the governor, while others were to be under the jurisdiction of the governor and cabinet, the whole cabinet, part of the cabinet, or individual cabinet members. This raised so many possible combinations of control that executive responsibility would have been only further blurred. However, in 1969, under pressure from its leadership, who sensed the possible hazards for executive authority, the legislature passed a major executive reorganization act which reduced the number of executive agencies to twenty-two, and gave the governor direct authority over half of them. The Florida governor now had administrative authority in many areas where before he had none. Whether this reorganization will increase the governor's administrative responsibilities in substance as well as in form, or whether it is not a thoroughgoing enough reorganization to make any real difference in his powers, remains to be seen. It should be noted, however, that the governor's power to remove officials from office has been limited by the new constitution. He is now required to obtain senate confirmation before suspending state officers he appointed.

Three other major changes in the governor's office bear mentioning: two have constitutional sanction, while the third results from statutory law. Section 8 allows the governor, along with only three cabinet members, to grant pardons and restore civil rights except in cases of treason or impeachment. This effectively abolishes the old Pardon Board. The governor has also acquired the right to engage in certain executive reorganization procedures unless specifically disapproved by the legislature. Finally, and perhaps most important, the old Budget Commission (consisting of the whole cabinet) no longer exists. Instead, the governor now has the right, and the responsibility, to compile and submit an executive budget to the legislature without the involvement of the cabinet. The significance of this development for gubernatorial leadership is readily apparent. Not only does control over the budget increase the governor's leverage within the administration, it theoretically enables him to establish a set of state priorities, define state problems, and develop public policy and programs in a coherent, consistent manner.

In conclusion it should again be emphasized that the constitutional setting provides only a framework for gubernatorial politics. It does not, by itself, determine gubernatorial behavior. In the past, as the following chapters will show, strong Florida governors have been able to overcome, at least to a degree, many of the limitations imposed on them by the constitution. Weaker governors, however, have in some cases been overwhelmed by the executive structure within which they had to operate. It is still too early to tell what full effects the new executive provisions of the 1968 constitution, with subsequent amendments and enacted statutory law, have had, and will have, on gubernatorial politics. It does appear, however, that the governor's power is substantially greater under the new constitution than it was under the 1885 document. Certainly, Governor Reubin Askew acted vigorously within the office and expanded it in new directions. While this may be a function of his style and ability as a leader, it also appears to be a result of the office's increased powers and responsibilities. The future seems promising for executive leadership in Florida.

5

The Executive Office in Florida

THE governor, to paraphrase Clinton Rossiter, must not only reign, but he must in some sense rule, as well. Rossiter was referring to the president, and while the governorship should not be thought of as a miniature presidency because of qualitative differences in the scope, prestige, and powers of the office, there are some parallels in their functions.[1] The governor is the chief executive, the principal administrator, of the state. He is responsible for running the executive branch of the state government smoothly, efficiently, and effectively. Services must be delivered: roads widened and paved, schools adequately staffed, taxes collected, law and order maintained. If there is a breakdown somewhere in the machinery of state government, the governor is ultimately responsible. Even if he has trouble controlling the executive branch, he must shoulder at least a substantial portion of the blame when things go wrong.

In spite of the importance of the governor's administrative functions, they are not always widely recognized and, in fact, they are often largely invisible. This is true especially in a state such as Florida where the executive is very fragmented by the cabinet system and the governor has great difficulty controlling his administration. It is precisely this lack of control which helps bring about the lack of visibility. In situations of executive fragmentation and decentralization, there is little accountability of bureaus and agencies, and they have considerable latitude to operate quietly away from the public's eye.[2] Moreover, as long as state services are provided in a reasonably effective manner, the public pays little attention (education seems to be the exception). Only when the governmental machinery breaks down, or there is a scandal, do citizens take notice. Thus, there is a sort of paradox for the governor concerning the politics of the executive branch. Although carrying out executive functions is important to the governor's overall "rating," his effectiveness is least likely to be noticed when everything is running smoothly. Deficiencies attract attention, but it is the kind of attention which is likely to alienate and antagonize citizens.

The notion of "running the machinery of state government," while intuitively understandable, is nonetheless vague. What does the governor do as an administrator? In Florida, as in other states, government is formally divided into three parts: the legislative, the executive, and the judicial. It is the executive's job to see that laws and judicial decisions are implemented and their intent carried out. In a formal sense, the executive also acts as a check on power excesses of the two other branches, especially the legislative.

To aid the governor in carrying out his constitutional duties, a host of departments and agencies have been created which are charged with the day-to-day operation of the government. Obviously the governor cannot operate all (or even some) programs by himself, and therefore a bureacracy has developed which theoretically acts as an extension of himself. In addition, there are other executive offices, in Florida called the cabinet, which, because of their considerable collegial decision-making ability, share some of the executive power. Whether or not the bureaucracy actually functions as the "arm" of the governor to do his bidding, and whether other executive officers form a true partnership with the governor in carrying out executive functions are questions that will be explored in this chapter. The important point for the moment is that although the governor does not have all the executive authority, as the chief executive officer he does bear the responsibility for it. And the public never ceases to remind him that he does carry this responsibility.

How, then, can the governor administer the state most effectively? What are his specific problems in controlling his administration? At least four major difficulties can immediately be discerned; others will be pointed out in the sections which follow.[3]

First is the problem of entrenched bureaucracy.[4] Agencies and bureaus in the executive branch quickly achieve set patterns of operation; in general, the older the bureaucracy, the more rigid is the pattern of activity in it. Changing that pattern is difficult, and a governor who wishes to revise or revamp the activity pattern of an agency must usually expend considerable time, energy, and political resources in doing so. Success, moreover, is by no means assured, because bureaucracies have a way of rolling with the punches and continuing previous patterns of operations even under the guise of new directives and plans. Bureaucrats, in addition, build up a systematic routine of association with legislators (especially those on relevant appropriations and substantive committees) and interest group clientele. This triadic relationship is usually stable over time, and is extremely important in policymaking as well as in program implementation. For a governor to influence bureaucratic operation successfully, he must somehow intervene to change the pattern of this triangular relationship as well as the internal politics of the agency itself. Finally many bureaucrats in state agencies are protected by civil service or other merit systems from "political pressure." While this undoubtedly has produced many desirable outcomes, it also serves to isolate and insulate bureaucrats from gubernatorial initiative. They can effectively ignore his calls for change by pulling their civil service mantles about them, and even embarrass him by charging "political interference."

Governor Napoleon Bonaparte Broward taking the oath of office on the steps of the capitol, January 5, 1905. Secretary of State H. Clay Crawford is directly behind Broward's elbow, retiring governor William Sherman Jennings directly in front of the column at the right. Broward was to become an extraordinarily dynamic governor whose support of the common man won him a large following. He is particularly remembered for his attempts to drain the Everglades. State Photographic Archives.

In contrast to the governor, bureaucrats often held office for a long time; as was noted in Chapter 4, members of the Florida cabinet tended to have very long tenures. Thus, they achieved both expertise about state government and politics as well as a sense of independence from the governor. Agency heads were likely to see governors come and go, and they recognized that they knew much more about state operations than either the incumbent governor, his predecessor, or his successor. They felt reasonably confident, then, in operating more or less as they chose.[5] Whether or not the two term extension will help the governor overcome these bureaucratic problems remains to be seen. No real pattern emerged during the Kirk administration. It does appear, however, that Askew's governorship was considerably enhanced both administratively and legislatively by his eight years in office. Undoubtedly the two terms have helped dispel some of the "revolving door" attitude which at least some state employees have had about the governor's office. However, if the experience of other states is at all illustrative, it would appear that it takes individual governors with the staying power of G. Mennan Williams (Michigan) or Nelson Rockefeller (New York) to challenge effectively bureaucratic expertise and longevity.

Perhaps most crucial to gubernatorial problems of administrative control is the structural and political fragmentation of the executive branch.[6] In only three states is the governor the sole statewide elected official; in every other state at least one other member of the executive branch is separately elected. Florida, it will be recalled, is a rather extreme example of executive fragmentation because of the cabinet system. Since the governor does not appoint cabinet members they are not beholden or responsible to him. In Florida, candidates for the cabinet do not even run on the same ticket as the governor. As a result, they usually insist on preserving their independence from gubernatorial candidates in their campaigns. Since cabinet members also have their own constituencies and a lengthy tenure in office, the result has been the same as mentioned earlier: they established considerable expertise in their own areas, their own bases of support, and significant autonomy from the governor within the executive branch.

Finally there is the dramatic difference in perspective between the governor and other members of the executive branch. The governor, by definition, must have a broad perspective. He has to survey all the needs of the state, define a set of problems, establish priorities, and choose among competing alternatives. The governor is probably the only member of the state government who is in a position to carry out this essential function of political leadership. Even other statewide elected officials cannot, for they generally become socialized by the agencies and departments they are supposed to lead. The heads of departments, agencies and bureaus, as well as lower level employees, do achieve a considerable expertise in their specialized areas, and their work is frequently marked by professionalism of the highest order. But this expertise is often achieved at the cost of acquiring tunnel vision. Their perspective becomes narrow and parochial.[7] They see state problems almost exclusively through the interests of their particular department; they view their own programs as deserving the highest priority, and they attempt to press those perspectives on the governor and legislature. Invariably, then, this difference in perspective between governors and agencies must lead to conflict over policy development and implementation.

The governor, of course, has at his disposal a number of means through which he can try to exercise some control over the rest of the executive branch. These resources vary tremendously from state to state, and scarcely any two governors can use them in the same way or even have access to them to the same degree. Reorganization as a political control device of the executive, for example, has scarcely been available to the Florida governor at all, largely because the cabinet system and the existence of the "little cabinet" tend to prevent consolidation and reorganization. Democratic party organization, moreover, has been largely nonexistent in Florida. Unlike governors of many other states, Florida's chief executive cannot exercise party control over top level appointees. However, he does, like his colleagues elsewhere, have other resources, and the effective use of these can be of considerable help to him. Such measures include use of patronage (including letting of contracts, building of roads and other state facilities, and appointments and suspensions) and budget powers. Each of these areas, as will be seen, is fraught with political difficulties. But they remain the principal devices of the governor as he tries to persuade the rest of the executive branch to cooperate with him. Interpersonal relations are extremely important too; how well the governor gets along with the rest of the executive branch can tremendously affect its willingness to work with him.[8] Thus the governor needs both "carrots and sticks," as well as a pleasing, ingratiating manner, in order to secure maximum cooperation.

THE FLORIDA GOVERNOR AND THE EXECUTIVE BRANCH

Like their counterparts in other states, Florida governors have been faced with the problem of molding an unwieldly executive branch in such a way as to implement their policy directives. This has traditionally been a very difficult matter, not only because of largely autonomous cabinet departments but because of the existence of a plethora of administrative agencies, many with overlapping or conflicting jurisdictions. In its most fragmented state shortly before executive reorganization in 1969, the Florida executive branch consisted of over 150 separate agencies. Given a short tenure, limited budget powers, and a traditional fear in the state of centralizing power in the hands of the governor, it is not surprising that many Florida governors regarded their administrative responsibilities as hopeless, and some performed them very badly.

Millard Caldwell was one of only a few Florida governors (including Collins and Askew) in this century to reflect at length on the complexities of trying to administer an executive branch which was designed to prevent it from being controlled by any one individual. While most Florida governors on one occasion or another expressed frustration with their administrative tasks, Caldwell's observations are important because they provide outsiders with a rare glimpse into how he, and undoubtedly other Florida governors, viewed their administrative tasks.[9]

Caldwell commented that the governor's administrative responsibilities, and difficulties, began even before he assumed office, because he had to arrange appointments to numerous commissions, boards, and agencies about which he was likely to know very little. It is an intimidating list to say the least: State Road Department, State Racing Commission, State Board of Health, Game and Fresh Water Fish Commission, State Board of Control, State Auditor, Improvements Commission, Milk Commission, Beverage Commission, Motor Vehicle Commission, Industrial Commission, Citrus Commission, State Chemist, Livestock Sanitary Board, Board of Forestry and Parks, State Marketing Bureau, Hotel Commission, Tuberculosis Board, Advertising Commission, Crippled Children's Commission, Council for the Blind, State Library Board, Budget Director, and Adjutant General.[10] Many of these boards and commissions made up what is known as the little cabinet, and the selection of appropriate members was thus extremely crucial for the governor in terms of his ability to control at least parts of his administration.

The list of appointments which so disturbed Caldwell did not stop with these major state positions, however. There were also a large number of appointments which the governor had to make to professional licensing

Governor Cary Hardee delivering inaugural address, January 4, 1921. An elegant figure with his pince-nez and cutaway, Hardee fit the popular image of a governor. His was a quiet and passive administration, however, basking in Florida's economic prosperity. State Photographic Archives.

boards, and other agencies and commissions which are responsible for local memorials or local improvements such as drainage districts. There were also other state and local positions which the governor had to fill upon vacancy of the office.[11] There are thousands of positions for the governor to fill, and while the opportunity for patronage is clearly vast, so are the problems. Reubin Askew commented that too much time is spent making the appointments, especially those at the local level, and he felt strongly that their number should be severely reduced and that local appointments should be made locally.[12]

Caldwell also pointed out the large number of cabinet level boards on which the governor must serve. These are administrative boards comprised of some or all cabinet officials, and it is their existence which gives rise to the oft-heard comment that Florida has a collegial executive. The major ones are the Budget Commission, Board of Commissioners of State Institutions, State Board of Education, Trustees of the Internal Improvement Fund, Board of Administration, Pardon Board, Board of Pensions, State Board of Conservation, Board of Drainage Commissions, Labor Business Agents Licensing Board, and the Agricultural Marketing Board.[13]

Again, the governor's major problem was that he had only limited knowledge of these boards and their functions and thus had to defer in making judgments to more expert members. In addition, the governor could not dominate these boards. He was but one member, although undoubtedly the most prestigious one, and he had but one vote. The lone exception was the Pardon Board, which could not take action unless the governor voted with the majority, and therefore he exercised a sort of limited veto over it. But in the vast majority of cases, the governor could only employ whatever powers of persuasion he had and hope for the best.

Governors other than Caldwell complained about the difficulties which this complex array of administrative boards brings to the office. Gilchrist, for example, noted wistfully that governors in other states did not have to bother with sitting on so many administrative boards, but rather could rely on boards which they appointed to carry out their wishes. Gilchrist went on to observe that having to serve as the chairman of the trustees of the Internal Improvement Fund took up a tremendous amount of time; as much, in his estimation, as all of his other administrative duties combined.[14] Fred Cone was a frequent critic of the administrative apparatus with which he had to deal.[15] Eventually he decided that it was unmanageable, and largely retired from any active participation in it.

Finally, Caldwell stressed the importance of the governor's ability to reorganize and streamline state administration. It was only through this process, he felt, that the governor could keep the state's administrative apparatus moving smoothly and efficiently. Caldwell also believed that administrative costs could be significantly reduced through reorganization.[16]

Yet here too, Caldwell observed, the governor was severely hamstrung. Most substantial reorganization required legislative approval, and it was not always certain that legislators would approve reorganization plans, especially if it appeared that the change might result in increased gubernatorial powers. Moreover, the legislature in Caldwell's administration (and up to 1968) met only biennially The problem was that for the governor's first legislative session (which occurred in April of his first year) he was not likely to know enough about how the state administrative machinery operated to put forward a significant or appropriate reorganization plan. Two years later, when the legislature again met in regular session, the governor was already a lame duck, and "the second legislature is generally unsympathetic to sweeping programs of a new order."[17] Also, of course, legislators, bureaucrats, and interest group clientele enjoy the stability of relationships built up over time and they are generally loathe to change it. Governors, hindered by a four-year term and a biennial legislature, and desirous of accomplishing more visible goals than the restructuring of agencies, have therefore largely left reorganization alone. Only Claude Kirk pushed a massive reorganization bill through the legislature, but in this he had public and legislative opinion on his side since the state legislature had just undergone a massive reapportionment in 1967.[18]

Although Caldwell did not make the point, it should also be noted that to create a successful reorganization plan a governor must have a real "sense" for administration. Some governors, such as Caldwell, seemed to have had a natural instinct for knowing how best to combine agency functions in a streamlined, effective structure. Others, such as Fuller Warren, Charley Johns, and Haydon Burns, seemed to have little understanding of how administrative structure, policy direction, and program implementation and operation were related.

THE GOVERNOR AND THE CABINET

In Chapter 4 the structure of the cabinet and basic set of relationships between it and the governor were outlined. To summarize briefly, it is not merely the existence of separately elected state officials other than the governor which makes the Florida executive unique, for some states have even more of these officials. Rather, Florida's uniqueness stems from the cabinet system which serves as a collegial decision and policymaking unit, acting as the governing board for several state agencies and functions. The list of commissions and boards, about which Gilchrist, Cone, Caldwell, and others complained , is suggestive of the range of functions with which the cabinet has been called upon to deal. Moreover, the cabinet and governing board system have bred decentralization of authority, dispersion of responsibility, and an incoherent administrative structure.[19]

For the most part governors and their cabinets have worked in reasonable harmony. Some chief executives have even stated that their cabinet members were a help to them. Collins, for example, noted that he relied on his cabinet for assistance, and it generally supported him, especially at critical moments.[20] In one instance, a jury had convicted Walter Lee Irvin, a young black man, of rape, and sentenced him to death. Collins, however, was not convinced that the prosecution had really proved its case, and with support from other cabinet members (acting as the Pardon Board) commuted the sentence. The decision was an unpopular one; it came at a time when racial feeling was at a fever pitch following the *Brown* decision, and Collins was desperately trying to prevent racial strife in the state. He foresaw what the Irvin conviction could lead to, and looked for ways to avoid increasing racial tensions while trying to see that justice was done. Popular belief was probably on the side of the jury. Nevertheless, members of the Pardon Board were quick to align with the governor and supported him strongly when he made his decision.[21]

For the most part cabinet members have remained quiescent in the face of gubernatorial initiatives. Traditionally, they seem to have taken the view that if the governor advanced a new policy that did not affect them or their departments, they would not oppose him. Governors, as Haydon Burns pointed out, would frequently tailor their demands to suit the cabinet, to adopt programs which they felt cabinet members would accept.[22] Undoubtedly this was often true, but it does not explain the cabinet's willingness to follow the dramatic leadership of the governor, such as in the Irvin case. The reason seems clear: cabinet members have usually been willing to give the governor substantial leeway, and to follow his leadership when their own interests were not directly involved. The governor, for his part, does not often intervene publicly in the affairs of cabinet departments. He recognizes the structural and political independence which cabinet officers have, and he respects it. Thus, for example, the governor ordinarily allows the commissioner of agriculture to establish policy in that area, and he does not usually try to dictate policies for banks and insurance, which are matters for the comptroller and treasurer. If the governor does intervene in affairs of a cabinet department, it is almost always with the knowledge of that officer. The intervention, moreover, generally results from important policy differences between the chief executive and the cabinet head, a realization by the governor that his self interest, or his conception of the state's public interest, is directly involved. Usually disagreements between the governor and cabinet will be worked out privately, although open conflicts do occur. Thus, agreement between the governor and other cabinet members results from a desire to cooperate and a mutual understanding that "territorial boundaries" will normally be respected. It is unquestionably this cooperation, which most observers of Florida politics overlook, that has enabled the state's executive branch to function relatively smoothly, especially when a "strong" leader occupies the governor's mansion. On the other hand, this respect for "territory" and willingness by the governor and cabinet officials not to impinge on each other's responsibilities has circumvented gubernatorial initiative. The governor is not free to act in any policy area he chooses, even one that might be of great importance to the state; he cannot dictate to cabinet members in their areas. This is a serious constraint on the potential range of gubernatorial policymaking.

On occasion, though, there has been open conflict between a governor and his cabinet, and verbal sparring matches have erupted. Fred Cone's criticism of the cabinet system has already been noted, but one additional problem should be mentioned. Early in Cone's term, he and the other members of the Pardon Board (the comptroller, attorney general, and commissioner of agriculture) had a sharp disagreement about the rules under which the board operated. Cone settled the matter by saying he did not make the rules and thus did not feel obligated to abide by them. For the rest of his term Cone and his cabinet kept each other at arm's length. [23]

Both Spessard Holland and Millard Caldwell often had public disagreements with their irascible attorney general, Tom Watson. Holland and Watson had numerous personal arguments. Malcolm Johnson noted that many of them were a result of Watson's belligerent attitude; in one instance, after exchanging bitter words with the governor, Watson invited Holland "to settle the dispute outside by more direct means than just a debate." [24] Johnson predicted that Watson and Caldwell would not get along any better, and he was right. Caldwell was especially irritated at the numerous lawsuits which Watson filed, and the costs they incurred. [25]

Collins also had problems with his cabinet even though it supported him most of the time. In 1957 the legislature at Collins' urging passed a central purchasing law. However, the governor felt it was too weak, and he sought, with cabinet support, to strengthen it in 1959. After holding two secret meetings with the cabinet he still could not persuade members to support him; the meetings were held, moreover, after Collins had publicly declared that he felt such secrecy was unnecessary. The following year the cabinet took advantage of a Collins trip to Washington and during his absence voted to approve $300,000 for repairs to the capitol; Collins had previously registered his opposition to the expenditure. [26] Finally, Collins sought to change the nature of the cabinet under constitutional revisions which he advocated during his administration. The sharp rebuke he suffered from cabinet members after trying to implement these changes has already been noted. [27]

Farris Bryant also encountered problems with his cabinet. The issues involved political appointments. In the first instance, Bryant sought to remove three state Conservation Department positions from merit system protection; he argued that they were, in fact, policymaking positions, and thus were exempt from the merit system. Bryant's words were echoed by Conservation Director Randolph Hodges. However, the move was blocked by members of the cabinet—Attorney General Richard Ervin, School Superintendent Thomas Bailey, and Agriculture Secretary Doyle Connor. Directors of the Road Commission and the Internal Development Commission also wanted Bryant's help in removing several positions in their respective departments from the merit system. However, because the cabinet disagreed sharply with the governor (Ervin argued that the Merit System Council should have acted before the cabinet was asked to take a position), Bryant could not help his own appointees.[28]

Although there were occasional splits between cabinet members and governors, there was never any real consideration given to changing the nature of the collegial decision-making system. Floridians wanted to retain the system, and cabinet members were very well entrenched. In addition, only rarely did a dispute between governor and cabinet members threaten to paralyze the decision-making apparatus; even with the running Holland-Watson argument the cabinet kept on operating (although both Holland and later Caldwell built their cabinet coalitions knowing they would invariably be opposed by Watson). If a governor foresaw trouble for one of his proposals to the cabinet, he would modify it, or drop it and perhaps resubmit it at another time when some groundwork had been laid. In general, however, this did not happen very often. Cabinet members, for their part, would allow governors to make speeches, set priorities, and establish alternatives. They realized this was a central part of gubernatorial politics and a perquisite of the governor's office. The cabinet would protest only when the governor violated traditional state norms or somehow impinged on the interest of individual cabinet officers or the collective body. While each governor and his cabinet have had their public and private differences, only once did a constitutional crisis threaten to bring the wheels of government to a halt. It occurred during Claude Kirk's administration. Kirk and his cabinet rarely agreed on anything. To a degree it was because of partisanship (Kirk was a Republican and the other cabinet members were Democrats); in part the disagreement was based on style (Kirk was flamboyant and publicity seeking, while the others were somewhat more restrained). Mainly, however, the continuous dispute was a result of Kirk's unwillingness to accept a cabinet veto of his administrative policies. Kirk essentially tried to run the state unilaterally. He wanted the cabinet to rubber-stamp all his proposals. Cabinet members, naturally, resented this.

The first real problem came in August 1967, when Kirk publicly announced that he wanted to abolish the cabinet system even though Floridians, according to Kirk's own private polls, favored it. Later his reasons became clear. Cabinet members blocked Kirk's move to hire a new state planning director and to get more money for the private war on crime he was financing. Kirk was livid. He said, "It's obvious that my ability as an administrator has been called into question. . . . If the cabinet would stop being partisan, perhaps they could go about the business of getting the state's work done." Finally, matters reached such proportions that Kirk ordered that his signature not be automatically fixed on expense checks for members of the cabinet and fifteen cabinet aides. He felt he should review the accounts before approving them. At the time, ironically, Kirk was under fire from the state auditor for misuse of expense funds.[29]

In spite of the difficulties, most Florida governors have publicly and privately supported the cabinet system. In fact, they had no choice. They could complain about it, but they knew they had to live with it. Too much criticism would have antagonized not only other cabinet members but legislators and citizens as well, all of whom seemed consistently to support the system. Most governors realized they must come to terms with the cabinet if they were to be at all successful.

Two Florida governors have suggested that the time has come to change the cabinet system. LeRoy Collins, who even criticized the cabinet while he was governor, carried his position even further. He argued that the cabinet no longer assists the governor, as it used to. Rather, the growth of cabinet departments and budgets, the acquisition of new functions, and the addition of large public-relations staffs have created a system of "little governors," each of whom places his own interests above those of the state. The cabinet, he felt, dispersed executive authority far beyond what was originally intended, and far beyond what is good for the state. Collins declared, "I know of no proposed model state constitution which embraces an elective executive cabinet such as we have, and most students of state government feel that it unreasonably dilutes the chief executive responsibility which properly should be that of the governor."[30] He concluded that the elected cabinet should be abolished.

Reubin Askew also advocated dropping the cabinet system in favor of governor-appointed executive officers. He regarded the cabinet system as an unnecessary obstacle in his effort to govern the state and an impediment to effective government in the post-Sputnik age.[31] A plan embodying his ideas was placed in the proposed new constitution drafted by the Constitution Revision Commission in January 1978. The entire document, however, was rejected overwhelmingly by voters in November 1978.

In keeping with the framework developed earlier, can we conclude anything about the governor's interaction with the cabinet, and does it contribute to the centralization of his administrative authority? Interaction for the most part has been harmonious. Within the areas not regarded by cabinet members as their own, governors can be reasonably certain they will not be opposed by these officials and can perhaps even gain their tacit approval. Jennings, Broward, Caldwell, Collins, and Askew, in particular, have been able to address politically controversial issues such as Everglades drainage, reapportionment, constitutional revision, and race relations without receiving public criticism by their cabinets. We wonder, then, whether other governors might not have been too cautious in attempting to consolidate cabinet support behind them; that is, could they have moved ahead without being concerned that their cabinets would undercut their support? Most Florida governors have dealt cautiously with and have been very anxious to avoid controversy involving the cabinet. Nevertheless, Florida's political history in this century suggests that bold direction by the governor need not always be compromised for fear of cabinet recalcitrance.

CONTROLLING THE ADMINISTRATION: PATRONAGE

An important device in controlling the administration is patronage, and the chief executives have been well aware of its usefulness in administrative affairs. For example, Governor Sidney Catts once said, "It is a mighty poor cat that won't look out for its kittens."[32] Catts was referring to political patronage when he made this remark, and it seems safe to say that every Florida governor in this century, regardless of his ideology, would in some measure agree with him. It should be realized that patronage can be used in both positive and negative ways; it can reward friends and punish enemies. Every Florida governor in this century has used patronage, in both manifestations, as a means of trying to control his administration and of influencing both legislators and local officials.

Patronage covers a broad range of behaviors and activities. Every day the governor is besieged with pension applicants, pleas for pardons or reduction of prison sentences, requests for building or improving roads, solicitations for jobs or state business, and removal of various officials. All of these can be considered part of the patronage system because they involve the granting or withholding of favors. Some idea of the vast amount of patronage controlled by the Florida governor can be obtained from referring back to the list of state commissions and boards appointed by him. This is just a partial catalogue; it does not include judges, for example, of which there have been several hundred in the state appointed by the governor.[33] Appointments are perhaps the most significant source of patronage because there are numerous positions to fill and numerous pressures exerted concerning these positions from other participants in the political system. This potentially affords the governor a tremendous opportunity to staff his administration with loyal supporters, or at least with individuals willing to follow his system of priorities. But as we shall see, the chief executive faces many dangers associated with the appointment process.

The overriding question concerning patronage and gubernatorial politics is the same one asked earlier in this chapter: to what extent does patronage help a governor administer the state more effectively, coordinate disparate agencies of government, and secure the cooperation of the bureaucracy and its interest group clientele? Theoretically, through use of contracts, appointments, and suspensions (the patronage areas of concern in this chapter), the governor can induce support for himself within his own administration by rewarding those who follow his leadership and punishing those who do not. It is even possible to bring a variety of bureaus into some reasonably coherent pattern, at least partially through patronage (although other administrative devices, such as reorganization and budgeting, would also be necessary).

The impact of patronage on a governor's administration is largely a function of the style that can be found on a continuum ranging from "merit system" on one end to "spoils system" on the other. A "merit system" style emphasizes a professional approach, using objective criteria such as relative costs and benefits in letting contracts and establishing qualifications in the case of appointments. It downplays partisanship or friends-and-neighbors politics. It should be stressed that such a style is still intensely political, but it represents the politics of a "good government" ethos. A "spoils system" type of patronage is that which deliberately carries out the old dictum "To the victor belong the spoils." Friends are rewarded, largely irrespective of costs or qualifications, and enemies are punished. Professionalism is downplayed and partisanship becomes a primary consideration in awarding patronage. Again, it should be emphasized that these systems represent extremes of a continuum, and it is unlikely that either would ever be found in "pure" form. Nonetheless, they do describe the range of behaviors and styles which can define gubernatorial approaches to patronage.

Patronage also takes place in a political environment; as was noted at the beginning of the book the setting of political activity usually determines what possibilities exist, what actions can reasonably be undertaken, and with what likely effects. In the case of patronage, setting becomes very crucial, because a particular style of patronage during one period might not be functional (in terms of increased administrative control) in another. Thus, a continuum showing the effects of patronage on the governor's administration ranges from "functional," in the sense of improving administrative control, to "dysfunctional" where it does not.

Patronage: Contracts

Governors have had considerable discretionary powers in letting state contracts. Centralized purchasing did not really begin in any systematic way until Collins' administration, although there had been laws prior to that time which provided in some measure for central purchasing.[34] The absence of central purchasing meant that governors could influence the letting of contracts to whichever companies they wished. Although this may have raised costs and promoted various kinds of diseconomies of scale, it did allow numerous opportunities for patronage. In addition, many executive departments' contracts did not have to be let on the basis of competitive bidding. Thus, governors were in a very strong position to use contracts to reward friends and supporters. For some agencies, especially the Road Department, contracts were at least as important as appointments and the actual selection of right-of-ways as mechanisms of patronage.

Contracts for insurance on state agencies have been especially prominent sources of patronage. Premiums on different policies run into the thousands of dollars annually. Governors, moreover, have not even tried to make a secret of the degree to which they influence the letting of insurance contracts. Spessard Holland, for example, wrote in a letter to Harry Holden, an insurance agent for the Standard Accident Insurance Company, that he would "try to help you in every way we can so far as insurance is concerned." Later, Holland had two men write a policy on two bridges built in the state, but the commission was divided with other insurance agents, in Holland's words, "so that just as many insurance friends as possible could be taken care of...."[35]

LeRoy Collins once noted that his office "on many occasions" supplied names of friendly insurance agents and companies to various state agencies. However, he was quick to point out, "I don't think of a single case where this office ever made a recommendation which resulted in high cost." Collins made his remarks in response to newspaper criticism of the way in which the state let insurance contracts. Indeed, governors had frequently been criticized for the way in which they used insurance (and other contracts) as patronage. At least one governor, Dan McCarty, did not approve of the procedure either. He publicly spoke out against the practice of the Game and Fresh Water Fish Commission, which awarded substantial insurance business to a company owned by senate president Charley Johns. He felt this was clearly a violation of public trust, although it should be pointed out that some of his views may well have been inspired by his political antipathy towards Johns.[36]

McCarty was probably unusual in his attitude toward using contracts as patronage devices. In terms of the continuum developed earlier, his approach is well toward the "professionalism" or "merit system" end. On the other hand, even governors such as Holland and Collins, normally thought of as professing a "good government" approach to state administration, did not hesitate to use patronage to reward their friends. Holland and Collins both occupy positions roughly midway along this continuum, especially when compared to Fuller Warren, who is clearly toward the extreme end of the "spoils system" side. Warren was extremely heavy-handed in his use of patronage, and on balance it probably did him more harm than good. Patronage did not help him control his administration, but instead it caused him considerable embarrassment.

In early 1950, it was revealed that the cost to the state of renting road construction machinery had increased to over $100,000 a month during the previous year. Warren had denounced excessive rates for renting this equipment during his campaign, but nonetheless rental contracts were important patronage instruments awarded by the Road Department without competitive bidding. During 1949 about $250,000 worth of contracts had been awarded to a company headed by A. F. Rich of Tallahassee. Rich, it turned out, had been chairman of Warren's inauguration committee.[37]

In itself this public disclosure was more annoying than politically damaging. However, it presaged a minor scandal, one that did embarrass the governor. In 1950, Charles V. Griffin, a close confidant and financial backer of Warren, broke with him when the governor rescinded Griffin's appointment as chief crime investigator in the administration. After the breakup, Warren dismissed a number of so-called "Griffin men" in the Road Department, including Robert Ghiotto and Arthur Sims, both of whom held high level positions. In August 1950, Ghiotto and Sims brought civil suits against the Road Department, apparently at the urging of Griffin, because of contract rental policies. The ensuing public disclosures of contracts let and rates paid were prominently displayed in the press. The embarrassment to Warren increased when Ghiotto and Sims won their suit over the rentals in spite of the efforts of the department's counsel and outside attorneys especially retained for the litigation. Their victory forced the Road Department to receive competitive bids before letting contracts.[38]

Competitive bidding did not stop the excesses in the Road Department. Indeed, LeRoy Collins was forced to invalidate all Charley Johns' road contracts which were not matched by federal funds, and could not "be justified by public welfare."[39] The contracts let by Johns during 1954 were $4.9 million over the Road Department's budget, and an additional $5.3 million in contracts had been planned.

Collins' action did not permit his administration to escape charges of wrongdoing, however. In 1960 gubernatorial candidate Farris Bryant, whose candidacy was opposed by Collins, charged that the Road Department was riddled with corruption. Subsequent investigations revealed eight state engineers had accepted bribes to approve shoddy road construction projects by the Cone Brothers Construction Company. The charges of bribery were never linked to Collins. He agreed that the road department employees had betrayed their trust and "must be and will be rooted out."[40] He also supported the suspension of the Cone Brothers Construction Company from further state projects. This incident points out the difficulty in reforming the road department after it had been the object of political manipulation. The employees had been accustomed to the mismanagement and the twisting of the law, and, not surprisingly, the merit reform instituted by Collins did not keep them from continuing to do so.

While Collins' reform reduced some of the manipulation of the department, it did not prevent the governors who succeeded him from continuing to intervene in the agency's affairs. For example, favoritism in the handling of toll road collections and in the letting of road contracts was charged against the administrations of Farris Bryant and Claude Kirk. The *St. Petersburg Times* quoted a letter from Governor Bryant to chairman John Hammer of the Turnpike Authority in which Bryant asked Hammer to remember his campaign backers when Hammer selected banks to handle toll road money. Two banks specifically designated by Bryant to handle these collections were First National Bank of Miami headed by Frank Smathers, brother of United States Senator George Smathers, and Florida National Bank of Orlando, headed by Ed Ball who had helped Bryant financially in the 1960 campaign.[41]

Claude Kirk apparently made extensive use of the road department in paying off friends and supporters of his 1966 campaign. Kirk's aides also established a Governor's Club to pay for his living, entertaining, and traveling expenses. In return for these contributions, the investors received a pair of blue cufflinks with Kirk's insignia, a small flag like the one Kirk flew on his limousine, an autographed color photo, state jobs, and state contracts. In December, 1969, $667,000 of the $820,000 that was paid in consulting contracts by the state went to firms or individuals who had contributed to Kirk's campaign. David Smith, a Pompano Beach businessman, refused to invest $2,500 in a Governor's Club membership when approached by a Kirk aide. He later stated that his refusal caused his road building company to be placed on the Department of Transportation's blackball list.[42]

These examples help illustrate the range of gubernatorial styles in letting contracts as patronage devices. They show that many governors have not hesitated to employ them in a manner which is characterized, in varying degrees, by spoils system styles. The question is, to what extent is this functional or dysfunctional in terms of administrative control? The answer seems to be that as long as scandal is avoided, the fact that "spoils system" politics is used does not hurt the governor and may help him . The public seems to expect and tolerate at least a certain level of reward-and-punishment politics. Only when there is evidence of conflict of interest, corruption, or extreme heavy-handedness in the use of contracts does the public take notice and cause the governor embarrassment. Warren, Johns, and Kirk are examples of this. And even a governor such as Collins, whose personal honesty and integrity were never questioned, found that his administrative abilities were called into account, and his public image somewhat tarnished, by a scandal resulting from the use of contracts as patronage.

Patronage: Appointments

As important as contracts have been in the politics of the executive in Florida, they still take second place to appointments. The governor may designate as many as 4,000 to 5,000 persons to positions during his administration. Not all of these appointments are overtly political, and many of them are to relatively minor and/or purely local positions. Not all of them prove satisfactory either; an individual may be incompetent, dishonest, or disloyal. And yet the fact remains that through appointments the governor can place in key administrative posts individuals whom he hopes will cooperate with him and respond to his definition of problems and his priorities. It is therefore an important mechanism in trying to control the fragmented executive branch and to help him implement his campaign promises.

Making appointments is by no means a simple matter. Governors themselves have pointed out most of the major difficulties. Ideological similarity or congruence is desirable, but not always possible. For political reasons governors sometimes have to make appointments which satisfy certain demands in order to gain other advantages. Thus, for example, LeRoy Collins fired his state prison director, Richard Culver, and appointed in his place H. G. Cochran, who was acceptable to Senator Charley Johns; he, in turn, agreed to cooperate (not for very long, as it turned out) with Collins on reapportionment.[43] In a state as large as Florida, geographical balance is important in appointments. Various regions must be recognized, and a balance must be struck between some of the traditional cleavages: north vs. south, urban vs. rural.[44] Since World War II various minority groups have had to be recognized through appointments. Fuller Warren was widely applauded for naming the first woman, Mrs. Jessie Ball Du Pont, to a high-level state agency, the State Board of Control; Fred Cone appointed the first woman sheriff more than a decade earlier.[45] On the other hand, LeRoy Collins received considerable criticism when he appointed black members to his racial advisory board; he argued, however, that matters would be discussed which directly affected the black community, and thus blacks should be included on the board. Reubin Askew actively sought to appoint blacks and women to a range of public offices, including Joseph Hatchett to the Florida Supreme Court.[46]

While the governor has to make thousands of appointments during his administration, unquestionably the most significant are those to the little cabinet. The little cabinet is not a formal institution. Traditionally it has consisted of those major state agencies whose directors and governing boards are appointed directly by the governor. It includes those Caldwell and Cone complained about, but it should be pointed out that some of the members of the little cabinet are much more important than others. The Road Board and the Beverage Commission were perhaps the most significant because of the number of possible patronage positions they provide: there are hundreds of road and beverage inspectors, numerous other employees who are not protected by civil service or merit system regulations, and of course, many, many contracts. In addition, roads and liquor licenses are themselves important instruments of patronage. Other agencies which ranked high in the pecking order of the little cabinet were the Racing Commission, Hotel Commission, Citrus Commission, Game and Fresh Water Fish Commission,

Governor Sidney J. Catts (seated, left front) with his family on the steps of the governor's mansion, Tallahassee. Catts appointed many members of his family to state positions, for which he was roundly criticized by Floridians. Loyalty to Catts underscored nearly all his appointments. The term "Catts and his kittens" emerged early in his administration because of such patronage tactics. State Photographic Archives.

and Board of Control (later, the Board of Regents). Each of these agencies has represented a crucial area in Florida's economic and social fabric, and thus an appointment to any one of them assumes a critical importance. If the governor can influence (and even control) the governing boards of these agencies, he can significantly influence policy development in these areas.

Before Millard Caldwell was inaugurated, the terms of gubernatorial appointees to the little cabinet did not necessarily correspond to the governor's. Thus, any governor would be confronted by a host of executive officeholders and appointees selected by his predecessor. It was customary for the holdovers to offer their resignations to the new governor, but it was by no means always done. Nor was there any easy way for an incoming governor to force the resignation of those he did not care to have in his administration; he had to wait until their terms expired. These holdovers often caused problems for governors: Fred Cone felt he could not work with his Citrus Commission because a majority of the members had been appointed during Dave Sholtz' administration. Sholtz himself became very impatient while waiting for some of Carlton's appointees to resign. He insisted: "An incoming governor is entitled to a free hand in appointing his department heads as well as members of boards and commissions." At the same time, however, each governor knew that at least some of his appointees would last beyond his administration into the next one; perhaps this was one of the few sources of consolation for governors facing a four-year term, no reelection, and no guarantees that what they tried to do would not be undone by the next governor. During Spessard Holland's administration, however, the legislature passed a bill providing that the terms of appointees to most commissions and agencies would correspond to the governor's, thus allowing governors to fill posts with "their people" right from the start.[47] At least one major agency remained under the old system, however; members of the Board of Control, later the Board of Regents, still serve terms which can overlap gubernatorial administrations.

One serious problem that has plagued all the Florida governors is the number of job seekers with whom they have had to deal. Even Governor Jennings found his correspondence overwhelmingly composed of letters from job applicants. Gilchrist once observed that he received letters from 200 to 300 applicants for public payroll jobs, and "many of the applicants were getting twenty-five or thirty men to endorse them."[48] Fred Cone campaigned on an "open-door policy," meaning that he wanted to be readily available to any citizen who wanted to see him. He quickly found, however, that too much of his time was being taken up in this way. It was not just the casual visitor who annoyed him: it was the job applicants. Twice he decided to limit his visiting hours, and once noted "If I could get rid of the job seekers I could attend to more of the state's business." Fuller Warren, who had made a similar rash promise during his campaign, quickly came to the same conclusion as Cone. Dan McCarty's office was not crowded with job seekers as Cone's and Warren's were, because he flatly refused to see them. Instead, he left most of the patronage appointments to his top level little cabinet officials. Charley Johns, however, liked to see people, and reporters noted that his office, like Warren's and Cone's, was always crowded with ten to twelve people, many of them wanting jobs.[49]

In making appointments, governors have been particularly concerned about finding both qualified and loyal people. These are not always the same, nor are they necessarily compatible values. They illustrate the relative emphases and styles of various governors in using appointments as patronage. All governors interviewed for this study agreed that regardless of any other considerations, appointments must be made on the basis of qualifications and capabilities. All recognized the dangers of appointing persons not capable of performing the required tasks. But politics largely determines what criteria constitute "qualifications and capabilities" necessary to perform a job. Indeed whether a governor tended more towards "merit system" or "spoils system" criteria in making appointments, the fact remains that the appointing process is an intensely political one with important implications and consequences for the governor's administrative control. As noted with contracts, different styles have different effects for this important area of gubernatorial behavior.

In appointing loyal and responsive men, the governor faces something of a paradox. There is a danger in surrounding himself exclusively with "yes men," because it can lead to a decline in the quality of leadership and an isolation from large issues facing the state. However, individuals who are too independent compound the governor's problem of trying to control an already fragmented and unwieldy administration. The difficulty is in finding people who strike the right balance between loyalty and independence, that is, those who "merit" appointment but who are also supporters of the governor. This issue has troubled many Florida governors, and on occasion they went to considerable lengths to find the right person for a particular slot. Both Spessard Holland and Millard Caldwell, for example, established an elaborate network of trusted friends and advisors across the state to help locate capable, loyal individuals.[50]

Holland, Caldwell, and McCarty probably represent the most extreme positions along the "merit system" end of the appointments-as-patronage continuum. Caldwell sought to upgrade the level of state appointments, and yet he also placed a great emphasis on loyalty. He once remarked that, other things being equal, he would regard the loyal supporter as a more desirable appointee than one who was not.[51] Caldwell, in fact, exemplifies very well some of the tensions which governors felt in this regard. He was genuinely concerned about upgrading the quality of state appointees, but he also wanted people around him whom he could trust. Thus, in his appointments to the little cabinet he named supporters, but only those whom he knew could handle the job. Ultimately, however, for Caldwell as for other governors, there were no guarantees; all they could do was screen carefully, make the appointment, and hope for the best.

Caldwell was also very aware of the political consequences of his appointments, and he never attempted to remove politics from the appointment process. Indeed, he tried as much as any governor to strengthen his administration through the political use of patronage. His criteria for making appointments, however, and for patronage generally, were definitely not those of spoils system politics.[52] Essentially Caldwell sought to enhance his administrative control by combining patronage with an effort to improve the quality of state appointments. Perhaps these dual goals are nowhere better seen than in his attitude toward the expansion of the state's merit system. On the one hand, Caldwell opposed the institution of a statewide merit system plan on the grounds it would reduce his administrative control. On the other hand, he did seek to enlarge its scope in those agencies already using merit criteria. Before his tenure, the state agencies monitored the merit systems in their respective departments. Caldwell attempted to consolidate them, arguing that uniform standards could be applied and the level of professionalism increased. He was successful in his attempt, and the Board of Health, State Welfare Board, and Florida Industrial Commission agreed to consolidate their councils. Caldwell left no doubt that he wanted to bring more agencies under the merit system and reduce the overt patronage used in the executive departments: "I see no sound reason why one Merit System Council cannot and should not serve the three agencies in which the merit system is now operating and, in addition, any other agencies of the state which may, by subsequent legislation, be placed under the Merit System principle. Such a Council would truly be representing the state and all of the employees subject to its jurisdiction. Duplication and overlapping services would be eliminated, certain economies effected, and the efficiency of the program enhanced."[53]

At the other end of the continuum in terms of styles employed in making appointments and consequences for their administrations are Sidney Catts, Fuller Warren, and Charley Johns. Each of these governors occupies an extreme position at the "spoils system" end of the continuum. Certainly no other governor created or encountered the furor over appointments that Sidney Catts did. Unlike his counterparts, Catts was not elected to the governorship as the Democratic candidate. He had been the Prohibition party's nominee. As such, Catts set about to punish the Democratic opponents who had denied him the party's nomination and to build a political power base for himself and his friends through the use of patronage. This brought him into conflict with many Democratic party regulars including his cabinet members. Superintendent of Instruction William N. Sheats and Catts became involved in a struggle over the appointment of rural school inspectors with one appointment coming up before the state supreme court and the court deciding for Sheats. This proved to be only a minor defeat for Catts as he managed to find many jobs for his allies, friends, and family at both the state and local levels. Such state agencies as the dental, the medical, and the road boards were taken over by Catts' people. At the county level, Catts did not hesitate to place his appointees as county probation officers, constables, school superintendents, and "even to membership on community school boards."[54]

Additional controversy arose when Catts insisted on appointing his children and his in-laws to office. His son, Sidney Catts, Jr., was named adjutant general of the Florida National Guard, a move that infuriated many since the younger Catts had never held a post higher than captain. Another son, Rozier, also became an officer in the National Guard, and Catts appointed his daughter Ruth as his personal secretary. Catts' oldest son, Edward Douglas, served on the state hotel commission, and his son-in-law was inspector of naval stores, secretary to the governor, and finally Duval County tax collector.[55]

While charges of nepotism and political cronyism often engulfed Catts' administration and would seriously hamper his legislative effectiveness, Catts' biographer does note that "many of Catts' appointees distinguished themselves." Be that as it may, Catts' indiscretions in attacking the party through his use of patronage and appointing relatives proved to be a very great liability to his governorship and his future political ambitions.[56]

Fuller Warren had been elected in part through the efforts of three very wealthy supporters: Louis Wolfson of Jacksonville, C. V. Griffin of Howey-in-the-Hills, and William Johnston of Miami. Each of these men contributed over $100,000 to his campaign fund, and each of them commanded a significant voice in Warren's administration, including the area of appointments.[57] State Senator Olin Shivers of Chipley remarked early in the Warren administration that "Fuller Warren will make a good Governor if his friends don't ruin him." Warren was under considerable pressure from his closest associates—especially Wolfson, Griffin, and Johnston—to appoint individuals acceptable to them. Repeatedly they sought to influence his choice of candidates for positions; in this they acted less as dictators than as referees establishing limits within which Warren had to choose. Thus, on the eve of his inauguration, shortly before a major appointment to the road department was to be announced, Warren received a telegram from Wolfson: "Sorry could not be in your meeting today. Think it very important Alfred McKethan [chairman of the State Road Department] interviews several men before reaching decision on chief engineer job. Rushing this matter may prove a great mistake." Warren then waited until Wolfson had returned from New York City before making the appointment.[58] While each of the three men was interested in appointments throughout the executive agencies, it appears that each had specific concerns as well: Wolfson with the Road Department, Johnston with the Racing Commission, and Griffin with the Citrus Commission. Griffin, however, had broader interests than those of the other two men. He apparently had a desire to promote "good government" in Florida, and it was at least in part this concern that caused him to try to support enforcement of the state gambling laws on behalf of the administration.

The hold which this triumvirate maintained over Warren's appointments reached such proportions that one newspaper commentator noted in early 1950 that the most serious problem with the administration was the lack of "Warren men" in it. *Miami Herald* columnist John Kilgore was moved to add: "Actually there is not and never has been a Warren administration, since it has been divided from the start, like all Gaul, into three parts—the factions led by C. V. Griffin, Louis Wolfson and William H. Johnston." The governor had been able to appoint very few of his own people to top level positions; as a result there were few individuals on whom he could personally rely.[59]

Warren's other major difficulty in making appointments was his apparent inability to judge people. For him, the major criterion for evaluating individuals for potential appointment was whether or not he liked them. Warren's selection of Frank Wright, a long-time friend and former publicity director for the University of Florida, as his assistant proved to be a mistake. Wright exhibited little ability in developing Warren's programs or policies, or in problem-solving. He quickly lost the confidence of other governmental officials in both the executive and legislative branches and, finally, of Warren himself. Wright resigned in 1951.[60]

Two other appointments also proved unsatisfactory and embarrassing. In October 1951, Warren placed Julius Jay Perlmutter on the Dade County Zoning Board of Adjustment. The appointment turned out to be an affront to Miami realtors. Perlmutter, at the time of his selection, was accused by the Florida Real Estate Commission of violating state laws for the conduct of a real estate business. Loyal Compton, Warren's press secretary, claimed that Warren had not known about the accusations at the time the appointment was made.[61] Later that month when former state Senator John Mathews of Jacksonville, a political colleague and ally of Warren, was appointed to the state supreme court, the *St. Petersburg Times*, normally a supporter of the governor, rebuked him for placing "one of the worst bigots" in Florida history in such a responsible post.[62]

To his credit, Warren did appoint a number of women to state boards and agencies: Mrs. Jessie Ball Du Pont to the Board of Control; Ida M. Knabb to the Florida Children's Commission; Mrs. Fred Baisden to the Board of Social Welfare, district nine; and Ruth Linda Sutton as justice of the peace, district three. On balance, however, Warren's male and female appointees were much more of a liability than an asset. Many of the people he selected proved unsatisfactory because of unethical behavior or incompetence.[63] To some extent Warren may have been the victim of bad luck. On the other hand, the conclusion is inescapable that some of the problems he incurred from weak appointments were the results of poor judgment or accepting the advice of his political cronies.

The conflict between "professional," or "merit system," styles in gubernatorial appointments and "spoils system" approaches is nowhere better seen than in the tremendous furor that arose during the brief Johns administration. The dispute resulted from the very different approaches toward patronage employed by Warren and Johns on the one hand, and Dan McCarty and LeRoy Collins on the other.

The Warren administration was notable for its use of spoils system criteria for distributing patronage. The Road Department, in particular, had become overloaded with inspectors and other appointed employees. Contracts had been liberally let and roads promised without much regard to cost. Other departments were, to lesser degrees, similarly operated.

Dan McCarty entered the governor's office promising to clean up the mess. In his attitudes toward patronage he went even beyond the criteria espoused by Millard Caldwell: while the faithful had to be rewarded, it had to be done in a businesslike, professional way, and certainly the spoils system could not be tolerated. In his inaugural address he said he would clean out the state government, and added, "I am determined that ours will not be an administration of 'sounding brass and tinkling cymbal'; nor one tainted with any kind of dishonesty." By the next day he had eliminated 400 jobs from the Road Department and halted $6 million in road projects.[64]

Within a few days it was clear to all state employees that McCarty meant business. Massive reorganization efforts began in the Road Department, Beverage Department, and State Industrial Commission. Employees were dismissed, contracts reexamined or cancelled, and every effort made to roll back what were perceived to be the excesses of the Warren administration. Legislators quickly became irritated at McCarty because of the firings and cancellation of projects, but the governor was unruffled. While he told them they had a right to make suggestions and recommendations, he would not tolerate any legislative interference with his executive prerogatives. He took an active role in the affairs of his little cabinet, insisting that all of their policies conform to the overall set of goals and priorities he had laid out for the state. Besides reorganization, he tried to advance the system of centralized purchasing and to establish more rigorous and uniform personnel practices in the little cabinet agencies.[65]

McCarty died in September 1953; although he was one of Florida's youngest governors he had suffered a crippling heart attack the previous February. His death prevented him from completing his ambitious administrative and legislative programs. His successor as acting governor was Charley Johns, president of the state senate and a prominent member of what later came to be known as the Pork Chop Gang.

Quite naturally Johns was tentative during his first few days in office. He seemed hesitant to make any decisions, either administrative or otherwise. However, it did not take him long to begin to move in such a way as to put his own stamp on his administration. It was clear too, that it would be much different from what McCarty had intended. In a letter to Earl Powers, chairman of the State Turnpike Authority, he directed that all work on the Florida Turnpike (a major project begun under McCarty) cease until he could familiarize himself with the plans. Similarly, he implied that he was not committed to McCarty's programs when he said that while he proposed no major housecleaning, he did think all of McCarty's appointees owed him the courtesy of tendering their resignations. In itself this was unusual since Johns was never elected governor in his own right. He also added that if members of the little cabinet failed to hand in their resignations, he might ask for them.[66]

Johns was not telling the truth about all of his plans. In fact, he did intend to make some major changes, and within a short time the little cabinet was in an uproar. By mid-October Johns publicly called for the resignation of the Racing Commission, Game and Fresh Water Fish Commision, Turnpike Commission and other members of the little cabinet to give him a free hand in running the state. A feud quickly developed between Johns and three McCarty appointees: Richard Simpson, head of the Road Board, Hotel Commissioner Jack Humphrey, and chairman of the Industrial Commission, James Vocelle. Simpson even went so far as to say he would not resign until a new governor was elected (a special election was to be held in May 1954).[67]

Matters deteriorated even further. Johns moved to suspend members of the little cabinet who would not resign (the governor has power to suspend, but not remove, some state officials). However, a 1934 state supreme court ruling prevented him temporarily from moving too rapidly. The court had held that before appointees could be ousted, detailed charges had to be filed which encompassed one or more of the following: malfeasance, neglect of duty, misfeasance, commission of a felony, drunkenness, and incompetence. Johns said he was aware of this, and preferred to ask for resignations in face-to-face discussions with McCarty appointees. His stratagem apparently failed. In the middle of November he suspended the members of the Racing Commission and Turnpike Authority, charging them with malfeasance and extravagance.[68]

By this time other public officials, and public opinion generally, had mobilized against Johns. There was tremendous hostility to what he was doing. McCarty had been seen as a highly competent and well-intentioned governor following the inept Warren, and after his death this public impres-

State Senate President Charley E. Johns takes the oath of office from Chief Justice of the Florida Supreme Court John E. Mathews to become acting governor of Florida on September 29, 1953. Johns, senator from Starke and member of the Pork Chop Gang, succeeded Dan McCarty, who died after a long illness. Johns's questionable gubernatorial initiatives led to a major confrontation between his supporters and those of the deceased governor. Accompanying Johns is his son, Jerome. State Photographic Archives.

sion remained strong. Prominent individuals from both the public and private sectors began to criticize Johns very sharply for undoing what McCarty had worked so hard to accomplish. Morale among public employees sank incredibly low; as one analyst pointed out, the cloud of tension and fear among state employees caused by the prospect of instant dismissal prevented virtually all of them from working at anything even close to peak efficiency.[69]

Johns seemingly paid no attention. He suspended the Road Board and Hotel Commission, then appointed his own. By the end of the year, the little cabinet was in complete disarray. Legislators were demanding that Johns call a special session to deal with the suspensions. But Johns simply ignored his own colleagues (he remained president of the senate while serving as acting governor). Some legislators even began to speak of impeachment. John McCarty, who had served as an aide to his brother, started talking as if he might run for governor in the special 1954 election to try to implement his programs.[70]

John McCarty decided not to run, but Senator LeRoy Collins, a close friend of the McCarty family and a loyal political ally, did. In the three-way race among Collins, Johns, and Brailey Odham of Sanford, much of the campaign debate centered around Johns' conduct of his administration. When Collins won, he immediately promised that he would provide hearings after his inauguration for the ousted McCarty appointees. He also said that measures were needed to protect state employees against political reprisals.[71]

His fears were well founded. In the wake of Johns' defeat "job jitters" began to hit many little cabinet departments, especially the Road Department. There was concern that there would be reprisals and firings to make room for Collins' supporters. By mid-June, just a few weeks after the runoff election, seven Beverage Department agents had been fired, and six new ones hired. The agency head, Everette McKenney, denied that any politics were involved, but many people recalled that during the campaign Johns had said one of the fired agents was "tearing his shirt for Collins" and that the man's brother had been a prominent official in Collins' campaign.[72]

The patronage turmoil continued into the summer when Johns ordered that the insurance policies of the Game and Fresh Water Fish Commission be awarded to a firm owned by his Marianna campaign manager. However, the commission gave them to a Tallahassee company, the Shuford-Collins agency, which was owned by McCarty supporters. Johns then threatened to remove the members of the Game and Fresh Water Fish board, and later refused to sign the check covering the premium, which amounted to some $40,000 for the year. The Tallahassee agency, however, said it would carry over the policy until Collins became governor. Johns' response was, "Every dog has his day."[73]

Johns also intervened directly in the purchase of his Cadillac limousine, ordering his Road Board head to buy it from a firm in Graceville. He fired forty-six employees of the Tag Department (even making the announcement himself, rather than through his appointed tag director), and ordered the Road Department to buy its insurance from a favorite supporter of his, even though lower bids had been received from other agencies. He ordered all meat for state prison camps to be purchased from the same meat packer, which caused a tremendous uproar among meat packers; there were additional outcries when prison officials disclosed that rotten meat and eggs had been delivered to the prison camps. By early September Johns suspended two officials of the Game and Fresh Water Fish Commission over the insurance policy problem. Upon their ousting, they called Johns the "biggest liar in Florida" and "the worst political despot in the modern history of Florida."[74]

Johns' response to the severe public criticism of his actions was either to ignore it or blame everything on the press. Public indignation by the middle of the fall, 1954, had become so acute that Collins decided to hold hearings on the Johns suspensions before his inauguration. He announced that they would take place in mid-December, and invited Johns to testify. Johns, however, did not attend, calling them a "farce" and "kangaroo hearings."[75]

At the hearings the officials Johns had fired denied the charges against them and instead accused the governor of smear tactics. They alleged that political considerations had been Johns' primary motivation and that the current suspicion which surrounded the Road Board resulted from his "dishonorable requests." As examples they mentioned Johns' demands for a supplemental agreement on a contract with a road builder who said he wasn't making enough money, a reevaluation of a piece of land owned by a friend on the Jacksonville Expressway right-of-way, and the granting of an engineering contract to a firm which he favored but at a cost some $100,000 higher than other bids.[76]

While the outcome may well have been decided in advance, Collins claimed that the hearings showed there were no grounds for removing the seventeen officials whom Johns had suspended, and he said he would reinstate them. Johns retired from the governorship under a dark cloud, returning to the senate for the rest of his active political career. Throughout this struggle, Floridians demonstrated their opposition to the blatant misuse of gubernatorial patronage powers. Patronage was acceptable to the voters but only as long as it was used subtly.[77]

What can be concluded about the effects of appointments on executive control of administration? It should be reemphasized that Caldwell, McCarty, and Collins were every bit as "political" in their use of appointments as patronage devices as were Catts, Warren, and Johns. Nonetheless, these different styles had very different consequences for gubernatorial control of the executive branch, and the general effectiveness of these men as governors. All governors, as suggested earlier, sought to reward the faithful. But the public places limits on how far these rewards can extend. Incompetence, corruption, or heavy-handedness bordering on the scandalous will not be tolerated. Johns, who carried this style to its limits, completely lost control of his administration because of resentment which developed within the executive branch. He, Catts, and Warren additionally lost the favor of the public as well, because it became disenchanted with the obvious political manipulation that marked their practices. Holland, Caldwell, McCarty, and Askew were all perceived by the public as trying to professionalize the executive branch. The public was far more supportive of the administrative behavior of these governors than of those such as Cone, Sholtz, Bryant, Burns, and Kirk, each of whom could be placed toward the "spoils system" end of the continuum. For them, appointments, like patronage generally, were mostly dysfunctional.

It is not easy to determine whether governors who used the spoils system experienced administrative difficulties and a loss of public support for that reason alone, or whether they would have had problems running the executive branch even if they had tried to be more "professional" in their appointments. But we can observe that governors who were heavy-handed, who violated norms of honesty and integrity in running executive agencies, or who appointed incompetents to office were generally not well regarded while in office, nor have ensuing years necessarily brought about a reassessment of their abilities. Finally, it should be noted that the limits of public acceptability of different styles of patronage shifted after a period of excess. The governors succeeding Catts, Hardee and Martin, were much less flamboyant, more business-oriented, and certainly more subtle, in their use of appointments. McCarty and Collins were regarded as much more professional in their patronage styles than either Warren or Johns. Finally, Askew was also perceived as upgrading appointments in the years following Bryant, Burns, and Kirk, each of whom blatantly used the spoils system. Thus a sort of "ebb and flow" pattern marks the governors' use of appointments as patronage, with many governors tending toward the spoils system styles. Following periods of abuse, however, the public supported enthusiastically those who acted professionally in their use of appointments to control their administrations.

Patronage: Suspensions

Suspensions are the opposite of appointments, but they represent a kind of reverse patronage. Legally, Florida governors can only suspend public officials from office for cause. Those who can be suspended are appointed state and local officials (the governor cannot suspend legislators or other members of the cabinet). He cannot, however, remove the individuals from office; only the state senate has that power.[78] The appropriate grounds for suspension were listed earlier. Although in theory it might seem easy to demonstrate the existence of such grounds, in practice it is not. The burden of proof is clearly on the governor, and unless he can show just cause for a suspension, he is likely to find public opinion and other state and local officials mobilized against him.

Governors have differed sharply in their attitudes toward suspension of public officials; probably this is because each sees the inherent problems involved in the act somewhat differently, although they are all aware that danger is present. The governor always seems to be criticized after a suspension, because citizens, and other public officials, often feel that he either acted too precipitously or not quickly enough. Some governors have acted quickly and frequently in suspending officials; Carlton suspended fifteen in four years.[79] Holland also moved with great vigor, only to have the ousted officials reinstated by the senate or reelected. Others moved very slowly, cautiously, and with great reluctance. Thus, the merit system-spoils system sequence outlined earlier does not quite apply to suspensions as patronage devices, probably because of its inherently negative character. Nonetheless, it is possible to define different gubernatorial styles in this area, and to assess their relative functionality for administrative control.

In general it can be said that the attitudes and actions of governors concerning suspensions fall somewhere on a continuum defined by Caldwell and Collins. Caldwell took a very cautious view of suspensions, particularly of local officials (the vast majority of all suspensions are at the local level). He, like Fred Cone and Fuller Warren, felt that the state ought to move slowly and carefully in intervening in what were primarily local affairs. As a result, Caldwell stated clearly that he would only suspend a local official who had been indicted by a grand jury; otherwise, he felt, it was the responsibility of the local citizens to vote the individual out of office or force his resignation.[80]

Collins, however, took a different view. He felt it was the responsibility of the governor to act swiftly in suspending officials, at either the state or local level, if they were suspected of wrongdoing and that only by decisive action could public confidence in governmental institutions be maintained. Moreover, to wait for a grand jury to act was not merely to delay, but to cause damage to government.[81]

Several instances can be cited to show how governors have used their powers of suspension and some of the political costs of that use. When Napoleon Broward suspended Sheriff Robert Jackson of Hillsborough County, he was severely criticized by the Democratic Executive Committee there, which also passed a resolution censuring him for replacing Jackson without consulting either the committee or the people of the county.[82] The traditions of localism and local autonomy in Florida politics have often prevented governors from taking swift action when the possibility of a local suspension arose; public criticism often follows this intervention, as was the case with Sidney J. Catts.

Catts had made it clear in his inaugural address that he would root out corrupt and immoral officials. No one realized, however, the degree to which he would use his suspension powers. As his biographer tells us, Catts removed over one hundred county and state officials during his four years as governor, including the entire Volusia County Board of Commissioners, and the sheriffs of Duval, Pinellas, Escambia, Monroe, Sumter, Citrus, and Clay counties. State historian William J. Cash observed that local officials lived more in fear during Catts' administration than at any other time in Florida's history.

Although he "removed officials for valid reasons," his widespread use of his suspension powers also proved to be a boon to political friends. In the process he alienated many legislators. State representatives were particularly irked that Catts had ignored them in making his decisions, especially when it meant the removal of people they had helped get appointed to office. Led by the state senate, legislators responded by refusing to support Catts' suspensions, reimbursing those suspended, threatening Catts with impeachment for abuse of power, and considering a constitutional amendment to limit the governor's removal power. His legislative program was also emasculated in the process.[83]

On the other hand, the failure of a governor to move decisively on a local suspension can cause severe problems. This has been particularly true when issues of law enforcement and gambling were involved. For many years Florida had strict antigambling laws, reflecting, in part, the strong fundamentalist religious strain and rural orientation of the state's politics early in the century. However, county sheriffs have frequently failed to enforce these laws, permitting not only gambling but sometimes organized crime to move into certain areas of the state. In general, revelations of this kind have been met with cries of outrage by the citizenry and have frequently forced governors to insist publicly on enforcement of laws, sometimes even accompanying their pious remarks with threats of suspensions.

Still, there were always political dangers for governors involved in the suspension of sheriffs, for they have often been powerful political figures. The experience of Fuller Warren in this regard is instructive, and it illustrates all of the administrative problems of this well-meaning but fundamentally inept governor. The issue concerned organized crime.

Warren had promised to suspend promptly any official accused of permitting gambling in his county and to hold a hearing later. But instead he spoke out sharply against the Kefauver and Miami crime commissions because of their criticisms of him and their implications that he was neglectful of his duty, and that, perhaps, he was even indirectly supportive of gambling. As a result, Warren was reluctant to carry out his own promise, and this hesitation drew heavy criticism from the press, legislators, and the general citizenry. Finally, after months of charges and attacks, he suspended five sheriffs—James A. Sullivan, Dade County; Walter Clark, Broward County; Alex Littlefield, Volusia County; Frank M. Williams, Polk County; and H. Isle Enzor, Okaloosa County. When he later reappointed three of them because the allegations could not be proved, he was again subjected to intense criticism.

In contrast to Warren's bumbling indecisiveness, LeRoy Collins moved quickly and firmly to quell political problems among county tax assessors. Like many governors before and after him, Collins was concerned with state and local finance. He saw clearly that local governments could raise substantial additional revenues only if property taxes were assessed at higher levels than they usually were. Florida tax assessors have traditionally assessed property at very low levels, thereby depriving local government of significant amounts of money. This irritated Collins. In 1957 he called for the level of assessments to be raised to "full cash value," or, he said, he would use his constitutional authority to enforce his order.[84] He was immediately opposed by the county assessors, who accused him of meddling in their affairs, and by legislators, who claimed they did not wish to see local taxes raised.

Collins, however, was adamant. In meetings with county officials he said he would do everything in his power to see that full assessments were made. He even threatened to suspend those who failed to uphold their obligations. Most of the assessors paid him little attention. The state, after all, had never before tried to tell them how to carry out their responsibilities. They were quite surprised and dismayed, when, in late September, 1959, Collins suspended Mrs. Mary Walker, the Seminole County tax assessor, because she refused to assure the governor that she would prepare a "competent" assessment roll. His dramatic action had the desired effect; the other assessors quickly agreed to the governor's order.[85]

Suspensions, to underscore a point made earlier, seem to cast a pall on the governorship. Rarely has a governor benefited politically from such actions. The public seems to believe that a governor who resorts to suspensions is not in full control of state agencies and departments; if he were, the problem causing the need for a suspension would never have arisen. Suspension of local officials is generally not well received if the public is convinced that the governor is "meddling" in local affairs. The chief executive would seem to profit most from quick and decisive action in this area; if he is slow to act in the face of apparent violations of acceptable behavior by local (and presumably state) officials, his own sense of public morality might be called into question.

EXECUTIVE AGENCIES AND GUBERNATORIAL ATTITUDES

What were the attitudes of governors toward their little cabinets? To what extent did they intervene directly in the affairs of their executive agencies? The variation is large, and not every governor treated all departments in the same way. For example, as suggested in Chapter 9, governors have been inclined to maintain a "hands off" attitude toward the Board of Control, but the Road Department has frequently been manipulated by them.

In general, the degree to which they intervened in their executive departments seems to have depended on the attitudes of the governors towards patronage, the confidence they had in their appointed heads, and the importance (political and otherwise) they placed on the functions of the particular department. Those who were greatly concerned with patronage, and who regarded it as a central element in their administrations, tended to intervene more than those who did not. Thus, for example, Fuller Warren and Charley Johns, both of whom based their administrations on spoils system politics, took very active roles in the affairs of certain state agencies.

Johns, as mentioned earlier, intervened in executive departments frequently to influence such matters as the purchase of cars, the location of roadside parks, and the awarding of insurance contracts. Catts went even further when he gave state jobs to members of his family. Fuller Warren's case was not quite as extreme but it did represent much the same set of attitudes.

At the other end of the spectrum were Caldwell and McCarty. Caldwell took a more direct interest in patronage than did McCarty, but part of the reason may well be that the latter served only nine months of his term. Both, however, were interested in upgrading the quality of state appointees, and both were far more willing than Catts, Warren, or Johns to allow those whom they appointed to the little cabinet to make major decisions concerning appointments, contracts, and other patronage issues. Both, in fact, only rarely intervened in the affairs of their executive departments, preferring to appoint men who they felt could be trusted with the affairs of the department. McCarty wanted his appointees to run their respective departments without hindrance from him. Caldwell, in speaking of the Citrus Commission, elaborated a position which marked his approach to running his whole administration: "It has been my policy to undertake to secure the best men possible for appointment to this body and then permit them to proceed to work for the best interest of the citrus industry without interference from me."[86]

Most governors have occupied a position somewhere between Catts-Warren-Johns and Caldwell-McCarty on the issue of intervention. In general, most only interfered in their agencies or tried to direct proceedings when their own interests were directly affected. Usually this occurred when the agency or department did something which did not meet with the governor's approval, or failed to do something he wanted. Otherwise, governors were generally busy with legislative and cabinet duties, speechmaking, conferences, etc., too busy, in fact, to take an immediate and controlling interest in the affairs of all 150 agencies (since 1969 there have been twenty-five "superagencies").

An instance from Fred Cone's administration illustrates the behavior of other Florida governors in this century. Cone held a very passive view of the governor's office, and in this regard he is not a "typical" Florida governor. On the other hand, he sometimes contradicted his own view when he felt his interests were directly involved. He did not hesitate to remind the Budget Commission of its responsibility to hold expenditures down, for example, and he used his item veto freely. Similarly, he was not inclined to become involved in administrative affairs, preferring to let his appointees run their agencies. He did require undated letters of resignation, but otherwise he rarely tried to tell his appointees what to do. He was, however, deeply concerned about organized crime and gambling in Florida, and therefore he followed the activities of the Racing Commission very closely; he did not want bookies and other gamblers in the state and felt that racing should be tightly controlled.[87] Likewise, he became embroiled in two disputes with his Citrus Commission. The first was over general policy direction. The commission, when Cone assumed office, was dominated by Sholtz appointees, and Cone, who received many complaints about citrus production, shipping, and marketing practices, was anxious for policies to be reviewed.[88] He could not get the commission to cooperate with him, and eventually he publicly criticized its members: "I have been governor for six months and none of the Commission has been to see me—I might as well talk plain. No one has conferred with me. No one has written to me, and I want to know what the policies are, how much money is handled. What it is spent for and what the people got for it." Finally, after public indignation was aroused, the board and Cone did meet, and they had relatively little difficulty finding common ground for agreement. Later, when Cone appointed five members of the commission, he again argued publicly with the board. Three of his appointees refused to sign undated letters of resignation, and Cone had to find three other appointees, referring to the first ones as "antagonistic." The commission sharply protested the governor's "efforts to turn the Florida Citrus Commission into a political machine."[89] Again, however, Cone met with the board, and the dispute was settled. During the remainder of his administration Cone continued to take some interest in the Citrus Commission, but he never again intervened so strongly. No issue, in his view, arose that caught his interest or attention sufficiently to warrant involvement.

BUDGETING

Governors have additional means for trying to control agencies, perhaps the most important of which is budgeting. From a theoretical standpoint, the budget can be a powerful executive tool for running the administration. The budget, after all, is perhaps the most crucial policy determinant in government. It is a way of buying a particular future, of allocating funds for some purposes but not for others, of indicating which state functions are more important than others. Through the budget, moreover, cooperative agencies (i.e., those willing to follow the governor's leadership and work with him) can be rewarded with more substantial incremental raises in funds allocated, whereas recalcitrant agencies can be pressured, or even punished, by a refusal to increase their budgets.[90]

The implied assumption is that the governor has control of the budget, that it is truly an executive budget reflecting his wishes and priorities, and that he does not have to share this authority with other state officials. For most of this century the nation's governors often had to share budget-making authority with members of the legislature. It was impatience with this system that finally led Governor Al Smith of New York to fight for, and succeed in obtaining, the first executive budget.[91]

During this century, Florida, unlike other states, always had an executive budget, but it had an important qualification. Although the governor did not have to share budget-making with the legislature, he did have to share it with the rest of the cabinet.One of the most important functions of the cabinet was to act as the State Budget Commission, which would prepare a budget every two years and send it to the legislature for approval. The governor sat as a member of the Budget Commission and was its chairman. He could establish a system of legislative and program priorities, and as long as they did not infringe on the interest of the cabinet members, they would generally be accepted. Similarly, a governor's campaign promises, while not in any sense binding, did, along with program priorities, help establish parameters within which discussion of the budget would take place. But even within these constraints imposed by the governor, the Budget Commission still had considerable room for maneuver and agreement. While the governor was undoubtedly influential in the budget process, even at the executive level he certainly did not dominate it. This system continued until 1968, when the chief executive was finally given exclusive control of the budget and the Budget Commission was abolished.

The mechanics and politics of the Budget Commission can quickly be described and the governor's relatively modest role easily understood. The Budget Commission would convene toward the middle of January in odd years (the budget was to last two years). When a new governor had just taken office, this meant only a few weeks following his inauguration. He knew very little about the state agencies and their programs, concerning which he was asked to make budgetary decisions. Meetings lasted several hours, usually daily, for about four to six weeks. Members of executive agencies, legislators, and interest groups would attend the meetings; bureaucrats would make formal budget requests. The commission, after meeting in executive session, would decide on the allocation (request) for each agency and department, and then the budget would be printed and delivered to legislators several weeks before the new session began.

The whole budget process under this system was completely political. As one recent governor said, it was nothing but logrolling and mutual accommodation.[92] Cabinet officials would each protect the allocation for their own departments and would act as advocates for increases. Thus, they served as both judge and jury. Each would confine his interest to that of his own department, and rarely, if ever, questioned the use of funds or allocations for other departments. Cabinet members had often been attending these sessions for years, as a result of their long tenure, and had established fairly clear sets of mutual expectations and methods of operating which were seldom, if ever, violated. The governor could ask questions, but he knew relatively little about the inner workings of the departments. By the governor's third year, he had learned a good deal about state operations; however, by then he was a lame duck.

Under this system there was no possibility of a complete "root and branch" budget review, or of the governor's utilizing the budget as an instrument of policy determination or executive control. From his perspective it was hardly even "muddling through," for he had relatively little to say about what budget allocations were made.[93] It is fair to conclude that between 1900 and 1968 the budget process in Florida served to fragment, and not strengthen, the governor's executive and administrative capabilities. It was only through the item veto, discussed in the following chapter, that the governor exercised any sole, direct control over the budget process.

One important development in devising a more systematic budget was the creation in 1945 of the post of professional budget director. Very early in his administration Caldwell, along with the comptroller, state auditor, budget commission secretary, and several members of the legislature, advocated the creation of the position of a full-time budget director. The post was established in order to create a uniform system of budgeting (until then each department had its own system) and accounting for state funds. Caldwell, in particular, stressed the need for uniform budgets and someone to keep a constant check on state spending. The presence of the director, while a big step in making the budget a more comprehensible and integrated document, did not fundamentally alter the politics of the budgetary process.[94]

It should also be noted that throughout most of this century legislators complained about the budget process. They felt, not without justification, that they lacked sufficient information to deal intelligently with the budget when it was delivered to them. In order to try, even in a small way, to improve this situation, Governor McCarty decided to invite members of the legislature to the Budget Commission hearings to listen, ask questions, and be informed.[95] Collins continued the practice, but ultimately it was abandoned. Both senators Charley Johns and Doyle Carlton complained that they were simply wasting their time. They argued that the rapid-fire presentation of budget requests—in one meeting fifty-six agency requests were examined and approved in less than four hours—along with limited information available contributed little to their ability to handle the budget. It is noteworthy that even with the addition of large permanent staffs for house and senate appropriations committees, legislators still feel unprepared to deal with the governor's budget.[96]

In 1968 the new constitution contained a provision allowing the governor greater budget powers. He no longer has to take a back seat to other members of the cabinet in preparing the budget. In addition, because the process is now conducted annually, the governor has greater opportunities for more regular analysis of state operations.

The full impact of this change in the budget process is not yet known. It is clear, however, that it remains intensely political. Substantial lobbying, trading, and bargaining still go on inside the governor's office as the budget is prepared. Available evidence also suggests that the budget remains largely incremental in character; that is, last year's budget provides the principal guidelines for this year's budget. There is little overall "root and branch" analysis of the total budget; this is the way matters have been throughout this century. In addition, the legislature can still make substantial changes in the governor's budget. He can lobby legislators to follow his wishes, but in the event they do not the governor can only accept their changes or use his item veto.

However, there are some clear differences between the older and newer patterns. The governor now maintains much closer control over the design of the budget. He is the center of the communications network concerning the budget, and if bargains are struck and accommodations made, he is instrumental in creating them. In his second administration Reubin Askew used his lieutenant governor, Jim Williams, as his chief budget aide. Graham has not followed suit. If this practice continues, not only will it give the lieutenant governor an important function but it will place an important executive official in the position of full-time overseer of the yearly budget process. On balance, it appears that the executive budget which Florida has finally obtained will strengthen the governor's executive powers.

Last, it should be observed that what happened in Florida is atypical of what happened in other states throughout the twentieth century regarding the governor's budget powers. As both Allen Schick and S. Kenneth Howard point out, the national trend has been toward greater centralization of gubernatorial control of the budget. The usual explanation given for this development is that it created greater control for the governor over his administration, helped "rationalize" policy formulation, and allowed the most efficient branch of government to respond quickly to state problems.[97] As we have noted throughout this work, however, the trend in Florida has largely been to prevent greater accretions of power in the governor's office. Florida's new budget procedure may mark a significant change in this historical direction.

CONCLUSIONS

Although performing executive duties is one of the most important parts of the Florida governor's responsibilities, we have here only suggested the enormous difficulties involved. The presence of a fragmented executive branch, with separately elected cabinet officers, prevents any real consolidation of executive authority. Even more important, the presence of collegial decision-making in the form of numerous boards and agencies means that the governor must divide his time and energies and seek to build coalitions with officials who may be indifferent, or even hostile, to his priorities and programs. This is true even though the governor and cabinet have generally worked reasonably well together in this century. Contrary to popular belief, the cabinet is not a wholly uncohesive body; especially in the years prior to the rapid expansion of state government and activities beginning in the late 1950s, the cabinet often served to help the governor, to act as a sounding board, and to provide information to him. But the fragmentation of authority and decentralization of power were still present in spite of the cooperation that existed. What often happened was that the governor had to temper his program to what other cabinet officers would accept and had to use his skill in interpersonal relations to persuade cabinet members to work with him.

Reorganization, patronage, appointments and suspensions, and the budget are the principal means through which the Florida governor can try to control his administration. Yet each of these mechanisms has the potential to create more problems than it solves. The governor's powers of reorganization are limited by statute as well as by close relationships between legislators, bureaucrats, and clientele groups. The entrenched bureaucracy itself prevents any simple or easy reforms. Patronage through contracts and appointments is at best an uncertain means of control, and no governor can be sure that any desired end can be achieved through its use. However, it is true that "professional" or "merit system" criteria and styles in patronage are more functional than the "spoils system" style. Finally, until 1968 the Florida governors' budget power was seriously circumscribed, and although the new authority to create an executive budget undoubtedly increases his administrative powers, it is not yet clear how much additional authority it gives him over the rest of the executive office.

Once more it should be emphasized that Florida does not fit a pattern found in other states regarding gubernatorial efforts to control state agencies. Observers of state politics have noted that throughout this century other states have adopted a steady procession of "progressive" reforms which were designed to increase the governor's executive powers.[98] These include governmental reorganization, increased appointment powers for the governor, policy clearance, and tighter budget controls. Florida has adopted some of these reforms, but there is by no means any steady progression in their development. Before 1968, few of them had really been implemented. State agencies have been reorganized, but Caldwell may be right in that it will make little functional difference for governors' executive authority. While budget powers have increased, the chief executive's ability to make key patronage appointments has not changed very much. Further research and time are needed to find out if the "progress" in gubernatorial powers in Florida really will have a substantial impact on bureaucratic-gubernatorial relationships.

Thus the Florida governor is faced with a different situation in trying to operate smoothly the machinery of state government. Confronted by fragmentation and competing executive officers, and lacking the power to act unilaterally, the governor has often found his administration hard to control. For administratively weak governors, such as Fuller Warren, the effect on the chief executive's career can be devastating. Even for administratively strong governors, such as LeRoy Collins and Reubin Askew, the effect can be frustrating. It is not surprising, therefore, that Florida governors have often preferred to turn their attention away from administration to matters that are more malleable and more politically rewarding.

6

The Governor and the Legislature

THE governor's office and the state legislature were established by state constitutions as coequal bodies. They were expected to function in an adversary relationship to insure that the rights of the public were properly protected. Although Florida had been ruled by Spain for over two centuries, its political institutions reflected the nation's English heritage.

For most of the nineteenth and twentieth centuries the Florida executive and legislature have operated as equivalent branches. During the twentieth century, in particular, the governor has seldom dominated the legislature. The inability of the Florida governor to assume a leadership position in this century was somewhat unique for the nation. In nearly every state, including many in the South, the position of governor became one of prominence and leadership as the century progressed. In most states, this development was a consequence of constitutional alterations in the office, especially those provisions for reelection, budgetary powers, and increased administrative control. These structural changes appear to have enhanced gubernatorial powers, sometimes at the expense of the legislature. In addition, as the population increased throughout the nation, demands by the public for more services forced the legislature to surrender some of its privileges and establish more power in the executive office. As a result, the nation witnessed the emergence of such powerful and influential governors as Alfred E. Smith and Nelson Rockefeller of New York, Huey Long of Louisiana, Alf Landon of Kansas, Earl Warren of California, Jimmy Carter of Georgia, and many others.

Florida's governors, like their colleagues in most southern states, however, remained essentially weak when compared to northern governors in industrialized states. The weakness of the office reflected, in large part, the limitations imposed by the constitution of 1885. While the constitution permitted the governor to seek reelection, he had to sit out one term before he could do so. Not one governor was reelected under this condition in the twentieth century. In addition, the constitution provided only for biennial legislative sessions. The legislature met in April and May of the governor's first and third years in office, leaving him only one hundred and twenty days to secure passage of his campaign promises. The smallest conflict with the legislature could cripple many of his programs.

Despite the restrictions placed upon the executive office by the constitution, none was especially unusual for the late nineteenth century. Indeed, in many respects Florida's constitution was quite typical of this era and was similar to constitutions elsewhere.[1] Although the constitution was not atypical of the period, its continuous existence over eighty-three years was. Many states modified their constitutions during the twentieth century to make the governor more responsive to the people and to alleviate mounting socioeconomic problems. Florida's chief executive, however, remained tied to the "horse and buggy" constitution of 1885 until it was finally rewritten in 1968.

SOURCES OF GUBERNATORIAL-LEGISLATIVE TENSION

Constitutional provisions account for only part of the tensions which have existed between the Florida governor and the legislature. In fact, political elements largely determine the web of interconnections between the two. The purpose of this section is to explore the nature of these tensions and the reasons for them.[2]

On the most abstract level, the Florida executive and legislative branches are natural adversaries simply because they have been structured to share policymaking responsibilities. In the American constitutional system, power is shared, not separated; this is true both vertically, in the case of the federal, state, and even local governments, and horizontally among the executive, legislative, and judicial areas of government.[3] This sharing of power with respect to the creation of public policy necessarily requires these separate institutions to cooperate. Yet, inherent in their cooperation are differences involving conflicts of ideology, priorities, methods, and roles which must be resolved before policy can emerge.

Similarly, the governor and legislature act from rather different perspectives. The governor has a broader point of view than do members of the legislature, since he represents the entire state. Legislators, however, reflect relatively narrow interests and far more homogeneous populations than does the governor. The legislator must look to his district first, and the whole state second; he is more likely to reflect specialized interests than is the governor. The effect is that legislators inject a rather parochial influence in policymaking, as opposed to the more catholic perspective of the governor.

Given the fact, then, that governors and legislators share policymaking responsibilities, but have such different orientations, conflict and tension between them seem inevitable.[4]

A third source of tension concerns the decentralization and fragmentation of power in the legislature.[5] While we have seen that power is hardly centralized in the hands of the Florida governor, it, nonetheless, appears more concentrated there than in the legislature. Permanent alliances have been unusual in that body (the Pork Chop Gang was a rare exception). Legislative committees have only recently begun to function in any systematic, collegial way; the more common practice in the past was for each chairman to run his committee out of his hip pocket. Chairmen themselves operated largely as independent barons. Legislative leadership has only occasionally been strong; the speakership of the house and presidency of the senate usually have changed every two years, preventing continuity or the firm establishment of power bases. When legislative leaders were strong, they were not necessarily allies of the governor. Often men seeking higher public office themselves, they cooperated with the governor only when they saw fit to do so, and they have not hesitated to oppose him. The effect of this fragmentation, decentralization, and fitful leadership has been to prevent the governor from cementing permanent ties to the legislature, and to force him to strike a series of bargains with individual members, thereby limiting his flexibility and ultimately his policy effectiveness.

The norms and rules of the legislature act as additional stumbling blocks for the governor interested in policy formulation. In part because of the decentralization and fragmentation of the legislature, but also because of the methods by which it operates, that body seems creaky and inherently slow to operate.[6] It is by nature conservative; this is true even if, as has generally *not* been the case in Florida, the members are imbued with a liberal ideology. Thus it is far easier to prevent policy development in the legislature than to implement it. Nearly all Florida governors, even those who were not policy architects, have felt frustrated and irritated by the inability or unwillingness of the legislature to act and their own limited ability to make the legislative machinery turn on their behalf.

In many states the political parties have served as an important linkage between the governor and legislature, a sort of bridge which potentially could help smooth some of the other sources of gubernatorial-legislative tension. In fulfilling this function, parties serve to organize and cement relationships (both alliances and opposition!) between governors and legislators, coordinate policy proposals, and hold legislators and governors accountable, if only to a small degree, for their actions.[7] In Florida, however, this linkage has not existed. Parties have been very weak; indeed in a one-party, multifactional state they can hardly be said to exist at all. Thus parties have not served to connect the two branches of government. Personality groups and ad hoc factions, rather, have existed in place of parties. Because of their temporary, transitory nature, the governor has been unable to rely on them as devices for promoting policy development, and he has thereby been deprived of a potential mechanism for easing tension between himself and legislators.

These sources of tension exist mainly for the governor who wants to create new policy. There are other matters, however, which arise from the governor's office and which often serve to alienate legislators.[8] In particular, they see him infringing on their legislative responsibilities by attempting to influence their deliberations. Similarly, Florida legislators have resented such gubernatorial devices as special sessions, not only because they are forced to extend their stay in Tallahassee, but also because until 1968 only the governor could determine the agenda of those special sessions; topics which legislators might wish to consider could not be placed on the agenda unless the governor agreed. Legislators have also disliked the governor's use of the veto and item veto (for appropriations bills). While it has occasionally been possible for them to override a veto, it has not been the normal practice to do so, and legislators tend to feel frustrated and angered by gubernatorial rejection of their decisions. Finally, the budget has been a frequent source of irritation between the governor and the legislature. While the governor has only recently gained a firmer hand on the budget, there have been sharp disagreements between the legislature and the governor about the overall size and shape of the budget and, more importantly, which branch would exercise the final word on specific appropriations.

Last, perhaps there is an element of jealousy between the governor and the legislature that breeds conflict and discontent. The governor, after all, commands more respect than the legislature. The media generally afford him more attention than any other part of state government. Legislators, as politicians, want to share in this respect and publicity. They realize, however, that the public looks to the governor for leadership and solutions to urgent problems, rather than to them. It is not unreasonable, then, that a certain measure of jealousy should enter the relationship, causing additional tensions and conflicts which have to be resolved if cooperation is to be secured.

GUBERNATORIAL STRATEGIES TOWARD THE LEGISLATURE

What can the governor do to create a more positive relationship with the legislature? The Florida governor has a number of techniques and strategies at his disposal: for our purposes these can be grouped into three categories.[9] The first consists of legislative conferences and addresses. They are basically devices for communicating the governor's priorities and agenda to the legislature. Conferences are often held prior to beginning the session and throughout the period of legislative deliberation. The goal of conferences and addresses is the same: to indicate to the legislature what the governor sees as the state's problems and his proposals for resolving them.

A second set of techniques for improving relations with the legislature is lobbying and alliance-building. Through these devices the governor actually seeks to build support for his agenda and proposals and to convince legislators that they should follow his leadership. The distinction between lobbying and conferences, then, fades, particularly once the session begins. Lobbying can consist of direct communication between the governor and individual or small groups of legislators or it can involve contact through intermediaries such as aides or important constituents. The chief executive has also resorted to the appointment of "legislative representatives" on the floor of both houses, or influenced the selection of legislative leadership. On the other hand, he may choose not to play such a direct role in legislative affairs and instead build alliances through more relaxed, passive actions such as letter-writing and press releases.

A third set of techniques includes the use of patronage, special sessions, vetoes, and referenda. Patronage is an attempt to use inducements to gain legislative support, to reward those who cooperate and punish those who do not. The calling of a special session is an attempt by the governor to force the legislature's attention to a specific set of issues. It is something of a "last resort" technique, to be used by the governor when he cannot secure legislative cooperation during a regular session. The threat of a veto or its actual use is another "strong-arm" tactic, designed to force the legislature to do the governor's bidding or to reject previous decisions. Finally, referenda are efforts by the governor to pursue an issue by bypassing the legislators and appealing directly to the voters. Sometimes this does not take the form of a specific issue or policy proposal but consists of an attempt by the governor to influence the election of friendly, or the defeat of unfriendly, legislators.

Although not really part of gubernatorial strategies for influencing the legislature, biennial legislative sessions have provided governors with a number of possibilities, both positive and negative, for working with the legislature. The fact that the legislature met only twice, for sixty days on each occasion (barring special sessions) during a governor's administration, unquestionably limited the results the chief executive could expect from that body. However, it may also be that such infrequent sessions allowed the governor potentially greater freedom to create policies free from legislative constraints.

In the following sections we seek to explore in some detail the ways in which Florida governors have used these techniques in dealing with the legislature, and to assess their effectiveness. In order to carry out this latter task, we have rated the overall effectiveness of such strategies. Not every administration used these techniques to the same degree. As a result we have concentrated on the governor's overall effectiveness, rather than attempting to rate him on each technique.

Gubernatorial-Legislative Relations: Conferences and Addresses

To improve their relationship with the legislature, some governors have met with legislative delegations even prior to assuming office. Since the Democratic candidate, chosen in the May primary, was assured of victory over his Republican opponent in the fall (until 1960), he had plenty of time to begin drafting his legislative program. These prelegislative conferences were important in refining legislative programs. With only two sessions to implement a legislative package, such conferences were usually a decided asset to a governor. Spessard Holland, for example, met with his legislative supporters during the fall of 1940 in preparing his legislative program. Millard Caldwell followed the same approach in the fall of 1944.[10] Askew met with close legislative supporters in 1970 to plan his program.

Most Democratic gubernatorial candidates also used the fall campaign to air their legislative proposals more fully in an effort to mobilize voter support. Napoleon Broward, for example, campaigned in the fall of 1904, urging support for both his Everglades drainage program and his candidacy. In the 1944 campaign Millard Caldwell seldom mentioned his Republican opponent. Instead he concentrated on explaining his legislative programs, especially his public school funding plan.[11]

The governor's first formal contact with the legislature occurred at the opening of each session when he presented his legislative package. The message to the legislature was an effective way to set the tone for a new administration and establish personal contact with legislators. A good first message has been particularly important to governors who have lacked legislative experience and whose leadership, consequently, was somewhat suspect by legislators. The most effective address, from the legislative point of view, appears to be the "plain, straightforward outline," which was filled in and enlarged upon as the session proceeded.

During the first years of the twentieth century, the message was usually read to a joint session of the legislature by the speaker of the house of representatives. In 1911, Governor Albert Gilchrist established the precedent of personally reading his message. Gilchrist, however, droned on for four and one-half hours and left many legislators wondering if the new precedent was worthwhile. Nevertheless, the trend continued and became accepted throughout the nation after President Woodrow Wilson personally delivered his State of the Union address to the U.S. Congress in 1913. In 1929 Doyle Carlton, a former state legislator, committed his forty-nine minute message to memory; his presentation was uniformly praised by the press and legislators. His address pointed out, however, that effective legislative relations depended on much more than a good legislative address or previous legislative experience. Subsequently Carlton experienced serious problems with the legislature.[12]

The twentieth-century governors have traditionally used the legislative address to detail their plans for the state. The message reflected the campaign promises of each with occasional additions. LeRoy Collins had made constitutional revision and reapportionment the major issues of his campaign in 1956, and these items became the heart of his program during his second term in office. Similarly, John Martin had campaigned on a platform emphasizing the need for new road construction, and this issue highlighted his legislative address.[13]

Most gubernatorial programs have been excessively wide-ranging. This is due to the absence of a viable party organization and the need for a gubernatorial candidate to appeal to diverse Democratic coalitions in seeking the party's nomination. Cary Hardee, for example, called for everything from reapportionment, economy in government, and conservation of natural resources, to dipping cattle for tick diseases. Sidney Catts sought such diverse programs as a prohibition amendment, graduated income tax, boys' and girls' industrial schools, taxation of church property, a franchise tax on corporations, a state bureau of labor statistics, a state insurance commissioner, and a ceiling on interest rates charged by loan companies.[14] Despite the breadth and diversity of these programs, most governors have concentrated on their major campaign proposals once the legislators began their deliberations and have left the minor recommendations to their own fate. The restrictions of the biennial legislative sessions mandated this approach. Napoleon Broward emphasized the Everglades issue to such an extent that his other recommendations were often overlooked. Collins' battle for legislative reapportionment had the same effect. Haydon Burns' administration became completely embroiled in his proposed road bond issue.

How well have legislative conferences and addresses served to aid governors in dealing with the legislature? Agenda-setting and the presentation of policy proposals have provided legislators with a set of guidelines and specific proposals with which they must deal. They have also set a tone for the new administration. But they alone have not insured success for any governor unless they were accompanied by additional persuasive techniques.

Gubernatorial Strategies: Lobbying and Alliance-Building

Once the legislature has begun its day-to-day deliberations, Florida governors have employed a number of different devices to build support in the house of representatives and senate. Some governors have intervened directly into the affairs of the legislature. Napoleon Broward, for example, actively solicited senatorial support for Senator Thomas F. West's bid for senate president. Broward told his close friend William James Bryan that West had been a strong supporter of his gubernatorial campaign and would greatly facilitate his legislative program if elected president. Unfortunately for Broward, West lost to Park Trammell and Broward's interference seemed to insure his defeat. Most governors have avoided interfering directly in legislative affairs and feared so alienating the legislature as to impair their legislative programs. For example, Broward's successor, Albert Gilchrist, refused to intervene in the battle between Senator F. M. Hudson of Miami and Senator Joseph Humphries of Bradenton for the senate presidency.[15]

To insure a fair hearing for their proposals and to facilitate their passage, however, a number of governors have designated legislators in each house as their intermediaries. Spessard Holland utilized two former members of the house of representatives, Jephtha Marchant and Henry Sinclair of Polk County, as well as Raymond Sheldon of Hillsborough County, chairman of the House Appropriations Committee and member of other important committees in the house, for this purpose. Sidney Catts relied heavily on three close supporters—representatives W. J. Roebuck and Arthur Gomez and Senator James E. Alexander.[16] LeRoy Collins, a former legislator, used a number of different people in both houses although all were from urban counties. Farris Bryant, who also served many years in the legislature, often selected, to sponsor bills, senators or representatives who were friends of his administration but had demonstrated some interest in the measure. Bryant felt that this approach helped expand his base of support in the legislature. Significantly, however, by the second session he had decided to single out specific floor leaders to speak on his behalf. Reubin Askew worked through the legislative leaders in both houses and through representatives who were genuinely interested in his programs. It was Askew's view that the selection of floor leaders challenges the authority of legislative leaders and consequently does not facilitate passage of a governor's programs.[17]

All governors have also relied on the personal approach to win legislative support. A number of them, including Millard Caldwell, wrote letters to legislators prior to each session soliciting their views on state problems. Caldwell noted that his letters won him the respect of many legislators who felt the governor was genuinely interested in their ideas. Doyle Carlton used a slightly different approach. In 1931 he wrote an open letter to legislators urging a constructive term and cooperation between the legislature and his office. Following a policy established by others, Spessard Holland personally went to Pensacola to honor Senator Philip Beall, senate president, who had been designated the outstanding Democrat in Escambia County in 1942. Holland made the trip to honor Beall and to solidify his support in the senate. Holland also sent telegrams to several victorious legislators in the fall of

1942 congratulating them on their victories and stating his interest in working closely with them in the 1943 session. In 1913 Park Trammell, to generate support, released part of his program to the legislators before the session convened.[18] A former member of the legislature, Trammell felt that the representatives did not like having the governor's entire set of recommendations dumped in their laps on the first day of the session.

While governors have generally found these personal approaches to be helpful, nearly all have also felt it necessary to utilize other techniques to insure passage of their programs. David Sholtz had his aides and cabinet members lobby on the floor of the house and senate in defense of his programs. Napoleon Broward delivered a special message to the legislature on his Everglades drainage plan to emphasize its particular importance to his administration.[19] Sidney Catts was seen by reporters on a number of occasions collaring representatives outside committee rooms.

While the lobbying efforts by most governors have not been as visible as Catts', their actions have been just as real. Reubin Askew noted in 1973 that: "It might not have been obvious but I was active, especially in the last week." Askew's aides were often seen talking to senators and representatives on the floor prior to the call for order, and standing near doors to committee rooms. One of Askew's favorite lobbying devices was to meet either individually or with groups of legislators in his office, and discuss informally his legislative strategy. He also met periodically with critics to discuss their opposition to his proposals. Askew remarked that this approach usually helped him immensely because the office had a way of impressing even the most reluctant opponent. During the last week of the 1973 session, Askew's lobbying efforts paid dividends: in that five-day period the legislature approved the governor's major proposals including the acquisition of Big Cypress Swamp, establishment of a little Federal Trade Commission act to block deceptive trade practices, improvement of workmen's compensation benefits, creation of a statewide grand jury, and revision of the state election code.[20]

For the most part, the Florida legislature has reacted as negatively to heavy-handed lobbying as it has to no lobbying at all. Claude Kirk's constant criticism of the Democratic legislature and his blustering manner brought about an open revolt in the legislature in 1969 that virtually stymied his entire program. When, for example, Kirk could not balance the budget but refused to reduce spending, he tried to blame the Democratic leadership for excessive spending and the need for additional taxes. The conflict resulted in a shouting match in the governor's chamber between Kirk and House Appropriations Chairman Ralph Turlington of Gainesville. Turlington accused Kirk of "lying" to the public and failing to understand fiscal matters. Turlington became so angry he finally had to be removed physically from the meeting by his colleagues for fear he would punch the governor. The legislature decided to cut Kirk's appropriations bill rather than increase taxes.[21] Thereafter, Kirk enjoyed little success in the Democratic-controlled legislature.

While Kirk encountered difficulty for his overbearing style, Fuller Warren and Haydon Burns were criticized for their failure to provide effective leadership. Both men abandoned their programs after the legislature expressed opposition to them. Warren made an abbreviated effort to rally public support for his tax proposals through radio addresses and public speeches. He also sought to dramatize the state's financial plight by mortgaging his automobile and by postponing payment of his salary. These two acts, however, did more to irritate legislators than to cajole them into voting for his proposals. Several legislators publicly ridiculed the governor; one, in particular, claimed angrily that Warren's actions were "asinine" and "utterly ridiculous." When the legislators continued to attack his tax plan, Warren quietly let the matter drop. Burns apparently could be equally indecisive. The editor of the *Tampa Tribune* noted that Burns did much less political "arm-twisting" than previous governors.[22] According to one prominent legislator, Burns immediately retreated from his programs whenever they were criticized by the legislators. In the cases of Warren and Burns, their actions proved disastrous. The legislature proceeded in both instances to ignore most of the governors' other recommendations.

The historical record shows rather clearly that, with the exception of LeRoy Collins, the legislature has preferred governors with definite objectives and programs. Fred Cone and Farris Bryant, who were also criticized publicly by members of the legislature for their lack of leadership, saw many of their recommendations ignored by the legislature.[23]

Once opposition to the governor or his programs has emerged in the legislature, Florida's governors have resorted to a variety of approaches to placate the opposition or to undermine it if necessary. One of the most frequently used methods has been a direct appeal to the voters. Napoleon Broward took his fight for drainage of the Everglades to the people, and after a long struggle was able to convince them of the importance of the program. LeRoy Collins appealed to the public to oppose a bill which would free presidential electors from being bound by the voters. He called the bill "political prostitution" and urged the public to call on their representatives to defeat the measure. [24] The proposal was subsequently rejected by the legislature.

In their effort to reach as many people as possible, governors began using radio and, more recently, television. The radio report to the public became very popular following the example set by President Franklin D. Roosevelt in his "fireside chats" during the depression. Governor David Sholtz used the same approach during his tenure. Sholtz' talks seemed to remove the worst fears of Floridians. They also benefited him politically. In 1933 he persuaded his listeners to send telegrams to their representatives supporting his legislative proposals.[25] The legislators initially reacted indignantly. Within two weeks, however, they had approved nearly all of Sholtz' recommendations.

More so than any other governor to that time, LeRoy Collins made extensive use of radio and television, particularly during his many battles with the legislature over reapportionment in the 1950s. While Collins was, perhaps, Florida's most effective governor in his use of the media, he was unable to utilize these techniques to overcome the "pork-chop" opposition to

Fuller Warren on the stump. A brilliant speaker with a magnetic personality, Warren eschewed the routine details of the governorship. But he loved to go out on the hustings, and in this way he was extremely effective. Photo from his book *Speaking of Speaking: Articles, Addresses, and Other Strident Stuff* (St. Augustine: Record Press, 1944).

his plan. Not all governors have enjoyed Collins' success with the media. Farris Bryant, for example, tried to mimic the Collins style by conducting a weekly series of radio shows entitled "Ask the Governor." He and his aides regarded the shows as a promotional effort to win public support for the governor's programs. In Bryant's case, however, the technique backfired when the series had to be cancelled for lack of listeners.[26]

Lobbying and alliance-building appear, overall, to be effective means of creating a cooperative spirit between governors and legislators. Governors utilizing these techniques have enjoyed considerably more success with the legislature than those who have not. Much depends, however, on the style of gubernatorial lobbying and the nature of the proposals a governor submits, since the legislative "mood" and the "climate" of public opinion strongly influence how they are received.

PATRONAGE, SPECIAL SESSIONS, VETOES, AND REFERENDA

A much more effective way for governors to influence legislative results has been through the use of patronage and the endorsement of legislative "pet bills." Prior to World War II, the governor of Florida could appoint legislators to state positions. Most legislators who received such appointments needed the extra money to make ends meet. With the legislature in session for one hundred and twenty days, legislators had the time to devote to other state positions. Nearly all the governors made it a practice to reward their loyal supporters. Sidney Catts, for example, appointed Representative W. J. Roebuck state convict inspector, Senator James E. Alexander circuit judge in the seventh judicial circuit, and Representative Arthur Gomez county solicitor in Monroe County. Thirteen key legislative supporters of Governor Spessard Holland were appointed to either honorary or salaried positions in state government.[27]

The governor has so many appointments at his disposal at both the state and local levels that there are numerous ways he can reward his followers. David Sholtz utilized his patronage powers to secure legalization of slot machine gambling in 1935 despite major opposition in the house of representatives. One of its members, D. R. "Billy" Mathews of Alachua County, recalled that "certain members of the legislature were given jobs by the state and then would vote like the governor would want them to vote." The slot machine bill was initially defeated in the house on the first roll call, but a parliamentary maneuver forced reconsideration on the following day. The bill then received a favorable majority after Sholtz' aides and his floor leader, S. P. Robineau of Dade County, met with several representatives and promised them or their friends government positions. Only Fred Cone opposed using his patronage powers to reward legislative supporters. As he put it: "It's not my idea of good government for men to have two jobs, especially members of the legislature. It's bad business—bad government." The policy of appointing legislators to government positions was not ended until 1945 when the state supreme court ruled that dual officeholding was unconstitutional.[28]

The governor has also exerted considerable influence in the legislature through his support or lack of support for local legislative bills. These measures usually deal with matters relating to a certain county or city. A legislator traditionally makes a number of promises to his constituents while campaigning for a senate or house seat. To insure passage of such measures and, thus, to facilitate the representative's reelection, many legislators have sought the governor's endorsement of the proposal. The *Tampa Tribune* noted in 1917 that legislators who sought Governor Catts' support for their personal bills were lined up outside his office as the legislative session neared its end.[29] Many governors exchanged their endorsements for the legislators' support.

When governors have been confronted by a particularly obstinate legislature, they have most frequently resorted to the threat of a special session. This was especially effective because Florida's legislators were anxious to get home to take care of their businesses or farming interests. It was also a fairly effective threat before the capitol was air-conditioned. Florida's long, hot and humid summers made the confines of the legislative chambers particularly unpleasant. In his battle with the legislators over reapportionment, Millard Caldwell used the steamy summer weather to his advantage. He noted that after 53 especially unpleasant days, most members were ready to accept his offer of a compromise on reapportionment.[30]

LeRoy Collins, who engaged in the longest running battle with the legislature over reapportionment, resorted to the special session on three different occasions to force it to accept an equitable plan. Collins, however, was faced with an air-conditioned capitol building and a pork-chop faction who promised to oppose his plan until "hell freezes over." Collins' effort to browbeat the legislature by use of the special session seemed to alienate him further from the rural representatives rather than effect a fairer reapportionment measure.

The governor could also pressure legislators through his power to veto legislative measures and to issue item vetoes of the appropriations bill. The veto has been a powerful weapon for the governor, especially in the days of biennial legislative sessions. When the governor vetoed a bill after the legislature had adjourned, the representatives had to wait two years before they could move to override his decision. Few gubernatorial vetoes were overturned in those days. Fred Cone, for example, vetoed 154 bills in the 1939 session, more than triple the number vetoed by any other governor, and the legislature failed to overturn any of them. However, as of 1968, the annual session has impinged rather significantly on this gubernatorial prerogative. Reubin Askew enjoyed five years as governor without having one of his vetoes seriously challenged, but during the 1976 session an increasingly independent legislature passed several bills over his veto. Similarly, Claude Kirk, who had numerous conflicts with the Democratic legislature during his last two terms in office, saw nearly every one of his vetoes overridden by legislators. Indeed, Kirk's "cavalier use of the veto and his broken promises" thwarted all hopes for compromise with his legislative opponents.[31]

When a legislature has balked at passing a major gubernatorial proposal it has occasionally recanted by agreeing to submit the plan to the people. The use of the referendum has had mixed results, however. Broward campaigned throughout the state on behalf of the Everglades drainage proposal only to see it narrowly defeated by the voters. Broward's efforts, however, were ultimately successful. By the time he left office he had convinced the public of the importance of this program.

After a difficult struggle in the legislature, Haydon Burns' $300 million road bond plan was also submitted to the voters. The legislative opposition to the plan was so widespread that several representatives, led by senators Lawton Chiles and Reubin Askew, actively campaigned against it. Burns, who had built his reelection bid around the bond issue, was unable to counter the arguments of his legislative nemeses, and the referendum was rejected by the voters.[32]

Not all governors saw their programs defeated by a referendum vote. Reubin Askew, who had attained the governorship on a platform which emphasized a corporate income tax, persuaded a divided legislature to approve the constitutional amendment and submit it to the people. In a highly publicized campaign, Askew was able to overcome the opposition of many business leaders and some legislators and secure ratification for his proposal. This victory during his first term of office strengthened his gubernatorial leadership; for the next three years the legislature endorsed nearly all his recommendations.

Those governors who have been unable either to persuade the legislature to approve their programs or submit them as referenda have, on occasion, resorted to more militant action. Napoleon Broward and Sidney Catts sought to purge the legislature. Broward urged the public to hold their legislative delegations strictly accountable for their actions: "people should organize, or have at least semi-annual meetings" and pass resolutions instructing their representatives how to vote. He also contemplated hiring a detective to keep an eye on "Grafters" and "Lobbyists" during the legislative session. He was "determined to have honest and legitimate legislation or none at all." Fortunately for the success of his legislative program, Broward decided not to hire a detective and word of his intent did not reach the floor of the house or senate. Sidney Catts was so provoked by the 1917 legislature that he threatened to go out on the stump to get a good legislature elected. He subsequently ordered the state treasurer not to pay any legislator per diem or travel expenses until an appropriations bill was passed.[33]

Most governors have avoided such direct conflict with the legislature. The traditional view has been that this approach takes on the semblance of a personal vendetta and the legislature is likely to rebel against such interference. The implications of President Franklin Roosevelt's unsuccessful purge of Congress in 1938 and its disastrous consequences for his New Deal programs have not been lost on Florida governors. In addition, the legislature in Florida has been an independent branch since 1885 and has always reacted in a hostile manner to any attempts by the governor's office to impinge directly on its authority.

A more typical response by governors to legislative opposition has been a public denunciation. Fuller Warren, for example, read a radio message to the people of Florida during the Christmas season in which he personally thanked seventy-eight legislators for their support of the sales tax. He ignored the fifty-five who had opposed it. Other governors, such as Napoleon Broward, Sidney Catts, Millard Caldwell, and LeRoy Collins, toured the state, criticizing the legislature or individual members for their opposition to gubernatorial programs. Spessard Holland used his Governors Clubs in the various counties to support pro-Holland legislators in the 1942 Democratic primary.[34]

Are patronage, special sessions, vetoes, and referenda effective devices for the governor in promoting cooperation with the legislature? The record appears to be mixed. Patronage seems to be the most effective of these techniques. With it the governor has been able to offer inducements to legislators in order to gain their support. Jobs, of course, have not been available as patronage devices for legislators since the mid-1940s. But the governor is able to provide contracts, appointments, support for local bills or bills of special interest to particular legislators, highway and other public programs, and endorsements for legislators seeking reelection. Special sessions have not always worked to the benefit of the chief executive. Although he could establish agendas and force legislators to remain in session until action was taken, the governor generally had to compromise on his initial proposals because of the nature of the opposition. Moreover, the resentment which many legislators felt at being coerced by the governor to meet and act had negative consequences for any future dealings between the two. Certainly this was the case with LeRoy Collins and Fuller Warren and was somewhat less true for Millard Caldwell. As a consequence, few governors have resorted to the special session. Vetoes, referenda, and attempts by the governor to "purge" legislators have been uniformly criticized by members of the legislature. They have been inclined to view these measures as attacks on their institutional integrity. Gubernatorial use of the veto or an effort to bypass the legislature and appeal directly to the voters is almost certain to elicit a negative reaction.

BIENNIAL SESSIONS: LIABILITIES AND ASSETS

The biennial legislative sessions up to 1968 probably were the greatest handicap Florida's governors encountered. Each governor knew he had, at most, two years to leave his legislative mark on the state. He, therefore, had to move quickly to insure the passage of his programs. Generally speaking, if a governor did not secure the adoption of most of his programs during his first session, he did not obtain their passage at all. The momentum he built up in the Democratic primary and the November election usually carried over into his first legislative session. The legislature apparently felt obliged to give the newly elected governor a thorough hearing during his first session. Millard Caldwell's reapportionment plan and part of his school program succeeded during his first term as did Fuller Warren's citrus code revision and cattle fencing proposition. Neither governor, however, enjoyed much success during his second legislative session. The same could be said of nearly every governor up to Reubin Askew. For example, although LeRoy Collins was a forceful legislative leader during most of his administration, his last legislative session saw an unbridled pork-chop majority ignoring all his recommendations except those that would benefit their constituencies.

By the second session the legislature felt it was under no mandate to approve any new programs. In addition, several legislators used the second session to boost their candidacies for the governor's office or for some other high state position. As a result, these members, who were usually the legislative leaders, showed little inclination to endorse a lame duck's program. Governors who alienated the legislators during their first session either because of their lack of ability or their heavy-handed manner were frequently confronted by a distinctly critical legislature during their second session. Doyle Carlton, who was severely criticized by legislators for the worsening economic condition of Florida and declining revenues during the depression, found his entire program blocked by the legislature during the second session. Carlton created additional difficulties for himself by vetoing a tax on racetrack gambling. His opposition to this plan alienated representatives from the big counties in Florida who saw the measure as a way to get additional funding for their communities. Representative John Mathews of Jacksonville led a walk-out of thirty big county members from the house of representatives in the fight over this funding plan. The legislature finally adjourned in 1931, refusing to accept Carlton's budget and unable to come up with one of its own. In the special session, Carlton called the legislature a "liability instead of an asset," but was forced to accept its compromise tax proposal.[35]

Fuller Warren, who was similarly criticized by the legislature during his first and second legislative sessions, was able to secure the passage of only one major proposal in the second session. His sole accomplishment was the passage of a bill calling for the unmasking of the Ku Klux Klan, and that measure had been originally introduced in the first session. No other governor, however, encountered the opposition faced by Sidney Catts. His personal attacks upon members of the legislature and his appointments of family and friends to high office sparked intense criticism from legislators. When he hired detectives to investigate the use of alcohol by his legislative enemies, the opposition became unrestrained. During the special session of

1918 the senate repassed a bill that Catts had vetoed; it provided payment for state and local officials whose suspensions by the governor had not been upheld by the legislature. The senate also refused to sustain Catts' suspension of hotel inspector A. L. Messer, whose job had been given to the governor's campaign henchman, Jerry Carter. In all, approximately one-third of Catts' suspensions were overruled by the senate. In another slap at Catts' use of patronage, the house of representatives voted to abolish the Hotel Commission and to cut the salary of the adjutant general. Catts was the only governor in the twentieth century to have a message expunged from the senate and house journals. He was also censured by the senate for accusing one of its members of drinking in the chamber. Catts became so unpopular that the 1919 legislature refused to allow his message to be read and simply ordered it printed.[36]

Although restricted in what he could accomplish legislatively, the governor was fairly free to do as he saw fit in the two years the legislature was not in session. One state senator, who served under the biennial and annual legislative systems, felt the governor had more power and independence under the old system. Without the legislature to oversee the governor's activities, the senator was of the opinion that the governor could do administratively what he could not do legislatively. In particular, the senator argued that the governor was able to manipulate the road, prison, and education programs as he wished.[37] The senator's remarks have to be tempered by the fact that many twentieth-century governors spent their last year of office campaigning for another elective post. Consequently, their actions as governor were quite circumscribed during their fourth year. Thus, rather than setting agendas for their successors or defining problem areas for the future, most Florida governors have gradually faded from public view during their final months in office and have not utilized their freedom from legislative restraints in an effort to outline new directions for the state.

REAPPORTIONMENT

Probably no other single issue has caused governors more difficulty in dealing with the legislature than reapportionment. The principal source of frustration in the struggle has been Article VII of the 1885 constitution. As Manning Dauer, political scientist and author of the 1967 reapportionment plan, has noted: "The constitution provided for equal apportionment on a population basis in the state Senate, but accompanying this provision was a limitation of each county to no more than one senator."[38] The result was a situation whereby in 1900 35 percent of the state's citizens elected over one-half of the senators. This figure actually decreased rather sharply throughout the twentieth century as the representatives of rural North Florida refused to surrender their seats to urban South Florida. By 1950, only 13.6

percent of the population elected over one-half the number of senators. In 1961 the percentage had declined ever further to 12.3 percent.[39]

The house of representatives operated under similar constitutional restraints. Each county was guaranteed one representative, with a maximum of three for any one county. As a result, the house too was badly malapportioned. In 1900, 36 percent of the population elected one-half the number of state representatives. By 1950 this figure had decreased to 18 percent, and by 1961 to 14.7 percent. A 1955 study of all forty-eight state legislatures except Arizona revealed that the typical legislature was controlled by approximately 35 percent of the voters. The study also revealed that the situation was steadily worsening. As the data on Florida show, the state was considerably below the national average.

Few of the pre–World War II governors concerned themselves with the unrepresentative nature of the legislature. While the constitution of 1885 required the governor to recall the legislature if it failed to reapportion itself every ten years, the document did not give him an active role in the deliberative process. Moreover, all the governors and their aides have considered reapportionment to be an especially dangerous issue. To force reapportionment on unwilling legislators (and nearly all were, since some were bound to lose their seats) had traditionally insured legislative retaliation, and very few governors were willing to jeopardize their legislative programs by pressing an issue which offered them no political benefits. Furthermore, all of the governors prior to 1952 were from the northern, rural areas of Florida or had been elected with substantial rural support. Not surprisingly, they were unwilling to alienate such an important part of their constituency by insisting on reapportionment. Most followed the policy of Governor Albert Gilchrist, who reminded the legislators of their constitutional duty but chose not to insist that they obey it.[40]

In 1923 the legislature, responding to the dramatic growth of South Florida, reapportioned itself for the first time in this century. The new amendment, however, still left only 27 percent of the population with a majority of the representation. The disparity in senate representation, for example, remained extreme: the thirty-fourth district (Hillsborough County) with a population of 133,384 had one senator, while Nassau County with a population of only 4,694 also had one senator.[41]

As they had in the past, the governors generally ignored the new constitutional mandate to call the legislature into special session. In 1935, for example, Governor David Sholtz refused to take such action after the legislature demonstrated that it was not predisposed to reapportion itself.[42]

Millard Caldwell was the first governor to insist that the legislature obey the law. His position apparently reflected his political differences with the legislature. According to Caldwell only four members of the 1945 legislature had supported his candidacy for governor. The others allegedly had backed his opponent, Lex Green. Many of these same men attacked Caldwell's legislative program and raised his ire for what he considered to be their narrow-mindedness. Caldwell's support of reapportionment also reflected his view of the law; he was a strict constitutionalist and felt that the legislature was obligated by state law to reapportion itself: "it may not be my job to determine what reapportionment is . . . but some reapportionment must be accomplished."[43]

His recommendation to Speaker of the House Evans Crary of Martin County and President of the Senate Walter W. Rose of Orange County was ignored until just before adjournment. He then advised both legislative leaders that "unless they moved on reapportionment he would call them back immediately into special session."[44] Both men noted that previous governors had let the matter drop and they advised him to do the same.

Three days after the legislature adjourned, Caldwell reconvened it in special session and promised the legislators they would stay in session until they adopted a reapportionment plan.[45] June and July 1945 were particularly hot, sweltering months in Florida and the non-air-conditioned capitol made them especially uncomfortable.

The negotiations dragged on through the heat. After two executive sessions and several sectional caucuses, legislative leaders from North and South Florida told Caldwell they were hopelessly deadlocked. In a radio address, Caldwell called on both sides to "abandon their positions of adamant disagreement" and meet "in fair discussion and [with a] give and take attitude." He told the legislative leaders that he would not accept continuation of the status quo. He offered no formula for them to follow, however, and added that he had no intention of recommending a reapportionment plan to the legislature. The constitution "neither requires nor suggests that the governor advise the legislature in what manner reapportionment should be accomplished."[46] On July 25, after fifty-three days of discussion, the legislature agreed to give South Florida two senatorial districts previously held by the North. Caldwell signed the measure noting that "perhaps it's the best possible under the circumstances."[47]

Nevertheless, the measure, which complied with the 1923 constitutional amendment, still left many communities in Florida grossly underrepresented. Hillsborough County, for example, continued to have the maximum of three representatives although its population had increased by over seventy thousand in the preceding twenty years.

From 1945 to 1955 the condition was further exacerbated as Florida's population grew rapidly with the end of World War II, particularly in the urban, southern sections of the state. In 1954, for the first time, Florida elected a governor, LeRoy Collins, who was from an urban area in North Florida (Tallahassee) and whose political power base was in urban South Florida. As noted earlier, Collins had been elected due, in large part, to the support he received in South Florida. His promise to work for a more representative legislature, his commitment to public education, and his racial moderation were highly regarded by South Floridians.

Collins' views of the constitutional requirements for reapportionment were quite different from Millard Caldwell's. Where Caldwell believed he had a constitutional obligation to insist that the legislature obey the law, Collins, reflecting the needs of his constituency, not only insisted that reapportionment be carried out but directly involved himself in the legislative process to insure that it was carried out equitably.

By 1955, 8 percent of the population could elect a majority of the state senators and 17.1 percent could elect a majority of the representatives. Collins was convinced that only through his direct intervention in legislative affairs could a fairer realignment be achieved. In his 1955 legislative address he made reapportionment the first priority of five major areas of governmental reform on which he sought legislative action. He told the legislators that he would keep them in session until a suitable reapportionment plan was devised.[48]

In traditional fashion, the legislature ignored Collins' request and adjourned its regular session on June 3, 1955, without passing any plan. True to his promise, Collins immediately reconvened the legislature, noting in a compromising tone that while the regular session had been constructive, the legislature had failed to meet its constitutional obligation on reapportionment. The leaders of the house of representatives appeared willing to make some adjustment toward increasing the size of their body and giving the additional seats to the larger districts in the state. But members of the senate were adamantly opposed to any change. Many senators from the smaller districts of North Florida, including W. Turner Davis of Madison, S. Dilworth Clarke of Monticello, W. Randolph Hodges of Cedar Key, and Newman Brackin of Crestview, bitterly attacked Collins for trying to dictate a reapportionment plan. These men, who controlled the senate's leadership, assumed, correctly as time would prove, that their districts would be eliminated by reapportionment. Reluctant to support reapportionment under the existing constitutional requirements, rural legislators attempted to circumvent the constitution by an amendment which would have provided a senator for each of the sixty-seven counties and a house based principally on population. The proposal permitted 30 percent of the population to elect a majority of representatives as opposed to 18 percent under existing guidelines. However, the fairness of the plans was misleading; the population of Florida was increasing so dramatically that the 30 percent figure would have declined to less than 25 percent by 1956. It was hardly surprising, therefore, that the voters rejected the plan (288,575 to 187,662) when it was submitted to them in the 1956 general election.[49]

Collins refused to retreat on this issue. Unlike Caldwell, he was deeply involved in the legislative deliberations. He met regularly with delegations from South Florida to map strategy and from North Florida to request some compromise. He also informed the special session that he would veto a house proposal which sought to merge Liberty and Wakulla counties with Jefferson County, and would provide Monroe and Bay counties with a senator. Collins had publicly promised to veto any bill which failed to separate Sarasota and Manatee counties (the two fastest growing counties in Florida) into two senatorial districts.[50] Despite Collins' stand, the senate supported the house bill and challenged Collins' constitutional right to veto a reapportionment measure. The state supreme court quickly upheld the governor's right to veto such a bill.

After his veto of the reapportionment bill, Collins, in his monthly radio and television address, called on the people of Florida to contact their legislators, "particularly those senators who have blocked fair reapportionment up to now."[51] The governor's public appeal only further incensed rural senators who felt that such matters should be kept within the confines of the capitol (a sort of gentleman's understanding). They also resented what they considered the governor's arm-twisting methods.

The political lines between the representatives from North and South Florida were now being more firmly drawn. Collins' decision to force a reapportionment plan through the legislature and his highway construction projects for South Florida had marked a decisive turning point in the rural versus urban split in the legislature. Prior to this protracted fight over reapportionment, the legislators from the two sections of the state had managed to work together with some degree of harmony. In fact, the 1954 house of representatives had designated Ted David from Hollywood as its speaker for the 1955 session. However, as the session wore on, animosities increased and the battle lines were drawn. South Florida legislators whose districts stood to benefit by reapportionment allied themselves with Governor Collins. Out of this controversy emerged the Pork Chop Gang composed of legislators from rural North Florida who, according to former state senator Verle Pope of St. Augustine, "took a blood oath to stick together, and did that on all legislation."[52] They also agreed never to elect another urban legislator to the senate presidency or house speakership. Their power was enhanced by their almost complete control of the legislative hierarchy. Not only did porkchoppers hold the senate presidency, but they also served as chairmen of nearly all the major committees in the house and senate, and controlled a majority of the membership of each committee. They were especially powerful in the senate where they controlled 21 or 22 of the 38 members. Their domination of the senate and near majority in the house had serious consequences for Collins' legislative programs. The president of the senate and speaker of the house appointed all committees and referred bills to appropriate committees. By stacking committees they could insure the committee's loyalty, indeed its subservience. In addition, when referring a bill to committee, the senate president could assign it to more than one committee if he wished. The bill was then handled by the committees in the order in which it was received. In a sixty-day session it was virtually certain that such a bill would never emerge from the committee. A two-thirds vote of senate members was necessary to bring such a bill to the floor for a vote. While the speaker was somewhat less powerful in assigning bills, he could refer an appropriations measure to the finance and taxation and the appropriations committees and to one other committee if he so chose.[53] With such power rural representatives were able to block effectively the demands of Collins and the representatives of South Florida (now nicknamed the Lamb Chop Gang).

Collins, however, refused to slow his drive for reapportionment. He spoke to a rural audience in Dunnellon, where Senator L. K. Edwards, Jr., one of his leading opponents, resided. Collins characterized his and the pork chop opposition to reapportionment as "greedy and selfish." He further contended that the smaller counties were defying the constitution by refusing to reapportion the senate and house. Collins' speech angered many of the pork choppers, particularly the president of the senate, W. Turner Davis of Madison, who defended his colleague Edwards against what he termed the "insults" of Collins.[54]

On September 29, 1955, after 120 days, the longest legislative session on record adjourned after failing to pass a reapportionment plan acceptable to Collins. He immediately notified the departing legislators that he would oppose the reelection of all those who had blocked reapportionment. Former Governor Millard Caldwell, who had been an active observer of the struggle, criticized Collins for involving himself too deeply in an issue that fell within the purview of the legislature.[55] Collins did, however, perceive the office of governor quite differently from Caldwell. He regarded the governor as the direct representative of all the people of the state, and, therefore, he was obligated to see that their desires were fulfilled by the legislature, especially in the area of adequate representation.

Collins' message to the legislature in 1957 had once again been an endorsement of reapportionment. In particular, he urged the legislators to adopt the findings of a constitutional advisory commission chaired by former senator Wallace Sturgis. According to the plan, the number of senators would be increased from thirty-eight to forty-two. House seats were to be allocated to the counties on the basis of one representative per 175,000 people and an additional representative for each 150,000. The proposal included a provision which permitted the governor to turn the issue of reapportionment over to the state supreme court for solution if the legislature failed to prepare a plan. The pork chop delegation demonstrated little interest in Collins' proposal. Instead, it moved to adopt a plan which would create a

45-member senate and 114-member house, but would still leave control of the legislature overwhelmingly in the hands of the rural areas of the state.[56]

Collins, who apparently felt that this change was the best he could get from the legislature, decided to approve the constitutional amendment and campaigned actively on its behalf. In reflecting on this proposal later in his career, Collins remarked that while the amendment left much to be desired, he thought some change, no matter how small, would improve chances for a more equitable reapportionment in the future. In late July, however, the supreme court removed the reapportionment amendment from the ballot along with the proposed constitution.[57]

The resentment of the pork chop members towards Collins was unrestrained in the 1957 legislative session. Incensed by his abortive effort to unseat them and better organized after a series of meetings prior to the 1957 session, the pork chop delegates could hardly restrain their glee as they defeated most of Collins' legislative program.

In 1959 Collins made a last ditch effort to reapportion the legislature. Reflecting his frustration over the reapportionment struggle, he called on legislators to provide Florida with honest representation or split it in two. The pork chop forces, well aware of their power, ignored his petition; senate members voted immediately to revise the 1955 plan which Collins had rejected.[58]

Collins launched one last lobbying effort for reapportionment, meeting with individual legislators and legislative delegations on weekend retreats. Led by Charley Johns, Collins' gubernatorial opponent in 1956 and a senator from rural Starke, the pork chop legislators accused Collins of violating the constitution by trying to "coerce the 1959 legislature to reapportion its membership in accordance with his personal rules."[59] The legislature's use of the constitution to criticize Collins' role in the struggle facilitated their cause. To the people of Florida in the 1950s, the separation of executive and legislative branches of government was highly regarded and Collins' alleged violations of this tradition weakened his case in the eyes of many Floridians.

Legislators did agree on a plan to establish a 103-seat house and a 44-member senate with control still predominantly held by the pork chop delegation. Although he was not satisfied with the proposal, Collins, nevertheless, approved it and campaigned for it. As in 1957, he regarded this initial change as ultimately leading to a more effective reapportionment. Despite Collins' endorsement and his campaigning efforts, the voters decisively rejected the plan, 177,955 to 146,601. The large counties of South Florida, particularly Dade, Hillsborough, Broward, and Pinellas, overwhelmingly rejected the plan, which they regarded as grossly unfair to themselves.[60]

Collins' successor, Farris Bryant, endorsed legislative reapportionment and a new state constitution, but he had been a close ally of the pork chop group during his days in the legislature, and he did not pursue these recommendations very vigorously. As Senator S. Dil Clarke of Monticello, one of the founders of the Pork Chop Gang, put it shortly after Bryant's inauguration: "We won't have any trouble with him." Clarke and his allies passed a plan which was quite similar in effect to the 1959 reapportionment amendment. On November 3, 1964, the voters overturned this proposal by a majority of almost 300,000 votes with counties like Pinellas voting five to one against it, and Dade and Broward two to one.[61]

Despite the division between the pork chop forces and the majority of Floridians, it had become increasingly clear by 1964 that some form of reapportionment would be enacted. The United States Supreme Court had made it clear in *Baker* v. *Carr,* 369 U.S. 186 (1962), that it considered reapportionment subject to judicial review. The Court followed up that opinion with the landmark *Wesberry* v. *Sanders,* 376 U.S. 1 (1964), in which the justices employed the "one man, one vote" principle to declare void a 1931 Georgia congressional apportionment law. Four months later the Court in *Reynolds* v. *Sims,* 377 U.S. 533 (1964), struck down an Alabama reapportionment law which violated the principle of one man, one vote.[62] The Florida legislature was ordered by the federal courts to reapportion in accordance with this decision.

Responding to the Court's directive, Governor Haydon Burns called reapportionment "mandatory" but, concerned about his reelection campaign, he maintained a strictly hands-off policy and let the legislative leaders decide the course of reapportionment. Burns did call the legislators into special session in June, 1965, but, instead of supervising the legislative proceedings, he took a ten-day vacation in the Bahamas. In 1966, responding to increasing public and Court pressure, the legislature adopted a reapportionment plan that required almost 48 percent of the population to elect a majority of the house members and 48.4 percent to elect a majority to the senate.[63] The new law reflected a major change in the nature of representation in Florida. It did not, however, satisfy the Supreme Court.

In 1967, the Court ruled in *Swann* v. *Adams,* 385 U.S. 440 (1967), that the 1966 law was unconstitutional. The justices questioned "peculiar deviations" in the Florida law. For example, in the house of representatives both Flagler and St. Johns counties composed a district 18.24 percent below the size of the average district, while Polk County had four representatives with a 15.27 percent variation above the average. This established a spread of 33.51 percent from the largest to the smallest district in the house. In 1967, under the Court's direction the legislature removed these irregularities and created a house of 119 members with 49.6 percent of the population electing a majority and a senate of 48 members with 50.9 percent of the population electing a majority.[64]

The Supreme Court's intervention in this troublesome issue saved sub-

Governor Haydon Burns signs the Tampa Port Authority Sports Bill on May 28, 1965. Burns ratified a number of these public works programs in 1965 in an effort to generate support for his coming reelection bid in the spring of 1966. Public, legislative, and newspaper criticism of Burns's governorship, however, reached such proportions that his reelection bid was in serious jeopardy. State Photographic Archives.

sequent governors from the political difficulties encountered by Collins. The Pork Chop Gang had demonstrated that it was determined to protect its position no matter how unrepresentative the legislature became. It seems certain that future governors who had the same political base as Collins (which was inevitable given the geometric growth of urban South Florida) would encounter the same problems Collins did with the Pork Chop Gang. Furthermore, the alliance of rural North Florida legislators had coalesced with the fight over reapportionment and these men had decided not only to block further reapportionment but had also begun shaping programs between 1960 and 1967 that were designed to benefit their own section of the state often at the expense of other sections.

RESURGENCE OF THE LEGISLATURE

While Florida's governors have considerable power to influence the proceedings of the legislature, they have never directed state affairs in the fashion of Huey Long or Nelson Rockefeller. As we mentioned earlier in this chapter, the constitution of 1885 was chiefly responsible for this situation. Once the restrictions were removed in 1968, experts assumed that the executive office in Florida would follow the pattern set in other states; specifically powers would increase, and the governor would begin to set policy and legislate for the state. This has not been the case, however. No sooner had the constitution of 1968 been adopted than the Florida legislature moved to strengthen its power vis-à-vis the governor. The reorganization act of 1969 provided legislative committees with a permanent staff to advise them on gubernatorial programs and assist in the preparation of new laws and a budget. These permanent staffs have enabled the legislature to maintain its independence despite the strengthening of the governor's position by the 1968 constitution.[65]

The effect of the staff system was unclear during the first few years since it was only in the formative stages and the staffs were too small to be very effective. In addition, the legislature was quite amenable to Governor Askew's leadership after the difficulties encountered during Claude Kirk's administration. From 1970 to 1974, the legislature heartily endorsed the governor's fiscal and legislative proposals with very few exceptions. In 1975, however, the legislature once again asserted itself, particularly in fiscal affairs.[66]

The meaning of this legislative questioning and the emergence of the staff system was made clear in 1976. The senate leadership met in January and February, and with the assistance of their staff drafted their own budget. The senate then used this budget, rather than the governor's proposal, as its guide in preparing their fiscal package.[67] The action by the senate leadership severely impinged on the governor's ability to utilize the executive budget for state policymaking. All the consequences of this development are not immediately clear, but on the surface, at least, it does present a real threat to gubernatorial leadership in the state of Florida.

The change in attitude by the legislature reflected a national trend which, by 1974, involved questioning the power of executive leaders at both state and national levels. The Vietnam War, the rise of the "imperial presidency," and finally Watergate served as catalysts for this criticism, especially at the national level. By the early 1970s many state legislatures had achieved a new degree of professionalism. Increased salaries and more facilities for elected members, full-time professional staffs, annual sessions, year around operation, and indeed reapportionment made legislatures more efficient, and effective, instruments of government.[68] While the benefits to Florida of increasing legislative effectiveness can scarcely be gainsaid, it is ironic that public questioning of executive power and the emergence of the legislature should have occurred at almost the same time that the executive office in Florida was beginning to enjoy the fruits of the new constitution.

THE GOVERNOR AND THE LEGISLATURE: AN ASSESSMENT

What can be said about the Florida governor and his relations with the legislature? How effective has the governor been in negotiating with the legislature, and what determines the degree of his effectiveness? The preceding sections have demonstrated how particular strategies have worked, or not worked, for governors. The single issue of reapportionment, moreover, has highlighted both the problem areas inherent in gubernatorial-legislative relations and the assets and liabilities of various gubernatorial techniques in dealing with the legislature.

We think it fair to state that the overall effectiveness of Florida governors in their dealings with the legislature depends on two fundamental factors: the degree of involvement with the legislature and the style or quality of that involvement. In addition, certain situational variables seem to be crucial in deciding governors' legislative effectiveness.

The degree of involvement determines the extent of communication between the two bodies. Not all of the communication has to be directly between governors and legislators. But without the transmission of gubernatorial desires and wishes, priorities and programs, the legislature will have little sense of direction. Even when legislators complain that the governor is too much involved in legislative affairs, that he is infringing on their prerogatives, they still expect him to provide specific policy directions. Governors who did not provide this guidance, such as Fred Cone, were criticized by legislators for their lack of leadership.

We have placed governors on a continuum of legislative involvement in order to observe the relative influence which this factor has had on their effectiveness. The ends of the continuum are represented by "ongoing/continuous" involvement on the one hand and "infrequent/discontinuous" involvement on the other. The "ongoing/continuous" end of the continuum includes such governors as Jennings, Broward, Catts, Caldwell, McCarty, Collins, and Askew. All of these men had very frequent contact with legislators, both during sessions and during periods when the legislature was not meeting. Occupying positions toward the middle of the continuum are Martin, Carlton, Sholtz, Holland, Warren, Bryant, and Kirk. These men interacted with legislators during the session but only infrequently at other times. Toward the other end of the continuum are Gilchrist, Trammell, and Burns, whose involvement with the legislature was infrequent even when it was in session. At the far end of the "infrequent/discontinuous" section of the continuum are Hardee and Cone. They intervened rarely in legislative matters.

Not all of the governors occupying positions toward the "ongoing/continuous" end of the continuum were effective in dealing with the legislature.

But no governor who had infrequent contact or who maintained an aloofness from the legislature could be considered effective in terms of cooperation with the legislature. Hardee was an ineffectual leader; Gilchrist, Trammell, Carlton, and Burns submitted proposals to the legislature but were very ineffective in lobbying for their passage and eventually abandoned them; Cone refused to get involved at all.

The second determinant of gubernatorial effectiveness concerns the style or quality of the governors' involvement with legislators. Style in this context refers to the manner in which the governor lobbies and builds alliances; how he uses patronage and other forms of inducements; the extent to which he shows respect and consideration for legislators' needs and interests; and his use of strong-arm tactics and threats. Here again we use a continuum to indicate the range of gubernatorial behavior and its relative effectiveness.

On the one side are the governors who have demonstrated an amiable style in dealing with legislators. These men sought cooperation through friendliness; they tried to avoid unpleasant confrontations or, if they occurred, abandoned their proposals to avoid personal animosities. Midway along the continuum are diplomatic governors. They tried to work with legislators as partners in a common enterprise. When conflict occurred, they sought compromise through negotiation. They were cognizant of legislators' needs, and, at least publicly, respected them as members of the policymaking process. At the other end of the continuum are governors demonstrating a heavy-handed style. They often regarded the legislature as a hindrance to, or at least a brake on, their policymaking initiative. They did not fear confrontation with the legislature; indeed, they seemed to relish it on occasion. While most governors whose style was heavy-handed were eventually forced to compromise, most did so only grudgingly, and some actually preferred an impasse which they loudly publicized as the fault of the legislature. The most extreme examples of this style in dealing with the legislature were the governors who publicly berated or ridiculed legislators.

Governors who employed an amiable style, such as Trammell, Hardee, Martin, Carlton, Sholtz, Cone, Warren, Bryant, and Burns, have not always been the most successful. Hardee, Carlton, Cone, and Warren offered so little leadership that even though they began their administrations with good legislative relations, by the end of their tenure legislators had lost respect for them. Trammell, Sholtz, Bryant, and Burns maintained good rapport with legislators, but each had relatively modest legislative goals and in his desire to maintain good relations did not insist on the adoption of controversial measures.

Governors at the heavy-handed end of the continuum, Catts and Kirk, also experienced little success with legislators, although for entirely different reasons. They confronted legislators, publicly assailed them, berated them, and were dictatorial in their use of rewards and punishments. Legislators quickly came to resent these governors, and for the most part refused to cooperate with them.

Another set of governors occupied a middle ground. Jennings, Broward, Gilchrist, Holland, Caldwell, McCarty, Collins, and Askew conducted well-conceived and deliberate negotiations with legislators throughout the sessions. Interestingly, none of them was afraid of confrontations with legislators. But the difference between these men and Catts and Kirk was that they never allowed the confrontations to reach the point of rigidity, where there was no room to maneuver, and neither side had a graceful "out." McCarty and Askew, for example, were well-liked by legislators because of their past legislative experience, the consideration and respect they showed legislators, and their desire to "work things out" rather than publicly trumpet a stalemate.

What does this suggest about style in determining governors' effectiveness with the legislature? Clearly the purely amiable style does not work; legislators want leadership, not just friendship. The governor must not be afraid to push and prod legislators along. But he cannot do so in a heavy-handed manner. He must be fair and respectful in his public attitudes, regardless of his private opinions. Even when a governor's personal feelings might bristle, he cannot descend to the point at which public denunciations become personal attacks on the integrity of the legislative institution or individual members.

Perhaps, then, the most effective governors, from the perspective of gaining cooperation with the legislature, are those who work closely with it on a regular basis, but who do not attempt to railroad their proposals through. The governor who is the diplomat, who attends to legislators' concerns, who takes an interest in the affairs of the legislature on a regular basis, and who is not afraid to challenge it on important matters (and we emphasize important) is most likely to be successful. The governor who fails to become involved, even when his style is amiable or diplomatic, is not likely to be successful. The heavy-handed governor, whether or not he involves himself with legislators on a regular basis, is likely to be perceived as the least successful. Thus Jennings, Broward, Holland, Caldwell, McCarty, and Askew appear to have had the greatest success. Collins ranks only slightly behind them, largely because his proposals on constitutional reform, reapportionment, and race relations were too advanced for legislative and public acceptance. Catts, Warren, Burns, and Kirk seem to have had the worst relations with legislators, and generally failed to accomplish very much with them. Other governors had, in greater or lesser degrees, mixed results.

CONCLUSIONS

The ability of the governor to influence and direct legislative deliberations in the state has reflected the quality of gubernatorial leadership. Men who have sought to lead and have had the political skills to do so have been able to persuade the legislature of the wisdom of their programs.

In retrospect, we would have to say Florida's gubernatorial leadership in legislative matters has varied dramatically in quality. The lack of strong, continuous gubernatorial leadership has especially undermined relations with the legislature. In part, this is a result of the tradition of an independent legislature and the constitution of 1885. A more important reason, however, appears to be the lack of party structure in the state and the ability of men with relatively little political experience, especially experience in working with legislators, to win the Democratic popularity contest in the spring. The 1968 constitution and the emergence of a viable Republican party may yet lead to a stronger party system and a more rational method of selecting candidates. But the result up to now has frequently been ineffective gubernatorial leadership not only in legislative matters but in all major policy issues.

Part III

Gubernatorial Initiatives

HAVING studied some of the structural and functional bases of the Florida governorship, in the following section we explore a number of specific policy issues. Through an examination of particular problems confronting the state and the ways in which governors have responded to them, it will be possible to assess more completely the impact governors have had on the state, which governors have been the most effective leaders, and what accounts for their success. In addition, we examine from the perspective of the executive office how Florida arrived at its policy positions on selected issues. To do this, we deal, successively, with economic and fiscal affairs, race relations, education, and criminal justice. Although other issues, such as agriculture, might also have been chosen, we believe these represent the most important and recurrent topical areas with which Florida governors have had to deal during this century. Thus, materials in this section add to and clarify the information set forth in the first two parts of this book.

7

Economic Development

BUT for the wild, devil-may-care boom of the 1920s, Florida's economic development was a slow and arduous process until the 1940s. In response to the economic difficulties of the state during this period, Florida's governors were very conservative in their approach to fiscal matters. In cooperation with the legislature, they made a continuous effort to manage the government on a businesslike basis. This policy has strongly influenced the governor's role in shaping economic growth, taxation levels, the labor union movement, and environmental programs

ECONOMIC GROWTH AND TAXATION

Governor Doyle Carlton's statement in 1929 that "economy in public expenditures is essential to our future development" was a common theme and could have been stated by any governor up to and including Robert Graham in 1979. Hand-in-hand with this economic philosophy has been a commitment by nearly every governor to hold the line on taxes. Spessard Holland saw the low tax base as an important attraction to northerners. He proposed that the state redouble its efforts to attract settlers by placing a constitutional ceiling of two mills on intangibles.[1] Similar versions of Claude Kirk's observation: "There will be no need for any new taxes" have been heard throughout the century.

These laissez-faire economic views are in part a carryover from the nineteenth century when Florida was a very poor, largely uninhabited state. During the late nineteenth and early twentieth centuries, the state put considerable effort into attracting new residents by selling its public lands. The sale of lands was also envisioned as a way to raise capital to build a more extensive transportation and communication system. In dealing with such a shaky economy, the state's political leaders have placed great emphasis on balanced budgets. Indeed, the 1885 constitution forbade the state from operating with a deficit. This fiscal policy has been heartily endorsed by politicians throughout the twentieth century and was rewritten into the 1968 constitution.

The rural, frontier-like nature of the state was very evident in the early 1900s. Florida's average population per one mile of railroad was only 163 compared to an average of 541 in the North, 485 in the South, and 204 in the relatively unsettled West.[2] This condition prevailed despite a 42 percent increase in Florida's population during the first decade of the twentieth century. Economically the state enjoyed a measure of prosperity due in large part to the success of the phosphate and citrus industries, each of which produced one-half the supplies in the United States.

Florida's general revenues during the first decade steadily increased although the state operated usually with less than $2 million per year. The chief source of state revenues was the General Revenue Fund, which included taxes on such items as licenses, insurance premiums, and corporate charters, a one mill tax for schools, and the leasing of state convicts. State income was spent principally on operating the government and the schools and on health and welfare.[3]

The only call for new taxes during this period was made by Governor Broward. He requested a tax on franchises because they were so "valuable." He also suggested that the state equalize its tax burdens by having the state and counties assess their constituents for their own purposes: "I am convinced that this lack of equalization in assessments will never be corrected until the subjects of taxation for state and county purposes are separated." Broward estimated that the revenues raised under his plan would total nearly $300 million as opposed to the $142 million then collected. He pointed out that county values ranged from 40 percent to 90 percent of full cash value.[4] Broward's concern for equalizing taxes was expressed by several other governors during the century, but the legislators, reflecting the concerns of their counties, were unwilling to approve such legislation until the late 1960s.

Florida's steady economic growth continued into the second decade of the century despite World War I. The population increased by nearly 29 percent. Florida's phosphate industry and naval stores remained in great demand during the war years. In 1915 Governor Park Trammell viewed the state's future with cautious optimism, noting the steady economic progress over the past decade. Rather than call for more government programs to assist the common man (in the manner of President Woodrow Wilson), however, he urged economy in government and a reduction in the tax millage because he felt the accumulation of a large budget surplus "might tend to extravagant and unnecessary appropriations."[5] The only new source of state revenue during this period was road taxes, and all this money was earmarked for road construction (the state's second greatest expenditure in 1920).

By the end of the decade, Florida had built up a $1.9 million surplus. Governor Catts followed Trammell's lead and called for a reduction of taxes for the "heavily taxed." Catts did attempt, however, to make the tax burden more equitable by closing loopholes and by urging inheritance, income, and franchise taxes.[6] Reluctant to tamper with the state's slow but steady growth and to impede the immigration of the rich and of corporations, the legislature rejected Catts' tax program. The emphasis remained on continued economic growth in what legislators and governors of the period considered an undeveloped state.

The state's only debt throughout the period 1910–20 was a small $601,506, all of it held in educational bonds. Nevertheless, even this sum concerned Governor Cary Hardee who recommended in 1921 that the bonds be retired through the establishment of a sinking fund with money provided by interest accumulated through state deposits in banks.[7] The legislature approved the plans and the state appeared to be in excellent financial shape as it entered the 1920s.

Florida took another financial step at the beginning of the new decade which had long-range significance for its tax policies. In 1921 the legislature approved a one cent per gallon gasoline tax. This marked a gradual trend away from the property tax as the state's chief source of revenue. Thereafter, Florida would swing increasingly toward sales and excise taxes which were geared to the social and economic objectives of increased population, tourism, and industry.[8]

Florida roared into the twenties with the economy leading the way. Americans were anxious to vacation in Florida during the winter and enjoy the warm climate and the luxury of West Palm Beach and Miami. Tourists and new residents flocked into the state, and the population increased by nearly 500,000 in the decade with nearly 300,000 arriving in the first five years. South Florida, in particular, felt the effects of this immigration. Miami grew from a town of 29,751 residents to a city of 110,637, and Tampa grew from 51,608 to 101,161. Nine new counties were created in South Florida from 1921 to 1925. Railroad construction increased dramatically to assist in the transportation of northerners, and the public road system grew from 748 miles in 1924 to 3,254 miles by 1930.[9] The citrus industry also enjoyed phenomenal growth.

The most dramatic change, however, occurred in land values. Lands both above and below water, which could not be given away prior to 1920, were being bid on as if they were rich in oil. Swamps, woods, bogs all increased in value as the public sought to get rich quick. After all "how could you lose on land investment" went the saying. William A. Baillett, writing in *Barron's* magazine, noted that there must be enough lots laid out in Florida to house half the population of the United States.[10]

Light-headed with economic success, Floridians went mad over the possibilities of even greater growth and riches. Counties bonded themselves to the hilt and then some as they sought to outdo one another in providing the services and facilities for the incoming tourists and residents. The bonded debt for the counties grew from $13.5 million in 1913 to $86.2 million in 1922, to $365 million in 1926, and to $532.5 million in 1931. Florida's county debt in 1931 was twice that of its nearest rival in the South (North Carolina).[11]

Only the state government proceeded with any degree of caution during this period. Through Governor Hardee's sinking fund scheme, the state had collected $140,000 toward paying off its $601,506 bonded school debt. Hardee tried to dissuade the counties from turning so heavily to bonds for construction. He cautioned Floridians that they were "in the anomalous position of demanding more and more of government each year and at the same time demanding less taxes."[12] However, Hardee and his successors, apparently confident of the state's continued economic boom, did not take any additional steps to limit the size of the bonded debt. Indeed, the 1926 collapse seems to have caught the governor as unprepared as it did the average citizen.

Signs of a decline in the Florida boom appeared as early as 1925 when newspapers and magazines warned investors about land promises in Florida. Critics also began belittling the tourist industry, characterizing many of the state's facilities as primitive. The 1926 and 1928 hurricanes followed by the depression and the fruit fly pestilence added the final coup de grace to Florida's short-lived economic boom. Per capita income plummeted by 58 percent from the end of the boom in 1926 to 1933. From 1926 to 1931 state and local tax collections fell from $62.23 to $47.84 per capita, or a decrease of nearly 25 percent. State banking resources declined from $593 million in 1925 to $60 million in 1934 with 45 national and 171 state banks failing. In April 1929, the Mediterranean fruit fly attacked the citrus groves in Florida, infesting nearly 72 percent of all trees.[13]

While economic matters had always been of principal concern to the governors, they had never been quite so pressing and persistent as they were during the depression. Indeed, financial concerns completely engulfed the Carlton administration. Elected on a fiscally conservative platform in which he called for reduced property taxes and debt relief, Doyle Carlton asked the legislature to eliminate "every useless expenditure," and abolish "every unnecessary office. . . ." He began by reorganizing the Department of Motor Vehicles and eliminating sixty-six positions. By the end of 1929 he had reduced salaries by $748,000.[14]

Faced with a $2.5 million state deficit, Carlton was forced to seek additional taxes from the legislature. He rejected a sales tax as inequitable and too expensive to collect. Instead he urged the adoption of an additional five cents gas tax—two cents to be allotted to the Road Department, another two cents to counties for the retirement of bonds, and the final cent to be distributed to counties with one-third going for roads and two-thirds for schools.[15]

To facilitate the state's recovery, Carlton proposed an increase in experimental and extension stations to assist agricultural production and to improve marketing procedures. He also urged an active program of industrial recruitment. He noted that "Florida has little to tax. Unlike many of its sister States, it does not have industry to properly share the costs of government." In order to protect bank depositors against losses in the future, he recom-

Governor John Martin in Ormond Beach, Florida, in 1925 to meet with the state's most prominent tourist and the nation's leading industrialist and philanthropist, John D. Rockefeller, then age 86. The two men discussed the state's tourist and land boom. Unfortunately for Floridians the boom collapsed a year later. State Photographic Archives.

mended that the state oversee the banking community. Finally, he wanted to
restrict the bonding powers of local government to prevent the recurrence of
such fiscal chaos, and to continue road construction only on a pay-as-you-go
basis.[16]

Carlton's tax plan encountered considerable opposition from counties
which had small debts and felt they were being forced to assume the financial
burden of the counties with large debts. On two different occasions, Carlton
addressed a hostile legislature urging passage of his tax measures and
defending himself against charges that his plan would benefit the bond
houses. In June, he called the legislature back into special session to provide
funds for schools and general fund appropriations. The longest legislative
session to that time adjourned on June 29, 1929, having approved the
governor's recommendations with an additional one cent tax going to schools
and universities.[17]

Carlton's problems were far from over, however. The state's economy
continued to deteriorate over the next two years and in 1931 Carlton found
himself again pleading before the legislature for additional taxes. Opposition
quickly emerged to his request for an extension of the six cents gas tax.
Representative John E. Mathews of Duval County denounced the governor's
economic figures: "I say advisedly that all the State owes is not the old debt,
but is a new debt contracted by this administration." Nerves were often on
edge during the many heated debates over the size of the tax increase and the
method of allocation. At one point a fistfight broke out in the house when the
majority attempted to lock out minority members and adopt a tax program.[18]

Representative J. Tom Watson of Hillsborough called for Carlton to
provide the legislature with "leadership." But Carlton, apparently overwhelmed by the magnitude of the depression and the constant criticism of the
legislature, refused to assume the mantle of leadership. He told the legislators at the special session in June: "If the program that has been offered
does not meet with your liking, then for God's sake provide one that does."[19]

Accepting the governor's charge, the legislature, in session for nearly 100
days, raised the gas tax from six to seven cents with the extra cent going to
the state's general treasury to make up for a reduction in property taxes.
(Property taxes were reduced from fourteen mills in 1930 to four and
seven-eighths mills in 1931.) The legislature also legalized pari-mutuel
betting at horse and dog tracks over Carlton's veto and created a state tax
commission and a state purchasing agency to enable the legislature to
prevent further wastefulness in government. The acts were clearly aimed at
Carlton and what the legislature regarded as his fiscal incompetence.[20]

Despite the fiscal battles during Carlton's administration, economic
conditions in Florida continued to deteriorate. Per capita income had drifted
downward from $510 in 1929 to $289 in 1933. By the end of 1933, 26 percent
of the population received public assistance; 22 percent of the white popula-

tion, or 226,868 people, and 36 percent of the black population, or 155,239, were on relief.[21]

The financial collapse in Florida had a profound psychological effect on its citizens. Led by the governors, many of them blamed the depression on irresponsibility in government and urged a return to fiscal restraint and balanced budgets at the state and local levels. Florida's depression governors, Doyle Carlton, David Sholtz, and Fred Cone, strongly supported this economic viewpoint. As Carlton observed: "it is well to keep government out of business but business principles should be employed in government."[22] Business conservatism thus influenced gubernatorial economic concerns as it had never had, even in the business-oriented 1920s.

Such an economic philosophy meant that efforts to relieve the plight of unemployed Floridians had to be put aside in order to restore the state to economic solvency. In his inaugural address, Sholtz called the state's activities a "business," and asserted that in seeking to manage the state's affairs he would ask three things: "1. Can the state afford it? 2. Does the state have the money to pay for it? 3. Can the state get along without it?"[23] None of the questions, of course, offered any real hope for the unemployed.

Sholtz commented subsequently that for Florida to recover from the depression its citizens had to be put to work. But then he added that "this relief work must be tapered off until it is halted entirely" and department heads should "skeletonize" their staffs.[24] The employment he had in mind would have to be provided by the federal government.

Sholtz did work closely with President Franklin Roosevelt to bring New Deal funds into the state and, in this fashion, restored a measure of prosperity. Nearly $58 million in federal funds was pumped into Florida by 1935. The New Deal monies and programs reduced relief rolls from 16,000 in 1933 to 4,000 in 1935. In Sholtz' final report to the people of Florida, he thanked the president and his administration which, he said, had substituted "food for words, work for idleness, hope instead of despair." He pointed out that the New Deal had cared for the unemployed by "sending millions upon millions of dollars into our state for that purpose without the matching of a single dollar by the state." Because Florida failed to contribute to the relief effort at all, its unemployed received an average of only $10.80 a week as compared to an average of $44.61 in New York where the state contributed 40 percent of the relief effort.[25]

In addition to the New Deal, the poor and unemployed in Florida were also aided by the creation of the State Board of Public Welfare which did away with Florida's antiquated "poor laws" and provided Floridians with a measure of welfare assistance. Sholtz' administration also facilitated their lot by providing free school textbooks and workmen's compensation for accidents. Although unsuccessful, Sholtz did push for increased expenditures for public welfare.[26]

Unlike Sholtz, Fred Cone was not an admirer of the New Deal, particularly its economic policies. He proposed to reduce the state budget back to the 1934 level. He characterized the growth in state departments as "astounding and rotten," and recommended a spending cut of $9 million. He also refused to provide state matching funds for federal programs to revitalize old and add new facilities at state institutions. The legislature, however, passed a $7.3 million budget with an increase of $800,000 going largely to schools, but not before Cone had vetoed 154 appropriations

TABLE 7.1. Florida's Federal Aid and State Receipts, 1920–48 ($)

Fiscal year	Federal aid	Other receipts	Total state receipts
1920	393,770	8,453,063	8,846,833
1925	1,336,759	28,621,631	29,958,390
1930	998,326	41,392,172	42,390,498
1934	5,751,586	29,181,068	34,932,654
1935	3,253,098	33,340,816	36,593,914
1936	2,859,979	41,272,740	44,132,719
1937	2,655,209	45,861,448	48,516,657
1938	5,626,989	48,041,453	53,668,442
1939	7,668,903	54,139,310	61,808,213
1940	12,244,870	56,296,250	68,541,120
1941	13,856,028	62,286,071	76,142,099
1942	17,303,884	65,674,359	82,978,243
1943	14,277,396	54,183,969	68,461,365
1944	17,781,805	71,229,445	89,011,250
1945	17,709,073	73,468,887	91,177,960
1948			217,000,000

SOURCE: *A Survey of Florida Tax Conditions with Recommendations for Improvement by the Florida Taxpayers Association, Inc.,* Research Staff, 1947, in P.K. Yonge Library of Florida History, University of Florida, Gainesville.

bills—three times more than any other governor. To Cone's credit he opposed any additional taxing of the poor.[27] Despite his dislike of the New Deal, he also accepted federal aid to Florida which kept the state solvent during the mid and late 1930s (see Table 7.1). The depression, in addition to the many problems it created, also accelerated an inequitable fiscal trend in Florida, one that has persisted to the present. In 1935 over one-half of the state's income (50.98 percent) came from excise taxes on such items as gasoline, beverages, and cigarettes.[28] Efforts to tax Floridians on their ability to pay never won gubernatorial approval during this period despite the example set by the New Deal.

The depression placed another fiscal burden on Florida. As was the case in California, many of the nation's unemployed migrated to Florida looking for work on farms and in citrus groves, and for a warm, sunny climate. Much like California, Florida showed little concern for the plight of these migrants. Governor Sholtz declared that Florida was not responsible for these transients and was "making every effort to keep out of the state those for whom we are not responsible." Doyle Carlton and Fred Cone endorsed Sholtz' view.[29]

World War II brought recovery to Florida as it did to the rest of the nation. The savings of individual Floridians almost tripled during the war and immediate postwar era, and for the first time in the state's history Floridians knew real prosperity.[30] Government employment and federal expenditures to improve the highway program, construct army and naval bases, and build coastal defenses particularly helped spur the state forward.

Wartime governor Spessard Holland emphasized a stabilization in state finances during this period of uncertainty, putting the road debt on a sound basis and refinancing and retiring the Everglades drainage debt. To assist Florida in preparing for the postwar period, Holland commissioned the Brookings Institution in Washington, D.C. to evaluate the state's financial condition. The institution's report suggested that Florida adopt a uniform and fair tax assessment, a strict and equitable collection of taxes, elimination of homestead tax abuses, a new tangible personal property tax, and creation of the office of state tax commissioner to act as referee between county officials and property owners.[31] The tax commissionership was established as part of the comptroller's office. Because of the war, however, the legislature decided to forego the remaining recommendations and Florida found itself fiscally unprepared to deal with the tremendous growth it experienced after the war.

Millard Caldwell, Florida's postwar governor, was a vigorous practitioner of conservative government and labeled his inaugural address a "report to the stockholders on our business of state government." Nevertheless, Caldwell was a strong supporter of a more equitable tax program. Specifically, he opposed the adoption of a sales tax and urged the creation of a tax study committee. He also persuaded the legislature to fund the state public school system through a Minimum Foundation Program.[32] This act helped alleviate the severe deterioration of the public school system, and, ultimately, provided Florida with a respectable school program.

Fuller Warren, elected in 1945, continued Caldwell's support of education and, in particular, his effort to equalize the tax burden. Faced with an empty treasury resulting from fiscal pressures on the state caused by rapid postwar population growth, and committed by his campaign pledge to veto any general sales tax, Warren, with the assistance of University of Florida economist Clement Donovan, prepared a radically progressive tax program.

Warren's budget proposed taxes on private utilities, the phosphate and petroleum industries, insurance companies, banks, small loan companies, and corporation charters.[33] The recommendations were, in fact, close to

Warren's political philosophy. If Warren was not himself a populist, he nevertheless was in sympathy with many populist programs. In his message to the legislature, he had declared: "The soundest and fairest of all principles of taxation is that taxes should be levied according to the ability to pay. That principle has not been followed in Florida."[34] Indeed, as he had previously noted, Florida's businesses paid only 11 percent of Florida's total taxable income in 1948 as compared with a national average of 18.3 percent, while Florida's consumers paid 77.4 percent against an average of 55.1 percent in the nation as a whole.

The proposed revenue package would correct these imbalances and implement Warren's view that previously untapped sources of revenue should carry their share of the burden. Politically, however, the tax package was a disaster. The breadth of the tax recommendations alienated nearly all entrenched economic interests in the state. The proposed taxes on phosphates, banks, petroleum, forest products, and tourists, for instance, drew the ire of the representatives whose counties depended on one or more of these enterprises. The tax package was so hastily and poorly prepared that some of the most important levies did not appear in the bill before the legislature. Warren was ultimately forced to abandon his fiscal proposals and accept, instead, a sales tax of 3 percent, giving Florida the highest rate in the nation at the time. The passage of the sales tax represented a victory for one of the most influential men in Florida—Ed Ball, trustee of the billion dollar Du Pont estate in Florida. In 1935 a Du Pont employee who sat in the legislature introduced the first sales tax bill only to have it defeated by a mere five votes. A move to pass an income tax, which Ball opposed vigorously, never got out of committee. Ball regarded the income tax as potentially devastating for the vast Du Pont fortune in Florida and favored the sales tax as a way to stymie the drive for an income tax. Ball had won a similar victory ten years earlier when the state voted to repeal its power to levy taxes. The law was adopted by a statewide referendum with Ball mobilizing the Du Pont estate fully behind the measure.[35] Warren's defeat on this program appears to have set back the forces of fiscal reform for some time. No such fiscal reform package was presented to the legislature again until the inauguration of Reubin Askew in 1971.

In part this reflected the conservative, probusiness outlook of the governors who were elected after 1952. Fiscal conservatism was also one of the few areas of agreement between the conservative, rural, pork-chop legislator and the urban, business-oriented legislator. Perhaps even more importantly, Floridians were also basking for the first time in an era of steady economic growth and were, consequently, opposed to new taxes. Not insignificantly, Florida's sales tax and other taxes provided the state with sufficient money in this period due to the tremendous growth in population and tourism. No new taxes were deemed necessary and fiscal reform was simply overlooked.

Florida's tremendous growth throughout the 1950s (the population increased by over two million), and the upsurge of its tourist industry, brought a new wealth to the state. It also resulted in increased demands on state and local government to meet the economic, social, and educational needs of these people.

Governor Collins urged the legislature to reorganize its fiscal programs to meet the increasing demands on the state and county governments. He proposed a consolidation of major tax collecting functions in a new division of revenues. The revenue division would be part of the cabinet with separate budgeting, auditing, and central purchasing power.[36] Collins' plan was defeated by the pork-chop delegation in the legislature who were committed to retaining budgetary controls in their hands.

Collins was able during his term of office to increase greatly spending for educational programs. During his term such expenditures grew by over 8 percent to 62.25 percent of the budget. However, Collins' administration, fiscally conservative like those of his predecessors, failed to meet the needs of the lower class during this period. State aid for public welfare was reduced by nearly 3 percent to 7.89 percent of state expenditures.[37]

The decade of the 1960s brought to the governor's office men who had substantial campaign support from the business community, who sought to protect their constituents' interests, and who had been businessmen themselves. As a result, they had very conservative fiscal policies. Governor Farris Bryant, for example, greatly expanded the highway program and conducted a very active advertising program for the tourist industry, both of which offered benefits for the businessman. He also resisted the national trend to provide funds for slum clearance and urban renewal, and opposed the use of federal funds for education. In his tax program, he ignored the inequities in the existing system and urged an extension of the 3 percent sales tax. As he put it: "I am just as conservative and economical as I always was. I don't want a wild spending spree."[38] Bryant did, however, expand the state university and community college system begun by Collins, but the funds went largely into building construction.

Haydon Burns, who served a brief two-year term as governor but was eligible for reelection, held the line on taxes so as not to offend any voters, but he willingly supported a legislative appropriation package which went over $1 billion dollars for the first time in the state's history. Following Bryant's lead, Burns also pursued an ambitious road program which would have bonded the state for $300 million. The plan, however, was rejected by nearly 150,000 votes.[39]

Having nearly the same constituency as Bryant and Burns, Claude Kirk announced on taking office that he would "operate state government without new taxes."[40] He made no effort to improve the regressive tax structure and retained his predecessors' commitment to programs designed to help the business community. During his last year in office, sales tax revenues amounted to over 60 percent of state income, and beverage and cigarette taxes were the major sources of revenue. All three men were among the most conservative and probusiness governors Florida has elected in this century. All were self-made men and were heavily influenced by their own pasts. Bryant and Kirk had been very successful in the business world before seeking the governorship. Burns was closely affiliated with Ed Ball and the Du Pont interests in Jacksonville. In addition, Burns had great admiration for the business community and its role in making Jacksonville a modern metropolis.

Governor David Sholtz (center) riding with President Franklin D. Roosevelt and Jacksonville Mayor John T. Alsop. Sholtz liked Roosevelt, and while he disagreed with many of the president's policies he was happy to receive New Deal programs and funds during the bleakest days of the depression. Such federal funding made it possible for Florida to meet its bills and provide a few welfare programs. State Photographic Archives.

By the end of the 1960s Florida had grown to seven million people and the wealth of the populace had increased by over $11 billion from 1965 to 1970 (up from $14 billion to $25 billion). The dramatic change in the state's socioeconomic picture also brought a change in its gubernatorial leadership. Reubin Askew, who had been elected on a reform platform, announced at his inaugural that he would urge the legislature to adopt a corporate profits tax, close tax loopholes, and veto any increase in what he characterized as a "regressive sales tax." In his legislative address, he reiterated his support for these issues and also called for a severance tax on phosphates. Despite the tremendous profits made by this industry, it had never paid one dollar in taxes. He also endorsed a one cent increase in the sales tax: "For too long, Florida has given special breaks and favors to the politically influential."[41]

The severance tax on phosphates had been debated in the legislature for many years and had been routinely defeated. For sixteen years the measure had failed to reach the floor of the senate despite the efforts of Senator J. Emory Cross of Gainesville. During this period no governor endorsed the tax and most opposed it. Claude Kirk, for example, had been elected with the support of the phosphate interests and he personally opposed such a plan.

Askew's election in 1970 once again revived interest in the plan. He presented his tax proposal to the 1971 legislative session, calling for a 5 percent tax on the gross sales value at the point of production and allotting a 20 percent credit for land reclamation. The industry proposed a 100 percent credit for land reclamation. After two months of discussion the legislature agreed to a 5 percent tax with the industry receiving 50 percent for land reclamation of old mines and 25 percent for new mines.[42]

The enactment of a corporate income tax proved to be a more difficult task. The legislature met in special session in January 1971, to remedy the projected $250 million deficit facing the state. Both houses approved the corporate tax proposal but not by the necessary three-fourths vote to permit a special election in the fall. As a consequence, the referendum would not be submitted to the voters before November 1972. Between the January session and the regular April session, support mobilized for a special election in the fall on the corporate tax plan. On May 4 the legislature agreed to the proposal and the election was set for November 2.

Askew immediately named a 42-member blue-ribbon committee to lead the fight for ratification. Ben Hill Griffin was its chairman, and several prominent businessmen were members. Askew's proposal had been vigorously opposed in the legislature by Associated Industries, an organization of businessmen led by Ed Ball of the Du Pont corporation in Florida and the Davis brothers of Winn-Dixie Stores. Amply endowed by its membership, Associated Industries continued its campaign against the tax, alleging, among other things, that ratification of the corporate tax would lead eventually to the adoption of a personal income tax and would restrict business development.[43]

Relying heavily on his own personal popularity with the public and the failure of corporations to pay their fair share, Askew spoke throughout the state about the reasonableness of this plan. He argued that "Florida imposed the fifth highest level of taxes on small businessmen in the country, but large corporations were taxed at an average of $.27 per $1,000 of income, whereas the national average was $6.51 per $1,000 of income." Askew concluded from these figures "that large corporations were not paying their fair share of taxes in the State of Florida." A state economist noted that only two other states did not have corporate income taxes—Ohio and Texas. Both, however, forced the corporations to contribute to the state treasury through stiff franchise or net worth taxes. Florida, on the other hand, required corporations to pay a corporate stock tax which amounted to only 0.5 percent of state revenues as compared to the 6.7 percent in Ohio and 5.7 percent in Texas. Ably assisted by Ben Hill Griffin and his committee, the governor's proposal scored a resounding victory in the fall elections; 816,642 votes were cast for the referendum as opposed to 337,217 votes against.[44]

While the adoption of the corporate and severance taxes removed two of the worst inequities in the tax structure, Florida remains a state whose taxation policies are designed to increase population, tourism, and industry. Nearly fifty-seven cents of each state dollar comes from the sales tax today compared to a national average of twenty-nine cents. At the end of 1973 the corporation tax contributed only 8 percent of the state revenues as opposed to nearly 9 percent for the beverage tax, while the severance tax generated a mere $5 million.[45]

Askew was slow to urge additional fiscal reforms because of the severe inflation in 1973 and 1974 followed by the recession of 1975. The governor and his aides were reluctant to make any changes that might further undermine business confidence during those troubled economic times. Another reason appears to be Askew's basic fiscal conservatism. He opposed a personal income tax and encouraged a reduction in county property taxes from 10 to 8 mills.[46] Finally an increasingly independent and conservative legislature refused to consider any new taxes, let alone fiscal reform. Legislative attention during the post-1975 period has been confined principally to tax exemptions as a way to attract new industry into the state.

LABOR UNION MOVEMENT

The economic and fiscal conservatism of Florida's governors also has adversely affected the labor union movement in the state. Organized labor and Florida governors have not enjoyed an especially good relationship during this century. In part, this reflected the nature of the Florida economy. As a primarily agricultural state throughout most of the century, and with many workers in the service sector of the economy, Florida has never had a large number of blue collar workers. Among all the states, Florida ranks last in industrial development and percent of workers in unions.

In political terms, the absence of large numbers of workers and the inability of labor unions to establish strong bases of statewide support have worked against labor's having a strong input into Florida politics. In addition, Florida's governors have generally discouraged a viable union movement in an effort to make the state more attractive to northern industry.

In 1939, for example, Fred Cone vetoed a bill setting up a state Department of Labor. Cone objected to the expense involved and also claimed that the department's functions were being adequately performed by other agencies. More revealingly, however, Cone pointed out that under the terms of the bill the state president of the American Federation of Labor would become a member of the department, and Cone opposed this because the president would not be accountable to the public.[47] The governor failed to make a similar argument about appointing representatives of the citrus industry to the Citrus Commission.

The lack of gubernatorial support for the labor movement was most clearly enunciated by Millard Caldwell during an organizing effort by the AFL-CIO in Florida. Caldwell regarded these union efforts as "the kind of Northern intrusion the South has often observed in the past." He added that he felt it was of the same order as the North trying to tell the South how to handle its race problem.[48]

The state's labor unions have also encountered almost uniform opposition from the governor's office during strikes. In April 1908, for instance, a strike by streetcar workers in Pensacola dissolved into a series of riots when the company tried to bring in strikebreakers. At the request of Mayor C. C. Goodman, Napoleon Broward sent in a detachment of state militiamen on April 11. While the state troopers restored calm, they also undermined the workers' cause by protecting the strikebreakers and the owners' property. Broward also forced the mayor to revoke a rally-holding permit which he had granted to the unions.[49]

During an often violent cigar-makers strike in Tampa in 1910 and 1911, Governor Albert Gilchrist visited the city and met with business leaders and strikers. The workers were protesting discriminatory wages and were demanding a closed shop in the cigar industry to protect their interests. Management was supported by the business and professional elite of Tampa, who formed a citizens committee. This committee directed the efforts to sabotage the strike, often relying on violent methods. After listening to both sides, Gilchrist blamed the strikers for the violence and praised the city leaders for their efforts to end the labor difficulties.[50]

Spessard Holland took a more militant antilabor stance during World War II. When factories in Tampa reported that a labor shortage of 1,750 men was hampering production despite the availability of 1,500 ablebodied workers in the area, Holland proposed that housing authorities expel all workers from public housing if they refused regular work. He also suggested that the police "persuade" loafers to return to work "or to leave town" to make room for others.[51]

In 1968, Claude Kirk was faced with a statewide walkout of teachers, which proved to be one of the nation's most important examples of teacher militancy.[52] Traditionally among the most docile of public employees, by the mid-1960s teachers were organizing and seeking bargaining rights through their professional associations, generally either the National Education Association (NEA) or AFL-CIO affiliated union, the American Federation of Teachers (AFT). In Florida, the NEA-affiliated Florida Education Association

(FEA) had publicly criticized the poor quality of the state's schools through-out the 1960s, and by 1967 was calling for an increase in state taxes to provide additional support for education. The FEA's demands were echoed by Superintendent of Public Instruction Floyd Christian.

The governor's response, however, was to deplore the FEA's "fear tactics" and "coercion and rattling of sabres." During the regular 1967 legislative session he not only opposed increased taxes for schools but actually called for a cut in educational expenditures. Teachers and other state officials were furious, and criticized Kirk sharply. The FEA publicly censured him, and by early June the NEA had invoked sanctions against Florida and urged teachers to boycott the state's schools.[53]

Kirk and the FEA continued to trade charges, and it was only in 1968, after the governor-appointed Commission for Quality Education recommended massive increases in aid to schools and higher teacher salaries, that he agreed to call a special legislative session. Teachers were very disappointed in the results, however, especially the small pay raise and the Kirk-backed bill linking tax increases for schools with a popular referendum. Confident that the crisis was over, the governor left for California in pursuit of the 1968 Republican vice-presidential nomination.[54]

The FEA, however, rejected the education proposals and called for a statewide teacher walkout beginning February 19, 1968. At first Kirk refused to negotiate with teachers or even suspend his political campaign: "We in Florida do not plan to turn over education to a union—it is un-American to turn education over to the union." But the walkout was effective and lasted three weeks. Kirk eventually was forced by public pressure to negotiate with the teachers, and after another special legislative session he allowed a $310 million tax package to become law. The governor's recalcitrance in dealing with the teachers had fostered hostility and distrust among state educators and had encouraged rather than discouraged support for a strike.[55]

Only Sidney Catts, Fuller Warren, and Reubin Askew endorsed the labor union movement in Florida. Sidney Catts had sought labor's backing during his campaign and had been elected with considerable labor support in 1916. Throughout his four years in office he proved to be a consistent supporter of organized labor's efforts in the state. During a strike by the city firemen and communication workers over layoffs in Jacksonville in the summer of 1919, Catts pledged to workers that he would fight against the "absolute monarchy and autocracy" of the city commission whose members were trying to coerce the workers into giving up the strike. Personally addressing workers in Jacksonville he assured them that they had his backing and urged them to continue to obey the law.[56]

Catts also became deeply involved in a violent strike by phosphate workers. According to Catts' biographer, the War Labor Board had investigated charges of labor exploitation by companies in Polk and Hillsborough counties and had endorsed a shorter workday and the right of collective bargaining.[57] Counsel for the phosphate industry, Peter O. Knight, had rejected the recommendations. Nearly 3,500 miners walked off their jobs in April 1919. The strike was marked by violence; several workers and bystanders were murdered by company guards. Catts toured the strike area during the summer, expressing his support for the miners. On July 14 he addressed a meeting of two thousand workers in Tampa and threatened phosphate owners with suspension of their charters for defying the will of the legislature and governor. He promised to have Attorney General Swearingen

Governor Albert Gilchrist (seated, center) meeting with the staff of the Florida National Guard. Gilchrist made active use of the guard for strike-breaking during his years in office. The guard proved to be of great benefit to business leaders who were trying to break such strikes. State Photographic Archives.

investigate the actions of the owners. Catts became further embroiled in the conflict when he mobilized the Gainesville National Guard and stationed it in Mulberry, which was located in the center of the strike area. In August he removed Polk County Sheriff Logan after miners complained he was supporting the owners and could not maintain order.

J. M. Langford, chosen by Catts to replace Logan, was more cooperative and sympathetic to strikers. Langford informed the companies privately that if they would cooperate with him as much as the strikers, he could maintain order and peace. When the violence continued, local leaders demanded that soldiers be sent, but Catts refused after Major John Crary of the National Guard told the governor that the trouble was caused by guards who were shooting to prolong the trouble and thereby preserve their jobs. Under increasing political and public pressure, Catts finally restored Logan as sheriff and renounced the affair.[58]

During his governorship Catts also supported such worker-related bills as workmen's compensation, reform to prevent child labor abuse in industry, the establishment of a Bureau of Labor, vocational education, and a laborer's lien bill. All these measures were defeated by the legislature in that antilabor era.[59]

Recipient of the labor vote in 1948, Fuller Warren encouraged the growth of labor unions in the private sector and generally defended their viewpoint in the state. During a walkout by Tampa bus drivers in 1949, Warren ridiculed the company's settlement offer: "three cents reminds me of a penny tip I was offered many years ago when I was a bellboy." He supported the drivers' demands for an eight-hour day and a twenty-five cent per hour pay raise, and he generally praised their conduct during the strike. However, when the strike appeared to threaten Tampa's economy during the Christmas season, Warren encouraged the workers to return to work in exchange for his support during mediation. Reubin Askew strongly endorsed union representation for public employees and urged its establishment in his fourth year of office.[60] Despite Askew's endorsement of labor unions in principle, the majority of legislators and voters still regard labor representation for public and private employees in Florida as an issue to be avoided.

While Catts, Warren, and Askew appealed to and received the support of labor in their gubernatorial campaigns and in turn supported labor during their governorships, neither man pressed for the repeal of right-to-work laws. The power of the business community and the conservative set of beliefs governing state politics have not permitted any Florida governor to make such proposals. In addition, it is doubtful that any of these governors was sufficiently committed to the union cause to press for such a change.

TOURISM AND TRANSPORTATION

In contrast to the labor union movement, tourism and transportation have been two sectors of special interest to twentieth-century governors because they help to underwrite the economy of the state and because they provide governors with patronage positions. Tourism is also important in another sense—it helps to highlight one of the governor's symbolic roles. Throughout this century and particularly since World War II, Florida governors have frequently acted as ambassadors and salesmen for the state's tourist industry.

The entire state is heavily dependent on the tourist industry; it is a major source of revenue, bringing in over $6 billion per year in 1973–74.[61] Thus, an off year in this industry can severely affect state resources. The road construction industry has been a lucrative economic venture for private construction companies since 1920. The Hotel and Restaurant Commission and the State Road Department (the Department of Transportation as of 1967) are the principal state agencies that regulate these two industries. They have also been used traditionally by governors to provide jobs for friends and political supporters.

Throughout the twentieth century, every governor has conducted an advertising campaign, either personally or through various state agencies, to bring people to Florida. One of the earliest and most vigorous promoters of Florida was Governor Albert Waller Gilchrist. He traveled throughout the North praising the state before such organizations as the Tammany Society and the Alaska-Yukon Exposition. He also made a practice of writing three letters a month to newspapers in other states telling their readers about the beneficial aspects of living in or visiting the state. In a letter to *The Chicago Examiner* entitled "Florida the Marvelous," he described the "beautiful, salubrious climate, and good fertile earth."[62]

This praise, indeed almost worship, of the state's climate was echoed throughout the century. The newspapers seemed to take an almost fiendish delight in showing pictures of blizzards in the North while Florida enjoyed a heat wave. Although more exaggerated than most, Governor Doyle Carlton's statement that Florida's "climate . . . is the dream of multitudes" was generally accepted by other governors.[63] In 1925 the legislature appropriated $50,000 to the commissioner of agriculture to use in attracting tourists. Advertising was also implemented by the Hotel Commission, which had been established in 1913.

Every governor has taken part in this ambassadorial effort to attract more tourists and business to Florida. Some, like LeRoy Collins, Farris Bryant, Haydon Burns, Claude Kirk, and Reubin Askew, have journeyed to Latin America, Europe, and Japan. Others, like Sholtz and Gilchrist, have confined their travels to the northern United States. Because of the importance of tourism to the state's financial well-being, it has been taken very seriously by governors. John Martin, for example, called on the Chambers of Commerce to cooperate with him to stop the "robbery" of motorists through traffic fines. David Sholtz condemned the high prices that tourists were charged in Florida and warned that the industry could be crippled if such gouging continued. The extent of gubernatorial interest in and scrutiny of the tourist trade was made clear by Mrs. Spessard Holland's drive to provide for clean restrooms in filling stations and in bus and railroad depots.[64]

Of all the governors, Fuller Warren was the most adept at selling Florida to the nation. A man of great vitality and gusto, he genuinely enjoyed speaking to large crowds and telling them about the advantages of Florida. He coordinated a year-round advertising program during which he traveled around the country speaking about Florida and sending crates of Florida citrus to each of the other forty-seven governors. Even road construction was planned to encourage tourism. Warren once remarked that we "design every project with tourist traffic in mind."[65]

Warren's comment lent credence to the accusation leveled by certain cities that Florida would go to any lengths to attract tourists. There was a measure of truth to this charge; in 1935, for example, the legislature adopted a ninety-day divorce law, reducing the divorce residency requirements from one year. The express purpose of the act was to win the lucrative divorce trade away from Arkansas and Nevada.[66] The more traditional approach, however, has been the practice of the Advertising Commission (now the Development Commission) to buy space in northern newspapers during the winter and show pictures of lovely, tanned young ladies enjoying the sun and beautiful beaches of Florida. As advertising became more sophisticated, most governors realized that Florida's climate and physical environment would sell themselves and bizarre laws and madcap advertising simply were not necessary.

Governors continued to promote Florida's tourist industry, however, and to seek out companies which would facilitate its growth. Governor Haydon Burns worked closely with the Disney Corporation in its effort to acquire land secretly in the Kissimmee area. Burns' administration also agreed to divert $5 million over five years from the highway fund to build roads around the planned Disney complex. Fifty million dollars in primary road funds were also designated for the Orlando area. Burns regarded the location of this attraction in Florida as a potential economic bonanza to the state. The economic ramifications of Disney World, however, exceeded even his administration's optimistic forecasts. From 1969 to 1970, before Disney World opened, to 1971–72, restaurant income in the ten-county area surrounding the complex climbed by 39 percent, hotel and apartment income by 40 percent, amusement admissions by 93 percent, and variety store sales by 61 percent. In addition, $470 million was spent in new hotel and motel construction and 160,000 jobs were created indirectly by the Disney complex.[67]

To facilitate the state's tourist business and its growth, the governors placed great stock in the road program. The chief executive did not play an important role in the road program until 1915. In that year the legislature, at the request of Governor Park Trammell, established the State Road Department composed of five board members appointed by the governor with the chairman elected by the membership. Four of the board members came from the four congressional districts in Florida and one at large. Initially, the Road Department merely acted as a source of information for the counties which designed and built the roads. However, in 1917 the legislature decided to enlarge the powers of the department, permitting it to authorize construction and maintenance of a system of state and state-aided roads. Momentum for this change had been provided by Congress' adoption of the Federal Aid

Road Act in 1916 which laid the foundation for the cooperative Federal-State Highway Program. Funds for state roads initially came from the General Revenue Fund. In 1923 the legislature adopted a three cent gasoline tax to fund road building with two cents going to the state road department and the other penny going to the counties on an equal basis.[68]

With the money generated by this increased gasoline tax, Governor John Martin directed a substantial increase in road construction during the twenties. Martin had promised during his campaign "to build roads from one end of the state to the other, before the people now living are in the cemetery."[69] Martin saw the new roads as an important way to attract new industry and additional tourists. The northern press had been particularly critical of Florida's poor roads and had repeatedly warned motorists of this danger to their lives and property.

The major thrust was provided by the adoption of the Federal Highway Act of 1956. Florida had 1,164 miles of the planned 41,000 mile highway program. Under this program Florida's federal road funds increased substantially, moving the state from thirty-eighth in federal funding to eleventh in 1958. The road department also benefited by Governor Collins' implementation of the merit system. In January 1956, Collins ordered that 4,626 employees of the road department be placed under the Florida merit system and that their replacements be hired on a nonpartisan, competitive examination basis.[70]

A fundamental change in Florida's approach to road construction did not occur until Haydon Burns' administration. Burns had decided in 1964 to make a $300 million road bond issue the heart of his legislative program. He also planned to use the measure to gain legislative and public support for his 1966 reelection bid. Immediately, however, the proposal ran into difficulty. Legislative leaders called it one of the worst-written bills they had ever encountered. This charge added weight to allegations made during the gubernatorial campaign that Burns lacked the political experience to be an effective governor. More importantly, however, legislators resented Burns' use of the road board and members of the little cabinet as lobbyists in the legislative corridors and back rooms. Senator D. D. Covington of Dade City said two road board members told him his district would not receive any new roads if he opposed the plan. Senator Ed Price of Bradenton characterized Burns' efforts as "the worst example of power lobbying by a governor I have ever seen. . . ." Nevertheless, Burns was able to garner enough votes for his bill but only after he agreed to submit the measure to the voters as a constitutional amendment. The *Tampa Tribune* reported he had secured Senator George Tapper's vote by agreeing to four-lane highway 98 in Tapper's district and suggested much of the bill's support had come in this fashion.[71]

Despite the bill's passage its implementation was by no means assured. It

Before modern highway motels were built, tourist camps, like the one pictured here, sprang up all over Florida. This "Tin Can Tourist Camp" located in or near Gainesville dates from the time of World War I, when traveling became more popular and automobiles more numerous. Tourism became a major economic factor in Florida during this era and contributed greatly to the development of South Florida. State Photographic Archives.

still needed the voters' approval in November, and a powerful block of legislators led by Senators Lawton Chiles, John McCarty, Reubin Askew, and Representative Ralph Turlington in coalition with several major newspapers, the *Tampa Tribune, St. Petersburg Times,* and *Miami Herald,* declared their opposition to the plan. Generally they characterized it as an enormous barrel of pork which Burns planned to use to win reelection, and a nice but hardly necessary construction program. The *Tribune* also argued that no emergency existed in the state's highway system since the money had been appropriated for the extension of the Sunshine Parkway and the four-laning of 500 miles of other roads out of current revenues.[72]

Burns tried to counter their opposition by personally leading the campaign for the road measure and hiring W. Howard Frankland as coordinator. Frankland, a former vice-chairman of the road board, was a native of Tampa where opposition to the plan was most intense. Burns hoped Frankland's appointment would generate enthusiasm for the plan in the area.[73] It did not.

Although Burns was a diligent campaigner, he was not a very effective speaker nor was he a personally magnetic figure. As a consequence, he was unable to overcome the arguments of the opposition and to convince voters of the program's importance. The plan and Burns' reelection hopes were dashed by a vote of 421,644 to 272,300.[74]

Despite the manipulation and periodic graft and corruption that have plagued the road department, it has still managed to build one of the most impressive interstate and intrastate road systems in the country, and often under some of the worst conditions. The Tamiami Trail, which extends across the Everglades from Miami to the Gulf coast, and the bridges from Miami to Key West are only two of many projects which were built under incredibly adverse conditions. In addition, the road department has helped underwrite one of the cornerstones of the state's economy, the construction industry. Its importance in this area has most recently been acknowledged by Governor Askew who, in his 1976 legislative program, opposed any tax increases except on gasoline so that his highway program could be completed and the depressed construction business revitalized.[75]

Tourism and highway construction remain important to the governor because they still permit him to reward his supporters through jobs and contracts; he has more control over these than any other areas in state government, and they are still very important to the state's economic vitality. The governor's role in selling Florida's tourist industry remains a significant part of the chief executive office. It may seem like a trivial duty but the state's economy is so dependent on this industry, as was evidenced during the 1974 recession, that the governor is obligated by the public to assist the promotional effort. The manipulation of the road department declined under Reubin Askew's leadership and will probably continue to do so during the post-Watergate era with voters demanding increased government accountability and with a Government in the Sunshine law. Nevertheless, because the chief executive needs patronage to facilitate his election and to meet his campaign promises, the road program will continue to fulfill, to some degree, the individual needs and promises of each governor.

ENVIRONMENT

During this century conservation of Florida's natural resources and, in recent years, protection of the environment have been closely associated with efforts to develop the state's economy. From the first decade, Floridians were aware that drainage of the Everglades and preservation of water supplies were vital elements in the state's growth. Not insignificantly, the state's resources in the early twentieth century were insufficient to accomplish these goals. By the late 1960s concerns with conservation shifted toward ecological issues. During this period tensions both in Florida and throughout the nation arose between those favoring rapid and essentially unregulated expansion of the economy and those who felt this seemingly unlimited and unregulated growth might ultimately pollute water, land, and air to such an extent that life would be imperiled. In Florida, as elsewhere, governors were called upon to resolve these issues.

Environmental issues have always been of special significance in Florida where almost one-third of the land is below water. The southern section of the state had been virtually uninhabitable for most of Florida's history due to the floodwaters of Lake Okeechobee. The second largest lake in the United States, Lake Okeechobee was 22 feet above sea level and overflowed its banks annually, turning more than 4 million acres into marshland. The problem was how to drain this land for settlement and keep the 730 square mile lake from overflowing. As the population grew in size during the late ninteenth century, the Everglades drainage issue became increasingly more important.

Drainage of these areas had first been proposed in 1838 by General Thomas S. Jesup, who was in Florida fighting the Seminole Indians. Jesup reported that the lands were exceedingly rich and he recommended that they be drained and reclaimed. An 1848 report by Buckingham Smith, a St. Augustine lawyer and Florida historian, to the United States Senate discussed the feasibility of draining the Everglades.[76]

In 1855 Governor James Broome approved a legislative act establishing the Board of Trustees of the Internal Improvement Fund of Florida. The act consolidated all lands in this area and placed them under the control of the governor, comptroller, treasurer, attorney general, and register of state lands. There was no activity on the drainage issue, however, until Governor Bloxham's first administration in 1881, when Hamilton Disston, a wealthy tool manufacturer from Philadelphia, agreed to drain and reclaim land in certain areas. Disston had built only twenty miles of canal when he was forced by a shortage of funds to abandon the project.[77] There was no further construction for another twenty years.

In 1900, under the leadership of Governor William Sherman Jennings, interest in the project was revived, and the state became actively involved in the planning effort. One of the major difficulties in the way of reclamation had been the confusion over land titles. In 1897 the Interior Department had revoked Florida's right to 2,942,000 acres of land "because it was thought to impinge upon the rights and interests of the Seminole Tribes." One of Governor Jennings' major accomplishments was to encourage Washington to turn over almost 3 million acres to the state.[78]

In his 1903 message to the legislature Jennings urged legislative funding for the drainage effort. He also traced the history of the Everglades and made special reference to the benefits of reclamation, especially the richness of the land for farming. Jennings' message was an educational tour de force on the Lake Okeechobee area, complete with maps, charts, and drawings. He made special reference to the loss in state income from the destruction of crops by flooding.[79]

Jennings also facilitated the drainage project by hiring Charles G. Elliott, a drainage engineer for the United States Department of Agriculture, to research the feasibility of drainage and reclamation south of Lake Okeechobee. Elliott reported that canals dredged to a depth of 0.3 to 0.4 feet per mile from the lake to the coast would permit adequate drainage.[80] Although no actual drainage or reclamation took place during the Jennings years, he was responsible for reviving interest in the project and for educating the public and legislature to the benefits to be derived from an Everglades drainage program.

Jennings' successor, Napoleon Broward, had campaigned on a platform calling for a state drainage program. In the 1905 special session of the legislature, Broward pointed out that "at a comparatively small expense the . . . region can be entirely reclaimed, thus opening to the habitation of man an immense and hitherto unexplored domain perhaps not surpassed in fertility and every natural advantage by any other on the globe." He then explained in careful detail how and where the drainage canals could be built. The clarity and thoroughness of Broward's presentation convinced legislators of the wisdom of such a plan. They passed the first comprehensive law establishing a Board of Drainage Commissioners to oversee the construction of drainage and reclamation. The money for the plan came from an acreage tax of 5–10 percent per acre to be assessed on the lands in the drainage district. The proposal was designed to raise $200,000 a year. Money was also raised through the sale of reclaimed lands. Broward estimated that it would cost $250,000 and take eighteen months to build one canal.[81]

The establishment of a permanent board of drainage commissioners was

Governor William Sherman Jennings and his father-in-law, Senator A. S. Mann, in a "Florida Automobile" about 1903. Jennings and Mann were returning from Daytona Beach to Tallahassee when they paused in St. Augustine to have this publicity photo taken. State Photographic Archives.

submitted to the voters in November 1906. Broward, who according to one man "sweats dope about the Everglades and drainage," campaigned throughout the state for the measure. He pointed out the richness of the land and its potential value to settlers. He also argued that the commissioners would protect the region from the railroad interests who were "out to steal the lands." Broward's proposal was bitterly attacked by representatives from the railroads and big business who sought to develop the land at their own convenience and for their profit. J. E. Ingraham, vice-president of the Florida East Coast railroad, called Broward's criticism of the railroads "unjust, unfair, and most undeserved." The *Florida Times-Union,* the leading spokesman for the business community, claimed that the proposal would foster a political dictatorship and lead eventually to "state liquor traffic and state insurance."[82] The governor would also have as a result enormous patronage at his disposal.

Bombarded by critical advertisements from railroads and business, the drainage amendment was defeated by five thousand votes. Despite the defeat, Broward promised to continue the fight: "They have beat me, but I am not through fighting yet . . . I will have another constitutional amendment offered at the next session of the legislature, and I will have some bills put through which will cause weeping and gnashing of teeth in certain quarters."[83]

True to his promise, Broward submitted a drainage proposal prepared by former Governor Jennings. Approved by sizeable majorities in both houses, the act established a board of drainage commissioners, determined a drainage district, and authorized a continuance of Everglades drainage and reclamation. It also continued the annual tax of 5 percent per acre and authorized use of this revenue for financing the drainage program.[84]

Drainage and reclamation proved to be slow and arduous during Broward's term of office. Only 13.2 miles of canal had been built by the end of his administration. Broward's contribution to the drainage project, like Jennings', however, went well beyond the physical construction of canals. Indeed, while Jennings reawakened the public's interest in the project, Broward convinced Floridians of the necessity of drainage. He had the unique ability to explain in detail the finer points of drainage and reclamation to legislators and experts, but he also could make the Everglades project very understandable to the average citizen. Broward told Floridians that several states had managed to restrain the Mississippi River and that the people of Holland had built dikes to hold back the ocean. The Everglades project, he commented, was insignificant by comparison. He was also able to counter the arguments of the railroad and business interests who wanted to control and direct the drainage program. Broward argued that to permit "the natural resources of a state to be needlessly or recklessly or willfully wasted would be to deprive the state and its citizens of the many advantages incident to proper use of such natural resources, even though they be the property of individual owners."[85]

After Broward left office he continued to fight for his drainage program and he made it a major issue in his United States Senate victory of 1912. His battle on behalf of the Everglades project and his widespread popularity among Florida voters made drainage a major political issue throughout the remainder of the decade and well into the 1920s despite the election of governors who lacked his enthusiasm and commitment to the project.

His successor, Albert Waller Gilchrist, for example, did not appear on the basis of his gubernatorial campaign to be a supporter of drainage. Gilchrist was elected with considerable support from the railroad and business community who favored private development of this land. As a result, it was expected that he would do little to facilitate the drainage program. However, he proved to be a strong defender of the project in the midst of a considerable controversy over whether it should be extended.

Gilchrist reported after assuming office that the costs of drainage were much higher than anticipated and that the state would need assistance from private contractors to complete the project. Another source of difficulty, he mentioned, was the large number of land companies selling unreclaimed land that they falsely alleged had been drained.[86]

Despite these problems, Gilchrist, reflecting the public's support of the drainage efforts, chose to expand the program during his governorship. He also defended drainage against its critics, at one point taking newspaper reporters on a tour through South Florida to show them and the public that progress was, indeed, being made and that the entire project was not just a boondoggle.[87]

Following the direction provided by Broward and Gilchrist, Governor Park Trammell's administration, which also lacked enough funds for the drainage project, proposed a plan to set up experimental farms to aid the state's agricultural industry and to increase the value of the Everglades lands. In addition, Trammell proposed the creation of local drainage districts to enable private landowners to cooperate in canal construction. His most ambitious proposal, however, sought to empower the Everglades Drainage District with authority to assess taxes, borrow money, and issue bonds. The legislature agreed to permit the commissioners to issue bonds up to $6 million. While World War I temporarily impeded the bonding arrangements, Trammell's program raised $3 million through the sale of bonds by 1917, and reclamation of some land became a reality over the next few years.[88]

During the tremendous land boom of the 1920s, the Everglades attracted numerous investors and settlers. By 1925, despite floods in 1922 and 1923 from heavy rains, there were nearly 25,000 people residing near this area. The collapse of the land boom the next year, however, set the area back severely and brought an end to the state's role in reclamation. By 1926 Florida's fiscal credit was so impaired that it could not provide financial assistance for further drainage. The two hurricanes in 1926 and 1928 destroyed what the land boom collapse failed to destroy. After the 1928 hurricane the federal government with a little financial assistance from the state assumed responsibility for the Everglades. Under the leadership of

United States Senator Duncan Fletcher, the Florida legislative delegation persuaded its colleagues in Congress to include the drainage of the Everglades in the Rivers and Harbors Act of 1930. The War Department began construction on the flood control project in November 1930.[89] Since that time, the planning for this area has been chiefly the responsibility of the United States Army Corps of Engineers, and most of the money has come from the federal government.

In 1942 Governor Spessard Holland was able to restore solvency to the state's drainage and reclamation project through a loan from the Reconstruction Finance Corporation.[90] Despite the government's financial support and Holland's economic reforms, however, the Everglades project has yet to be finished although over 2,000 miles of canals with more than sixty-five major spillways and dams have been built.

The Everglades drainage project proved too ambitious for an economically immature state. Nevertheless, Florida's gubernatorial leadership had been able to persuade the public of the importance of this area and of the need for the state to play a decisive role in its management and development. The state's inability to develop the area fully was not a failure of its gubernatorial leadership. The economic collapse of the 1920s, which brought the Everglades project to a halt, was so severe that all governmental programs suffered until the end of World War II. However, Florida's fiscal problems probably helped the drainage program in the long run. They brought in the federal government, thus insuring the massive funding needed for the project as well as a more carefully planned and developed drainage effort.

An issue which had been discussed almost as long as Everglades drainage but without the same intensity was the construction of a cross-Florida barge canal. The idea has been considered since the early nineteenth century as a way to open up the west coast for development and to establish new markets. Prior to World War II the army engineers had made twenty-eight surveys of possible canal routes in Florida. In preparation for the war, Congress authorized the construction of the canal but, largely because of more pressing matters, money was never allocated for the project, and it was placed on the "deferred" category list.[91]

Interest in the project was revived under Governor Farris Bryant in 1960. Bryant, who had the backing of many local business and political leaders, persuaded President John Kennedy to ask Congress for an appropriation of $1 million for the canal. Bryant apparently won Kennedy's support by implying to Warren M. Goodrich, chairman of the Democratic Executive Committee, that the president's support of the barge canal would help him carry Florida in the 1964 presidential election.[92]

In 1964 President Lyndon Johnson initiated construction of the canal from Yankeetown on the Gulf coast to the St. Johns River basin and then to Mayport on the east coast. By 1970 barely one-third of the $200 million venture had been completed when it came under heavy attack by environmentalists. William M. Belk, a marine biologist for the Florida Department of Air and Water Pollution Control, stated that the barge canal would be "the most devastating project ever undertaken in Florida." Belk and other environmentalists argued that the canal would destroy wildlife and fisheries and endanger water resources. The battle loomed as a major confrontation between supporters of unrestricted economic development and "wild-eyed" environmentalists when Governor Kirk suddenly intervened. Elected on a probusiness platform, Kirk had, nevertheless, expressed concern for the state's environment during his campaign and in his first legislative address. He suggested that construction be delayed until more studies could be made. Secretary of Interior Walter J. Hickel also endorsed a delay of fifteen months in construction at the suggestion of the Bureau of Sports Fisheries and Wildlife.[93] The undertaking was permanently halted in January 1971, when President Richard Nixon impounded all funds for the project.

Governor Reubin Askew's election insured that the project would not be continued during his term of office. An advocate of environmental protection, Askew retreated from his initial desire to challenge Nixon's action and opposed any further construction on the canal. In February 1977, the Florida cabinet, under Askew's leadership, formally ended the venture.

The response of environmentalists and the leadership of governors Kirk and Askew on the barge canal issue opened up a new period of environmental action in Florida. Prior to 1967, Floridians and their political leaders had been caught up in the economic and population growth of the postwar period with virtually no one warning of the environmental consequences of such growth. In addition, Florida's pork-chop legislators who dominated state politics from the mid-1950s to 1967 were closely allied to the paper and pulp interests and land developers in the state. The emergence of an urban dominated legislature following reapportionment led to a significant change in legislative policy regarding these interests.[94]

Kirk was the first governor to reawaken public interest in environmental planning. After his inauguration in 1968, he appointed a water quality advisory commission and announced that he intended "to devote major attention to all areas of preventing air and water pollution." He also established a ten-member governor's advisory council on marine sciences and technology. To highlight his interest in oceanographic research, Kirk, with characteristic flamboyancy, planted a state flag on the ocean floor off the coast of Miami. In response to the state's massive population expansion, which threatened to disrupt all environmental improvements, Kirk proposed that growth be reduced by placing the Florida highway patrol "at our border checking visas of those who want to come to work in Florida."[95]

With the assistance of Governor Kirk, environmentalists belonging to the organization known as Conservation 70s persuaded the legislature to adopt

President Harry Truman in Florida to dedicate the Everglades National Park. The visit and the establishment of the park demonstrated the increasing role played by the federal government in the Everglades drainage program. Behind Truman and to his right stands Governor Millard Caldwell; directly to his right is U.S. Senator Spessard Holland. Photo from Nixon Smiley, *Florida's Yesterday's* (Miami: E. A. Seemann, 1974).

forty-one conservation bills. The laws governed such areas as alligator killings, sewage outfalls, a statewide wilderness system, submerged lands, pollution enforcement, oil spills, environmental education, DDT, endangered species, and aquatic plant control.[96] For the first time in Florida's history, its political leaders endorsed the principle of environmental protection.

Governor Askew consolidated and enlarged upon the gains made by Kirk. He believed Florida, like California, to be in "great danger" of becoming a "paradise lost." In September 1971, Askew launched his environmental campaign by sponsoring a statewide conference on Water and Land Management in South Florida. Askew commented later that he used the conference "as a way to get legislative and public support for water management." Accompanied by considerable fanfare the conference also generated ideas that would be instrumental in the creation of five major environmental bills. These acts provided for planning and regulation of environmentally endangered lands and water resources; consolidated the Department of Natural Resources, Pollution Control, and Trustees of the Internal Improvement Trust Fund into one agency; and provided $200 million for the purchase of environmentally endangered lands.[97] In November 1972, the public approved by referendum the allocation of such lands and the selling of bonds to acquire recreation space.

Askew used the environmental funds to buy the Big Cypress Swamp. He also remained a persistent defender of the environment. Although he refused to endorse any proposals to stop or limit the state's population growth because of the democratic nature of American society, he believed steps had to be taken to protect the environment in the face of such growth. As he stated, "Florida is forever facing choices between trees or towers, creeks or canals, marshes or marinas, water or waste, beaches or barriers . . . men or machines, and greenlands or ghettos." In the face of these alternatives, his plan was to buy up endangered lands, beach and greenbelt areas, and to regulate pollution.[98]

The change in the gubernatorial position on environmental issues reflects, in large part, the change in public attitude. Very few governors, with the exception of Jennings, Broward, Kirk, and Askew in this century, have provided leadership on environmental questions. The role of the public, particularly in recent environmental developments, appears to have been essential in sparking gubernatorial action and effecting stronger legislation. A survey of state voter concerns on growth, energy, pollution, and other environmental matters by Cambridge Research Survey in 1973 revealed that 67 percent endorsed the state's use of eminent domain to take environmentally endangered lands, and 74 percent endorsed the need for greater environmental protection in South Florida.[99]

While the Florida voters and their governors have demonstrated a renewed commitment to environmental protection since 1967, these matters are still secondary to economic concerns. After the severe recession of 1973 the legislature rejected a measure to protect coastal and inland wetlands out of concern for the state's continued growth. In addition, communities which had contemplated placing limits on their size decided against doing so when unemployment increased dramatically.

CONCLUSIONS

Although the gubernatorial approach to state fiscal, economic and labor, and environmental matters does appear to have changed somewhat under Askew's leadership, it is difficult to attach any meaning to it for the future. What has been clear up to this point is a policy, although largely unformulated, of fiscal restraint, balanced budgets, and economic conservatism. Florida's governors during the twentieth century have been in almost total agreement on the need for minimal taxes and minimal spending. There has been a willingness among them to allow inequities in the tax structure to stand and to refrain as much as possible from taxing businesses. Efforts to impose a state graduated income tax have received no support from the governor's office. The governors have shown a willingness to spend for roads, tourism, and education, and to treat other social services as luxuries for the most part. The attitude of each governor on these matters has reflected his own personal views and the nature of his constituency, which has been largely middle and upper class, conservative, and business-oriented.

As we demonstrated in Chapter 2 the governors have been almost entirely self-made men. They achieved economic success through business and politics, they strongly reflected the values of American business, and they strenuously endorsed efforts to bring more business and industry into the state. These efforts have seen Florida's governors traveling around the nation and the world to attract new investment. Reubin Askew visited Japan and Europe in an example of boosterism.

The failure to provide more social services has also reflected the governor's personal views and his constituency. Since blacks have constituted the poorest population in Florida, the ruling white hierarchy has felt little or no pressure to help the poor. This attitude appeared to be changing due to Askew's leadership and a more informed black electorate. The public has also held the labor movement in very low esteem, largely because it was seen as a threat to business growth. As a consequence, the governors have helped block its development.

Business concerns still dominate gubernatorial policymaking in Florida and this circumstance shows no sign of diminishing in the future. The state's economy continues to be overly dependent on tourism and construction, two areas which are highly susceptible to fluctuations in the economy and which, as a consequence, encourage a conservative fiscal policy.

Underlying this economic conservatism has been the business background of nearly all governors and a population which wants to avoid the economic chaos of certain northern states. Fiscal and economic conservatism is thus anchored deeply in the state and shows no sign of abating in the near future. Such conservatism and rigidity have also characterized the racial setting in Florida for most of the twentieth century.

8

Race Relations

FLORIDA'S pattern of race relations was established during the antebellum period. White Floridians, nearly all of whom resided in the northern section of the state, strongly endorsed the superiority of the white man and the enslavement of the black man. The passing of slavery with the conclusion of the Civil War initially caused considerable social and political dislocation in the state. Florida's blacks worked closely with white Republicans to govern the state for ten years. This political development came to an abrupt halt in 1877 with the end of military Reconstruction in Florida. However, the reemergence of the Democratic party failed to result immediately in a segregated society. Apparently many white Floridians felt that an attempt to resurrect such a segregated community would result in northern military retribution.

DEVELOPMENT OF SEGREGATION

Nevertheless, gradually over the next thirty years, the white population moved to reassert its supremacy. In 1889 the state legislature adopted a poll tax and a multiple ballot law which provided separate voting places for state and national elections. The two laws effectively removed blacks from the voting rolls.[1]

Florida's turn-of-the-century progressive governors were one with their white constituents in the view that blacks were an inferior race and should be segregated. William Sherman Jennings, for example, criticized President Theodore Roosevelt for dining with Booker T. Washington. Jennings contended that the president's action encouraged "the negro to demand social equality that cannot be granted him. Personally I regret the matter exceedingly." During Jennings' third year in office intermarriage was forbidden between white persons and Negroes. Jennings' successor, Napoleon Broward, shared his view of black inferiority. However, Broward disagreed with Jennings and other white Floridians in their proposal for alleviating the state's racial problems. Rather than enact more encompassing segregation laws, Broward, echoing the aim of the American Colonization Society in the early nineteenth century, recommended that Congress purchase territory either foreign or domestic and transport blacks to this land where they could live among themselves and govern themselves. No blacks would be permitted to migrate back to the United States. It was Broward's view that educating blacks would result in acute racial problems because blacks would feel frustrated by their secondary status in white society. The result, as he foresaw it, would be racial violence unless something was done soon to prevent it.[2]

Because Florida was critically short of labor in the early twentieth century, the legislature never endorsed such a proposal. However, its members did pass legislation to restrict and regulate the activities of blacks. During Broward's four years in office four Jim Crow bills were adopted providing for separate colleges and universities (1906), separate seating areas on street railroad cars (1905), separate ticket windows (1907), and making miscegenation illegal (1906).[3] The legislators also proposed two bills to disenfranchise blacks in 1907 and 1909. On both occasions they passed the senate to the delight of standing-room-only galleries but were rejected in the house. In these two instances house members felt that Congress would react angrily to such legislation, and might pass another Reconstruction "Force Bill." The belief was also widespread that the federal courts would reject such a measure.[4]

Governor Albert Gilchrist endorsed the racial views of Broward, his predecessor, although he did so in a more paternalistic, "Bourbon" fashion. As the son of a former large slaveholder, he viewed the separation of the races as "simply a question of the preservation of Anglo-Saxon civilization." He added, however, that white rule must "be just." To Gilchrist's credit he was sincere in this statement. He ordered the sheriff of Lake City to let qualified Negroes vote after it was rumored that a white mob was preventing blacks from voting on a prohibition amendment. He also took a strong stand against lynching which had become an accepted form of punishment for blacks in many areas of the South. The sheriff of Leon County had been murdered, apparently by a Negro, Mick Morris, in March 1909. After Morris's capture several citizens threatened to remove him from jail and lynch him. Although the matter did not fall within his jurisdiction, Gilchrist warned the people of Leon County not to pursue the lynching talk. He added that any who may try to lynch Morris "will be punished to the utmost." The governor's leadership helped restore calm to the community and permitted Morris a fair trial.[5]

Unfortunately, Park Trammell, Gilchrist's successor, did not follow his example. Four blacks were lynched during Trammell's administration and he took no action to prevent the crimes or to punish the guilty parties. In addition, he failed to denounce the acts or to have the attorney general's office conduct an investigation.[6]

The Trammell view of race relations was endorsed and enlarged upon by Sidney J. Catts. He viewed blacks in much the same way as other southern demagogues did; they were distinctly inferior to whites, not to be trusted with democratic responsibilities. "I have frowned upon and would not tolerate," Catts declared, "a negro vote coming in to settle the Democratic fuss." For Catts and many other Floridians the place of blacks in the state had to be carefully delineated so that there could be no question about their inferior position with respect to whites. "I do not believe in higher education for Negroes," he told a campaign crowd, "when there are thousands of white children who get only two or three months a year of schooling." "The Negro is," he concluded, "an inferior race."[7]

Despite these views, Catts and other Floridians became concerned about the heavy migration of blacks to northern states; over 40,000 left the state's northern counties alone. Responding to the alarms raised by lumber and turpentine interests in the state, Catts urged blacks to stay in Florida and called for a unity among the races. But when the NAACP asked Catts to see that whites who lynched two blacks in 1919 were punished, Catts reverted to his old ways: "Your Race is always harping on the disgrace it brings to the state by a concourse of white people taking revenge for the dishonoring of a white woman, when if you would . . . [teach] your people not to kill our white officers and disgrace our white women, you would keep down a thousand times greater disgrace."[8]

While not enunciated quite so emotionally or openly by other governors, this view of black-white relations was generally shared by all Florida governors until the *Brown* decision. Governor Doyle Carlton, for example, wrote his Road Department chairman, Robert W. Bentley, suggesting that white working conditions be changed. He noted that whites were laboring in mud and water "which only a negro seems able to stand."[9] Reflecting his rural, deep South roots, Fred Cone took this view one step further when he refused to support a $4,000 annual salary for the president of Florida A & M College for Negroes because "no Negro is worth $4,000 to teach school." While David Sholtz was more paternalistic in his racial views than Cone, his reluctance to send in the National Guard to protect Claude Neal, a black man accused of murdering a white girl in Marianna, Florida, resulted in the state's most brutal lynching. The sheriff of Marianna sought to protect Neal by transferring him secretly to a jail in Brewton, Alabama. The next day, however, a white mob removed him from Brewton and lynched him after torturing him for hours. Sholtz called the act "deplorable" because, he noted, his administration would have promptly and legally executed Neal as it had done in a similar case. Sholtz subsequently directed a half-hearted investigation which failed to result in any arrests.[10] The state's governor agreed with the legislature when it refused to pass legislation unmasking or outlawing the Ku Klux Klan, and when it denounced Mrs. Hoover for entertaining a black congressman at the White House.[11] While some governors such as Carlton decried lynchings and others such as Spessard Holland took steps to prevent them, they all supported racist attitudes and permitted the existence of a climate of opinion that allowed such acts to take place. Only Fuller Warren opposed racism. He sponsored legislation to unmask the Ku Klux Klan, winning legislative approval in 1951.

The pervasiveness of racism in Florida affected other nonwhite groups as well as blacks. Two Italians were lynched in Tampa on September 20, 1910, after being taken from two deputy sheriffs. They were alleged to have assassinated a local citizen. The lynching became an international incident when the Italian government demanded and Governor Gilchrist refused an indemnity for one of the lynched men who was still a citizen of Italy.[12] In 1912 and 1913 the possibility of extensive Japanese colonization in Florida greatly upset the white population. Governor Park Trammell suggested that the state adopt an alien land law forbidding Japanese landownership. The proposal never became law, however, as the threatened "Japanese invasion" never materialized. In 1932 racism combined with economic factors to force the eviction from Florida of Philippine migrants. Forty-five Filipino farmers, who worked for very low wages, fled their homes when a mob of 200 white workers threatened their lives. The farmers retreated to Cuba where, despite Governor Doyle Carlton's promises of protection, they decided to stay with their families.[13]

THE BROWN DECISION AND ITS AFTERMATH

Despite such long-standing racial traditions, Floridians did not react emotionally when the United States Supreme Court delivered the *Brown* decision on May 17, 1954. There was no public outcry even though the decision was announced in the midst of a close gubernatorial primary, and it might have been expected that the candidates would try to capitalize on the emotionalism of the moment. However, both candidates, LeRoy Collins and Charley Johns, seemed unsure of its effects and, while endorsing segregation, let the matter drop. Most editors and other politicians who addressed the issue urged calm and restraint. For example, Florida's former governor and then senior U.S. Senator Spessard Holland said he hoped the decision would be met with "patience and moderation," and that there would not be any "violent repercussions" in the state. In an editorial the *Tampa Tribune* held that the *Brown* decision was inevitable and should be accepted, even while calling it "deplorable" because it overturned law, custom, and social order in states maintaining segregation.[14] By and large, however, Floridians seemed to have relatively little to say about the decision in the days and weeks immediately following it.

The reasons for this mild response were to be found in the state's social and economic structure. Florida had a relatively small percentage of blacks (21.8 percent in 1950) compared to its southern neighbors; as V. O. Key, Jr., pointed out, the smaller the percentage of blacks in a state's population the less chance there was for intense racial animosities.[15] In addition, the diversity of Florida's population, with many immigrants from the northeast and midwest settling in the urbanized, southern region of the state, tended to moderate racial hostility. Florida's heavy economic dependence on tourism also provided a steadying influence that helped explain the mild response to the Court's decision. Perhaps as significantly, the tone of Florida's race relations had been established long ago. The place of the black man had been clearly defined and racial appeals by politicians were unwelcome in such a fixed social setting.

But this is not to say that the *Brown* decision had little impact in Florida. Since in the spring of 1954 Florida was one of only four states with no school integration whatsoever, the decision had grave implications for the state's traditional pattern of public education.[16] It had equal importance for the state's politics. Prior to 1954 race played a small role in Florida politics, but after that date Florida governors found themselves increasingly confronted by the state's racial problems.

The Supreme Court's decision in *Brown* v. *The Board of Education of Topeka, Kansas,* 347 U.S. 483 (1954) placed racial issues at the forefront of Florida gubernatorial politics for the first time since 1916. During the years following the *Brown* decision, each governor found his administration caught up in the problems of integration, civil rights, and busing.

Florida's governors have been in a position as legislative, executive, and moral leaders to assist the public's acceptance of these issues. However, while no Florida governor urged passage of an interposition resolution or advocated a persistent policy to exclude blacks from white schools in the manner of a George Wallace of Alabama, only two governors, LeRoy Collins and Reubin Askew, made conscientious efforts to ease racial turmoil in the state following the *Brown* decision.

Although Collins had endorsed segregation in his gubernatorial campaigns, of 1954 and 1956, his emphasis on peacefulness and upholding the law suggested that he was far more flexible on racial issues than were many of his fellow public officials. He was able to enunciate such views because his political support came from moderate South Florida. His inaugural address on January 8, 1957, established a new tone in Florida and, perhaps, throughout the South, on racial issues. Collins told Floridians that integration was coming, and the state would do well to accept it gracefully. He said he would preserve segregation as long as possible, but "the Supreme Court decisions are the law of the land." He added that whites must "face up to the fact that the Negro does not now have equal opportunity"; accordingly, blacks are "morally and legally entitled to progress more rapidly." Collins admitted that he did not have all the answers to racial questions, but he added: "Haughtiness, arrogance, and forcing of issues will not produce the answer. Above all, hate is not the answer."[17]

Through his own rhetoric and actions he attempted to set the course he hoped Florida and the South would follow. In a speech before the Southern Governors' Conference in 1957 he declared the solution to racial problems was dependent "largely upon bettering the living standards of Negro people. And the improvement cannot be brought about in an atmosphere of racial furor."[18]

In November 1957, *Time* magazine criticized Collins for being a man of words, but not deeds, on the race issue. An examination of Collins' relations with the legislature on race suggests that this was not the case. During his last four years in office he consistently emphasized through messages to the legislature, the programs he submitted to it, his use of the veto, and other actions that he was determined to steer Florida on a course of moderation on racial issues.

Collins' legislative program on race actually began with his acceptance of the Fabisinski Committee proposals in July 1956. The committee, which Collins had appointed in the spring, was charged with finding and recommending ways of legally maintaining segregation in Florida. It proposed a four-point program permitting county school boards to assign pupils to schools on the basis of individual needs; regulating the assignment of teachers; giving the governor power to promulgate and enforce rules needed to maintain law and order during use of public parks, buildings, and other facilities and to prevent domestic violence; and clarifying the governor's powers to declare an emergency.[19]

Collins called a special legislative session in mid-July 1956 to take up these recommendations, which he publicly endorsed. He made it clear to the legislators that he would not accept any programs dealing with segregation except those which the committee and he were proposing. But some legislators, especially representatives Prentice Pruitt of Monticello and J. Kenneth Ballinger of Tallahassee, resented Collins' tone and position. They wanted to introduce strong anti-integration laws and they resisted the idea that only Collins' bills could be considered by the legislature. His proposals on segregation were quickly passed, but the legislature persisted in considering more stringent measures. Collins feared the potential divisiveness of these discussions and felt they could force the state into a direct confrontation with the federal government on race, which he wanted to avoid. On August 1, he adjourned the legislature, using as his justification a little-known constitutional provision empowering the governor to do so when both houses could not agree on a time for adjournment. When news of Collins' action reached the floor of the legislature, Representative Farris Bryant of Ocala, later governor of Florida, was in the middle of a speech introducing an interposition resolution. It was precisely this kind of measure Collins wanted to avoid.[20]

During the 1957 regular session of the legislature the governor tried to continue his moderate racial policies. In his speech opening the session, he called for only one additional law on race, and none on segregation. He felt the bills passed the previous summer provided Florida with sufficient resources to handle its racial problems.[21]

The legislature, however, had other ideas, and proceeded to give Collins his only major defeat on racial matters. An interposition resolution was passed by a near unanimous vote over the governor's strong objections. Collins had no power to veto such a measure. However, he wrote a note registering his opposition directly on the resolution; he observed that what the legislature had done "stultifies our state" and concluded "It will do no good whatever and those who say it can perpetrate a cruel hoax on the people." Collins did, however, veto the so-called "last resort" school bill passed by the 1957 legislature; it would have closed the schools rather than integrate them. He did sign the only racial measure he requested from the 1957 regular session; it established a governor's racial advisory group. He also signed a bill passed by the October special session which required that the public schools be closed if federal troops were sent in to force integration.[22]

In 1959 Collins blocked thirty-three anti–school integration bills introduced in the legislature. Some of these were drastic: they would have created systems of private schools financed with state funds; others would have closed the schools rather than integrate them; still another bill would have made teaching in an integrated school a criminal offense.[23]

Collins sought only minimal, and moderate, legislation on race. His emphasis, moreover, was on preventing legislative excesses on racial matters; he was determined to keep Florida from following the path of some of its southern neighbors. Thus by taking a negative view of much that the legislature wanted to do, Collins was able to prevent the state from taking an extremist position on race.

Even though Collins managed to maintain moderate racial policies throughout his administration, he did not bring about significant school desegregation. Collins was pledged to maintain segregation in the public schools, but he repeatedly insisted that the pupil placement law was the only legal way to do so. When he left office in 1961, only one school district (Dade County) was desegregated.

Collins was criticized in some circles for not pushing harder on school desegregation. The fact is, however, that he did make an effort to convince local school officials that some school desegregation should be attempted at a time when the federal government was applying no pressure on the state to do so. In part he felt that some desegregation would strengthen the legal foundation of the pupil placement law. But he had also begun to realize that school desegregation was inevitable. During the fall of 1958 Collins met quietly on several occasions with local school officials to secure their cooperation in a limited effort to desegregate some schools. Financial inducements and assistance were apparently offered to cooperating districts. By mid-December, however, Collins dropped these discussions. He said no volunteer district or community could be found, and he felt that there was no place in the state where school desegregation could be accomplished without provoking resentment and violence. Thus, he declined to push the issue further, maintaining that decisions regarding school desegregation would have to come from local districts. In mid-February 1959, Dade County did announce that four black students would be enrolled in an all-white elementary school; Collins applauded the decision, although he noted it was purely a local one.[24]

In desegregation of higher education Collins' record is also mixed. He led the fight in 1956 to keep Virgil Hawkins, a black, out of the University of Florida College of Law. He even promised to plead the state's case before the United States Supreme Court if necessary. However, in late January 1959, Collins proposed that graduate programs at Florida A & M University be eliminated in favor of creating integrated ones at Florida State University and the University of Florida. He maintained that the cost of operating graduate programs made this the most realistic course of action. However, his proposal was immediately attacked. House Speaker-designate Thomas Beasley said there was "no chance" Florida A & M programs would be shut down, holding that "the people of Florida were willing to pay whatever is necessary to maintain segregation." It was in the face of this kind of resistance and threats of violence that Collins elected not to force the desegregation of Florida's public educational facilities.[25]

The three governors who succeeded LeRoy Collins had taken strong stands in their campaigns against integration, civil rights, and busing. Not surprisingly, they had made little effort to promote racial equality in Florida. Farris Bryant, who succeeded Collins, had announced his intention of reappointing Collins' statewide biracial advisory committee with Cody Fowler, a Tampa lawyer, again serving as chairman. Fowler refused to accept the appointment, alleging that Bryant wanted only men "whose opinions would be congenial with his own." Bryant later announced he had chosen a successor to Fowler, but he refused to name him. The committee was subsequently dissolved.[26]

Bryant also blocked federal programs which appeared to be designed, at least in part, to promote integration. Thus, he opposed federal aid to education in Florida because the state might be forced to submit to federal integration guidelines in order to receive federal funds. Additionally, Bryant refused to let the state cooperate in a study of equal job opportunities for blacks as requested by the Civil Rights Commission.[27]

Under Governor Burns there were few changes in the racial policies established by Bryant. Burns made nc effort to establish a biracial advisory committee and took few steps to promote racial harmony. In addition, he was a leading critic of the Civil Rights Act of 1964 and Voting Rights Act of 1965.

To the credit of both governors, they took no militant steps to block school integration. While governors Ross Barnett of Mississippi and George Wallace of Alabama tried personally to halt school integration in their states, Bryant and Burns allowed it to take place gradually and quietly. During Bryant's administration, for instance, twenty counties in Florida integrated their public schools. He refused to make inflammatory statements on local school issues despite pressure from his political supporters. An opponent of strong federal and state government, Bryant argued: "It's the American way to leave the solution to people in their areas." In addition, although both men relied on racial appeals to win their elections, not one of these governors resorted to such emotional or demagogic rhetoric once they were in office. Burns appointed several blacks to office, including Clifton Dyson, the first black man to sit on the Board of Regents, and allowed the desegregation of the state's schools to continue. In his first message to the legislature, he also denounced prejudice and bigotry, arguing it had "no place in our government."[28]

Claude Kirk's election in 1966 offered little change in the racial policies pursued by Bryant and Burns. Although he had campaigned against busing to achieve school desegregation, Kirk also had played down racial issues by alleging: "I won't even admit there's a problem. We don't have color in Florida."[29] Despite the flamboyance and theatrics of his first three years in office, he initiated few racial policies that set his administration apart from those of Bryant and Burns.

The election of Reubin Askew in 1970 brought about a significant change in the leadership provided by Florida governors during the 1960s. Elected on a reform platform, Askew promised in his inaugural address: "Equal rights for all our peoples, rural as well as urban, black as well as white."[30] Askew entered office in the midst of the busing dispute. He personally felt that the emotional controversy over busing would further damage the public school system by speeding up the white exodus to private schools. In late August 1971, he received a petition with 40,000 signatures asking him to request Congress to call a constitutional convention to prohibit busing as a means of achieving racial balance in the public schools. In response to this proposal,

Governor Askew told a summer graduating class at the University of Florida that busing was "an artificial and inadequate instrument of change. Nobody really wants it—not you, not me, not the people, not the school board, not even the courts." However, he went on to say "the law demands, and rightly so, that we put an end to segregation in our society," and he saw busing as a necessary element in achieving this goal.[31]

Askew's speech was made more remarkable by Alabama Governor George Wallace's appearance barely seventy miles away in Jacksonville, Florida. To a cheering crowd of thousands, Wallace said President Nixon would force him to run for president if he did not halt busing by executive order. At the same time former Governor Claude Kirk was leading a Parents Against Forced Busing group in Pinellas County. He would later become national chairman of the organization.[32]

In February 1972, the Florida legislature, meeting in special session, took up the busing issue and quickly passed a measure adding it to the presidential primary ballot of March 14; the straw vote asked Floridians if they would support a constitutional amendment prohibiting forced busing. Governor Askew agreed to sign it but only after the legislature dropped the adjective "forced" and agreed to a companion referendum asking voters if they supported quality education for all and opposed a return to a dual system of public schools.[33]

Apparently determined to prove to himself and the nation that Florida was not a racist state, Askew raised $32,000 to conduct a speaking tour and persuaded Florida's religious leaders to join him in the campaign. With remarks that he would repeat throughout his tour of the state, Askew reiterated his personal dislike of busing to a festive audience at a state fair in Orlando. Yet he added that through "busing and other methods, we've made real progress in dismantling a dual system of public schools in Florida." He noted that racial issues had in the past frequently obscured the more important "economic and environmental problems of the people, both black and white." He closed by saying "it's time we told the rest of the nation that we aren't caught up in the mania to stop busing at any cost . . . , that we know the real issues when we see them, and that we no longer will be fooled, frightened, and divided against ourselves."[34]

When the straw ballot was held the antibusing resolution was heartily endorsed by Floridians 3 to 1. However, the straw vote on equal opportunity for all children regardless of race, creed, or color passed by an even wider margin of 4 to 1.[35] The results were, at best, only a partial victory for Askew. Most critics of integration, including Wallace supporters in Florida, had apparently decided that a negative vote on the second issue would have no influence on Washington and might even dilute their opposition to busing (since Congress and the White House would probably view such opposition as racially motivated). Nevertheless, Askew's efforts had gained him and his state much favorable publicity throughout the nation, only part of which was diminished by the results of the straw vote.

Askew's legacy to improved racial relations in Florida went well beyond his leadership in the busing issue. Upon taking office, he authorized an employee survey which disclosed that the vast majority of black employees in state government held menial positions and more than 89 percent were receiving wages below the poverty level. Shortly thereafter, Askew issued an executive order establishing an affirmative action plan to correct the under-representation and underutilization of blacks in state government. The first progress report published in 1972 revealed that the number of blacks in state government had doubled and that blacks had attained several responsible positions. Some of the more prominent black appointments made by Askew include: Mr. James Gardener, member of the Board of Regents; Dr. Claude Anderson, Education Coordinator; Mr. Calvin Map, Dade County judge; Mrs. Athalie Range, member of the Council on State Housing Goals, Florida Legal Services Board, and the Inter-American Center Authority; and Joseph Woodrow Hatchett, first black justice of the state supreme court since Reconstruction. His purpose in appointing blacks to high office was, as he put it, because "I want to, in some specific ways, give some hope to young black people that the establishment is not inherently hypocritical." Askew's campaign against the busing referendum and his appointment of blacks to prominent positions in state government appear to have helped alleviate the frustrations of black Floridians and restore racial tranquility to the state. Acts of racial violence virtually disappeared from the public scene in the 1970s.[36]

Askew also aided blacks and the poor generally by opposing any increase in the regressive sales tax and raising the limit for family assistance from $155 to $176 a month. In addition, he favored a complete revamping of the state's tax base. In an interview with *Ebony* magazine, Askew commented that "With almost blind reliance on consumer taxes in Florida, we're hitting the lower and middle-income families—thus many black families—far too hard." While the governor readily noted the problem, his administration was unable to bring about significant tax relief, with the single exception of the corporate tax.[37]

The progress in race relations made under Reubin Askew's leadership points out the important role a governor can play in affecting the state's racial environment. The meaning of executive leadership was never more evident than during the racial turmoil of the 1950s and 1960s.

CIVIL PROTEST AND DESEGREGATION

It was LeRoy Collins' leadership in the late 1950s which prevented the sit-in demonstrations from deteriorating into violent confrontations. In 1956 and 1957 the NAACP attempted to desegregate the city buses in Tallahassee.

Collins denounced the NAACP effort as a "miscarriage of ambition." He argued that blacks should be concerned "with other conditions of far more importance than where people sit on buses." In January 1957, he suspended Tallahassee bus service for nearly two weeks in order to preserve public order after rocks were thrown and shots were fired at the homes of blacks involved in the desegregation effort.[38]

Collins expressed the same attitude toward lunch-counter sit-in demonstrations in 1960. Daytona Beach, Tallahassee, Tampa, Sarasota, and St. Petersburg all had sit-in demonstrations during that year. Collins, who was strongly motivated by legal considerations, stated: "I hate to see demonstrations of this kind. They lead to disorder. Disorder leads to danger to the general welfare and I hope we will not have any more of it." He appealed directly to the people of Florida to restore racial harmony: "We must find responsible community leaders who can provide leadership for social adjustments which we must make. ..."[39]

But while he was sharply critical of the tactics of blacks, Collins reserved his strongest language for white Floridians who refused to recognize the winds of change, and particularly those who continued to engage in the repression of minority groups. When a synagogue and black elementary school in Jacksonville were bombed in late April 1958, Collins was outraged: "This is not just an invasion of the personal property rights of those directly injured. It is a serious crime against every citizen of Florida. It is a trampling underfoot of the freedom and security of American justice. Anyone who would perpetrate such a wrong like this has such a diabolical mind and intent that he is a common enemy of all, regardless of race, color, or religion."[40]

At the same time that he was openly criticizing black sit-in tactics in the spring of 1960, he went before the public on television to express his thoughts on segregation. He reiterated his commitment to law and order. But he also stated what was unquestionably a unique view for a Florida governor. Collins said he believed it was "unfair and morally wrong" for white store owners to encourage black patronage of some departments in their establishments but to deny blacks service in others. Legally, he said, they can do that, "But I still don't think [the store owners] can square that right with moral, simple justice."[41]

Later in the year, when severe racial turmoil flared in Jacksonville, Collins went personally to the city to see what could be done. He observed that the violence may have been between "colored trash and white trash" but all the people of the city must share the blame: "I am sure it must be easily observable to the people of Jacksonville that conditions there are not what they should be in the Negro community. Their housing is extremely poor. Their recreational facilities are extremely limited, and certainly the people of Jacksonville have been aware that there has been growing tension in the last several months. . . . You cannot try to sweep the trash under the slums and expect to avoid difficulties, because slums breed difficulties, slums breed crime, vice, and disorder."⁴² Collins' fairness and moral suasion were instrumental in bringing a temporary halt to sit-in demonstrations in Florida. The racial protests, however, did not pass with his governorship, although the leadership he provided did.

In the summer of 1963 the sit-in demonstrations and antisegregation marchers came to St. Augustine, Florida. In several violent and near-violent encounters between whites and blacks, one white was killed, four blacks were wounded, and many were injured. The racial disorders eased during the fall and winter. In the spring of 1964 Dr. Robert Hayling, a black dentist and St. Augustine leader of the Southern Christian Leadership Conference (SCLC), invited northern college students to St. Augustine during the summer to help with the "struggle for human rights."⁴³ Hundreds of students and newsmen began arriving in early March to prepare for the expected confrontation with the local police and citizenry.

Governor Farris Bryant had already made it clear to Floridians, both during his campaign and after, that he opposed sit-in demonstrations. He argued in the campaign that they violate the right of private property and the "fundamental constitutional guarantee that no citizen's property shall be taken from him without due process of law." He stated to the United States Senate Commerce Committee that if a traveler is free not to buy because he doesn't like the owner's mustache, accent, or race, "the owners of the property ought to have the same freedom. That's simple justice."⁴⁴

When the demonstrations began in St. Augustine in March, the local police quickly arrested the demonstrators, including Mrs. George Endicott Peabody, mother of the governor of Massachusetts. Violence followed in May when white mobs pelted antisegregation marchers with rocks and bottles. As the confrontations among police, white militants, and integrationists accelerated, Martin Luther King, Jr., promised "a massive assault on segregation" in the city with a nonviolent army from Savannah, Georgia, Birmingham, Alabama, and Wilmington, North Carolina. Bryant, who was attending a national governors' conference in Cleveland, Ohio, condemned the violence but only sent in forty-five state troopers to assist the embattled local police force. He refused to allow United States marshals to intervene.⁴⁵

Events in St. Augustine worsened when King arrived to direct the integrationist drive and J. B. Stoner, an Atlanta Klansman, showed up to lead the segregationists. Adding to the confusion, Sheriff L. O. Davis of St. Augustine named Halsted R. (Hoss) Manucy, leader of the Ancient City Hunting Club and a militant segregationist, one of his special deputies to maintain order in St. Augustine. Bryant visited the area and described it as "very explosive and very tense" but did little to encourage the forces of compromise. He did send in an additional 80 troopers and issued an order banning night demonstrations but only after local leaders asked him to do so. The ban, however, was overturned by federal Judge Bryan Simpson who suggested instead "enforcement, arrests and charges against these hoodlums [segregationists] everybody seems afraid of."[46]

Violence erupted again when white militants assaulted a group attempting to integrate St. Augustine Beach. There followed a series of wade-ins at the beach and at motel pools in town. Under considerable pressure from President Johnson, Governor Bryant finally stepped in and announced the establishment of a four man biracial committee of St. Augustine citizens to restore communications between blacks and whites.[47]

Conditions in St. Augustine were still tense when President Lyndon Johnson signed the Civil Rights Act on July 2. The new law forbade discrimination in all places of public accommodation such as hotels, restaurants, and theaters. It also served as a catalyst which threatened to disrupt the fragile truce as militant whites bitterly denounced it. Adding to the confusion was Governor Bryant's ill-timed statement that he felt the same about civil rights as he did about taxes: "I don't propose to collect taxes and I don't propose to enforce civil rights."[48]

Shortly after Bryant's announcement, segregationists in St. Augustine began enlisting business support to refuse service to blacks. Dr. King returned to the historic city and promised to march and protest until the law was obeyed. Bryant, meanwhile, had not only failed to convene his biracial advisory committee but had also failed to appoint any members. He also rejected the help of former Governor LeRoy Collins, then serving as President Johnson's Community Relations Service Director. The Community Relations Agency had been established by the Civil Rights Act to help mediate social crises in southern communities. Instead of violence once again becoming the order of the day, however, federal Judge Bryan Simpson took control of events in St. Augustine through a series of injunctions and orders.[49]

Governor Bryant's role in the St. Augustine crisis had done little to improve black-white relations in Florida. Even after the crisis was resolved he continued to be a thorn in the side of the civil rights movement. Rutledge Pearson, president of the NAACP in Florida, remarked that compliance with the Civil Rights Act in Florida had been "encouraging." He added, however, that "It would help if the governor of Florida would take a position of upholding the law, and encouraging people to obey it."[50]

With the settlement of the St. Augustine crisis, racial tensions appeared to be resolved in Florida. In fact, of course, they had only subsided temporarily. The reasons for racial conflict were still present: law enforcement discrimination, poverty, economic discrimination, inadequate schools, and high unemployment. In 1967 the calm that had characterized Florida's racial relations for three years came to an abrupt halt. Within the space of a few summer months, black Floridians in seven cities took to the streets, openly challenging the police and civil authority, and, in the process, destroying property and injuring several dozen people. While the riots in Florida paled in comparison to the violence and destruction in Newark, N. J., or Detroit, Michigan, they still shocked most Floridians. Particularly startling was the riot in Tampa which lasted four days and was ranked by the National Advisory Commission on Civil Disorders as one of the most intense in the nation.[51]

The causes of the riots in Tampa, Clearwater, St. Petersburg, West Palm Beach, Deerfield Beach, Lakeland, and Riviera Beach were complex and often unique in each area. But the failure of Florida's governors in the 1960s to recommend any programs that might alleviate the general plight of the poor only exacerbated black frustration and anger in the cities.

Claude Kirk, one of the governors during this period, responded to the crisis by deploying National Guardsmen when requested by local officials. He also visited the areas. In Tampa, employing his own confrontation politics, he stormed into a church meeting of 200 blacks and asked for an end to the looting and violence. In return he promised a thorough investigation of the shooting of a black youth by police. It was this youth's death that had sparked the riot. Kirk's promise appears to have had a temporizing effect on the black community, although the riot might well have run its course by that time.[52]

Somewhat later Kirk commended 130 black youths from Tampa who had patrolled the riot area urging blacks to stop the violence and return to their homes. However, he never made any recommendations to the legislature in 1967 or thereafter that might have improved the social and economic conditions of the poor. Instead he supported the enactment of one of the severest antiriot laws in the country. The law made rioting a felony punishable by up to two years in prison.[53]

Kirk also contributed to racial disharmony by interfering in the Manatee County school desegregation controversy of 1970. In January United States District Court Judge Ben Krentzman ordered Manatee school officials to begin busing students to achieve a ratio of 80 percent white to 20 percent black students in each school. When the judge's order went into effect on April 6, Kirk responded in surprising fashion by suspending both the school board and Superintendent of Schools Jack L. Davidson, and personally seizing control of the schools. Kirk apparently sought to bolster his gubernatorial reelection bid in 1970 and to test President Nixon's statement which criticized busing. Judge Krentzman ordered the schools returned to the county school officials and Governor Kirk to appear before him to explain his actions. Kirk refused to appear, claiming Krentzman had "overstepped his bounds." He also defied the court by again suspending both educational bodies. Kirk warned federal officials that there might be a loss of life if they attempted to serve him with a subpoena. On April 11, Krentzman found Kirk guilty of contempt and fined him $10,000 a day until he surrendered control of Manatee County's schools. The following day Kirk bowed to the judge's demands and directed the school board to implement Krentzman's desegregation order.[54] Kirk's role in the Manatee incident only further turned the public against busing. It also created chaos in the Manatee County school system, and it was several years before the tensions there were alleviated.

The gubernatorial leadership during these periods of racial turmoil suggests that the racial climate had been effectively moderated or worsened, depending on the quality of that leadership. While the *Brown* decision did generate white resistance and hostility in Florida, as it did in all southern states, LeRoy Collins' moral leadership in the 1950s enabled Floridians to avoid the difficult adjustments experienced in such states as Alabama and Mississippi. His commitment to upholding the law and his sensible, moderate leadership in race relations ensured that there would be no "Little Rock" in Florida. (The Little Rock crisis saw President Dwight Eisenhower send in federal troops in 1957 to oversee school desegregation. In response, Governor Orval Faubus closed the schools in 1958.)

Gubernatorial leadership in the 1960s on racial issues never matched that of Collins. However, Bryant and Burns did manage to steer Florida through the troubled waters of the early '60s without resorting to demagoguery. Although Kirk did act in such a manner in April 1970, his was not a racially demagogic administration. The Manatee crisis stands in marked contrast to the other racial policies his administration pursued. Nevertheless, the problems encountered by Kirk as well as by Bryant and Burns pointed out the inherent contradiction of a candidate pursuing a racially oriented campaign, and trying to provide positive, peaceful leadership on racial issues once in office. During a period of racial crisis, such as that in St. Augustine in 1963 and 1964 and Manatee in 1970, a governor who had resorted to emotional appeals was unprepared and ill equipped to deal with racial turmoil. He found himself mistrusted by the black community and unable to appease his white constituents without using the police power of the state.

Reubin Askew benefited from the racial policies of his predecessors, as well as from the changing public attitudes on race. His personal decision to take a progressive stand on race relations also led to a dramatic shift away from the type of gubernatorial leadership that characterized the 1960s. The question today is no longer whether the Florida governor will assume a racist posture but whether he will pursue programs and policies broad enough in scope to permit black Floridians to participate fully and equally in the range of opportunities the state can provide. Although Askew started the state in the right direction, no clear-cut solution has yet emerged to this problem.

CONCLUSIONS

Race has been an issue that lay just beneath the surface in Florida gubernatorial politics for most of the twentieth century. The governors, with the exception of Collins and Askew, have not questioned the racial segregation and discrimination that have existed since the late nineteenth century. In part this view of race relations reflected their own personal views and in part it reflected political expediency. Florida is a southern state and its racial heritage has been very much a part of the southern tradition. Most of the governors have been from rural parts of Florida or other southern states, and it is precisely these areas where racial segregation was most firmly entrenched and maintained. Prior to 1970 no man could hope to win the governorship as a racial moderate and no one tried. Even LeRoy Collins was forced to mask his racial moderation in the 1956 Democratic primary.

But racial issues did not dominate or overwhelm Florida gubernatorial politics. While a gubernatorial candidate typically referred to the "niggers" and the importance of keeping them in their place, few carried the rhetoric into the governor's office. Sidney Catts had conducted a racially demagogic campaign in 1916, but once elected his tone was notably more subdued. Even during the turmoil following the *Brown* decision, the governors avoided racial extremism. As a southerner Bryant personally opposed school desegregation while Burns and Kirk sought to make political capital from the race issue. Nevertheless, all three men bowed to court decisions.

Because Florida's governors have been largely self-made men, economic matters rather than racial concerns dominated their administrations. The factors that inhibited Florida's development in the twentieth century were, they thought, economically related, not racially related. LeRoy Collins and Reubin Askew sought to put racial matters behind so that both races could focus their attention on economic development. Having come from an economically deprived background which gave him a sympathy and understanding for the plight of black Floridians, Askew was personally as well as economically motivated to rectify the injustices faced by blacks. The personal backgrounds of Florida's governors and the needs of the state were thus crucial in Florida's ability to avoid racial extremism.

While racial issues have heavily influenced the nature and style of gubernatorial politics in Florida, they have yet to receive the attention commanded by educational matters even during the post-*Brown* era.

9

Education

SKIP one generation in education and our people would lapse into servitude. Organized society performs no function so vital to its perpetuity as the education of the youth who in a few short years will arbitrate the destinies of the world." When Governor Doyle Carlton spoke these words in 1929, he was both echoing and anticipating the position which Florida governors had taken, and would take, on education in the state. Like economic development and efficiency in government, education has been a perennial issue in Florida gubernatorial politics, one which no governor has been able to sidestep or avoid. And like prosperity in the private sector and economy in the public, education has been an issue which all governors have had to favor. The political climate and traditions of the state have never permitted any Florida governor to oppose education outright. Even though not all Florida governors have favored education to the same degree, there has been a remarkable consistency in the public pronouncements they have made about it. In 1907 Governor Napoleon Bonaparte Broward stated, "... the capacity of the white man's brain for development and education must not be limited by anything else than our power to provide training and opportunity." More than sixty years later racism had disappeared from gubernatorial rhetoric, and Governor Reubin Askew was speaking of both blacks and whites when he considered the impact of education and schools on improving people's lives in a message whose content was similar to Carlton's: "To beat 'the life' [of squalor]—to make one's own life, and to insure a better life for all has been the vitality—the spirit of our schools. This spirit must prevail."[1]

Education, then, has traditionally been an important policy issue in Florida, and one to which governors have often pledged their support. However, and perhaps more importantly, it is also a policy area in which the rhetoric of Florida governors has been much more noticeable than dynamic leadership. Indeed, it is the thesis of this chapter that, with few exceptions, the support which Florida governors have given education has been largely of a symbolic nature. While they have recognized the critical role which education plays in building a stronger society and improving the life of the individual, Florida governors have not sought to commit or utilize the state's resources to establish excellence in its systems of lower and higher education.

Throughout the twentieth century Florida has ranked low, in comparison to other states, in its support for education. Several statistics illustrate this point. Table 9.1 shows Florida's ranking during the twentieth century in comparison to other states on expenditures per pupil as a function of average daily attendance (ADA) in elementary and secondary schools. In 1973, Florida ranked twenty-fifth among the states in terms of the percentage of per capita expenditures for students as a function of personal income in the state.

TABLE 9.1. Florida Expenditures per Pupil in Average Daily Attendance (ADA)

Year	Expenditure ($)	Ranking among All States
1919–20	36.16	41
1929–30	50.61	42
1939–40	58.35	41
1949–50	181.37	36
1959–60	317.64	37
1963–64	394.95	35
1969–70	732.39	26
1971–72	868.37	30
1975	1,147.00	23

SOURCE: Bureau of the Census, *Statistical Abstract of the United States, 1975* (Washington: Government Printing Office, 1975), p. 75.

In 1971–72 Florida ranked forty-third in the nation in expenditures for higher education as a percentage of personal income; by 1977–78 it still ranked thirty-ninth on this measure, and fortieth on per capita appropriations.[2] Thus, it seems inevitable to conclude that while Florida governors have endorsed education and have been glad to make glowing speeches about its importance, they have not been willing to provide the necessary leadership to pay for it.

In some ways Florida governors have been only partially responsible for this situation. There is a strong tradition in the state for economy-mindedness, and Florida government has been notable for its low tax, low service level orientation. It has been impossible for education, by itself, to buck this tide. Education has been perceived by governors as but one policy area (albeit a visible and popular one) crying out for ever greater levels of scarce public resources. In addition, Florida had been a poor state for most of the pre–World War II period (1900–1920, 1926–41) and this had also detrimentally affected school funding. Education budgets had been tempered accordingly to fit in with total fiscal demands and available state revenues. As will be seen below, the governing structure for education in the state has also been idiosyncratic, to say the least. As a result, governors have not always been in the best possible position to direct educational policymaking. But even without these extenuating circumstances, there has been little leadership by Florida governors to move its systems of education beyond the minimal levels acceptable to its citizens. The state's chief executives have even opposed particular programs or pieces of legislation which might have improved public education. It must be concluded that if Florida has failed to establish educational systems of excellence, with a few very notable exceptions its governors must share some of the blame.[3]

DECISION MAKING IN EDUCATION

Educational decision-making in Florida has traditionally been decentralized and collegial in character.[4] The governor frequently has no direct control over educational policy but rather must assume a role that enables him to participate in, but not necessarily dominate, decision-making.

The cause of this decentralized policymaking structure has been the cabinet system.[5] The commissioner of education (prior to 1968 he was called Superintendent of Public Instruction) has sat as a member of the cabinet, although he was neither appointed by nor responsible to the governor. Like other members of the cabinet he has his own statewide constituency. While his longevity has not been as great as that of other cabinet members, there have been only seven education commissioners since 1900 compared to twenty-one governors during the same period.[6] The commissioner of education is responsible for running the state Department of Education. As the head of this vast bureaucracy (it is the largest state agency, employing nearly 137,000 people) he has been in a significant position to influence educational policy quite independently of the governor.

The commissioner of education reports to the cabinet which acts as the State Board of Education. In other states, the board (if there is one) is usually appointed by the legislature or governor or both, but this has not been the case in Florida. Until 1968 the Board of Education consisted of all members of the cabinet except the comptroller and commissioner of agriculture; since then all seven members sit on the board.[7] The board has a variety of duties and responsibilities, but essentially it must approve all educational policy decisions not requiring legislative action. It cannot appropriate money for the schools, for example, but it can recommend the construction of new educational institutions or changes in the curriculum. This has given it vast authority over educational policy.

The governor appoints the state Board of Regents (previously known as the state Board of Control), the governing agency for public higher education in the state. As such, the regents have been more open to gubernatorial leadership than any other education-related agency in the state. Nevertheless, the regents have exercised considerable independence from the governor during their relatively short existence, particularly in the area of budget requests for higher education, and cannot be regarded as simply the "tool" of the governor in this area. At least one governor, Reubin Askew, has publicly criticized the regents for failing to respond to his leadership.[8] Also, the Board of Education has authority over the regents, and the legislature, particularly in recent years, has played an active role in policymaking for higher education. Thus the governor's voice even in this area has been significantly lessened.

Finally, Florida governors have been faced with a set of beliefs about public lower and higher education which can be found elsewhere in America: "politics and schools don't mix."[9] Citizens have traditionally been reluctant to permit direct intervention by political figures into education. Schoolmen at both lower and higher levels have fostered this set of beliefs, since it provided them with greater independence and freedom to maneuver without having to account for their actions. While in recent years some of these attitudes have been eroded, they have by no means disappeared, and until the late 1960s their influence could be felt very strongly. Thus, Florida governors have had to proceed very carefully. Too strong a role in educational policymaking has usually met with resistance from professional educators, legislators, and segments of the general population (especially editorial writers). The result has been that gubernatorial policy initiative in education has been relatively circumspect and often surrounded by considerable fanfare designed to depoliticize any proposals made. For example, one finds in Florida considerable gubernatorial reliance on blue-ribbon citizens' committees on education which, nevertheless, usually propose what governors want them to.

PUBLIC SCHOOL FINANCE

Perhaps the most crucial educational policy area in which the state exercises authority is school finance. Even though public education is locally administered, it is actually a state function, and the state has the power to influence all aspects of school operation. While many factors determine the kind of education a state provides, money is clearly a principal determinant of its quality.[10]

In Florida, as in other states, approximately half of all public school resources have been provided by the state through grants of money to local school districts.[11] The state has also influenced the amount of resources raised locally, through regulation of millage on ad valorem property taxes. It has been in the area of school finance, especially the amount of state aid provided to local schools, that Florida governors have been especially influential.

In their rhetoric, Florida governors from the beginning of this century have generally claimed to favor full funding of the schools. In his inaugural address William Sherman Jennings called for "the most liberal support and development" of the public schools. Four months later Jennings was to repeat this request in his message opening the 1901 session of the legislature, and the same request for "liberal appropriations" appears in his 1903 legislative message.[12] Similar language can be found in the inaugural speeches and legislative messages of many later Florida governors.

Likewise, from early in the century governors have had to look for fiscal mechanisms to provide sufficient funds for schools. Most of the state funds for public schools in Florida came from earmarked sources, and when these sources have proved insufficient new devices have had to be found. Thus, as early as 1915 Park Trammell recommended that revenues from hunting licenses issued by the state game department go directly to the Rural School Fund (the sum only amounted to about $25,000) instead of being invested in securities and having the interest go to the schools. Throughout this century the problem of raising sufficient revenues for schools has been a part of the larger question of raising sufficient revenues for the state as a whole. The opposition to a sales tax which extended over much of this century (and to some extent continues even to the present) and the ongoing antipathy towards personal income taxes have prevented the development of a sound tax structure in the state to finance schools and other essential services. Coupled with the low tax, low service belief system that has marked Florida politics, governors have often been forced to rely on makeshift, stopgap measures to provide revenues.[13]

The amount of money available for schools has not been just a matter of gubernatorial prerogative. Even more crucial is the relative wealth of the state at any particular time. Governors, regardless of the priorities they place on education, or their desire for "full funding" and "liberal appropriations," have been constrained by available resources.[14] Perhaps nowhere was this better seen in Florida's history than during the 1920s and 1930s, when funds for schools dramatically reflected the changing economy of the state.

During the early 1920s Florida enjoyed the fruits of a fabulous land boom, and schools benefited from this prosperity. John Martin's administration significantly increased school appropriations and those for other state services.[15] A measure was also passed which provided free textbooks for all students in the first six grades of public school. But this age of prosperity for the state and its schools did not last very long.

Florida suffered terribly during the depression; the economic woes for education began with the collapse of the land boom in 1926. The best indicator of the schools' fiscal problems was the rapid decline in assessed property values: most school revenues came from the property tax, revenue which had been totally dependent on assessed property values. Between 1926 and 1930 assessed property values in Florida fell from $623 to $441 million.[16]

Doyle Carlton was Florida's governor beginning in January 1929, and it was his responsibility to lead the state during the early years of the depression. A fiscal conservative, he felt the best way to improve the state's financial situation was to cut expenditures. He also opposed any new taxes to raise funds for the schools and other services. He was especially opposed to a general sales tax, which he felt was discriminatory, and the legalization of pari-mutuel betting, which he thought immoral (the legislature approved this measure anyway, over Carlton's veto). Eventually the gasoline tax was raised in order to provide more funds for education and other state services.[17]

But conditions in the schools continued to worsen. Many school districts had to shorten school terms when they ran out of money. Teachers were asked to take salary cuts and in several cases they went unpaid. While no school districts failed to open in 1933 and 1934, more than half the districts owed teachers some back salary. When David Sholtz took office in 1933 the situation was chaotic: "The state superintendent's budget in 1933 included $312,408 to pay back salaries. Teachers in [some] places took reduced pay to keep the schools open a full term. Others cut out such 'nonessentials' as home economics, physical education, art, music, and manual training. St. Petersburg tried charging tuition and begging those without children to pay it for children whose parents were unable to pay. A final measure of the extent of the problem was revealed when the [Federal Emergency Relief Administration] granted $610,210.82 to school districts in fifty-five counties to pay back salaries to 4,461 teachers."[18]

But like his predecessor, Governor Sholtz did not feel the state could, or should, increase its financial commitment to the schools. In 1933, he requested $5.5 million for public education and threatened to veto any bill appropriating more. He also promised to remove "A certain group of school officials" who were trying to lobby for more funds.[19]

The legislature ignored Sholtz and appropriated $7.5 million. However, when it failed to increase state taxes, the actual amount of funds available to the schools was $5.4 million, less than Sholtz had originally requested. Teachers and other professional educators were furious with the governor. They openly blamed him for the state's failure to support the schools and the increasing economic plight of teachers.[20]

Sholtz remained unsympathetic to their demands. He rejected their calls for more funds, and flatly turned down a request for a special session to raise money for schools. He urged local school districts to do what business had been forced to do during the depression: reduce costs and collect delinquent accounts. In particular, he urged schools to collect local poll and property taxes, which, he argued, would greatly increase revenues available for education: "Put business management into operation of the school system, see that the teachers are paid regularly fair living salaries, collect your taxes and I tell you there will be no school problem in Florida." Teachers and other professional educators found little consolation in these words; in 1934 some 6,000 Florida teachers were on relief.[21]

By 1935 the state's financial outlook had improved slightly, and in his budget message Sholtz suggested that either a three cents gasoline tax or a 3 percent sales tax be used to supply additional revenue for the schools. The legislature, however, resisted adopting either tax and chose not to act when Sholtz failed to press for his school finance program. As a result, the legislature's appropriation was $1.5 million less than the $10.5 million Sholtz had requested. Professional educators and their allies bitterly criticized the governor for failing to provide adequate school funds. To save face, in 1936 Sholtz appointed a committee to study school funding and report to the next legislature, by which time there would be a new governor. Sholtz avoided dealing with educational matters during the rest of his administration.[22]

While state finances have often limited the size of a governor's commitment to education, Fred Cone, whose administration was perhaps the most fiscally conservative of all in this century, in his first message to the legislature in 1937 called for "real money" for the schools. However, he also insisted on strict economy in all branches of government, and was unalterably opposed to any new taxes. During that same session Cone vetoed a teacher retirement bill, charging that it would simply drain the state's resources and that it discriminated against other state and local employees.[23]

In 1939 Cone again said he wanted "full funding" for the schools, but he opposed new taxes and any increase in the total appropriation for general government. Even before the legislative session began it was clear that school funding was the principal problem facing the legislature. But Cone provided no leadership on this matter. Instead he suggested strict enforcement of the existing tax laws. As a consequence, Florida's schools were financially strapped for the entire year and were in danger of having to close before the end of the school year. Without any guidance or prodding from Cone, the legislature passed an $11.4 million appropriation bill, plus an additional $2 million just to bail the schools out on an emergency basis.[24]

Although most Florida governors have not been as active in the support of education as their rhetoric suggests they might, there have been two occasions when governors were directly responsible for the development of significant, indeed innovative, policies in school finance. These were the Minimum Foundation Program (MFP) in 1947 and the Florida Education Finance Program (FEFP) in 1973. These programs were significant because they not only provided mechanisms for getting more state monies into the public schools, they also permitted consolidation of a diverse system of disbursements for the schools into a much more efficient and accountable procedure. For the period prior to 1940, it is virtually impossible to tell how much state money Florida poured into county schools, because disbursements were made on a fragmented, programmatic, strict line item basis (e.g., salaries, textbooks, etc.). As a result, it is not always possible to tell just how much money went to the schools. Beginning in 1940, however, and especially after 1948, it became possible to trace the origin and disbursement of state money for schools. But most important, the amount of money available to the schools began to increase sharply, as these figures from the comptrollers' *Reports* for the various years show: 1940 (county schools only), $12,749,780; 1950 MFP, $47,498,000; 1960 MFP, $181,031,031; 1970 MFP, $660,512,041; 1975 MFP, $1,324,263,847.

THE MINIMUM FOUNDATION PROGRAM AND THE FLORIDA EDUCATION FINANCE PROGRAM

Even before he became governor, Millard Caldwell had committed himself to the improvement of education in Florida. A major portion of his campaign platform was devoted to schools, and he was deeply concerned about the need to upgrade their quality in the years following the Second World War: "There's no more important problem facing Florida citizens than the critical condition of our schools."[25] In his campaign Caldwell stated he would "Guarantee to all Florida counties, rich or poor, the best trained teachers and the best equipped schools" by increasing state aid, instituting an equalization formula for distributing that aid, earmarking surplus state funds for teacher retirement, reforming teacher tenure provisions, increasing teacher retirement benefits, providing for suitable teacher sick leave, and extending both public school and higher education facilities. He later repeated these same pledges in his inaugural address.[26]

After Caldwell won the nomination for governor in 1944, he appointed a fifteen member, blue ribbon Florida Citizens' Committee on Education, headed by S. Kendrick Guernsey of Jacksonville, with the help of incumbent Governor Spessard Holland and Superintendent of Public Instruction Colin English. The committee was charged with surveying the condition of education in Florida and with making recommendations for meeting the needs of the state's young people in the postwar years. It was clear to Caldwell that Florida was ill-equipped to handle the anticipated population boom in the decades following the war.

Although the Citizens Committee was not legally established until the legislature passed a concurrent resolution in 1945, it actually began its deliberations in late 1944. Caldwell followed the work of the committee very closely, keeping in constant touch with Guernsey and showing great interest in the proceedings. He took an active role in hiring the committee staff, which included Edgar Morphet, who was later to become one of the nation's leading specialists in educational finance, as executive secretary.

Even with Caldwell's urging and the best efforts of the committee members and staff, it quickly became apparent that a full-blown report and set of recommendations would not be ready for the legislative session beginning in April 1945. There was simply too much work to be done. The committee, therefore, issued a preliminary set of proposals in February 1945, which were designed to provide basic educational needs for the state. Essentially, its plan consisted of an $18.2 million package of state aid to the schools. Of this amount, $4 million would have to come from new state sources.[27]

In his message to the legislature opening the 1945 session, Caldwell specifically pointed to the recommendations of the Citizens Committee (which he had earlier endorsed), and notified legislators that he expected them to be passed into law. He proposed that the schools receive over $3 million just to catch up to the needs of 1945, and some $5.3 million each year to improve their overall quality. To pay for the increased state assistance to education, as well as other state services, Caldwell recommended a rise in the cigarette tax from three to four cents; an increase in the beer tax from seven-eighths cents per bottle to three cents; and a large hike in the gross utilities receipts tax from 1.5 percent to 10 percent. The taxes, he claimed, would raise an additional $14 million per year.[28]

The day after the opening of the session, Caldwell submitted several education bills embodying his proposals and those of the committee. The two major bills consisted of a teacher pay raise ($2.7 million) and a $3.9 million school appropriations bill, which would increase state aid from $800 to $1,050 per instructional unit. As one analyst noted, Caldwell set an unusually fast pace for the legislature by introducing these key bills so early in the session. Before the end of April the education package had passed both houses with only a whisper of opposition. The wealth of individual Floridians had grown dramatically during the war years, and the governor and legislature were committed to using a portion of that wealth to upgrade public education. Teacher salaries had been increased retroactively, and a record $11.2 million general state aid to schools had been approved.[29]

In January 1947, the Citizens Committee issued its final reports and recommendations, and they proved to be far more critical of Florida's educational conditions, and more comprehensive in terms of future plans, than had been expected.[30] The committee felt that Florida had not committed sufficient resources to education in the past and was not doing so then. It argued that if the state wished to provide greater opportunities for its citizens, it would have to increase dramatically the investment it made in education. But the mechanism for providing increased state assistance would have to be changed to what the committee called a Minimum Foundation Program, the MFP. This would be a joint state-county program designed to insure a "floor," a minimum level of educational expenditure, for every school district in the state. Thus the gap between the wealthiest and poorest districts would be reduced, and all students, regardless of where they lived or how much money their parents made, could be assured of at least a guaranteed minimum quality education. The committee also recommended that substantial administrative and structural changes be made in the state school system. These included a new, separate, nonsalaried state board of education with an appointed state school superintendent (thus replacing the cabinet system for governing the state's schools), nonsalaried county boards of education with an appointed school superintendent, and changes in the tax structure for raising school revenues. On the last point, the committee took pains to suggest that the state stabilize its system of finance to provide for adequate planning as well as adaptation to new educational needs. Finally, in a series of detailed reports and proposals the committee made very specific recommendations in areas other than the MFP, including the instructional program in elementary and secondary schools, vocational education, special services, handicapped and other exceptional children, school personnel (including teacher salaries), other education and school related agencies, the school plant, and higher education.

In his speech opening the legislative session in 1947, Caldwell made no specific recommendations on education other than to endorse the work of the committee. In mid-April a bill was introduced which embodied its recommendations. The measure provided for school appropriations of $33 million each year, or a $15 million annual increase; this figure pared $3 million from the committee's suggestion of $18 million at Caldwell's request. Even with the cut, the appropriation would still bring Florida close to the national average in educational expenditures. The bill also mandated some local school district reorganization and reform, especially in the area of personnel practices.[31] The proposal for a new state board of education and appointed superintendent was, not surprisingly, rejected; neither members of the cabinet nor the citizens generally seemed to want the educational governing structure upset.

Caldwell's bill was well received in the house, but the senate was much more hesitant about the increased expenditures. Members seemed especially concerned about the added expense burden on counties (the smaller, rural, underpopulated counties were particularly worried). Caldwell spent about a month in intense lobbying for the bill. He and the bill's senate manager, Senator LeRoy Collins of Leon County, also decided that they would tie the teacher pay raise bill to the whole package and accept no other amendments. Thus, senators would have to vote on a take-it-or-leave-it basis. Given that choice, and coupled with the efforts made by Caldwell and Collins to enlist the support of senators' constituencies to convince them of the bill's merits, the bill easily passed in early May.[32]

The final bill provided for a $50 million education package, comprising some $36 million from the state and $14 million from counties. Some school district reorganization at the local level was also mandated. But the heart of the bill was the MFP, under which even the state's poorest children were guaranteed a basic quality education. This program was eventually copied by other states, and remained the basis for funding education in Florida until 1973. Indeed, it was substantially changed only once in the intervening years; in 1963 the funding formula was amended so that the state contributed 75 percent of all MFP funds, and local effort contributed only 25 percent.

The MFP was regarded as a real innovation in the late 1940s, but by the late 1960s it appeared to be outmoded. At that time Florida was again facing another school fiscal crisis. The 1960s had seen a number of commissions appointed by Florida governors and legislatures, including the Governor's Committee on Quality Education (Bryant), the Governor's Conference on Education (Burns), and the Commission for Quality Education (Kirk). All of them consistently pointed to growing educational problems in the state. Most of the difficulties were a result of the dramatic rise in Florida's population and a need for increased revenues. But growing urbanization, and particularly the racial problems of the large cities, caused unprecedented tensions in the state's schools.

In 1971 Governor Askew appointed a twenty-two member group called the Governor's Citizens' Committee on Education.[33] Meeting over a two year period, the committee, working closely with the governor, designed a new mechanism for educational funding. It is noteworthy that when Askew perceived reform of the MFP to be necessary, he employed the same device, the blue-ribbon citizens committee, that his predecessors had used to smooth over potentially troubled political waters.

The program which the committee designed is called the Florida Educational Finance Program (FEFP). Its thrust is much the same as that of the MFP in that it attempts to provide equality in education for students regardless of where they live or what their specific educational needs are. Under the FEFP, funds are distributed to local school districts based on the number of full-time equivalent student hours, thus permitting more funds to go to crowded urban districts. The funding formula also takes into account program cost factors (since some educational programs are more expensive to operate than others), compensatory education supplements (which are aimed at educationally disadvantaged urban and rural students), district cost differentials, and the local tax effort.[34]

Askew was an enthusiastic advocate of the new FEFP formula as were many legislators. The bill, which he signed on June 26, 1973, actually increased state school operating funds by $32 million. He was especially pleased that the formula did away with many of the old restrictions on the use of state funds; thus under the new program local school officials have not only more funds available but greater flexibility in their use. "This is a giant step," said Askew as he signed the bill. "It completely rewrites the MFP and guarantees every school child an equal chance for a quality education."[35]

HIGHER EDUCATION

Elementary and secondary schools comprise a very significant portion of Florida's concern with education, but by no means the only part. Public colleges and universities also represent a substantial investment by the state in terms of resource commitment and policy development. In Florida, however, gubernatorial concern with higher education during the twentieth century has been less pronounced than with elementary and secondary education. Other than making budget requests for colleges and universities and perhaps an occasional speech on the importance of higher education, most Florida governors have not made any significant policy recommendations in this area. The reasons are not hard to find. The State Board of Control (later the Board of Regents) was responsible for overseeing the state's institutions of public higher education; its members are appointed by the governor with the approval of the state senate. Governors have generally found it more convenient, and less politically trying, to work through these boards to make policy recommendations than through direct involvement. Moreover, higher education is a policy area which seems to be especially sensitive to charges of political intervention, and most governors have preferred to keep colleges and universities at arm's length. Finally, until the post–World War II period there seemed to be little need for much gubernatorial leadership in higher education. The three state universities—two in Tallahassee and one in Gainesville—seemed to fulfill the needs of the state. Only with the rapid rise in enrollment following the war was it clear that Florida needed more institutions of higher education and new policies to satisfy state requirements. It was at this time that governors began to take a more active role in this policy sector than earlier ones had.

The most important development concerning higher education in Florida early in this century occurred in 1905 during Broward's administration. Until that time, Florida had an array of eight state-supported seminaries, colleges, and universities. They were only loosely connected, and there was little, if any, coordination among them. It could scarcely be said that Florida, at that time, had any real *system* of higher education. The Buckman Act in 1905 changed this situation. It created a five-member State Board of Control, which was to be responsible to the State Board of Education (the cabinet). The Board of Control was to be appointed by the governor, with members serving overlapping terms. The Buckman Act also abolished the previously existing eight institutions of higher education and replaced them with three. Florida Female College (later Florida State College for Women and then Florida State University), the University of Florida, and Florida Agricultural and Mechanical College for Negroes.[36]

While agreeing with the thrust of the Buckman Bill, Broward denied that it came at his suggestion. He claimed he did favor three universities built in the most populous regions of the state; at that time these were all in northern Florida and the Panhandle. The extent to which Broward may have influenced the Board of Control in its first major decision, the location of the University of Florida, is not known, unfortunately. Gainesville was victorious over Lake City on a close vote. Gainesville won, apparently, because it offered free water to the university, even though Lake City offered more land.[37]

Following the passage of the Buckman Act higher education received little gubernatorial attention until the Caldwell administration. Caldwell was interested in both lower and higher education, and he is the only Florida governor in this century who was willing to make the necessary commitment to upgrade all parts of the state's educational system to make them compare favorably with those elsewhere in the country.

Again, it was Caldwell's Florida Citizens' Committee on Education which made major policy recommendations that changed the course of higher education in this state. In its reports, the committee pointed to the growing demand for higher education in the state, especially in the years following the war, and said Florida was not in a position to meet those needs. Accordingly, in its major recommendations it proposed the establishment of coeducation at all public institutions of higher learning in the state, of another state university in the southern part of Florida, and of a true university system headed by a chancellor to coordinate and administer a statewide program of higher education. Not all of the committee's recommendations were immediately adopted. In 1947, the University of Florida was made coeducational. Florida State University was also created in that year from the old Florida State College for Women; it too became coeducational. Eventually the other recommendations of the committee were accepted by the state.

Caldwell's role in higher education did not stop with the Citizens' Committee. During his tenure as governor Caldwell was chairman of the Southern Governors' Conference. While serving, he was an advocate of what he called regional higher education. He felt that it would be difficult if not impossible for individual southern states to create systems of higher education which were both large enough and of sufficient quality to satisfy the growing needs of the region. As a result, he proposed that the southern states band together in a compact which would permit sharing of programs, facilities, and personnel in higher education, easy transfer of students and credits among member institutions, and general coordination of higher education efforts. Caldwell argued in a series of public statements that by engaging in this kind of enterprise, the southern states could provide services needed in higher education and avoid waste, duplication of effort, and the growth of an array of mediocre colleges and universities.[38]

Caldwell was only partially successful in his efforts to promote regional higher education. He did succeed in establishing the Southern Regional Education Board as a part of the Southern Governors' Conference; and the board continues to act as a coordinating device for higher education in the South. He served as the first head of the board, and after leaving the governorship continued to participate actively in its affairs. Caldwell did not succeed in persuading his fellow southern governors to make the same commitment to higher education that he did; he even had trouble getting them to pay the relatively modest dues ($3,000 per year at the start) needed to make the board work. He was also criticized by many blacks, because they felt that his regional higher education proposals would preserve racial segregation at colleges and universities which, in fact, seems to have been his intention. Nonetheless, Caldwell's efforts were recognized elsewhere in the country. Benjamin Fine, at that time the highly respected education editor of the *New York Times,* noted the development of regional higher education in the South and urged other sections of the country to emulate it.[39]

Equally important to the growth of state services in higher education was Governor LeRoy Collins' advocacy of a system of state-supported community colleges. It was the adoption of this program in Florida that brought about a true democratization of higher education in the state; it was now possible for people in all parts of Florida, and from virtually all income levels, to participate in some form of postsecondary education. Collins did not originate the idea of a state community college program. In fact, legislators and educators had publicly discussed the idea for some time. And yet it was Collins' support in 1955 which enabled the state to establish the Community College Council and Community College Advisory Board. The council set forth a plan for the community college system in the state; its report, called "The Community Junior College in Florida's Future," was released in 1957. The advisory board was to establish a long-range plan for building and coordinating community colleges prior to the 1957 legislative session.

But Collins had already committed himself to the development of community colleges. During the first days of his administration, in March 1955, he publicly stated that he opposed the construction of more state universities; he later modified his views on this point and supported the founding of the

Governor Millard Caldwell addressing a group of newspaper reporters in 1947 in the chamber of the Florida House of Representatives. Caldwell used the press skillfully as a means of persuading legislators to accept his programs. He was especially successful in gaining support for his far-reaching reforms in educational finance. State Photographic Archives.

University of South Florida in Tampa. But early in his administration he felt the existing institutions, including private colleges and universities, ought to be encouraged to expand. However, he warmly endorsed community colleges, arguing that the state ought to spend its limited funds for higher education expansion in this area because such institutions could educate people efficiently and effectively.[40]

The 1957 legislative session was something of a landmark for community colleges in the state. With Collins' support, the legislature approved a program to provide the whole state with community college facilities. Using the California system as a model, funds were provided for the existing four community college regions, six new institutions were established, and more were planned for the future (twenty-eight community colleges were eventually opened). The legislature also brought the community colleges under the MFP formula, although the mechanism for funding was different from that for the elementary and secondary schools.[41]

While the governor's role in higher education was an influential one, he was not free to direct it as he chose, as Collins came to realize. Collins advocated establishing a state university system headed by a chancellor, as

Caldwell's Citizens' Committee had recommended. The legislature, however, would have none of it. J. Wayne Reitz, at that time president of the University of Florida, openly opposed the bill. Collins was publicly critical of Reitz's position. He noted that the three other university presidents had not opposed his plan, and said Reitz was "out of step. ... The best I can determine he just resents having any professional leadership between him and the Board of Control." Reitz hit back at Collins the next day, saying the chancellor system would bring an unnecessary and costly bureaucracy to the governance of higher education in the state. Collins' bill was introduced in the legislature in late April 1957. It was immediately buried by legislative committees, and never emerged; undoubtedly the presence of many University of Florida alumni among legislative members, as well as the public opposition of the influential Reitz, persuaded many legislators to oppose it. The chancellor's office and university system were not actually founded until 1963, during Farris Bryant's tenure.[42]

It should not be assumed, however, that Collins' relationship with Reitz and other state university officials was generally critical or hostile. The opposite is more correct. Collins attempted to cooperate with university faculty and administrators as they sought to expand and improve higher education in the state. He was, in fact, instrumental in securing Reitz' appointment to the presidency of the University of Florida. In 1953, when the presidency became vacant following the death of J. Hillis Miller, the Board of Control, which had responsibility for the appointment, was leaning toward either an out-of-state educator or Dr. John Allen, a Floridian who was serving as acting president and who later became the first president of the University of South Florida. The faculty in Gainesville, however, was unhappy with these choices, and declared that Reitz was the only acceptable candidate. One of the leaders of the faculty communicated its desires to Charles Ausley, a former law partner of Collins, who passed along this information to the governor. He, in turn, spoke with members of the Board of Control, and later called the faculty member. Collins indicated that while he could not promise that Reitz would be appointed, he assured him that neither of the other candidates would be named. Shortly thereafter, Reitz did become president.[43]

During the 1960s higher education grew rapidly in the state. By the early 1970s there were nine state universities; enrollment in the institutions rose from 27,000 in 1960 to 110,600 in 1974. The development of the state's community colleges has already been noted; by 1974 about 430,000 students were enrolled in them. The political ramifications of higher education as a policy issue can ultimately be seen in the decision to build a nine-campus state university system and an extensive array of public community colleges. Universities and community colleges have often been used by governors as patronage devices to fulfill their campaign promises and smooth over their political difficulties in some of the state's regions.

Gubernatorial decisions to support additional higher education institutions did not result solely from these reasons; governors also felt, and rightly so, that great opportunities for higher education were needed in the state. But the political motivations which helped establish Florida's particular system of higher education cannot completely be discounted either. Thus one finds every Florida governor from Collins (who originally opposed the idea of more public universities) through Kirk strongly endorsing the establishment of more campuses throughout the state.

But the growth of the system was not without its problems. Farris Bryant, for example, seemed not to notice that the rapid development of higher education required administrators and faculty to have considerable independence in decision-making in order to assure its orderly growth. Bryant was willing to work through the Regents on some matters, but as with all state agencies he was generally so finicky about details and so fiscally conservative that he refused to delegate any responsibility. For example, Bryant insisted that he personally approve the appointment of any individual to any state position which paid more than $10,000 annually. In the case of institutions of higher learning, this included full professors, department chairmen, deans, and other administrators at this salary level. Normally these appointments were routinely handled at the institutions themselves. At one point the University of Florida was actively seeking a new chairman for the department of foreign languages, and agreement was reached on, and an offer made to, a distinguished scholar from out of state. When the appointment was submitted to Bryant, however, he delayed a decision for some months. Efforts to prod him into action were fruitless. Finally, the individual nominated could no longer wait for Bryant's approval, and he withdrew his name. The university then had to find another candidate. On another occasion, following a freeze in December 1962 which did serious damage to the citrus crop, Bryant declared a state fiscal emergency and directed that money appropriated by the legislature for faculty salary raises be withheld. Efforts by university personnel, other state officers, and public groups to change the governor's mind were to no avail. Bryant, it should be noted, did not try to hurt the universities or use them as political whipping boys. But neither did he try to help them. His fiscal conservatism and unwillingness to trust others' judgment may have impeded the development of flexible, accountable organizational structures and procedures in the university system which were needed to guide it through a period of rapid growth.[44]

Gubernatorial leadership in higher education seemed to be lacking at crucial times. Perhaps the most critical of such occasions occurred during the late 1950s and early 1960s when the Johns Committee was investigating higher education in the state. A special senate committee chaired by Charley Johns of Starke was established in the late 1950s to investigate the NAACP and communists in the state; the committee was formed despite the opposition of Collins, who said he thought that if it was to exist at all, it also ought to investigate the Ku Klux Klan. The committee never had a clearly defined task, especially in terms of its investigations of higher education. However, early on it sought to root out communists, homosexuals, and other allegedly subversive and un-American elements from the universities. The focus was primarily on the University of South Florida, but all the institutions were involved. Charges were made against individual faculty members, and resignations were forced. The curriculum was attacked; the activities of the Johns Committee became infamously branded throughout the nation as a witch-hunt.

In its report in early 1963 the committee made a number of serious allegations.[45] It maintained that the university administrators had invited known communist sympathizers to lecture or teach; that professors were teaching ideas contrary to orthodox religious principles; that professors were using "newsstand paperbacks" containing salacious material in their classes; and that there was homosexuality in the university system. Most of these charges were made on the basis of hearsay and similar dubious evidence. The effect of these charges is impossible to document conclusively. However, at the University of Florida alone more than a dozen faculty may have been investigated, and allegedly about that number left the university as a result.

Johns later regretted his role in the investigation, saying it was unproductive and injurious.[46] Nevertheless, the damage was done. Unfortunately, neither LeRoy Collins nor Farris Bryant spoke out in defense of the university system, its programs, or its personnel. Neither came to the aid of those faculty members who were forced out of the system although both men supported higher education. Yet neither was anxious to buck the tide created by the Johns Committee and defend higher education during what was surely its darkest hour in the state. While neither Collins nor Bryant probably wanted to dignify the Johns Committee's work by bringing public attention to it, it would appear that some defense of the system by the governor might have made the institutions, and the people in them, less vulnerable to the tactics being used against them.

A few years later the university system was again thrown into turmoil, this time by a dispute between Haydon Burns and the Regents appointed by his predecessor, Farris Bryant. The 1963 legislature passed a bill dissolving the old Board of Control and replacing it with a nine-member Board of Regents. Bryant did not make his nominations to the Regents until late in his administration. As a result, it was too late to have the senate confirm them before the beginning of Burns' tenure.

Burns felt that he was being burdened by Bryant's midnight appointees, and resented having a board over which he could exercise virtually no control. Accordingly, he filed suit to disallow the Bryant regents from occupying their seats. In mid-February 1965, the state supreme court ruled that Burns could ignore Bryant's appointees; all he had to do was withdraw their names before the senate met in April. Most observers felt that the Bryant regents would have to resign under those circumstances; they eventually did.

Burns, however, was seriously criticized for his action. Senator Ed Price of Bradenton accused him of throwing the universities into "total turmoil" by his action. Secretary of State Tom Adams roundly condemned Burns, noting that the express purpose of creating the regents was "to insulate higher education in this state from the day-to-day pressures of political harassment and involvement." By his actions, according to Adams, Burns had served to politicize the regents and create an atmosphere of confusion and mistrust. Similar charges were hurled at Burns by others in the state, and it was only after Burns appointed his own regents that matters quieted down.[47]

Of all Florida governors in this century, Haydon Burns seems to have had the most difficulty dealing with higher education. He intervened more regularly in the affairs of colleges and universities than most others, with the result that he was consistently opposed by members of the higher education profession and its allies.

During a conflict between Burns and University of Florida President J. Wayne Reitz over fiscal autonomy for the universities, Reitz even criticized Burns while the governor was visiting the university. Burns regarded fiscal autonomy as a "disaster," while of course it was strongly favored by university administrators. The governor felt that fiscal autonomy would result in the establishment of strong competition among the universities for higher levels of state appropriations. He also felt that a rational approach to university expansion would be "thrown out" as a consequence of this competition. Moreover, Burns maintained that university presidents would simply act in their own self-interest, rather than for the good of the whole system, or the state, under fiscal autonomy. Burns further antagonized the academic community by his insistence on selecting university presidents. He was appalled that so few of them had had any fiscal or administrative experience, and he felt that no one man could handle all the responsibilities of a university president without a strong management background. The academicians of course disagreed, and antipathy between Burns and the universities became so great that the faculty senate at the University of Florida censured him.[48]

Burns especially alienated educators by his action in the appointment of a president for Florida State University. A group of faculty met with Burns to draw up a list of possible candidates for the position. The original list consisted of over 100 names, which the faculty committee reduced to ten. It then presented the list to Burns for his final consideration. Burns' response was not to examine the list at all; he returned the files to the committee unopened, and he told the faculty members, "The employer does the hiring, and not the employees."[49]

Burns also took a direct role in the establishment of the University of West Florida in Pensacola and Florida Technological University (now the University of Central Florida) in Orlando. Originally, on a list of construction priorities given to Burns by the State Education Department these institutions were ranked low: numbers sixty-nine and seventy. However, at a cabinet meeting, Burns directed Chancellor Broward Culpepper to revise the list and see that the two universities ranked numbers one and two. This was done, and only then did Burns accept the list as one he would support.[50]

The years following Burns' governorship represented something of a respite for institutions of higher learning in Florida. Whereas Burns insisted on having a direct hand in university affairs, Claude Kirk was largely oblivious to them. The rapid growth of the system continued and even increased during the late 1960s, and Kirk largely let the universities, and regents, steer their own course. Only one significant conflict occurred. After the resignation of J. Wayne Reitz as president of the University of Florida in 1967, Kirk sought to have one of his friends and supporters, a prominent state businessman, appointed to the post. The nomination was made through a Kirk-appointed regent, Dr. Wayne McCall, a dentist from Ocala. Chester Ferguson, chairman of the regents, and other members of the board were interested in other candidates, including Stephen C. O'Connell, chief justice of the Florida Supreme Court. The consulting faculty committee of the university felt that O'Connell was the most acceptable of the candidates who could get regent support, and indicated this to Ferguson. After O'Connell was named, Kirk called for Ferguson's resignation. But the chairman, in a public statement reminiscent in tone and sentiment of Macaulay's poem "Horatio at the Bridge," defended his honor and the regents' selection. Instead, it was Dr. McCall who resigned from the regents. After this dispute, Kirk largely left the regents, and higher education, alone.

Reubin Askew was far more vocal in his support of higher education than either Burns or Kirk. During the first years of his administration he seemed especially anxious to move the system forward. However, he never submitted a substantially increased budget for higher education. Later, in the mid-1970s, when a severe recession hit the state, Askew no longer could commit even modest increments of money to expand and improve the universities. Nonetheless, he never singled out higher education for substantial budget cuts in the way in which other state officials (such as Dempsey Barron, former president of the senate) did. Moreover, Askew appears to have had a generally good rapport with university officials and the regents. He did not always agree with them, nor did he accede to their requests (especially budgetary ones) or involve himself in public disputes or conflicts with them. He sought to resist legislative encroachment into traditional university affairs. Although he signed the twelve-hour law (which requires a minimum classroom time for each faculty member), he did so reluctantly; and in 1977 he vetoed a bill which might have required censorship of certain kinds of films before they could be shown on campuses.[51]

SUMMARY

Education has been a crucial policy issue in Florida throughout the twentieth century. It has sometimes dominated a governor's administration. And yet the governor's role in this area, as policy leader, has been restrained. It has been limited by a governing structure which permits only indirect leadership in education, vesting power instead in the elected commissioner of education and State Board of Education. In addition, the value system concerning education prevents too active a role by the governor. Floridians generally, and professional educators in particular, seem very sensitive to political intervention into education. Governors of Florida, then, have trod very lightly in this policy area during this century.

In their rhetoric governors of this state have invariably been supporters of education. Millard Caldwell probably did the most to improve it significantly and to achieve the quality of educational systems found in other states. Caldwell saw that tremendous demographic changes faced Florida following World War II and felt they necessitated significant upgrading of educational services provided by the state. Governors such as Collins and Askew placed a higher priority on education and sought to improve it throughout Florida, but each felt constrained by budgetary problems, and thus limited the commitment which he was prepared to make to education.

Collins and Askew also expressed serious reservations about pouring additional sums of money into education. Their concerns were based principally on budgetary limitations. Other governors, such as Sholtz and Kirk, seem to have been disillusioned with professional educators as well as concerned with pressing financial matters. But whatever the cause, the result has been the same: in most gubernatorial administrations during this century, education has not had any special treatment in the budget, even while its prominence and importance as a policy issue, state service, and right of the citizens have been consistently recognized.

With Florida's rapid growth following World War II, governors have played a more active role in education. Prior to that time, policy proposals came mainly from professional schoolmen; these were made directly to the cabinet or legislature, often without much intervention by the governor. Governors in the first quarter of this century were only tangentially involved in the public school affairs since the school system was totally decentralized. In addition, there were only three schools of higher learning, each of which was very small and required small state appropriations. But the pressures of rapid growth on the state's schools and institutions of higher learning have forced most governors to take a more active role. Gubernatorial leadership in the area of school finance has been particularly necessary to insure that Florida could provide at least minimal levels of support, and educational quality, for the tremendous number of new citizens it gained yearly.

As the education budget has increased, education as a policy issue has become increasingly political. The prominence of education in the state's budget (education-related expenditures account for approximately two-thirds of the budget) has prompted the governor's intervention. This has been especially true during times of economic hardship in the state. But political developments within the field of education itself, including teacher militancy and unionization, accountability, race and busing, and for a period, student unrest, have all brought about additional gubernatorial participation in educational affairs. Public disillusionment with at least some parts of the state's educational system has added to the political atmosphere surrounding the schools, where previously there was none, or at least a very low key political atmosphere.

It remains to be seen what the long-term effects of increased gubernatorial involvement in the state's educational systems will be. However, it does seem clear that the gubernatorial role in education is likely to become an increasingly prominent one during the rest of this century. This is probably true even if Florida eventually changes its constitution and opts for an appointed, rather than elected, state commissioner of education. Education as a policy issue, it is often said, is now too important to be left to professional educators. If that is true, then the governor, as the chief elected official in the state, will have to play an ever more important role in directing its growth and in choosing new policy alternatives for the future.

10

Criminal Justice

THE direction and operation of prisons have not regularly been areas of prime concern to Florida governors. As long as criminals are kept safely behind bars and prevented from rioting, the governors have tended to ignore prisons and leave their administration to the superintendent of prisons and the directors of the respective state institutions. Only when controversy has surrounded some specific penal matters have the governors intervened.

The governors' failure to address prison matters during this century reflected the interests and needs of the public. The people of Florida have consistently demonstrated little interest in prison problems during the twentieth century. They have also expressed a desire to punish criminals rather than rehabilitate them. Consequently, the citizenry has seldom been concerned with stories or pictures of horrid prison conditions. The typical attitude of most Floridians has been that criminals go to prison to be punished, not to be coddled. Without exception, the twentieth-century governors have reflected this view.

THE CONVICT LEASE SYSTEM

Because of the public's attitude, the governors in the early twentieth century allowed the convict lease system to continue long after it had been acknowledged as a cruel and harsh exploitation of prison labor. Established in 1868, the convict lease system was a consequence of the major labor shortage in Florida during the nineteenth and early twentieth centuries. The shortage was particularly acute in such important industrial areas as lumbering, turpentine manufacturing, and phosphate mining. In fact, the convict lease system came into existence throughout the South during this period as a way to supplement or replace the loss of slave labor. Not only had the abolition of slavery hurt the labor situation, but many freed slaves decided to start their lives anew in the North. As historian Fletcher Green noted, the Civil War "halted the development of the penitentiary system; and the social, economic, and political unrest of the Reconstruction period fixed the lease system upon the South almost to the exclusion of other forms of labor." With state treasuries almost empty, prisons in ruins, and crime increasing, the lease method appeared to be the most desirable arrangement. Under the system, prisoners could be leased for five years although most businessmen utilized them for a shorter period of time. The worst conditions existed in the phosphate mines. One such mine in Elliston, Citrus County, was found by a legislative investigating committee to have such cruel and inhumane conditions "that would be hard to realize unless it could have been seen or heard." The eighty leased convicts suffered from a lack of food, clean clothes, and bedding, and were in poor health. Many convicts had severe lash cuts on their backs.[1]

Nevertheless, because of the labor problems, every governor endorsed the convict lease system in the early twentieth century. William Jennings did recommend changes but not to aid the prisoners. Jennings was disturbed by the small sums the state received for leasing convicts. Under his leadership syndicate bidding for prison labor was eliminated and the state's revenues were increased, often at the expense of the prisoners, however.[2]

Napoleon Broward defended the system, contending that 75 percent of the reports of cruel and inhuman treatment of convicts had originated in county convict camps or with county prisoners at state camps over which the Department of Agriculture had no control. He urged, however, that the legislature end the leasing of female, aged, and decrepit convicts. Prior to Broward's recommendation, these prisoners had been freely leased and companies were forced to pay the same rental to the state as they did for a healthy convict. In 1903 the Naval Stores and Commission Company, which operated thirty camps in turpentine farms and phosphate mines, built a hospital to care for these prisoners. The state offered no assistance in this matter other than to examine conditions at the hospital periodically. Broward and his commissioner of agriculture were particularly insistent on ending female leasing. The commissioner noted that he had "not found any State or civilized country that leases out its female labor except our own State." Broward also added a note of caution to the state's enthusiasm over the economic success of the lease system: "Penal laws and prisons [were] not to revenge upon the criminal his offense against society, but to reform him and make him a beneficial and producing element in the social system rather than a charge upon it."[3]

Few heard Broward's moral stirrings, however. His successor, Albert Gilchrist, for example, publicly defended the system at a meeting of the American Prison Association in Omaha, Nebraska. He characterized the work as rehabilitating; prisoners learned a trade while working in the fresh air. Gilchrist also pointed out at this meeting a most important feature of the lease system; it generated revenue for the state (approximately $340,000 to $350,000 per year). Florida was a poor state during this part of its history, and this source of funds was not inconsequential to Gilchrist's administration. During his governorship the state signed a four year lease with the Florida Pine Company which specified segregation of convicts, certain uniforms, and health care. Gilchrist resisted an effort to use the state convicts in a road building program because it was not profitable. He felt the county convicts could build the roads, and revenues raised through state leasing would provide the money.[4]

Despite the rosy picture painted by Gilchrist at the meeting, conditions were bad under the lease system and he and his predecessors knew it. Gilchrist had Mr. D. D. Clark investigate conditions of prisoners at the Sweat Turpentine Company near Olustee, Florida. Clark's report concluded that the condition of prisoners was "very bad . . . generally." He found one convict badly beaten and the other prisoners half-clothed, most without shoes. Their housing conditions were as severe. The Sweat Turpentine Company had no bathing facilities and the stockade lacked a roof. Apparently the rain was considered sufficient for bathing. The state consistently had trouble finding guards who would treat the prisoners decently. Salaries for guards were a meager $18 to $25 per month with board at the camp. Few able men remained guards for long.[5]

Despite the abuses in the system, Gilchrist did not ask the legislature to abolish it. The importance of the convict lease system to the economic well-being of the state and its industries was widely recognized and the legislature would not have approved its elimination even if Gilchrist had recommended it.[6]

Reform in the leasing system was also made difficult by the large number of prisoners who were black, over 80 percent in 1906. The white political leadership in Florida had little sympathy for the black convict. For example, in his report to Gilchrist, Clark noted disparagingly that white convicts slept in beds "which Negroes had vacated, and in the same bedding." The commissioner of agriculture defended the use of corporal punishment by those who leased prisoners since the prison class came from the "lower strata of the Negro race."[7] While addressing the American Prison Association, Gilchrist commented that 80 percent of the convicts were black as if this statistic provided a defense for the leasing system. In many respects, the convict lease system was the South's answer to the abolition of slavery and the consequential decline in available black labor.

The attitude toward black prisoners was clearly reflected in the response by the prison superintendent during a minor prison revolt in 1914. On November 12, some black prisoners brandishing bed slats ordered others not to leave when the door was opened in the morning for them to go to work. The prisoners demanded to speak to the governor about conditions before they would surrender. The superintendent had been in Lake City and arrived back five or six hours after the revolt began. He grabbed a rifle and entered the chamber where the rebels were seated. He ordered the men to lie on the floor and then fired a shot at the man he thought had engineered the protest, but missed him. The superintendent then shot and killed a prisoner who had not obeyed his order to lie down. A joint legislative investigating commission called the shooting "absolutely unjustifiable," but apparently no action was taken against the superintendent.[8] Florida's governors never questioned the convict lease system until the abuses became so bad that public opinion forced them to respond. Significantly, they reacted not to abuses of black prisoners but to the hardships of white prisoners.

Gilchrist's administration did rectify some aspects of the leasing system. For example, the use of old, infirm, and female prisoners was halted and the Sweat Turpentine Company was ordered to improve working conditions for white prisoners.[9] In 1912 the state purchased almost 17,000 acres near Ellerbe and Raiford to build a state prison for those prisoners not leased. No buildings were constructed, however, because the legislature failed to appropriate sufficient money.[10]

Gilchrist's successor, Park Trammell, urged the construction of a prison to house criminals since the state owned no buildings, stockades, or hospitals. He also recommended that prisoners be used in road building in the future. Trammell felt the state was unable to supervise the convict lease system properly and that the misuse of convict labor was widespread. The legislature approved the construction of a prison farm in 1913. The measure also divided convicts into two categories—Class I included all able-bodied men, Class II covered infirm and aged men and women. Counties were also permitted to use state prisoners in road construction for a $100 lease plus prisoner expenses. But the governors refused to abolish the convict lease system.[11]

Sidney Catts had given no indication of supporting an end to the lease system during his gubernatorial campaign. According to his biographer, however, his residing in DeFuniak Springs, Florida, "had exposed him to the abuses visited on convicts leased to the turpentine camps, and he was determined to improve conditions." His aide, Jerry Carter, also pleaded with Catts to endorse such a change. Catts appointed J. S. Blitch as superintendent of prisons. Blitch proved himself exceedingly able and farsighted. He introduced for the first time a rehabilitation program at Raiford prison and provided recreational and educational facilities for the prisoners. In 1917 the legislature approved a Convict Lease Act which assigned 300 convicts to the State Road Department, but any male convict not employed on roads or the prison farm could be leased privately for two years. In 1919, at Catts' urging, the legislature approved the end of leasing for state convicts although the leasing of prisoners continued at the county level.[12] The system was abolished at all levels only when it became a national scandal.

In 1923 Martin Tabert of Munich, North Dakota, died from a whipping after serving a sentence in the camp of the Putnam Lumber Company near Clara, Florida. Tabert had been arrested for traveling on a train in Florida without a ticket. His mother had subsequently sent a letter with money to the sheriff to pay for the offense, but the sheriff returned the letter unopened with a note, "Party Gone." On April 18, 1923, Tabert died after receiving 100 lashes at the Putnam Camp. The North Dakota legislature passed a resolution asking the Florida legislature to investigate and alleging that the sheriff and the lumber camp were involved in a conspiracy to convict men for minor offenses. Governor Cary Hardee, a proponent of the lease system, criticized the resolution for giving Florida "unwholesome publicity." Nevertheless, he suspended the Leon County sheriff and judge for their role in Tabert's confinement and death. The legislature, under considerable public pressure, created a joint senate and house committee to investigate Tabert's death. During the course of the investigation, the wife of a small town postmaster revealed that nine prisoners had been killed at the MacClenny camp of Senator T. J. Knabb of Baker County. J. H. Thomas, state prison supervisor, corroborated Mrs. Franklin's testimony, calling the Knabb camp "a human slaughter pen." Thomas claimed to know of nine or more deaths. Thomas also alleged that Knabb had offered him $1,500 to close the case of Paul White who died at the camp. Under continued pressure from the public and the press, and at the urging of Governor Cary Hardee, the legislature placed a ban on whipping prisoners. When the public demand for the elimination of the convict lease system did not diminish, the legislature formally abolished the system in May 1923, to take effect January 1, 1924.[13]

PRISON REFORM AND THE DEATH PENALTY

The nullification of the leasing system did not lead to better prison conditions. Shortly after its abolition, the state put the convicts to work on highway construction often under conditions as harsh as those encountered in the phosphate mines or the turpentine mills. Blacks continued to receive the worst treatment, laboring in malaria-infested swamps to build a highway system that would open up the state for land development and tourism. Doyle Carlton refused to allow white prisoners to work under such conditions.[14] In a real sense, therefore, the economic vitality of Florida was made possible by imprisoned blacks who provided the muscle for the state's development.

Despite the harshness of prison life in Florida and the occasional criticism of it by prison reformers and the press, little has been done to eliminate even its worst aspects. In fact, prison reform has received almost no support from the state's governors. Their failure to move in this direction reflects the lack of public interest in prison reform as well as the lack of financial resources to implement any such changes even if the governor were so inclined. Prison reform costs money and Florida could not afford it prior to World War II. The state's financially distressed condition simply prohibited improvements in an area that was not high on anyone's priority list.

John Martin was the only governor to propose significant improvements in the system. He urged installation in prisons of factories for making shoes and license plates. Martin believed it would be good business for the state, ease the burden of prison life, and help reform prisoners.[15] However, his proposals died with the collapse of the state's economy in 1925. Fred Cone asked the Prison Industries Reorganization Administration, a federal agency, to survey the Florida penal system. The report issued by their survey team in June 1939 urged the development and extension of educational and vocational training activities, adoption of a merit system for prisoners, expansion of prison industries, separation of the women's from the men's prison, and the establishment of several experimental minimum security farms. The report was never considered by the legislature because of the preparation for World War II, and many of the suggested reforms were not implemented until the 1970s. Doyle Carlton and Spessard Holland also took an active interest in prison conditions although they never encouraged reforms in the system. Both men, nevertheless, approached their duties as head of the Pardon Board in a conscientious manner. Carlton took a personal interest in older prisoners who lacked a lawyer or friend or relative to defend them before the Pardon Board. Holland directed the release of 508 men after a thorough investigation revealed they had served their sentences without problems and were ready to be returned to society.[16] Holland and his Pardon Board may have had additional reasons for releasing so many men. The state was seriously short of laborers during World War II, and they apparently sought to bolster the work force as well as to provide more men for the armed forces. To Holland's credit, he established the Parole and Probation Board system and modernized methods to oversee state prisoners.

While LeRoy Collins was never an exponent of prison reform, he did oppose the abuse of prisoners. In November 1958, he condemned the mistreatment of convicts at Raiford prison after reports disclosed that prisoners on death row were refused smoking privileges and often handcuffed to their cell doors for seventy-six hours at a time. Collins called such acts "indefensible."[17]

The lack of concern for prisoner rehabilitation continued throughout the 1960s. The three governors of that decade—Bryant, Burns, and Kirk—urged more money for law enforcement and stiffer prison penalties instead. Kirk strongly supported the "law and order" campaign conducted by President Richard Nixon's administration.

Initially, Reubin Askew seemed to offer a new direction in prison management. Upon taking office he urged that the "correctional system must be fully committed to the complete and efficient rehabilitation of offenders." In his first legislative address, he noted that 80 percent of those arrested in 1970 were repeaters—"people who have been punished before but not rehabilitated." He recommended an ambitious prison reform schedule including an extended work release program for twelve rather than six months, furlough visits home rather than twenty-four hour visits, an appropriation of $1.3 million for more parole and probation officials to supervise these programs, and $10.3 million for additional prisons.[18] The legislature agreed to all of the governor's recommendations.

By 1972, however, Askew's views on prison reform began to harden. Despite severely overcrowded conditions in the state's prisons, he failed to recommend additional appropriations for prison construction in either 1973 or 1974. By 1975 the shift in his views appeared to have become complete; he called on the legislature to adopt "stricter punishment for repeat offenders and mandatory prison sentences for the use of dangerous weapons in committing crimes." He also recommended swifter punishment of suspected felons. Of a like mind, the legislature passed a law requiring a three year to life sentence for all crimes committed with a gun. The legislators also approved additional funds for courts to reduce their case loads. To Askew's credit he did secure an additional $21 million for prison construction.[19] However, in 1975 most Floridians supported construction programs no matter what their nature to help the state and the construction business out of the recession. Askew also vetoed the "shoot to kill" bill in the 1976 session, noting that the bill would have made it legal for homeowners to shoot anyone trespassing on their property. Such legislation was considered too extreme even by many "law and order" advocates in Florida.

By 1976 Floridians, like most Americans, seemed much more desirous of punishing criminals and removing them from society than establishing effective rehabilitation programs. Governor Askew's changing views on prison reform seemed to reflect the desires of his constituents.

The gubernatorial position on the death penalty has been consistent with its position on prison reform. Every governor in the twentieth century has supported the death penalty; each has viewed it as an effective deterrent to crime. During his gubernatorial campaign, Albert Gilchrist took a strong stand endorsing capital punishment as a preventive to other murders. Virtually all governors since Gilchrist have echoed his view. This, of course, did not make the signing of a death warrant any easier for governors.[20]

Although the argument cannot be made without qualification, it does appear, that up to 1965 at least, the state's political leaders had little hesitancy about invoking the death penalty because most prisoners who were sentenced to death were black. When Farris Bryant was asked to comment on Florida's thirty-eight executions in 1963, a figure that ranked the state third in the nation, he replied that he had not studied the situation and, consequently, had no opinion about it. But Senator Ed Price of Bradenton who had studied the situation seemed to dismiss the statistics when he noted that over 50 percent of those executed had been Negroes.[21]

In 1971 the Supreme Court ruled in *Furman* v. *Georgia,* 408 U.S. 238 that the death penalty was cruel and unusual punishment because it was applied in an erratic and capricious manner. The justices noted that the death penalty discriminated against males, the poor, and blacks, and therefore it was unconstitutional. In Florida, however, Governor Askew had already asked the legislature for a moratorium on the death penalty until July 1973, so that a commission chosen by the house and senate could examine the issue of capital punishment. He remarked that as a legislator he had voted for the death penalty but as governor he had "serious doubt about the necessity and the rightness of the state deliberately taking lives. . . ." Askew added that under the present system if a jury recommends mercy a criminal gets life, but if a jury makes no recommendation a criminal is sentenced to death. He suggested that the jury be required to make a definite judgment.[22]

The committee subsequently recommended that the death penalty be continued, arguing that it had served as a deterrent to crime, and that a judge be empowered to employ the death sentence even when a jury recommended clemency. Askew endorsed the committee's findings and in 1972 the legislature reestablished the death penalty to meet the Supreme Court's objections. Florida was the first state to restore capital punishment.[23] In 1976, the Court approved Florida's new death penalty law, and in 1979, under Governor Bob Graham, John Spenkelink was executed.

CRIME PREVENTION

Unlike prison reform and the death penalty, crime has always been an area of major concern to Floridians and their governors. The governor in Florida in collaboration with the attorney general's office has directed the investigation and punishment of criminal activities in the state. Many governors have shaped the nature of criminal investigations by public pronouncements during their campaigns and in their inaugural and legislative addresses. Although the attorney general has been elected separately in Florida, he has usually been willing to follow the policy directives of the governor. No attorney general in this century has resisted the governor's wishes in the investigation and prosecution of criminal activities.[24]

Prior to World War II, the public was particularly concerned with crimes committed by blacks. Floridians, like southerners generally, were somewhat paranoid about such crime and often reacted to it with an unbridled emotionalism. As noted in Chapter 8, Floridians and their governors, with only an occasional protest, quietly acquiesced when blacks were lynched for crimes such as rape and murder. Park Trammell ignored these lynchings during his administration, thus seeming to encourage their continuance against alleged black criminals. David Sholtz acted in a similar manner in the case of the brutal lynching of Claude Neal who was accused of murdering a

In 1967 Governor Claude Kirk hired George R. Wackenhut (right), former FBI agent and head of a large private detective agency, to head his "War on Crime." Kirk had to abandon the project when Wackenhut's men exceeded their authority, ignoring basic civil liberties and bypassing well-established legal channels in the pursuit of criminals. P. K. Yonge Library of Florida History.

white woman.[25] As noted earlier, between 1900 and 1930 Florida led the nation in lynchings with a rate of 4.5 per 10,000 blacks. Interestingly, however, crimes committed by blacks in black neighborhoods often went unpunished. Only when crime touched white society were the criminals punished, usually swiftly and excessively.

The governors apparently viewed the lynchings and excessive punishment of black criminals as necessary. In the segregated pre–World War II society, it was essential that blacks know their place, and criminal punishment was seen as an important way of reminding wayward blacks of that place. Consequently, the governors seldom objected to the harsh punishment and treatment received by black criminals. Fears about black crime subsided somewhat by 1920 as the state began to enjoy the benefits of prosperity.

Beginning in that decade, but becoming more pervasive after World War II, Floridians' fears shifted to the establishment of organized crime in the state. The growth of tourism in South Florida had encouraged the spread of gambling, both legal and illegal, and led to charges of criminal profiteering.

In 1950, after a series of articles in the *Miami Herald* about organized crime in that city, the United States Crime Commission, chaired by Senator Estes Kefauver of Tennessee, and the Greater Miami Crime Commission each conducted extensive hearings into the allegations. Governor Fuller Warren had promised during his campaign to suspend promptly any official accused of permitting gambling in his county and to hold a hearing later. But instead he spoke out sharply against the Kefauver and Miami commissions because of their criticisms of him and their implications that he had neglected his duty by permitting such illegal activities to continue unabated. As a result, Warren was reluctant to carry out his own suspension promise, and this hesitation drew heavy criticism from the press, legislators, and the public. Finally, after months of charges and attacks, he suspended five sheriffs—James A. Sullivan of Dade County, Walter Clark of Broward County, Alex Littlefield of Volusia County, Frank M. Williams of Polk County, and H. Isle Enzor of Okaloosa County. When he later reappointed three of them because the allegations could not be proved, he was again subject to intense criticism. Some of the attacks against Warren were the result of questionable steps he himself took. After he suspended Sheriff Enzor, Warren replaced him with James A. McArthur, the man's son-in-law. "Only Fuller Warren would pull a stunt like that" was a typical outraged comment.[26]

Warren had been unable to judge the public attitude about crime during his administration. Instead of becoming actively involved in the effort to weed out mobsters or trying to educate the public about the realities of organized crime, Warren bungled his way through the entire investigation, occasionally lashing out at the director of the Miami Crime Commission, Daniel Sullivan, as a "hired liar."[27] His stance on the criminal investigations ultimately eroded his support and adversely affected his administrative and legislative leadership.

The furor over organized crime that permeated America and Florida during the early 1950s, proved to be a passing phenomenon and the remainder of the decade and the early 1960s were fairly tranquil. At the behest of governors Collins and Bryant charges were made and investigations were conducted by the attorney general's office into organized crime and the misuse of public funds. However, neither man made criminal investigation a primary goal of his administration and neither became involved in a controversy over suspension of local officials as Warren's administration had. Both Collins and Bryant felt it was the duty of local communities to oust their officials if they felt they were involved in questionable activities.

The anticrime battles of the Kefauver days seemed to be a thing of the past when the 1966 gubernatorial campaign began. However, Republican Claude Kirk chose to make vice in Dade County a major issue in his campaign against the Democratic nominee and former mayor of Miami, Robert King High. After his victory over High, Kirk immediately announced that he was opening a "command post" to continue his fight against organized crime. He refused, however, to divulge his plan of attack.[28]

On the day after his inauguration, Kirk announced the establishment of a "War on Crime" to be conducted under his direction by George R. Wackenhut, a former special agent of the Federal Bureau of Investigation and president of the Wackenhut Corporation, a nationwide private detective agency. Kirk announced that Wackenhut and his army of detectives would be paid by private contributions. The Wackenhut Corporation was one of the major detective agencies in the country; it was also a very conservative organization. Its monthly bulletin warned the public of the dangers of coexisting with communism, and it had gone so far as to link the Civil Rights Movement and the free speech movement at the University of California at Berkeley with communism.[29]

After announcing his war on crime, Kirk called on the legislature to establish a state Department of Justice under the governor's office to help him facilitate the elimination of organized crime.[30] Most Floridians endorsed Kirk's early anticrime activities, although he had presented no evidence to substantiate his charges of massive vice and gambling in Miami, and the role of the Wackenhut Corporation in the anticrime investigations was very unclear.

Within a matter of months, however, the nature of the investigation surfaced and Kirk was forced to abolish his private police unit. In April 1967, Secretary of State Tom Adams reported that he was being followed by Kirk's agents. Shortly thereafter, a United States Crime Study condemned Kirk's use of a private police force to stop crime. The report noted that these detectives lacked the necessary controls to protect individual rights. Robert Shevin, the attorney general, criticized Kirk for bypassing legitimate legal channels. In addition to the public criticism, Kirk's crime force was handicapped by a shortage of funds. By the end of April, his "War on Crime" was over $200,000 in debt and only $8,000 had been received in private contributions. Kirk's credibility was further impaired when he alleged that the underworld had placed a $50,000 price on his head for his efforts to destroy their operations.[31]

In May, Kirk acknowledged that his use of the Wackenhut Corporation had not been a "good idea," and he asked the legislature to provide $1.5 million for a special police force to fight organized crime. The legislature agreed to the proposal but chose to have the director selected by the cabinet. Kirk vetoed the bill because he lacked absolute authority over the investigation.[32]

The passing of the Kirk administration in 1970 brought an end to his highly publicized and questionable crime campaign. His successor, Reubin Askew, operated through the traditional law enforcement framework and refused to personalize the crime fight. Askew did, however, consider crime a serious problem in Florida and, with the assistance of Attorney General Robert Shevin, he established a project to involve the public in his anticrime program. Financed by a $750,000 federal grant, the project was intended to teach the public how to recognize and report crimes, to protect their property, and to improve relations with the police. Through Shevin, Askew also encouraged the state's attorneys to look closely at the records of suspected underworld figures in Florida. The governor similarly supported the creation of a permanent statewide grand jury to maintain a constant eye on organized crime.

CONCLUSIONS

The disparity in the state's approaches to prison reform and to crime has remained largely unchanged since 1900. The financial costs of improving prison life are still too high for a state recently racked by a severe recession. In addition, the vast majority of prisoners in the state are blacks and, despite an improvement in racial attitudes, Floridians have little sympathy for the plight of black convicts. The public and the governors are determined to make Florida as safe and secure from crime as possible. Furthermore, many people have moved to the state to escape the crime problems in the cities of the Northeast and Midwest. The governors have responded directly to the concerns of Floridians and the recent emigrés. As a result, criminals continue to be vigorously pursued, arraigned, prosecuted, and imprisoned.

Only Sidney Catts and Reubin Askew have seriously undertaken prisoner rehabilitation programs. However, Catts' personal concern and policy initiatives did not survive his administration, whereas Askew became sidetracked by more pressing economic concerns. Restricted by a brief four-year term before 1968, the other governors concentrated on what they perceived as more important policy matters.

Although Florida now has the second largest prisoner population in the country and the largest death row population, prison reform remains low on the priority list for Floridians. They consider education, employment, environmental protection, and crime prevention much more important. The governors have shaped their programs to meet these desires, and, as a consequence, prison reform and financial support for prisons have continued to languish.

As this and the preceding chapters make clear, the governor's role in policy formation has varied dramatically during this century. In the final chapter we appraise the quality of gubernatorial leadership and offer a general assessment of the role Florida governors have played in solving the state's problems.

Part IV

Appraisal

IN this final section we evaluate the personal qualities, attitudes, and political leadership of Florida's twenty governors in this century. We also compare the gubernatorial initiatives in the areas of economics, race relations, and social programs. Finally, we assess each governor's public ethics and the impact they have had on his administration and the state. In our view, all of these aspects of executive behavior and leadership must be analyzed and understood if a governor's administration is to be fully explained and understood. In the last part of this chapter we assess the ratings and make some observations on the future of Florida gubernatorial politics.

11

Florida's Governors: A Critical Evaluation

THIS final section is divided into three parts and is based on tables 11.1–11.4, which detail our estimation of a governor's leadership in several different but crucial personal and political areas. In part one, we have assessed the personal direction the governor has brought to the office, utilizing the hypothesis developed by political scientist James David Barber. The governor's personal appeal, character, psychological reward from the office, and style have been rated here. In part two the governor's accomplishments in administrative and legislative matters are evaluated. Governors are appraised on the basis of their perception of state problems and their ability to deal with them effectively. We have attempted to make our evaluations according to the standards of the times in which the man governed and not on the basis of contemporary standards. In the third part of this chapter we assess the governor's initiatives in the policy areas of economics, race relations, and social programs and conclude with a discussion of his public ethics. We believe a governor's effectiveness is influenced significantly by his ethical and moral leadership. It sets the tone for his governorship and influences the public's impression of his leadership. Following the ratings of each governor in the tables, we have expressed at some length our reasons for this evaluation. We have also evaluated the ratings and assessed the future of gubernatorial politics.

PERSONAL APPEAL

During this century Florida has had five governors (25 percent) who exhibited charismatic qualities: Napoleon Broward, Sidney Catts, Fuller Warren, LeRoy Collins, and Claude Kirk. Broward and Collins combined strong personal appeal with aggressive, forward-looking gubernatorial programs.

Catts and Kirk, on the other hand, were often demogogic in style and used their strong personal appeal to hide inadequacies in their programs and questionable gubernatorial decisions. Warren enjoyed considerable personal popularity but, after some initial legislative successes, both he and his administration became surrounded by controversy during the last three years of his term.

Four governors (20 percent) had gregarious personalities: Park Trammell, John Martin, David Sholtz, and Charley Johns. As opposed to being strongly charismatic, these men were "hail-fellow, well-met" types. They each enjoyed the social and public responsibilities of the office although they differed widely in their gubernatorial achievements. Eleven governors (55 percent) are classed as reserved in appeal: Jennings, Gilchrist, Hardee, Carlton, Cone, Holland, Caldwell, McCarty, Bryant, Burns, and Askew. These men tended to be quite formal in meeting the symbolic duties of the office. They were also very cognizant of the decorum, tradition, and prestige of the governorship. While charisma would seem to be the most influential of the three characteristics, this has not typically been the case in Florida. Of the five charismatic figures, only two, Collins and Broward, were effective governors. Floridians and their legislators seem to prefer a more reserved figure as governor and, traditionally, such men have governed the state more effectively.

ACTIVE OR PASSIVE CHARACTER

James David Barber's view of active and passive presidential character largely concerns the degree of vigor and strength exhibited in the chief executive's leadership. This view is also useful for examining and ranking the leadership of Florida governors, although we would add one additional dimension: The individual governor's conception of the office is extremely crucial in determining the active or passive quality of his administration. The governor who feels that it is his responsibility, because of his position, to lead the state forward, to find solutions to problems, and to establish a system of priorities is likely to be an activist governor. Alternatively, a governor who feels that he is a caretaker, or manager, or simply a symbolic head of state is not likely to extend the office very much or indeed be much more than a relatively passive leader.

Based on these concepts (see the Introduction for our definition of active and passive), we can conclude that Florida has had fourteen active (70 percent) and six passive (30 percent) governors in this century. In the active category are perhaps Florida's ablest governors: Jennings, Broward, Caldwell, Collins, and Askew. Each of these men took a very dynamic view of the governorship and sought as much as possible to lead the state in new directions and advance the public interest. Jennings and Broward were Florida's principal progressive governors, and they acted vigorously in such areas as election reform, curbing corporate power (especially railroads), and developing natural resources and land conservation. Not all of their proposals were accepted during their administrations, but the force of their leadership kept these issues on the public agenda for some years thereafter. Moreover, each extended the powers of the governor's office considerably, thus allowing greater "maneuvering room" for those who followed.

Although Millard Caldwell had a basically conservative economic philosophy, his leadership was active and energetic. Also, he held office just after World War II, when the state felt it necessary to upgrade services. Consequently, he became recognized as one of the most forceful governors in this century. He is most noted for the Minimum Foundation Program, which he established as a new mechanism for public school finance. He was also one of the few governors to push a reapportionment bill through the legislature (although the resulting change was minimal).

LeRoy Collins and Reubin Askew are best known for their vigorous moral leadership as well as for substantive contributions. Collins used the full force of his office to keep Florida on a course of moderate racial policies at a time when racial hatred was flaring elsewhere in the South. In addition, he greatly expanded educational opportunity and the economic base of the state. Askew in his first administration exerted similar moral leadership on the issues of school desegregation and busing and also urged a state corporate income tax, Government in the Sunshine, and environmental protection.

These five governors (25 percent) were activists who contributed greatly to the welfare of the state. But there are seven active governors whose contributions were not of the same magnitude. Sidney Catts and Claude Kirk expended enormous amounts of energy during their administrations, but most of it was negative or even dysfunctional in character, and little of a positive nature was accomplished. John W. Martin began as an extraordinarily active leader during the land boom of the mid-1920s, but when it ended and the bust came he suddenly became unable to act and scarcely did anything. David Sholtz in 1933 desperately wanted to guide Florida out of the depression, but the lack of state funds and his basic conservatism prevented him from leading a frontal assault on the state's economic woes. Dan McCarty in the early 1950s was a truly active governor during the nine months he served—a remarkable accomplishment considering how ill he was—but his contributions were limited by his short tenure. Finally, both Fuller Warren and Charley Johns were extremely active. Warren's efforts were mostly wasted, however, because while he sincerely wanted to help the state, he seemed unable to use the institutions of government to accomplish his goals. Charley Johns used all of his energy, and the mechanisms of

TABLE 11.1. Florida Governors, 1900–1978: Characteristics of Gubernatorial Leadership

Governor	Year Term Began	Personal Appeal			Character		Psychological Reward from Office		Style		
		Char-ismatic	Gregar-ious	Re-served	Active	Passive	Positive	Negative	Demogogic	Neo-Pop.	Reserved, Businesslike
Jennings[a]	(01)			X	X		X				X
Broward[d]	(05)	X			X		X			X	
Gilchrist[a]	(09)			X		X	X				X
Trammell[c]	(13)		X		X	X	X				X
Catts[b]	(17)	X			X			X	X		
Hardee[b]	(21)			X		X	X				X
Martin[b]	(25)		X		X		X				X
Carlton[b]	(29)			X		X		X			X
Sholtz[b]	(33)		X		X			X			X
Cone[b]	(37)			X		X		X		X	
Holland[c]	(41)			X		X	X				X
Caldwell[c]	(45)			X	X		X				X
Warren[b]	(49)	X			X			X		X	
McCarty[a]	(53)			X	X		X				X
Johns[c]	(53)		X		X			X	X		
Collins[b]	(55)	X			X		X				X
Bryant[b]	(61)			X	X			X			X
Burns[b]	(65)			X	X			X			X
Kirk[b]	(67)	X			X			X	X		
Askew[a]	(71)			X	X		X			X	
Total		5	4	11	14	6	11	9	3	4	13

a. Did not seek subsequent elective office. Total 4. b. Ran for but never elected to public office after governorship. Total 11. c. Ran for and elected to public office after governorship. Total 4. d. Ran for public office after first term as governor, and defeated once but elected once. Total 1.

government, to reestablish spoils system politics by rewarding his friends and punishing his enemies through the use of patronage. Farris Bryant and Haydon Burns were active, especially in patronage, contracts, and administration, though not in legislative proposals.

Six Florida governors (30 percent) must be classified as passive, although they varied considerably in this regard. The terms of Albert W. Gilchrist and Park Trammell followed those of activists Jennings and Broward, and their administrations are best seen as consolidation periods after the tremendous activity of the first eight years of the century. Cary Hardee was governor during the early years of the Florida boom, and he chose to remain in the distant background while the energies of the state were directed at an expanding private sector. Doyle E. Carlton was completely hamstrung by the depression. Not only did he not know what to do to meet the demands of the time, he did not believe that government has a legitimate role in solving welfare and economic problems. Fred Cone may have been the state's most passive governor. He refused to take any part in legislative affairs, saying that was the business of the legislature and not of the governor, and he refused to permit any expansion of the state budget or state services. Cone's illness also contributed to his passivity. Under other circumstances, Spessard Holland might have been an activist governor. However, he held office during World War II and directed Florida's attention to the war effort rather than to internal development or expansion.

PSYCHOLOGICAL REWARDS FROM THE OFFICE

In terms of personal satisfaction and psychological fulfillment, we have classified eleven governors (55 percent) as having a positive response to the office, while nine (45 percent) are classified as having a negative response. Of the eleven governors in the positive category, four—Jennings, Holland, Caldwell, and McCarty—enjoyed considerable legislative and administrative successes. The remaining seven had mixed legislative accomplishments, but the vast majority (excluding Martin) enjoyed administrative success. All these men liked being governor and liked the power that went with the office. In terms of administrative and legislative effectiveness, positive governors rank highest in our classification. Of the nine in the negative category, only Fuller Warren defied easy classification. He drew great pleasure from the public and symbolic aspects of the governorship but had considerable difficulty in his dealings with the legislature, administrative personnel, policy issues, and the press. Seven of the remaining eight men in this category shared Warren's frustrations with the governorship, especially in their dealings with the legislature. They also disliked the symbolic functions and trappings that went with the office.

STYLE

Another important component of our gubernatorial assessment is style. This is a difficult term to define, but generally we consider it to refer to the way in which a governor behaves in office and carries out his duties. Style signifies the "personality" of behavior, and just as individuals have personalities, so do the repeated characteristics of their behavior lend a "personality" to them. We have chosen three categories to describe the style of Florida governors: demagogic, neopopulist, and reserved or businesslike.

Definitions of demagogues vary, but perhaps T. Harry Williams' conception is best: the loud, flashy, at times crude politician who employs violent rhetoric, appeals at times to prejudice, and makes extravagant promises but generally cannot or will not deliver on them.[1] There were a number of demagogues in the South, especially during the first thirty years of this century. They tended to promote black disenfranchisement and use of the white primary, and exploited nativism, Protestantism, and racism. The great prototype was Tom Watson of Georgia, but others included Tom Heflin of Alabama, C. J. Vardaman and Theodore "The Man" Bilbo of Mississippi, "Pitchfork" Ben Tillman and Cole Blease of South Carolina, Eugene Talmadge of Georgia, and more recently George Wallace of Alabama.

Based on this view, Florida has had three demagogic governors in this century: Sidney J. Catts, Charley Johns, and Claude Kirk. Catts was a demagogue in that he exploited anti-Catholicism and southern racism. He was later charged with bribery, peonage, and counterfeiting, and was tried on some of these charges, but no jury, state or federal, would vote to convict him. He combined charisma with demagogy and low public ethics.

The same qualities—charisma, demagogy and low public ethics—characterized Florida's first Republican governor since Reconstruction, Claude Kirk (1967–71). A hard-driving businessman, he first ventured into politics in an unsuccessful bid for the U.S. Senate in 1964. In 1966 he handily won the governor's race. An amateur in politics, he disregarded the regular Republican organization. After a series of victory dinners which raised several hundred thousand dollars, he bypassed the party, put the money in personal expense and campaign funds, hired a Lear jet, toured the country, and sought the Republican vice presidential nomination in 1968. As governor he provided some leadership in environmental and conservation programs but ignored other problems such as a statewide school strike. His use of a private corporation to wage war on crime violated the state constitution. At first a moderate on integration, he changed as he faced reelection in 1970 and sought to block busing by taking over the school superintendency of Manatee County. Found in contempt by a federal court, he sought to capitalize on this but was defeated for reelection. All of these examples of his gubernatorial style contribute to his demagogic rating.

The third Florida demagogue, Charley Johns (1953–55), was a Democrat who also combined low public ethics with a racist appeal. One of the leaders of the so-called Pork-Chop Gang while a member of the senate, Johns felt that the state's rural, agricultural, and mining interests had to be protected against the encroachment of urban and metropolitan South Florida. His administration, moreover, largely consisted of a rather heavy-handed use of patronage in the form of state contracts and political appointments designed to maintain the system of cronyism by which he operated. He likewise was defeated for reelection.

The distinction between a demagogic and a neopopulist style is not always clear, because demagogues often rely on neopopulist appeals for support. However, the reverse is by no means necessarily true. As V. O. Key points out, neopopulists rely most on the "cause of the common man" for their support.[2] Usually this is reflected in an anticorporation, antibank, antiurban, anti–big government, prorural, proagriculture perspective; it often includes racist sentiments as well. Florida has had four neopopulist governors in this century, although fortunately none of them conducted himself as a racist.

Napoleon Broward was a tremendously exciting individual, possessed of a dynamic and forceful personality. More than any other governor, Broward gained the support of the "common man" in his fight to have the state develop the drained Everglades lands for all Floridians rather than have the railroad and large land interests develop this area for their private gain.

Fred Cone lacked any of the progressive, liberal tendencies found in many neopopulists. Indeed, he was extremely conservative in his attitudes toward government. However, even though he was a successful banker and businessman, Cone was very folksy, and at times seemed almost the country rube. His speeches and writings, for example, were designed to appeal to small town and rural Floridians and not to urban residents or big business interests.

Fuller Warren was a classic neopopulist. His goal was to make government alleviate human suffering, especially that of the poor. He believed that the cost of government should be borne by those who could most afford to pay. He felt very close to the common people, and regarded himself as one of them.

Reubin Askew's neopopulism was not based on folksiness or flashiness, but rather on a moral intensity that appealed to all segments of the Florida population. Askew was not a man of great personal warmth; to some he seemed stiff and formal. But his humble origins and almost evangelical espousal of traditional American religious and moral values enabled him to assemble a constituency that cut across a range of Florida voters. Because of his broad appeal, Askew could even articulate positions on controversial issues, such as school busing for desegregation, without apparent loss of his popular support.

Thirteen Florida governors (65 percent) in this century have been what we call "businesslike or reserved" in style. Other commentators have referred to this kind of governor as a "chamber of commerce" executive, a depiction which, although a bit narrow, is apt.[3] While there are significant variations in those who exhibit this style, all have shown remarkable similarities. Unlike Fuller Warren, who seemed to draw his strength from mingling with citizens, many Florida governors have been decidedly reserved, dignified, and distant. While few were haughty, most preferred to maintain a broad gulf between themselves and the public. Additionally, most were business-oriented since many of them were businessmen and/or lawyers before entering politics. Conservative, espousers of traditional American and southern verities, dedicated to private enterprise, aligned toward management and ownership of property rather than toward labor, most of the governors reflected the values of their humble origins and middle-class status.

There has been, however, considerable variation in the business-like style of this group of governors. Both Caldwell and Collins were quiet men, but their physical presences and extraordinary inner strength inspired immediate confidence. McCarty and Holland also reflected a moral intensity that inspired confidence. Gilchrist, Trammell, Hardee, Carlton, and Bryant were so dignified that at times they seemed pompous. Haydon Burns appeared confused and overbearing in his handling of the office. David Sholtz had the strongest credentials for the image of the "businessman-governor," but he was a gregarious man who enjoyed mingling with people. Thus, even though most Florida governors were businessmen and conducted themselves in a reserved manner, there was enough variation in their styles to warrant caution in ascribing the same characteristics to all of them.

GUBERNATORIAL EFFECTIVENESS

At this point we have completed consideration of the personal qualities of gubernatorial leadership, and we now turn to an assessment of gubernatorial effectiveness. The categories used for this evaluation are administrative leadership and legislative relations (Table 11.2).

Administrative leadership for Florida governors has been considerably more complex than it has been for their peers in most other states. The governors who have administered the state successfully have tended to be activists who have had extensive political experience either in elective office or in party politics. These include Jennings, Broward, Holland, Caldwell, McCarty, Collins, and Askew. In bringing progressivism to Florida, Jennings and Broward proved to be two extremely able, often dynamic leaders. Trammell governed during World War I and Holland and Caldwell during World War II, and they ably coordinated the state effort. Caldwell also helped ease the state through the difficult postwar adjustment. Although

TABLE 11.2. Florida Governors, 1900–1978: Gubernatorial Effectiveness

Governor	Admin. Leadership			Leg. Relations		
	Effective	Mixed	Ineffec.	Effective	Mixed	Ineffec.
Jennings	X			X		
Broward	X				X	
Gilchrist	X				X	
Trammell	X				X	
Catts			X			X
Hardee		X				X
Martin		X			X	
Carlton			X			X
Sholtz		X			X	
Cone		X				X
Holland	X			X		
Caldwell	X			X		
Warren			X			X
McCarty	X			X		
Johns			X			a
Collins	X				X	
Bryant		X				X
Burns			X			X
Kirk			X		X	
Askew	X				X	
Total	9	5	6	4	8	7

a. The legislature did not meet during his term.

Gilchrist lacked political experience, his leadership experience in the army and his sense of honesty and fairness provided the state with four years of good government.

Three of the five governors who enjoyed mixed administrative success—Martin, Sholtz, and Cone—served during the Great Depression. This was an era when a governor's conservative economic, probusiness outlook had disastrous consequences for Florida's populace. John Martin, for example, had been able to govern the state effectively during the prosperous years of 1925 and 1926, but when the land boom began to slip in 1926 his leadership was seriously impaired. Cary Hardee was little more than a caretaker governor during his four-year term. He was decidedly probusiness and basked in the prosperity of the early 1920s. He failed, however, to dissuade the counties from their increasing indebtedness and the problems this could create if the boom slowed. Unlike the others in this category, Farris Bryant had considerable political experience before he was elected in 1960. But he had so tied his campaign to the forces of big business in Florida that he was unable to govern the state without consulting them.

Four of the six administratively ineffective governors had little political experience. Catts came literally out of nowhere to win the governor's race. Kirk had served as Republican chairman for Richard Nixon in 1960 and had run for the U.S. Senate in 1964, but he had never held elective office. Warren had served two widely separated terms in the state house of representatives, and Burns had been mayor of Jacksonville for four terms but never held state office. The remaining two governors in this category showed an inability to govern for different reasons. Carlton seemed overwhelmed by the magnitude of the depression and turned to the legislature for direction. Johns had been a leader of the Pork-Chop Gang prior to becoming acting governor. His rural ties and his use of patronage to aid his friends dominated his actions as interim governor.

Within the category of legislative relations, effective gubernatorial leadership has been characterized by well-developed programs, legislative experience, and strong individuals who could cajole the legislators and, on occasion, mobilize public support in their behalf. Only four of Florida's twenty governors are in this category. Jennings won legislative and public support for his progressive programs and the Everglades drainage plan. Holland, Caldwell, and McCarty had long and prominent political careers before becoming governor. Holland's success was attributable in large part to the war, Caldwell's to his political wisdom and a well-prepared legislative program, and McCarty's to his close ties with legislative leaders and the inadequate leadership of his predecessor.

Eight of Florida's governors (40 percent) had mixed results in their legislative dealings and experienced a number of different problems. Martin and Sholtz saw their leadership frustrated by the depression. LeRoy Collins, an urban politician with strong support in South Florida, was forced to contend with a hostile pork-chop legislature that opposed his spending programs, legislative reapportionment, and racial desegregation. Despite his effective moral leadership, Collins' achievements were modest in terms of legislative success. Claude Kirk had to contend with a Democratic legislature which cooperated with him only on measures that it also favored, such as environmental protection, constitutional revision, and reapportionment. In sharp contrast to Kirk, his successor, Reubin Askew, enjoyed legislative successes unrivaled in the state's history during his first term. By his second term, however, the legislature had asserted its independence and Askew was unable to regain legislative support. Askew's initial success seemed to result, in part, from the legislature's frustration with former governor Kirk and its joy at having as governor one of their own, whose ability they respected.

Broward enjoyed little success with a conservative legislature outside of the Everglades drainage issue for which he gained support by going to the people. In contrast to Broward, Gilchrist sought few new programs and his policy of refusing to intervene in legislative matters insured the passage of very few of them. Trammell had an ambitious program but had very little success in winning support from legislators, many of whom apparently believed he was an ineffectual governor.

The third group of governors (seven in number, 35 percent) is classed as ineffective because either they created such hostility that the legislature was in near revolt or they lacked the ability and political savvy to use the office to win legislative support. Sidney Catts, Doyle Carlton, and Fuller Warren are in the former category for different reasons. Catts was bitterly despised by legislative leaders for his partisanship in making appointments, his direct interference in legislative affairs, and his autocratic manner. Carlton was opposed for his failure to provide Florida with the leadership the legislature expected during the depression. Fuller Warren's inability to defend his economic program and his inept handling of the Kefauver investigation of organized crime in Florida led to the same failures experienced by Carlton.

Farris Bryant and Haydon Burns showed an unwillingness to exert pressure on the legislature. Both men would give up their programs rather than fight the legislature or appeal to the public. Cary Hardee offered little legislative leadership or direction. Fred Cone personally believed the governor had no right to intervene in legislative deliberations, although he did reserve the right to reject legislative proposals if he felt they were unwise. In fact, he vetoed more bills than any other governor in Florida history. Charley Johns did not serve as governor during a legislative term.

GUBERNATORIAL INITIATIVES

In this section on gubernatorial initiatives, we have assessed the governors' impact on the three policy areas of economics, race relations, and social programs (Table 11.3). We rank them furthermore in terms of their liberal, moderate, or conservative attitudes on these policy issues. These terms are relative. As suggested elsewhere in this book, such labels must be used very carefully in the context of Florida politics. What is considered "conservative" in this state might be regarded as reactionary or antediluvian elsewhere. And "liberal" might look pale in comparison with the standards of such states as Wisconsin, Massachusetts, New York, and California. Florida is basically conservative, and what we regard as moderate or liberal is often movement along a basically conservative continuum, and not difference in kind or quality. Moreover, Florida has ranked so low, traditionally, on some measures of social services that any improvement will appear as a great leap forward, even though in other states it might appear as a small step indeed.

ECONOMIC ATTITUDES

We believe the demographic setting almost always places some limits on the governor's actions in regard to his economic attitudes. A prime example of this is that in our classification only one governor emerges as a liberal in economic philosophy. Florida has been a developing state from the beginning of the century. None of the early progressives could have been elected on Robert La Follette's Wisconsin gubernatorial platform, or that of the Non-Partisan League in North Dakota or of the Farmer Labor Party in Minnesota. The organized labor movement in Florida has been small throughout this century. Manufacturing has not developed substantially. The emphasis has been on growth in a frontier state. Revisions to the state constitution have been added barring a state income tax and a state inheritance tax. These factors have provided the setting in which fifteen governors (75 percent) qualify as conservative, four (20 percent) as moderate, and only one (5 percent) as liberal.

Jennings, Broward, Catts, and Askew represent the only economic moderates who have occupied the executive mansion in Florida. Jennings ran as an anticorporation and antirailroad candidate. As governor he succeeded in establishing a state railroad regulatory commission. He also started drainage of the Everglades and proposed land sales favoring farmers' purchasing small plots rather than policies aiding corporations. Broward attempted to rectify the grossly disproportionate tax burdens in each county and to tax new franchises to increase revenues for schools and other programs. Sidney J. Catts proposed tax equalization and encouraged labor to organize. Askew successfully implemented a corporate income tax and a severance tax on phosphate for the first time in the state's history, with revenues going to support schools and social welfare programs. He also increased state aid for the family assistance program.

Only Fuller Warren qualifies (barely) as an economic liberal. During his four-year term he tried to equalize taxes by requiring private interests to pay for the increasing needs of the state. However, the legislature, reflecting the conservative economic values of the state, rejected the proposal. Warren, an ineffectual leader, accepted this decision without a fight, and a compromise sales tax measure was passed by the legislature.

The least visible and least supported issue in the twentieth century has been the labor union movement. Because most governors have been self-made men and have had strong economic and social ties (through such organizations as the Chamber of Commerce, Kiwanis, and Rotary) to the business community, they have tended to be energetic supporters of a laissez-faire economy. Only Catts, Warren, and Askew have supported the union position in Florida in the twentieth century. Catts had pledged in his campaign that he would uphold the union cause against the "absolute monarchy and autocracy" of bankers and capitalists. In 1919 he supported the firemen in their strike against the city of Jacksonville and the phosphate workers in their walkout in Hillsborough and Polk counties. Warren also endorsed the union effort in his campaign and generally supported its cause during his governorship. Askew sponsored legislation that permitted the unionization of public employees.[4]

RACIAL ATTITUDES

On racial attitudes, Florida has had since 1900 sixteen conservative, two moderate, and two liberal governors; both liberals were elected after 1950. As with all policy decisions, the demographic makeup of the state has placed limits on gubernatorial initiative. Florida's pattern of race relations for most of the twentieth century was established in the late nineteenth century when it adopted a series of laws segregating the white and black races and removing blacks from the voting rolls. Since 1900, Florida governors have endorsed, with few exceptions, the continuation of racial segregation and discrimination.

TABLE 11.3. Florida Governors, 1900–1978: Gubernatorial Initiatives

Governor	Economics			Attitude toward Racial Matters			Social Programs		
	Cons.	Mod.	Lib.	Cons.	Mod.	Lib.	Cons.	Mod.	Lib.
Jennings		X		X					X
Broward		X		X					X
Gilchrist	X				X		X		
Trammell	X			X			X		
Catts		X		X				X	
Hardee	X			X			X		
Martin	X			X			X		
Carlton	X			X			X		
Sholtz	X			X			X		
Cone	X			X			X		
Holland	X			X			X		
Caldwell	X			X				X	
Warren			X		X				X
McCarty	X			X					X
Johns	X			X			X		
Collins	X					X		X	
Bryant	X			X			X		
Burns	X			X			X		
Kirk	X			X			X		
Askew		X				X			X
	15	4	1	16	2	2	12	3	5

Florida elected only one racial demagogue as governor in the twentieth century—Sidney J. Catts. Catts had repeatedly denounced blacks in his campaign and even called for their total disfranchisement. He also supported laws which would have carefully delineated the place of black Floridians so all would be sure of their inferior position.

The governors in the conservative category range from Napoleon Broward, who proposed a colonization program for blacks in Africa, to Farris Bryant, who denounced school desegregation, to Claude Kirk who closed the schools in Manatee County to prevent busing to achieve integration.

In the period before the *Brown* decision (1954), only Albert Gilchrist and Fuller Warren took moderate positions on racial issues. Despite his view that blacks are an inferior race, Gilchrist was essentially a paternalist who felt that white rule must "be just." Fuller Warren led a successful fight to unmask the Ku Klux Klan in 1951 and was the first governor in the state's history to entertain an interracial group in the executive mansion. He took the latter step after the murder of the secretary of the Florida NAACP.

Florida's only two liberal governors on racial issues have been LeRoy Collins and Reubin Askew. Collins was elected shortly after the Supreme Court rendered the *Brown* decision. While he said he personally opposed the decision, he blocked repeated efforts by the legislature to close schools to prevent integration. In his last two years as governor, he led an educational effort to persuade white Floridians that integration was inevitable and that they should begin preparing for it.

The election of Reubin Askew in 1970 brought about a new era of race relations in Florida. Askew expressed the unusual view for a Florida governor that busing was "a necessary element in achieving" integrated schools.[5] Despite Florida's straw ballot rejection of busing, Askew continued to move the state toward a biracial society. For example, he dramatically increased the number of blacks in state government, especially at the upper levels.

SOCIAL PROGRAMS

All Florida governors, without exception, have wholeheartedly endorsed the concept of public education. Most have regarded it as a central concern of the state. Very few, however, have done anything substantive to improve the quality of elementary, secondary, or higher education. In particular, they have not sought to provide enough money to allow for anything other than the barest minimum quality in the state's systems of education. Moreover, a few governors have acted in ways which were truly harmful to education in the state.

David Sholtz, for example, while himself a well-educated man, refused during the depression to consider extra state aid to keep hard-pressed local school districts solvent. As a result, the academic year was shortened, and several thousand teachers went on relief. Charley Johns pledged himself to segregation in the schools while he was governor, and subsequently as a legislator led a witch-hunt against homosexuals, communists, and other alleged undesirables in the state university system. Claude Kirk not only put his own children in private schools after criticizing the public schools, but later in his administration he had to be forced by other state officials and public opinion to negotiate with teachers who had carried out a successful statewide strike. Finally racism influenced the educational attitudes of a number of governors. Napoleon Broward, for example, thought education would cause blacks to forget their "correct" social position.

Only three Florida governors have truly been friends of education. Millard Caldwell unquestionably was the most important. He was the architect of the Minimum Foundation Program, a pathbreaking system of public school finance which eventually was adopted in other states. It was only through this program, which transferred part of the tax burden from the counties to the state, that all counties were able to adopt a nine-month school year. LeRoy Collins began the expansion of the Florida State University System and also strongly advocated the establishment of a large number of public community colleges. Reubin Askew not only established a new system of educational finance based on student needs, educational programs, and geographic location, but he steadfastly remained committed to school desegregation and busing at a time when public opinion was opposed to both.

The extent to which governors have emphasized prison reform is another indicator of their attitude toward social programs. Most governors must be ranked as "conservative" on this measure: most have taken a very hard line on criminals generally and have not advocated prison reform. Overcrowded prison conditions, brutal treatment, and prisoner deaths from beatings or shootings occasionally drew even national attention. Only in the administrations of Catts and Askew, however, were there any attempts to change conditions significantly. In the main, governors would call for an investigation following an incident or scandal and a report would be prepared and filed, but few if any real changes would ensue.

The picture is similarly dismal for old-age pensioners and welfare recipients. Florida has the nation's highest percentage of citizens over 65 years of age (17.5 percent), and throughout the century the state has been considered a haven for retirees and other elderly persons. Because of the potential voting importance of this group of citizens, Florida governors invariably promised to increase benefits for retirees. But, as in the case of education, the governors have not come forth with very much, except to increase the homestead exemption. Funds have not been made available for other than the most minimal benefits needed to keep the elderly quiescent. Moreover, in spite of the potentially important electoral position occupied by retirees in the state, it is safe to say that no governor has ever set forth a comprehensive public policy concerning the elderly, especially those who are poor and ill.

The same is true of welfare payments generally: aid to families with dependent children (AFDC) disbursements remain among the lowest in the nation. The state's most serious poverty problem, however, is probably that of the migrant workers. No Florida governor has successfully dealt with the citrus industry and organized agricultural interests to provide state assistance to this group of people. Only LeRoy Collins made a serious attempt to improve their conditions, but his efforts were stymied by the opposition of agricultural interests, who feared an end to a cheap source of seasonal labor.

PUBLIC ETHICS

In this last section we appraise each governor's public ethics and their impact on his administration and the state (Table 11.4). Generally Florida governors have demonstrated a reasonably high sense of public ethics, that is, for the most part they have conducted themselves in a way consonant with the public trust they have been given. Most have not sought large private gain through

TABLE 11.4. Florida Governors, 1900–1978: Public Ethics

	High	Medium	Low
Jennings	X		
Broward	X		
Gilchrist	X		
Trammell		X	
Catts			X
Hardee	X		
Martin		X	
Carlton	X		
Sholtz			X
Cone		X	
Holland	X		
Caldwell	X		
Warren		X	
McCarty	X		
Johns			X
Collins	X		
Bryant		X	
Burns			X
Kirk			X
Askew	X		
Total	10	5	5

their public office; most have also been aboveboard in their moral behavior while they were chief executive. Ten governors (50 percent) rank high, five (25 percent) medium.

Five governors (25 percent) rank low in public ethics. David Sholtz utilized his prior knowledge of the sale of state bonds and made a fortune from them after leaving office. Fuller Warren did not profit from his position; indeed, he left office as a rather poor man. However, some of his advisors and friends did benefit. For example, after Warren signed the cattle fencing law, which required ranchers to put wire fence around their land to keep cows from wandering onto highways, his associate, Louis Wolfson, nearly cornered the national market on barbed wire and profited immensely from his association with Warren.[6]

Perhaps the worst displays of low public ethics by Florida governors, however, came from Sidney Catts, Haydon Burns, Charley Johns, and Claude Kirk. It is not known whether Johns directly profited from his position. However, he thought nothing of voiding state contracts in order to award new ones to his friends and associates. This was especially true of insurance and road building contracts. Burns devoted great attention to instructing state agencies to purchase from his supporters. These supporters also received state contracts, consultantships, and law firm retainers.[7]

Following his election, Kirk sponsored a number of victory dinners for Republicans, raising $300,000. This money did not go to the political party, but rather to Kirk's expense funds for a nationwide campaign for the Republican vice presidency. Catts both exploited the office for his family and inflamed religious passions.

Even though most of the other governors were honest men, a few stand out because of their personal integrity and moral rectitude while in office. Napoleon Broward, Spessard Holland, Millard Caldwell, and Dan McCarty were all regarded as extremely upright men; Caldwell was so well respected that he was eventually appointed to the state supreme court and served for a time as chief justice. LeRoy Collins survived a major scandal in his Road Department in part because there was never any question concerning his own personal honesty. Reubin Askew's almost clerical piety and rectitude were well known throughout the nation.

Among governors who sought reelection or election to other offices, four of those with high public ethics were successful, one died in office, three never sought reelection, and two were unsuccessful. Of those with a moderate sense of public ethics, one was successful, four were defeated. Finally, of the five governors with low ethics, all were defeated in later bids.

CONCLUSIONS

What, then, does our analysis show? What most clearly emerges is the influential nature of the demographic setting. Regardless of personal style, beliefs, and behavior, the governor has to operate in very particular circumstances. His times, his environment, very strongly influence the opportunities he has, the pressures brought to bear on him, and the possibilities for creating and implementing new public policies. The conservative social and economic attitudes of the state, for example, provide a framework within which any governor, irrespective of his personal beliefs and desires, must operate. It is our contention that governors who could operate within this conservative setting, and who probably reflected it in their own values and ideologies, were most likely to be elected; this same setting influenced their behavior following inauguration. Thus, twelve governors (60 percent) out of twenty are classified as social conservatives and three are moderates; sixteen (80 percent) are racial conservatives and two are moderates; fifteen (75 percent) are economic conservatives and four (20 percent) are moderates.

Once elected, however, these conservative candidates typically found themselves bound by the demographic factors which had facilitated their election. Cary Hardee, for example, was elected as a businessman's governor. His administration was restricted by the laissez-faire attitudes prevalent in Florida during the 1920s. Florida's depression governors—Martin, Carlton, Sholtz, and Cone—had been elected after promising to balance the budget. Their administrations were literally overwhelmed by the depression as they attempted to alleviate the state's economic plight by pursuing these conservative fiscal policies.

What then was the role of Florida's five most progressive and effective governors? Did the demographic setting influence the behavior of these governors to the same extent that it did the others? The answer seems to be that it did not. There have been five—Jennings, Broward, Caldwell, Collins, and Askew—who sought to improve the effectiveness and expand the powers of the governorship. They worked within the framework of existing social norms and values, but because of personal beliefs, the force of their personalities and moral convictions, and their political skill in both symbolic and substantive areas, they were able to initiate new discussions of public policy, chart new directions for the state, and in some cases begin implementing programs in these areas. They were not successful in every endeavor they undertook; sometimes they were too far ahead of their fellow public officials and the general citizenry. But they expanded Floridians' notions of what future policy should be, and in so doing changed the environment, the situation, and the limits of public acceptability. The difference between these men and the more conservative, passive governors was the extent of their willingness to seek substantive changes, rather than just to accept certain demographic conditions and create only slight modifications of the status quo, as did most Florida governors during this century.

Even the leadership of the activist governors has been significantly affected by the time in which they held office. Jennings and Broward, for example, benefited indirectly from the emergence of progressivism and the dynamic leadership of President Theodore Roosevelt. Askew's racial moderation was accepted by Floridians in the 1970s because of changes that occurred as a result of the *Brown* decision, the civil rights movement, and actions of the federal government. The pressing social and economic needs of Floridians after World War II enabled Millard Caldwell to win support for his programs. Only LeRoy Collins clashed with the temper of the times when he supported reapportionment and racial moderation. Significantly, he lost on both issues.

Thus, the value system and particular circumstances of the state at any moment strongly influence who wins gubernatorial elections and how he functions in office. Personal styles, attitudes, and ideologies suggest what the governor will do within this framework once he is in office. Relatively passive, conservative governors have accepted the circumstances and sought only slight modifications. The more activist, dynamic, and ultimately more effective governors have not been confined by the framework or situation, but have instead been able to manipulate it and modify it significantly through their vision, moral persuasion, and political skill.

According to our analysis, the personal background of the governor does not influence his overall effectiveness as significantly as the demographic setting does. Obviously, we do not mean to suggest or imply that personal characteristics are irrelevant. Clearly such personal attributes as the governor's conception of his role ("character" in our scheme) and his acceptability (personal appeal and style in our model) significantly influence what happens during his administration. But personal data seem to be most important in the candidate's, and later the governor's, ability to meet the limitations imposed by the demographic setting. While most Florida governors, for example, have been either reserved or active, those who were the most active seem to have been able to modify the limitations of the setting most effectively. Similarly, governors receiving positive psychological rewards from their duties, particularly when combined with active characters, have generally been more effective than those receiving negative rewards.

What is of special interest is that governors with charismatic personal appeal and styles have not always been very effective. Only two such governors, Broward and Collins, can be considered very effective, while none of the gregarious governors ranks very high. Similarly, only two neopopulist governors, Broward and Askew, achieved above average success as governors. What this suggests is that simply being a pleasant individual, a backslapper, a charmer, or a person with rustic appeal does not insure success or effectiveness as a governor. Citizens and other officials may like these kinds of governors, but effective leadership requires more.

Moreover, demagogic qualities, while producing excitement, are eventually counterproductive. Catts, Johns, and Kirk generated a great deal of attention through their demagoguery, but ultimately lost the support of citizens because of their irresponsible behavior. Finally, when public ethics was combined with personal data, sharp differences emerged in the effectiveness of the governors. Those with low public ethics, even when they were charismatic, gregarious, demagogic, or neopopulist, quickly lost popular support. Governors such as Catts, Sholtz, Warren, Johns, Burns, and Kirk, while exciting and even fun to watch in office, ultimately came to be regarded as among the least effective governors, while Broward and Collins, who were powerful, magnetic personalities as well as men of great moral stature, were among the best. Jennings, Caldwell, and Askew perhaps lacked the vibrant personal qualities of these two men, but have been recognized as possessing the same moral qualities. Perhaps, then, in terms of their ultimate effectiveness, it is better for governors to be reserved, businesslike men of integrity. Charismatic governors with questionable ethics have enjoyed little success in this century.

We think it important to emphasize that the demographic setting which has influenced significantly the election and subsequent behavior of governors has not been limited to physical, economic, and social circumstances. It has included attitudes, beliefs, and value systems prevalent among the citizens. Governors who have reflected these values were most likely to be elected; this seems to account for the significant number of governors who have been, in varying degrees, ideologically conservative. On the other hand, the five most effective governors, all of whom were firmly rooted in prevailing belief systems of the state, were able by force of personality and political skill to bring about significant policy changes: development of the Everglades, the Minimum Foundation Program in education, a moderate racial policy, and a corporate income tax represented significant departures from past policies. Ideologically none of these governors (with the possible exception of Askew) could be considered liberal by national standards. And yet, perhaps precisely because they were regarded as supportive of traditional state values but were unwilling to accept them as immutable, they brought new leadership to the state.

Public values and attitudes, the record of previous administrations, and economic and social conditions have placed limits on what Floridians would accept as legitimate administrative behavior by governors, especially in the use of patronage and in governors' interaction with the cabinet. In the case of the legislature, prior experience with that body, as well as the predominant economic situation and outlook of the state, seem to be crucial. While service in the legislature was no guarantor of success for the governor (e.g., Cone and Warren), those governors with considerable legislative success (e.g., Jennings, Caldwell, and Askew) understood legislative operations and were generally respected by that body. These three men, as well as Broward and Collins, presented the legislature with concrete programs, fought for their passage, and appealed to the public when necessary instead of attempting to dictate to it (Catts, Kirk) or being intimidated by it (Carlton, Burns). Finally, no governor faced by stringent economic or fiscal limitations in the state (Martin, Carlton, Sholtz, Cone, Warren, and Askew in his second term) met with much legislative success.

A final point should be made in assessing a governor's subsequent political efforts. Twelve ex-governors ran for political office but were defeated (table 2.8); seven ran successfully after their term as governor (Broward, Trammell, Holland, Caldwell, Johns, Collins, and Askew); two were successful once and defeated once (Broward and Collins). Three governors (Jennings, Gilchrist, and McCarty) never ran again for office. What are the important aspects of our analysis? Four men were active (Broward, Caldwell, Collins, and Askew), two passive (Trammell and Holland). All had high public ethics. One (Collins) was reelected as governor but, because of later developments in the demographic setting, he was defeated for a U.S. Senate seat. All who won subsequent election were effective in administration and in legislative work and had positive relations with the legislature. On the other hand, four governors who were defeated for subsequent office had negative legislative relations and were ineffective as administrators (Catts, Carlton, Warren, and Burns). Johns was an ineffective administrator and never dealt with the legislature. Two, moreover, are categorized as demagogues (Catts and Kirk), three were low in public ethics (Catts, Burns, and Kirk). Activist governors who have had high public ethics and enjoyed administrative and legislative success have thus experienced future political gains. Those who have not have generally retired, seldom to be heard from again. Even before running for governor, those who succeeded in effectiveness generally can be classified as activist and positive with regard to personal attributes, and in relation to the demographic setting fit the times in terms of social, economic, and racial attitudes. One, Warren, who barely qualifies as a liberal in economic matters, had to abandon a partially liberal position when, in a conservative period, the more conservative legislature rejected his tax program and instead enacted a sales tax (with food and medicine exempted). Thus the demographic setting has placed limits on gubernatorial initiative.

THE GOVERNOR IN THE FUTURE

What of the future? The fundamentally conservative nature of the state's politics is unlikely to change very much in the immediate years ahead, and it is equally unlikely that Floridians will suddenly opt either to provide massive amounts of public funds for governors or to support dramatic new programs.

A resurgent Republican Party undoubtedly will stimulate competition in the state's politics, but it will be a conservative, rather than expansionist, thrust. All of this notwithstanding, it is likely that the governor will continue to be the central figure in the state's politics, perhaps even more so than he is presently. The problems of Florida will continue to grow as its population growth accelerates, and the governor will be the state figure who has to meet this challenge. The governor's centrality in the state's politics will become further entrenched if changes are made in the cabinet as LeRoy Collins and Reubin Askew have suggested. Such changes are not likely to occur overnight, but they will be inevitable if Florida is to have a governor capable of contending with the demands of the late twentieth and early twenty-first centuries.

Nevertheless, Florida's government will never be consistently successful at alleviating state problems as long as it depends heavily on the personal characteristics and abilities of the men in the governor's office. If the office and party framework remain structurally weak, there will continue to be, as there has been in the past, a great variation in the quality of men who are elected governor. This wide disparity in leadership will also continue to affect adversely the state's development. Some of these structural weaknesses can be changed through legislation and constitutional revision. Other changes in the office will occur as governors are forced to respond to the substantial socioeconomic developments of the last quarter of this century. Change is not inevitable, however, in the context of such a tradition-bound institution as the executive branch of Florida's state government. Florida has been unique in the restrictions imposed on the office by tradition, the constitution, and a fragmented political system. Because of these restrictions it has taken an unusual man to govern Florida effectively in the twentieth century.

Notes

1. See, for example, David Easton, *A Systems Analysis of Political Life* (New York: John Wiley, 1966).

2. Parts of this section draw heavily from work done by the authors in conjunction with Professor Manning J. Dauer, Distinguished Service Professor, Department of Political Science, University of Florida. We wish to thank Professor Dauer for stimulating our thinking and for allowing us to modify and use materials which he helped to develop. He is, of course, not responsible for any changes or reinterpretations which we have made. See Manning J. Dauer, David R. Colburn, and Richard K. Scher, "A Typology of Executives," paper delivered at the annual meeting of the Southern Political Science Association, Gatlinburg, Tennessee, November 2, 1979.

Numerous frameworks are available in social science for examining political behavior, but there are relatively few which specifically address executive leadership. We believe the best work toward understanding political executives has been done by James David Barber in his articles and his book *The Presidential Character: Predicting Performance in the White House,* 2d ed. (Englewood Cliffs, N.J.: Prentice-Hall, 1977). By modifying his framework we have developed an analysis which we consider informative for studying Florida governors.

3. These kinds of outputs include such items as recognition by governors of the legitimate demands of certain interest or ethnic groups, appointment of blue-ribbon advisory commissions and study groups, and proclamations and declarations. See Murray Edelman, *The Symbolic Uses of Politics* (Urbana: University of Illinois Press, 1967).

4. We do not include welfare policy here, especially old-age assistance, because it is not an area in which governors have been very active; other than advocating small increases in old-age assistance (especially during campaigns) and signing appropriations bills, governors generally have not made major efforts in welfare policy. The conservative nature of the state, especially in fiscal matters, has militated against anything more than a minimal commitment to welfare benefits and has prevented active gubernatorial involvement. Moreover, the legislature has usually responded (albeit slowly!) to demands of the elderly for increased benefits.

CHAPTER 1

1. The literature on modern southern history and politics is vast, and the citations in the chapter are suggestive only. Materials listed are those most relevant to this study and accessible

297

to others. See V. O. Key, Jr., *Southern Politics in State and Nation* (New York: A. A. Knopf, 1949), especially pp. 82–105, 298–311; Manning J. Dauer, "Florida: The Different State," in *The Changing Politics of the South,* ed. William C. Havard (Baton Rouge: Louisiana State University Press, 1972), pp. 92–164; Neal R. Peirce, *The Deep South States of America* (New York: W. W. Norton and Co., Inc., 1974), pp. 435–94; Charlton W. Tebeau, *A History of Florida* (Coral Gables: University of Miami Press, 1971).

2. Dauer, "Florida: The Different State," pp. 94–106.

3. Key, *Southern Politics,* pp. 82–105; Peirce, *Deep South States,* pp. 435–94; C. Douglas Price, *The Negro and Southern Politics* (New York: New York University Press, 1957), Donald R. Mathews and James W. Prothro, *Negroes and the New Southern Politics* (New York: Harcourt, Brace, 1966); C. Vann Woodward, *The Strange Career of Jim Crow* (New York: Oxford University Press, 1974); George Brown Tindall, ed., *The Pursuit of Southern History* (Baton Rouge: Louisiana State University Press, 1964); W. J. Cash, *The Mind of the South* (New York: Random House, 1960).

4. Key, *Southern Politics,* especially chaps. 1, 5, 14; Dauer, "Florida: The Different State," pp. 92–164; William C. Havard, "The South: A Shifting Perspective," and "From Past to Future," in Havard, *Changing Politics of the South,* pp. 3–36, 688–729; Alexander Heard, *A Two Party South?* (Chapel Hill: University of North Carolina Press, 1952); Harold M. Hollingsworth, ed., *Essays on Recent Southern Politics* (Austin: University of Texas Press, 1970); Allen P. Sindler, ed., *Change in the Contemporary South* (Durham, N.C.: Duke University Press, 1963).

5. U.S. Department of Commerce, Statistical Indicators Division, Felix Tamm, Chief, *Long Term Economic Growth, 1860–1970* (Washington: Government Printing Office, 1973), pp. 232–36; estimates from Richard A. Easterlin, "State Income Estimates," in *Population Redistribution and Economic Growth, U.S., 1870–1950,* vol. 1, eds. Simon Kuznets and Dorothy S. Tewnac (Philadelphia: American Philosophical Society, 1957).

6. (New York: Harper, 1944).

7. *Negro Yearbook, 1949* (New York: Macmillan, 1949), pp. 98–99. The actual number of lynchings was probably much higher than these NAACP figures.

8. Arthur F. Raper, *The Tragedy of Lynching* (Chapel Hill: University of North Carolina Press, 1933), p. 28.

9. Tebeau, *History of Florida,* p. 394.

10. Dauer, "Florida: The Different State," pp. 92–164.

11. Peirce, *Deep South States,* p. 472. In spite of their substantial numbers, Cubans have not yet been an important force in statewide electoral politics because of their recent arrival in the U.S. and lack of citizenship. It seems reasonable to predict, however, that as increasing numbers of Cubans become citizens, register to vote, and become active in politics and in other ways, they will emerge as a potent political force in the state.

12. Dauer, "Florida: The Different State," pp. 92–94; Peirce, *Deep South States,* pp. 435, 450.

13. "Florida: The Different State," p. 92.

14. *Florida Statistical Abstract, 1971,* (Gainesville: University of Florida Press, 1971), p. 18.

15. *Southern Politics,* p. 85.

16. Dauer, "Florida: The Different State," pp. 92–93, 124–44; Peirce, *Deep South States,* pp. 435–38, 464–71.

17. U.S. Department of Agriculture, Economic Research Service, *State Farm Income Statistics,* Supplement to Statistical Bulletin No. 547 (Washington: Government Printing Office, September 1975).

18. *Florida Statistical Abstract, 1967,* pp. 212–13; *Florida Statistical Abstract, 1975,* p. 237.

19. U.S. Department of Commerce, Bureau of Economic Analysis, *Survey of Event Business,* April 1964, April 1969, April 1975; *Florida Statistical Abstract, 1976,* p. 121.

20. Dauer, "Florida: The Different State," pp. 102–3.

21. "State, Local Taxes Still Heading Up," *U.S. News and World Report,* November 14, 1977, p. 82.

22. Dauer, "Florida: The Different State," p. 102.

23. U.S. Department of the Interior, Bureau of Mines, *Minerals Yearbook, 1972*, vol. 11, Area Report: Domestic; *Florida Statistical Abstract, 1974*, p. 357.

24. *Southern Politics*, p. 82.

25. Ibid., chap. 5; Dauer, "Florida: The Different State", pp. 92–164; Peirce, *Deep South States*, pp. 435–94. Florida has not had the extraordinary degree of "friends-and-neighbors" politics that has characterized Alabama politics: see Key, *Southern Politics*, chap. 3.

26. *Southern Politics*, p. 86.

27. Morris C. Haimowitz, "Population Trends in Florida" (Master's thesis, University of Florida, 1942), pp. 124–26.

28. Key, *Southern Politics*, p. 92; Dauer, "Florida: The Different State," pp. 119–24; Peirce, *Deep South States*, pp. 453–59.

29. *Southern Politics*, p. 92.

30. Ibid., pp. 92–96; Dauer, "Florida: The Different State," pp. 94–96, 124–44; Paul M. Cohen, "The Florida Poll," *Gainesville Sun*, January 18, 1976.

31. *Southern Politics*, p. 94. The conclusions of this study suggest that issues, while seldom crucial in elections, are on occasion more important in Florida politics than Key would allow. Yet our findings corroborate his, that campaigns are more personality than issue based (ibid., chap. 14).

32. Dauer, "Florida: The Different State," p. 111; Peirce, *Deep South States*, p. 447; Cohen, "Two Groups of Republican Voters"; Stuart Mandel, "The Republican Party in Florida" (Master's thesis, Florida State University, 1968); Gregory Lee Baker, "Intraparty Factionalism: The Florida Republican Party" (Master's thesis, University of Florida, 1977).

33. Cohen, "Two Groups of Republican Voters."

34. Ibid.

35. Ibid.; Dauer, "Florida: The Different State," p. 111.

36. See Earl Black, *Southern Governors and Civil Rights: Racial Segregation as a Campaign Issue in the Second Reconstruction* (Cambridge: Harvard University Press, 1976).

37. Dauer, "Florida: The Different State," pp. 106–13.

38. Ibid., pp. 119–24; Peirce, *Deep South States*, pp. 453–54; see also Manning J. Dauer, "Florida Reapportionment," *Business and Economic Dimensions*, March 1967, pp. 8–14.

39. Dauer, "Florida: The Different State," pp. 119–24; Peirce, *Deep South States*, pp. 453–54.

40. Peirce, *Deep South States*, pp. 435–39.

CHAPTER 2

1. See, for example, Lester Seligman, et al., *Patterns of Recruitment* (Chicago: Rand McNally, 1974) and Joseph Schlesinger, *How They Became Governor* (East Lansing: Governmental Research Bureau, Michigan State University, 1957).

2. Interview with Alma Warren, Gainesville, February 6, 1971, tape (8A) and transcript in University of Florida Oral History Archives, Florida State Museum, Gainesville.

3. Interviews with Millard Caldwell, Tallahassee, July 24, 1975; LeRoy Collins, Tallahassee, February 11, 1975; Farris Bryant, Jacksonville, August 26, 1975; Reubin Askew, Tallahassee, January 10, 1975.

4. Data for this table and subsequent sections came from the following sources (because data are drawn so widely and repeatedly from them, references will not be restated throughout the chapter): Biographical Boxes, P. K. Yonge Library of Florida History, University of Florida, Gainesville, hereafter cited as Biographical Materials, UF; Allen Morris, ed., *The Florida Handbook 1975–1976*, 15th ed. (Tallahassee: Peninsular Publishing Co., 1975), pp. 89–102; John R. Deal, "Sidney J. Catts: Stormy Petrel of Florida Politics" (Master's thesis, University of Florida, 1950); Juanita Gibson, "The Office of Governor in Florida" (Ph.D. dissertation, University of Michigan, 1958); Victoria Harden McDonnell, "The Businessman's Politician: A Study of the Administration of John Wellborn Martin, 1925–29" (Master's thesis, University of

Florida, 1968); Daisy Parker, "An Examination of the Florida Executive" (Ph.D. dissertation, University of Virginia, 1959); Samuel Proctor, *Napoleon Bonaparte Broward: Florida's Fighting Democrat* (Gainesville: University of Florida Press, 1950); Warren A. Jennings, "Sidney J. Catts and the Democratic Primary of 1920," *Florida Historical Quarterly* 39, no. 3 (1960–61): 203–20; Merlin Cox, "David Sholtz: New Deal Governor of Florida," *Florida Historical Quarterly* 43, no. 2 (October 1964): 142–52; Adele Setnor, "Recruitment Patterns of Florida Governors" (Honors thesis, University of Florida, 1975); *Tampa Tribune,* August 23, 1903; William Sherman Jennings Papers, P. K. Yonge Library of Florida History, University of Florida, Gainesville, Box 5, unidentified biographical clipping; ibid., Box 16; S. B. Roxx, "Governor Jennings of Florida," *Alkahest,* December 1903; *Tampa Tribune,* December 23, 1936; Millard F. Caldwell, "Honor and Service in Politics," 1953, David Levy Yulee lecture, University of Florida, January 12, 1953 (Gainesville: University of Florida Public Administration Clearing Service, 1953); *Tampa Tribune,* September 29, 1953.

5. Biographical material from this section came from Biographical Materials, UF; *Tampa Tribune,* January 4, 1909; Park Trammell Collection, P. K. Yonge Library of Florida History, University of Florida, Gainesville; Wayne Flynt, "Sidney J. Catts: The Road to Power," *Florida Historical Quarterly* 49 (October 1970): 107–28; *Florida Times Union,* January 9, 1929; Official Program, Inauguration of Governor Spessard L. Holland, January 7, 1941; *Tampa Tribune,* January 8, 1960, July 3, 1966, March 11, 1972; Morris, *Florida Handbook,* pp. 89–102.

6. Data for this section and the section on place of residence are found in the sources listed for notes 4 and 5.

7. Ibid.; U.S. Bureau of the Census, *Census of Population: 1970,* vol. 1, *Characteristics of the Population,* pt. 2, Florida—Section 1, Table 50, Florida 11–219 (Washington: U.S. Government Printing Office, 1973); ibid., census reports 1900–1960; Douglas W. Johnson, Paul R. Picard, and Bernard Quinn, *Churches and Church Membership in the United States, 1971* (Washington: Glennary Research Center, 1974), pp. 37–42; U.S. Bureau of the Census, *Census of Population, Census of Religious Bodies, 1936,* vol. 2, pt. 1, Denominations A–J, vol. 2, pt. 2, Denominations K–Z (Washington: U.S. Government Printing Office, 1941), pp. 118, 1090, 1136, 1387, 1438; *Census of Religious Bodies, 1926* (Washington: U.S. Government Printing Office, 1936), pp. 14, 15; Morris L. Haimowitz, "Population Trends in Florida" (Master's thesis, University of Florida, 1942), pp. 124–26.

8. Morris, *Florida Handbook, 1975-1976;* Biographical Materials, UF; see also David R. Colburn and Richard K. Scher, "Florida Gubernatorial Politics: The Fuller Warren Years," *Florida Historical Quarterly* 53, no.4 (April 1975): 390.

9. Biographical Materials, UF.

10. Morris, *Florida Handbook, 1975-1976;* Biographical Materials, UF; Proctor, *Broward,* pp. 99, 101, 102.

11. Morris, *Florida Handbook, 1975-1976.*

12. Ibid.; Setnor, "Recruitment Patterns."

13. Morris, *Florida Handbook, 1975-1976.*

14. "Public service" includes, but is not limited to, the holding of elected public office.

15. Morris, *Florida Handbook, 1975-1976;* Biographical Materials, UF; Setnor, "Recruitment Patterns."

16. Ibid.

17. Schlesinger, *How They Became Governor,* pp. 22–28.

18. Morris, *Florida Handbook, 1975-1976;* Biographical Materials, UF; Setnor, "Recruitment Patterns."

19. Ibid.; Interview with Farris Bryant, Jacksonville, August 26, 1975; Charlton W. Tebeau, *A History of Florida* (Coral Gables: University of Miami Press, 1971), pp. 467–68.

20. Morris, *Florida Handbook, 1975-1976;* Setnor, "Recruitment Patterns." Graham has been excluded from this category since he was governor of Florida at the time this book was written.

21. V. O. Key, Jr., *Southern Politics in State and Nation* (New York: A. A. Knopf, 1949), pp. 82, 96–100; Manning J. Dauer, "Florida: the Different State," in *The Changing Politics of the South,* ed. William C. Havard (Baton Rouge: Louisiana State University Press, 1972), pp. 117–19.

22. Schlesinger, *How They Became Governor,* pp. 9–10.

CHAPTER 3

1. For a more detailed examination of Florida during Reconstruction see Jerrell H. Shofner, *Nor Is It Over Yet: Florida in the Era of Reconstruction* (Gainesville: University of Florida Press, 1974); Jerrell H. Shofner, "Political Reconstruction in Florida," *Florida Historical Quarterly* 45, no. 2 (October 1966): 145–70.

2. Charles H. Dickinson to Napoleon Broward, November 10, 1904, in Box no. 2, Napoleon Broward Papers, P. K. Yonge Library of Florida History, University of Florida, Gainesville, hereafter cited as NB:UF; interviews with former governor Millard Caldwell, Tallahassee, July 24, 1975, with former Governor Haydon Burns, Jacksonville, Florida, July 21, 1975. Also see Farris Bryant Papers, Campaign Literature, Florida State Archives, Tallahassee, Florida.

3. Allen Morris, *The Florida Handbook: 1967–68* (Tallahassee, Florida: Peninsular Publishing Co., 1967), p. 309.

4. Interview with former governor Millard Caldwell, Tallahassee, July 24, 1975.

5. *New York Times,* October 25, 1954; Stuart Gene Mandel, "The Republican Party in Florida" (Master's thesis, Florida State University, 1968), pp. 77, 80.

6. Box no. 21, Democratic Executive Committee, 1931, Democrats, Doyle Carlton Papers, Florida State Archives, Tallahassee, Florida.

7. "Napoleon B. Broward, Candidate for Governor of Florida" p. 7 (pamphlet), NB:UF.

8. *Southern Politics in State and Nation,* p. 82.

9. Proctor, *Broward,* p. 82; *Tampa Tribune,* June 17, 1900; William Sherman Jennings Papers, Box no. 4, Nomination, P. K. Yonge Library of Florida History, University of Florida, Gainesville. Also see William T. Cash, *History of the Democratic Party in Florida* (Tallahassee, 1936). Cash covers the gubernatorial campaigns from 1904 to 1932 in a lively and informative fashion.

10. *Tampa Tribune,* June 20, 1900.

11. Jacksonville *Florida Times-Union,* June 23, 1900; Proctor, *Broward,* pp. 162–63.

12. Jacksonville *Florida Times-Union,* June 23, 1900.

13. Box no. 12, Primary, William Sherman Jennings Papers.

14. Napoleon Broward to Governor Charles Densen of Illinois, November 12, 1907, Letter Book, 1905–8, NB:UF.

15. *Broward,* p. 187; E. M. Semple to Broward, October 17, 1903, Box no. 1, NB:UF.

16. Dickinson to Broward, Box no. 2, November, 1904, NB:UF; Proctor, *Broward,* pp. 164, 165, 197.

17. Proctor, *Broward,* p. 183.

18. Ibid., p. 21.

19. Box no. 2, November, 1904, NB:UF.

20. Pamphlet on "N.B.B," NB:UF.

21. Proctor, *Broward,* p. 21.

22. Ibid., p. 202; Broward to Honorable J. W. Brody, February 19, 1908, Letter Book, 1905–8, NB:UF.

23. *The Metropolis,* July 23, 1907.

24. Jacksonville *Florida Times-Union,* March 5, 1908; Sister Mary Evangelista Staid, "Albert Waller Gilchrist, Florida's Middle of the Road Governor" (Master's thesis, University of Florida, 1970), p. 31.

25. Jacksonville *Florida Times-Union,* January 3, 1908; Staid, "Gilchrist," p. 39.

26. Jacksonville *Florida Times-Union,* January 3, 1908; Staid, "Gilchrist," p. 31.

27. Staid, "Gilchrist," p. 36.

28. Box S–T, Park Trammell Materials, P. K. Yonge Library of Florida History, University of Florida, Gainesville; *Tampa Tribune,* April 28, 1912. The second-place finisher, William H. Milton, refused to enter the second primary.

29. In 1909 Governor Gilchrist argued strongly in favor of a one-primary system because of the expense involved in a second primary (*Tampa Tribune,* January 7, 1909).

30. Mygnon Evans, "Florida's Fire and Brimstone Governor," *Florida Accent,* December 17, 1972; Sidney J. Catts Materials, Box no. 197, James B. Hodges Papers, P. K. Yonge Library of Florida History, University of Florida, Gainesville.

31. *Tampa Tribune,* January 19, 1916.

32. Sidney J. Catts Materials, Box no. 197, James B. Hodges Papers, P. K. Yonge Library of Florida History, University of Florida, Gainesville.

33. Ibid.; *Miami Herald,* June 2, 1940.

34. *Tampa Tribune,* March 4, 1916.

35. Dorothy Lord, "Sidney Johnstone Catts and the Gubernatorial Election of 1916," *Apalachee,* 1963–67, pp. 51–56; Wayne Flynt, "Sidney J. Catts: The Road to Power," *Florida Historical Quarterly* 49, no 2. (October 1970): 115.

36. Jacksonville *Florida Times-Union,* June 2, 1920.

37. Flynt, "Catts," p. 115.

38. Jacksonville *Florida Times-Union,* November 9, 1916.

39. Wayne Flynt, "William V. Knott and the Gubernatorial Election of 1916," *Florida Historical Quarterly* 51, no. 4 (April 1973): 430.

40. Jacksonville *Florida Times-Union,* June 2, 6,1920.

41. Martin was also the first candidate to solicit the women's vote. At the bottom of all political advertisements, his campaign aides inserted the phrase "The Ladies Are Especially Invited." See Victoria Harden McDonnell, "The Businessman's Politician: A Study of the Administration of John Wellborn Martin" (Master's thesis, University of Florida, 1968), pp. 36–43.

42. Catts Papers, Sermon Book, 1899–1905, University of Florida; *Tampa Morning Tribune,* May 15, 1928. The *Tampa Morning Tribune* became the *Tampa Tribune* on June 1, 1958, but the two names were still used after that date.

43. *Miami Herald,* May 22, 1928.

44. *Tampa Tribune,* May 29, 1932.

45. Ibid, June 3, 1932.

46. Ibid, June 19, 24, 1932; Merlin Cox, "David Sholtz: The New Deal Governor of Florida," *Florida Historical Quarterly* 43, no. 2 (October 1964): 143–52.

47. *Tampa Tribune,* January 3, 1936.

48. Ibid, January 19, 1936.

49. *St. Petersburg Times,* May 20, 1940.

50. *Miami Herald,* May 15, 1940; *Tampa Tribune,* May 17, 1940.

51. *Clearwater News,* May 17, 1940.

52. Jacksonville *Florida Times-Union,* April 20, May 1, 1940.

53. *Tampa Tribune,* March 30, 1944; Private papers of former Governor Millard Caldwell, Tallahassee, Florida.

54. The number of black voters increased significantly in the years following the 1944 decision, but blacks still only made up 9 percent of the electorate in 1960, and less than a majority actually voted.

55. See statistics in the introduction to this volume. Formal Announcement of Fuller Warren for Governor of Florida, 1948, Fuller Warren Papers, Florida Collection, Robert Manning Strozier Library, Florida State University, Tallahassee.

56. *Miami Daily News,* May 11, 1948; *Pensacola Journal,* May 12, 1948; *Ft. Myers Press,* May 24, 1948; Fuller Warren Papers, Florida State University, Tallahassee.

57. *Tampa Morning Tribune,* June 7, 1950; Griffin Press Clippings, 1950, Fuller Warren Papers, Florida State University, Tallahassee.

58. Morris L. Haimowitz, "Population Trends in Florida" (Master's thesis, University of Florida, 1942), pp. 124–26.

59. See chap. 5, this volume.

60. *Tampa Tribune,* May 14, 16, 1954.

61. Jacksonville *Florida Times-Union,* May 18, 1954.

62. *Tampa Tribune,* February 19, 1956.

63. Ibid., February 3, 1956; Jacksonville *Florida Times-Union,* February 3, 1956. The interposition resolution was an attempt to "interpose" the authority of the state between the Supreme Court and the schools, thereby rendering the Court's decision meaningless.

64. *Tampa Tribune,* April 26, 29, 1956.

65. *Miami Herald,* April 1, 1956.

66. Report of the Secretary of State, Tabulation of the Official Vote, Florida Primary Elections, 1956, P. K. Yonge Library of Florida History, University of Florida, Gainesville.

67. *Tampa Tribune, Orlando Sentinel,* April 21, 1960; Farris Bryant campaign ad., P. K. Yonge Library of Florida History, University of Florida, Gainesville.

68. *Tampa Tribune,* May 21, 24, 1960.

69. Ibid., April 24, 1960.

70. Campaign Literature, Farris Bryant Papers, Florida State Archives, Tallahassee, Florida; Bryant campaign ad., P. K. Yonge Library of Florida History, University of Florida, Gainesville. Earl Black, *Southern Governors and Civil Rights: Racial Segregation as a Campaign Issue in the Second Reconstruction* (Cambridge: Harvard University Press, 1976), p. 96.

71. Jacksonville *Florida Times-Union,* March 24, May 3, 23, 1964.

72. *Tampa Tribune,* Jacksonville *Florida Times-Union,* February 3, 1956; *Palm Beach Post,* May 11, 1960; *Miami Herald,* February 17, 1964; *Tampa Tribune,* May 22, 1964. High also charged that a past president of the NAACP had contributed $500 to Burns' campaign.

73. Jacksonville *Florida Times-Union,* April 5, 1956; *Tampa Tribune,* April 12, May 10, 1956. Robert Saunders, field secretary for the NAACP, praised High's civil rights record, noting that he had a "genuine interest in developing good race relations."

74. Haimowitz, "Population Trends in Florida," pp. 124–26.

75. *Tampa Tribune,* May 10, 1956; *Miami Herald,* May 16, 1956.

76. Report of the Secretary of State, Tabulation of Official Vote, Florida Primary Elections, May 5, 26, 1964, p. 12. P. K. Yonge Library of Florida History, University of Florida, Gainesville.

77. Black, *Southern Governors and Civil Rights,* pp. 342, 343.

78. *Tampa Tribune,* April 7, 1965.

79. General election returns for the office of governor from 1944 to the present are as follows:

		Democrat		Republican
1944	Millard Caldwell	361,007	Bert Acker	96,321
1948	Fuller Warren	381,459	Bert Acker	76,153
1952	Dan McCarty	624,463	Harry Swan	210,609
1954	LeRoy Collins	287,769	J. Tom Watson	69,852
1956	LeRoy Collins	747,753	William Washburne	266,980
1960	Farris Bryant	849,407	George Petersen	569,939
1964	Haydon Burns	933,554	Charles R. Holley	686,297
1966	Robert High	668,233	Claude Kirk	821,190
1970	Reubin Askew	984,305	Claude Kirk	746,243
1974	Reubin Askew	1,118,954	Jerry Thomas	709,438
1978	Bob Graham	1,406,580	Jack Eckerd	1,123,888

Despite a sizeable increase in the number of registered Republican voters in Florida since 1950, Republican candidates were still heavily dependent on Democratic votes if they hoped to be elected.

Registered Voters

	Democrats	Republicans
1950	1,060,560	60,595
1960	1,656,023	338,340
1970	2,024,387	711,090

SOURCE: *Report of the Secretary of State, 1949–50, 1959–60, 1969–70.*

80 *Tampa Tribune,* October 10, 21, 1964.

81. (New York: Harcourt, Brace & World, 1966), p. 394; interview with Haydon Burns.

82. *Tampa Tribune,* November 2, 1966.

83. See David Halberstam, *The Best and the Brightest* (New York: Random House, 1972), and Eric Goldman, *The Tragedy of LBJ* (New York: A. A. Knopf, 1969).

84. Matthews and Prothro, *Negroes and the New Southern Politics,* p. 377.

85. *New York Times,* November 26, 1967.

86. *Miami Herald,* August 20, 1970. President Nixon had called a meeting of leading southern officials to discuss school desegregation.

87. Ibid., September 25, 1970.

88. Ibid., September 15, 25, 1970.

89. Mathews promised, if elected, to implement an educational reform program emphasizing vocational education, an air and water quality program, and a seventeen-point crime-fighting program, but because of his drab campaign style, few voters bothered to study his platform (*Tampa Tribune,* September 9, 1970).

90. Ibid., September 2, 5, 1970.

91. *Miami Herald,* August 22, September 17, 22, 1970.

92. Ibid., September 17, 1970.

93. Ibid., October 9, 10, 1970. Kirk's low-cost housing plan had tremendous appeal in Pinellas County, which had the highest percentage of retired people in the state.

94. *New York Times,* November 6, 1974; *Gainesville Sun,* August 29, 1973.

95. *New York Times,* November 6, 1974.

96. Bob Graham, *Workdays: Finding Florida on the Job,* ed. Lawrence Mahoney (Miami: Banyan Books, 1978), pp. 1–130.

97. *Miami Herald,* September 14, 1978; *Tampa Tribune,* September 14, November 7, 1978.

98. *Tampa Tribune,* September 11, 1978.

99. Ibid., October 1, 2, 4, 5, 1978.

100. *Miami Herald,* October 6, 1978.

101. *Florida Times-Union, Tallahassee Democrat,* September 14, 1978.

102. *Tampa Tribune,* November 6, 8, 9, 1978; *Miami Herald,* November 9, 1978.

103. Matthews and Prothro, *Negroes and the New Southern Politics,* p. 398.

104. Herbert J. Doherty, Jr., "Liberal and Conservative Voting Patterns in Florida," *Journal of Politics* 14, no. 3 (1952): 412. For an assessment of the urban voting patterns in Florida see Numan V. Bartley and Hugh D. Graham, *Southern Politics and the Second Reconstruction* (Baltimore: Johns Hopkins Press, 1975).

CHAPTER 4

1. The 1885 constitution was actually Florida's fifth constitution beginning with the charter of 1839. Her most recent constitution had been adopted following the defeat of the Confederacy in 1868. It was through this document that the federal government sought to impose its will on wayward Confederate Floridians. The governor was given considerable power, including the right to succeed himself and to call special sessions of the legislature and adjourn them when the two houses were at loggerheads. He also had veto power over all legislation.

2. Charlton W. Tebeau, *A History of Florida* (Coral Gables: University of Miami Press, 1971), p. 288.

3. Ibid., p. 289; William C. Havard, "Notes on a Theory of State Constitutional Change: The Florida Experience," *Journal of Politics* 21, no. 1, (February 1959): 87.

4. See Francis Newton Thorpe, *The Federal and State Constitutions* (Washington: Government Printing Office, 1909), 2: 649–764.

5. See, for example, V. O. Key, Jr., *Southern Politics in State and Nation* (New York: A. A. Knopf, 1949), pp. 82–105; Manning J. Dauer; "Florida: The Different State," in *The Changing Politics of the South,* ed. William C. Havard (Baton Rouge: Louisiana State University Press, 1972), pp. 92–164; and Neal R. Peirce, *The Deep South States of America* (New York: W. W. Norton and Company, 1974), pp. 435–94.

6. A later dissent by former governor LeRoy Collins is noted below.

7. Manning J. Dauer, "The Constitution of Florida," University of Florida, Public Administration Clearing Service, 1950, Civic Information Series, no. 3, p. 4.

8. For a general critique, see Manning J. Dauer and William C. Havard, *The Florida Constitution of 1885–A Critique,* University of Florida Studies in Public Administration, no. 12 (Gainesville: Public Administration Clearing Service, 1955), pp. 39–48.

9. Dauer and Havard, *The Florida Constitution of 1885,* p. 43.

10. Allen Morris, *The Florida Handbook 1973–1974* (Tallahassee: Peninsular Publishing Company, 1973), pp. 85–133.

11. Address to the Legislature, 1933, Box 41, David Sholtz Papers, Florida State Archives, Tallahassee, Florida.

12. Dauer, "Florida: The Different State," pp. 119–24; Jacksonville *Florida Times-Union,* January 9, 1929.

13. Interview with LeRoy Collins, February 11, 1975, Tallahassee.

14. *Gainesville Sun,* August 9, 1967.

15. For accounts of some of these attempts, see D. H. Redfearn, "A New Constitution for Florida," *Florida Law Journal* 21 (January 1947): 2–13; Thomas E. David, "The Case for Constitutional Revision in Florida," *Miami Law Quarterly* 3 (February 1949): 225–34; and Richard E. Bain, *The Proposed Florida Constitution of 1958 and the Constitution of 1885: A Comparison* (Tallahassee: Bureau of Governmental Research, Florida State University, 1958).

16. *Miami Herald, Tampa Tribune,* October 26, 1955.

17. *Tampa Tribune,* October 23, March 12, 1955, October 9, 1956; Speech before the Constitutional Advisory Commission, October 22, 1955, Box no. 1, Speeches, October 6–December 16, 1955, Florida Collection, LeRoy Collins Papers, Main Library, University of South Florida, Tampa; Havard, "Notes on a Theory of State Constitutional Change," p. 94.

18. Madelyn L. Kafoglis, "Revenue Bonds and a New Cycle for Election of Governor and Cabinet Constitutional Amendments," University of Florida, Public Administration Clearing Service, 1963, Civic Information Series, no. 42, pp. 9–12.

19. *Tampa Tribune,* October 2, 1959, November 15, 1960.

20. Manning J. Dauer, "Florida Reapportionment," *Business and Economic Dimensions,* March 1967, pp. 8–14; Dauer, "Florida: The Different State," pp. 119–24.

21. *Gainesville Sun, Tampa Tribune,* April 27, 1967.

22. The following relies on Manning J. Dauer, Clement H. Donovan, and Gladys M. Kammerer, *Should Florida Adopt the Proposed 1968 Constitution? An Analysis,* University of Florida, Studies in Public Administration, no. 31 (Gainesville: Public Administration Clearing Service 1968); Gladys Kammerer, "Florida," in *Compacts of Antiquity: State Constitutions* (Atlanta: Southern Newspaper Publishers Association Foundation, nd), pp. 120–42; and Manning J. Dauer and Richard Scher, "Florida Constitutional Revisions of 1968 and 1972," paper delivered at the Southern Political Science Association Convention, New Orleans, November 1974.

CHAPTER 5

1. Clinton Rossiter, *The American Presidency,* rev. ed. (New York: Mentor Books, 1960), p. 17; Joseph E. Kallenbach, *The American Chief Executive* (New York: Harper and Row, 1966).

2. Analyses of this point are well known in political science literature, but most of the available research deals with federal and urban bureaucracies. See, for example, Alan Altshuler, *The Politics of the Federal Bureaucracy* (New York: Dodd, Mead and Co., 1968); Wallace S. Sayer and Herbert Kaufman, *Governing New York City* (New York: W. W. Norton and Company, 1960); Douglas M. Fox, *The Politics of City and State Bureaucracy* (Pacific Palisades: Goodyear Publishing Company, 1974); and Ira Sharkansky, "State Administrators in the Political Process," in *Politics in the American States,* ed. Herbert Jacob and Kenneth N. Vines, 2d ed. (Boston: Little, Brown and Company, 1971), pp. 238–71.

3. See Thomas R. Dye, *Politics in States and Communities,* 2d ed. (Englewood Cliffs, N.J.: Prentice Hall, 1973), pp. 163–89; Duane Lockard, *The Politics of State and Local Government,* 2d ed. (New York: The Macmillan Company, 1969), pp. 317–74; John A. Straayer, *American State and Local Government* (Columbus, Ohio: Charles E. Merrill Publishing Company, 1973), pp. 97–134; Coleman Ransone, *The Office of Governor in the United States* (University: University of Alabama Press, 1956); and Thad Beyle and J. Oliver Williams, eds., *The American Governor in Behavioral Perspective* (New York: Harper and Row, 1972), pp. 73–288.

4. Altshuler, *The Politics of the Federal Bureaucracy.*

5. Joseph Schlesinger, "The Politics of the Executive," in *Politics in the American States,* ed. Jacob and Vines, pp. 222–25.

6. This problem has been discussed in chap. 4; for a more general discussion see especially Dye, *Politics in States and Communities,* pp. 163–89.

7. Thomas Dye, "State Legislative Politics," in *Politics in the American States,* ed. Jacob and Vines, pp. 208–9; Anthony Downs, *Inside Bureaucracy* (Boston: Little, Brown and Company, 1967).

8. Interview with Governor Reubin Askew, January 10, 1975, Tallahassee.

9. While one might wonder whether the ways in which Caldwell saw the office and described what he did were different from his actual behavior, there seems to be a close parallel between the two. That is, the things he did as chief executive, and the problems which concerned him, closely resembled those matters which he discussed in this address and later published: Millard F. Caldwell, "The Governor's Duties and Responsibilities," an address before the Florida State Chamber of Commerce, December 2, 1947, published by the Florida State Chamber of Commerce (n.p., n.d.), P. K. Yonge Library of Florida History, University of Florida, Gainesville; interview with Millard Caldwell, July 24, 1975, Tallahassee.

10. Caldwell, "Governor's Duties," pp. 2–4. Most of these agencies no longer exist, having been reorganized, combined, or abolished.

11. Ibid., p. 5.

12. Interview with Governor Reubin Askew, January 10, 1975, Tallahassee.

13. Caldwell, "Governor's Duties," p. 4.

14. Jacksonville *Florida Times-Union,* January 8, 1913.

15. See for example, *Tampa Morning Tribune,* January 8, 1939.

16. Caldwell, "Governor's Duties," p. 5. It is of interest that Caldwell later changed his mind about the effectiveness of reorganization. Given the rapid growth of state government, which he deplored, Caldwell felt that shifting bureaus around might neither save costs nor promote gubernatorial control (interview with Millard Caldwell, July 24, 1975, Tallahassee).

17. Caldwell, "Governor's Duties," p. 5.

18. Citizens Conference on State Legislatures, *The Sometime Governments* (New York: Bantam, 1971).

19. For other problems inherent in the structure of the cabinet, see chap. 4; see also Manning J. Dauer, "Florida: The Different State," in *The Changing Politics of the South,* ed. William C. Havard (Baton Rouge: Louisiana State University Press, 1972), pp. 117–19; and Manning J. Dauer and William C. Havard, *The Florida Constitution of 1885: A Critique* (Gainesville, Florida: Public Administration Clearing Service, 1955), pp. 41–48.

20. Interview with LeRoy Collins, February 11, 1975, Tallahassee.

21. *Tampa Morning Tribune,* December 16, 1955, February 17, 1956.

22. Interview with Haydon Burns, July 21, 1975, Jacksonville.

23. *Tampa Morning Tribune,* March 10, 1937.

24. *Miami Herald,* January 7, 1945.

25. See, for example, *Tampa Morning Tribune,* August 13, 1947.

26. Ibid., April 3, 1959, June 8, 1960.

27. See chap. 4; *Tampa Morning Tribune,* October 26, 1955.

28. *Tampa Morning Tribune,* January 3, 1962.

29. *Gainesville Sun,* August 9, December 12, 1967; *Tampa Morning Tribune,* April 2, 1968.

30. Collins' addresses to the Florida League of Women Voters Conference on "Shifting Power Patterns in Our Political System: The Executive," March 23, 1976, Orlando, and Florida College Teachers of History, April 10, 1976, Gainesville; interview with Collins, February 11, 1975, Tallahassee.

31. Askew's views were presented at the League of Women Voters Conference in Orlando by James Apthorp, the governor's senior executive assistant, March 23, 1976; interview with Governor Reubin Askew, January 10, 1975, Tallahassee.

32. *Tampa Morning Tribune,* April 11, 1923.

33. Since 1972, when a constitutional amendment reorganizing courts in Florida was ratified, the number of judges to be appointed has been greatly reduced.

34. Both Millard Caldwell and Fuller Warren had discussed and proposed central purchasing systems, but no action was taken. The first real steps toward centralized purchasing were taken during Dan McCarty's administration (*Tampa Morning Tribune,* September 29, 1953).

35. Box 160, General Materials, 1941, Gi–Har. Letter from Holland to Harry Holden, July 21, 1941, Spessard Holland Papers, P. K. Yonge Library of Florida History, University of Florida, Gainesville; Box 180, General Materials, Hou–I, ibid.

36. *Tampa Morning Tribune,* January 13, 1953, March 7, 1958.

37. Ibid., January 20, 1950.

38. *Florida Times-Union,* August 1, 1950; *Tampa Sunday Tribune,* January 14, 1951.

39. *Tampa Tribune,* December 19, 1954.

40. Ibid., November 1, 1960.

41. Ibid., April 11, 1963.

42. *Gainesville Sun,* May 12, 1972; *St. Petersburg Times,* March 22, 1970.

43. *Tampa Morning Tribune,* January 13, 1953.

44. For discussion of these cleavages, see chap. 1.

45. David R. Colburn and Richard K. Scher, "Florida Gubernatorial Politics: The Fuller Warren Years," *Florida Historical Quarterly* 53, no. 4 (April 1975): 396; *Tampa Morning Tribune,* February 13, 1955.

46. *Tampa Morning Tribune,* May 23, 1957. See also chap. 8, this volume; interview with Governor Reubin Askew, January 10, 1975, Tallahassee.

47. *Tampa Morning Tribune,* January 4, 1933, January 2, 1945.

48. William Sherman Jennings Papers, P. K. Yonge Library of Florida History, University of Florida, Gainesville. Box 8 consists of large numbers of job requests. Letter from Gilchrist to Hon. Frank Clark, January 28, 1909, Albert Waller Gilchrist Papers, Official Papers of the Governor of Florida, Florida State University.

49. *Tampa Morning Tribune,* February 6, July 15, 1937, October 3, 1953.

50. See, for example, Box 160, General Materials, 1941, Gi–Har, article by Allen Morris, Spessard Holland Papers, and A–Com, letter from Holland to Erwin Clayton, January 27, 1941; Millard Caldwell Papers, P. K. Yonge Library of Florida History, University of Florida, Gainesville; Box 9 contains extensive records illustrating the degree to which Caldwell sought information about qualified applicants for state jobs. See also *Tampa Morning Tribune,* January 1, 1945.

51. Interview with Millard Caldwell, July 24, 1975, Tallahassee.

52. Ibid.

53. Letter from Caldwell to Leland Hiatt, state welfare commissioner, May 22, 1946, Millard Caldwell Papers, Florida State Archives, Box 214, Merit System Council, 1956.

54. Wayne Flynt, *Cracker Messiah: Governor Sidney J. Catts of Florida* (Baton Rouge: Louisiana State University Press, 1977), pp. 108, 111.

55. Ibid., pp. 112–15.

56. Ibid, p. 126.

57. Colburn and Scher, "Florida Gubernatorial Politics," p. 392.

58. *St. Petersburg Times,* March 29, 1949; *Jacksonville Journal,* February 25, 1950, in Fuller Warren Scrapbooks, P. K. Yonge Library of Florida History, University of Florida, Gainesville (hereafter cited as FWS:PKY); telegram from Louis Wolfson to Fuller Warren, December 6, 1948, uncatalogued Fuller Warren Papers, ibid.

59. *Jacksonville Journal,* February 25, 1950; FWS:PKY; *Miami Herald,* April 25, 1950.

60. "Frank S. Wright—Appointed by Governor Warren to be Assistant to the Governor," 1948, Fuller Warren Papers, Florida Collection, Robert Manning Strozier Library, Florida State University, Tallahassee (hereafter cited as FWP:FSU).

61. "Appointments by Governor Fuller Warren during 1949–1952," FWP:FSU.

62. Mathews had authored a white supremacy bill aimed at barring blacks from Democratic primaries. He had been an ideological comrade of the Ku Klux Klan and a leader of the Dixiecrat movement of 1948, according to the *St. Petersburg Times,* October 18, 1951.

63. *Miami Herald,* August 6, 1950.

64. *Tampa Morning Tribune,* January 7, 1953; *Miami Herald,* January 8, 1953.

65. *Tallahassee Democrat,* January 8, 9, 10, 1953; *Tampa Morning Tribune,* January 18, February 8, September 29, 1953.

66. Letter from Johns to Earl Powers, October 2, 1953. Charley Johns Papers, Florida State Archives, Box 300, Road Department—Turnpike, 1953; *Tampa Morning Tribune,* October 2, 11, 1953.

67. *Miami Herald,* October 11, 12, 1953; *Florida Times-Union,* October 13, 18, 1953.

68. *Tampa Morning Tribune,* October 20, November 11, 1953.

69. Ibid., November 15, 18, 1953.

70. *Miami Herald,* December 11, 12, 14, 15, 1953.

71. *Tampa Morning Tribune,* May 27, 1954.

72. Ibid., June 1, 19, 1954.

73. Ibid., July 2, August 14, 1954.

74. Box 311, Road Department Miscellaneous, 1954, letter from Cecil Webb, chairman of Road Department, to C. K. Ireland, purchasing agent for Road Department, August 11, 1954, Charley Johns Papers, Florida State Archives; *Tampa Morning Tribune,* August 22, 29, September 4, 1954.

75. *Tampa Morning Tribune,* September 8, 19, November 7, 11, 20, 25, 1954.

76. Ibid., December 14, 15, 1954.

77. *Tallahassee Democrat,* December 19, 22, 1954.

78. *Tampa Morning Tribune,* November 20, 1954.

79. *Florida Times-Union,* April 2, 1931.

80. *Tampa Morning Tribune,* December 29, 1946.

81. Ibid., January 23, 1959.

82. Ibid., January 1, 1909.

83. Flynt, *Cracker Messiah,* pp. 117–26.

84. *Tampa Morning Tribune,* May 26, October 25, 1957.

85. Ibid., January 10, February 9, 18, 1958, September 25, 27, 1959.

86. Box 230, Citrus Commission, 1948, letter from Caldwell to C. B. Fort, August 17, 1948, Millard Caldwell Papers, Florida State Archives. For additional information, see chap. 11.

87. Box 106, Racing Commission, 1937, Fred Cone Papers, Florida State Archives. This box contains an enormous amount of correspondence and documents indicating Cone's great desire to keep the state free of gambling.

88. Ibid., Box 98, Citrus Commission, 1937.

89. *Tampa Morning Tribune,* July 13, 25, 28, August 3, 1937, November 22, 1938.

90. See, for example, Aaron Wildavsky, *The Politics of the Budgetary Process* (Boston: Little, Brown and Company, 1964).

91. David R. Colburn, "Alfred E. Smith: The First Fifty Years, 1873–1924" (Ph.D. dissertation, University of North Carolina at Chapel Hill, 1971), pp.137–38.

92. Interview with Governor Reubin Askew, January 10, 1975, Tallahassee.

93. This distinction comes from Charles Lindblom, "The Science of Muddling Through," *Public Administration Review* 29 (Spring 1954): 79–88.

94. *Tampa Morning Tribune,* February 4, 1945; Millard Caldwell Papers, Florida State Archives, Box 196, Budget Commission, Miscellaneous, 1945.

95. Dan McCarty Papers, Florida State Archives, Box 292, Budget Commission, 1953, letter from C. Farris Bryant to McCarty, January 10, 1953.

96. *Tampa Morning Tribune,* December 18, 1958; interview with Representative Elaine Gordon, February 24, 1976, Gainesville.

97. Allen Schick, *Budget Innovation in the States* (Washington: The Brookings Institution, 1971); S. Kenneth Howard, *Changing State Budgeting* (Lexington, Ky.: Council of State Governments, 1973).

98. Herbert Kaufman, *Politics and Policies in State and Local Government* (Englewood Cliffs, N.J.: Prentice-Hall, 1963).

CHAPTER 6

1. C. Vann Woodward, *Origins of the New South, 1877–1913* (Baton Rouge: Louisiana State University Press, 1951), pp. 51–74.

2. Relatively few political scientists have systematically explored gubernatorial-legislative relations. The following sources are suggestive of the available literature that was consulted: John C. Wahlke et al., *The Legislative System* (New York: John Wiley, 1962); William J. Keefe and Morris S. Ogul, *The American Legislative Process* (Englewood Cliffs, N.J.: Prentice-Hall, 1964); Alexander Heard, ed., *State Legislatures in American Politics* (Englewood Cliffs, N.J.: Prentice-Hall, 1966); Malcolm E. Jewell and Samuel C. Patterson, *The Legislative Process in the United States* (New York: Random House, 1966); Malcolm E. Jewell, *The State Legislature* (New York: Random House, 1969); Thomas R. Dye, "State Legislative Politics," in *Politics in the American States,* ed. Herbert Jacob and Kenneth N. Vines, 2d ed. (Boston: Little Brown and Company, 1971), pp. 163–209; John A. Straayer, *American State and Local Government* (Columbus, Ohio: Charles E. Merrill Publishing Company, 1973), pp. 63–95; David Berman, *State and Local Politics* (Boston: Holbrook Press, 1975), pp. 79–102; Charles Adrian, *State and Local Governments,* 4th ed. (New York: McGraw-Hill Book Company, 1976), pp. 288–339; and Samuel C. Patterson, "American State Legislatures and Public Policy," in *Politics in the American States,* ed. Jacob and Vines, 3d ed. (Boston: Little Brown and Company, 1976), pp. 139–95.

3. The most lucid discussions of this fundamental principle of federalism can be found in Morton Grodzins, *The American System* (Chicago: Rand McNally, 1966), and Daniel Elazar, *American Federalism: A View from the States,* 2d ed. (New York: Thomas Y. Crowell Company, 1972).

4. Dye, "State Legislative Politics," pp. 208–9.

5. This point is frequently stressed in the literature. For instance, see Keefe and Ogul, *The American Legislative Process;* Patterson, "American State Legislatures and Public Policy," pp. 139–95; and Heard, *State Legislatures in American Politics.*

6. This point is also discussed in studies of state legislatures. See Berman, *State and Local Politics,* pp. 79–102; Dye, "State Legislative Politics," p. 208; Heard, *State Legislatures in American Politics;* and Donald G. Herzberg and Alan Rosenthal, eds., *Strengthening the States* (New York: Anchor Books, 1972).

7. Jewell, *The State Legislature;* Fred Greenstein, *The American Party System and the American People* (Englewood Cliffs, N.J.: Prentice-Hall, 1963); Frank Sorauf, *Party Politics in America,* 2d ed. (Boston: Little Brown and Company, 1972); Malcolm E. Jewell and David M. Olson, *American State Political Parties and Elections* (Homewood, Ill.: The Dorsey Press, 1978).

8. Wahlke, et al., *The Legislative System,* provide the best analysis of the perceptions legislators have of their roles in the political process.

9. See Straayer, *American State and Local Government,* pp. 63–95; Berman, *State and Local Politics,* pp. 79–102; and Adrian, *State and Local Governments,* pp. 288–339, for general considerations of these and other strategies. In a broader context, see Keefe and Ogul, *The American Legislative Process;* Heard, *State Legislatures in American Politics;* and Jewell and Patterson, *The Legislative Process in the United States.*

10. General Correspondence, 1940, Spessard Holland Papers, P. K. Yonge Library of Florida History, Gainesville; interview with Millard Caldwell, Tallahassee, July 24, 1975; also Box no. 8, Millard Caldwell Papers, P. K. Yonge Library of Florida History, Gainesville.

11. Samuel Proctor, *Napoleon Bonaparte Broward: Florida's Fighting Democrat* (Gainesville: University of Florida Press, 1950), p. 207; interview with Millard Caldwell, Tallahassee, July 24, 1975.

12. *Journal of the House of Representatives of the State of Florida, Regular Session, 1911,* pp. 25–119; Jacksonville *Florida Times-Union,* April 4, 1929. See chap. 7, this volume.

13. *Journal of the House of Representatives of the State of Florida, Regular Session, 1957,* p. 8; *1925,* p. 22.

14. Ibid., *1921,* pp. 10–31; *1917,* pp. 14–35.

15. Napoleon Broward to William James Bryan, March 10, 1905, Box no. 3, March, 1905, Napoleon Broward Papers, P. K. Yonge Library of Florida History, Gainesville; Staid, "Gilchrist," p. 67.

16. General Materials, P–Z, Box 166, 48Sh, Spessard Holland Papers, P. K. Yonge Library of Florida History, Gainesville; Wayne Flynt, "Sidney J. Catts: The Road to Power," *Florida Historical Quarterly* 49, no. 2 (October 1970): 125.

17. *Tampa Tribune,* January 5, 1963; interview with Reubin O'D. Askew, Tallahassee, January 10, 1975.

18. Box no. 8, Millard Caldwell Papers; Doyle Carlton to Harry Wells, November 25, 1930, Box no. 13, Democratic Executive Committee, Doyle Carlton Papers, Florida State Archives, Tallahassee; editorials, *Pensacola Journal,* General Materials, D–Hol, Holland Papers, 1943; Spessard Holland to Senator A. G. McArthur, May 7, 1942, Box no. 176, General Materials, Me–Ro, Holland Papers; Jacksonville *Florida Times-Union,* March 31, 1913.

19. Proctor, *Broward,* pp. 216–22.

20. *Gainesville Sun,* June 3, 1973; interview with Reubin O'D. Askew, Tallahassee, January 10, 1975.

21. Interview with person who wishes to remain anonymous, Tallahassee; *Orlando Sentinel,* October 2, 1967.

22. David Colburn and Richard Scher, "Florida Gubernatorial Politics: The Fuller Warren Years," *Florida Historical Quarterly* 54, no. 2 (April 1975): 400; *Tampa Tribune,* April 21, 1965.

23. *Tampa Tribune,* April 18, 1937, June 2, 1961.

24. Ibid., May 13, 1959.

25. Ibid., May 24, June 21, 1933.

26. Ibid., July 8, 1962.

27. Flynt, "Sidney J. Catts," p. 125; Folder—Key Men, General Materials, 1943, Box no. 182, I–Phon, Spessard Holland Papers.

28. Interview with D. R. "Billy" Mathews, July 14, 1970, Oral History, University of Florida, Gainesville; *Tampa Tribune,* January 31, 1937; *State of Florida ex rel., N. Vernon Hawthorne* v. *Marshall C. Wiseheart,* 28 So. 2d 589 (Fla. 1946). Also see Constitution of 1885, Art. 3, section 5.

29. *Tampa Tribune,* June 1, 1917.

30. Interview with Millard Caldwell, Tallahassee, July 24, 1975.

31. *Miami Herald,* July 16, 1967.

32. See section on "Roads and Tourism" in chap. 7, this volume.

33. Napoleon Broward to George Willicombe, April 16, 1907, Letter Box 1905–7,

Napoleon Broward to Governor Joseph W. Fook and Honorable W. P. Gerome, April 10, 1905, Box no. 3, Napoleon Broward Papers, P. K. Yonge Library of Florida History, Gainesville; Jacksonville *Florida Times-Union,* May 31, 1917.

34. *Orlando Sentinel,* December 27, 1949; Irvin Walden to Robert W. Davis, May 6, 1942, General Materials Me–Ro, Box 176, Holland Papers, 1942, P. K. Yonge Library Florida History, Gainesville.

35. See chap. 7, this volume; *Tampa Tribune,* June 5, 1931.

36. Wayne Flynt, *Cracker Messiah: Governor Sidney J. Catts of Florida* (Baton Rouge: Louisiana State University Press, 1977), pp. 153, 182–83; *Tampa Tribune,* April 14, 17, May 1, June 1, 1917; *Journal of the House of Representatives, 1919,* pp. 8–9.

37. Interview with former Representative Emory Cross, Gainesville, January 30, 1976.

38. Manning J. Dauer, "Florida: The Different State," in *The Changing Politics of the South,* ed. William C. Havard (Baton Rouge: Louisiana State University Press, 1972), p. 119.

39. Douglas S. Gatlin and Bruce B. Mason, *Reapportionment: Its History in Florida* (Gainesville, Fla.: Public Administrative Clearing Service, 1956), p. 13; Dauer, "Florida: The Different State," p. 122.

40. *Tampa Tribune,* May 7, 1909.

41. Gatlin and Mason, *Reapportionment,* p. 11.

42. Richard E. Bain, "Legislative Representation in Florida: Historic and Contemporary" (Master's thesis, Florida State University, 1960), p. 204.

43. Interview with Millard Caldwell, Tallahassee, July 24, 1975.

44. *Tampa Tribune,* June 1, 1945.

45. Ibid.

46. Ibid., June 2, 1945.

47. Ibid., July 10, July 25, 1945.

48. Gatlin and Mason, *Reapportionment,* pp. 13–14; *Tampa Tribune,* April 3, 1955.

49. *Miami Herald,* June 5, 1955; Dauer, "Florida Reapportionment," pp. 9, 10.

50. *Tampa Tribune,* July 9, 1955.

51. *Miami Herald,* August 9, 1955.

52. *Tampa Tribune,* March 2, 1972.

53. Loren P. Beth and William C. Havard, "Committee Stacking and Political Power in Florida," *Journal of Politics* 23, no. 1 (February 1961): 68, 70–73. The key legislative committees from 1955 to 1959 which were dominated by porkchoppers were: Senate—Finance and Taxation, Rules and Calendar, Constitutional Amendments, General Legislation, Education, and Appropriations; House—Finance and Taxation, Rules and Calendar, Constitutional Amendments, General Legislation, Public Schools, Appropriations, and Apportionment.

54. *Tampa Tribune,* September 6, 7, 1955.

55. Ibid., September 28, December 11, 1955.

56. William C. Havard and Loren P. Beth, *The Politics of Mis-Representation: Rural-Urban Conflict in the Florida Legislature* (Baton Rouge: Louisiana State University Press, 1962), p. 50; *Tampa Tribune,* October 8, 1957.

57. Interview with LeRoy Collins, Tallahassee, February 11, 1975; *Miami Herald,* October 24, 1957; Havard and Beth, *The Politics of Mis-Representation,* p. 62. In *Pope* v. *Gray,* 104 So. 2d 841 (Fla. 1958) the court ruled "daisy-chain" techniques eliminated the right of the people to originate decisions.

58. *Tampa Tribune,* April 10, 1959.

59. Ibid., April 11, 1959.

60. *Miami Herald,* April 21, 1959; *St. Petersburg Times,* November 4, 1959; Havard and Beth, *The Politics of Mis-Representation,* p. 67.

61. *Tampa Tribune,* January 4, 1961; *Miami Herald,* November 7, 1962.

62. Alfred H. Kelly and Winfred A. Harbison, *The American Constitution: Its Origins and Development,* 4th ed. (New York: Norton, 1970), pp. 1015–27.

63. *Tampa Tribune,* January 5, June 13, 1965; Dauer, "Florida Reapportionment," p. 10.

64. Dauer, "Florida Reapportionment," p. 10.

65. Thomas L. Neilson, "The Changing Role of the Professional Staff in the Florida

Legislature," paper presented at the Fourth Annual Meeting, Florida Political Science Association, May 17, 1975, Gainesville.

66. See chap. 7, this volume.

67. Interview with former Senator Robert Saunders, Gainesville, December 16, 1975. In one survey of legislative effectiveness, Florida was ranked fourth nationally. The changes the legislature had brought about were judged to have improved its operations considerably. See Citizens Conference on State Legislatures, *The Sometime Governments* (New York: Bantam Books, 1971).

68. Neilson, "The Changing Role of the Professional Staff."

CHAPTER 7

1. *Florida Times-Union,* April 25, 1929; Spessard Holland Papers, 1944, General Materials Gi–I, Box no. 185, Speeches on "Lower the Intangible Tax Ceiling," P. K. Yonge Library of Florida History, University of Florida, Gainesville.

2. Wallace Martin Nelson, "The Economic Development of Florida, 1870–1930" (Ph.D. dissertation, University of Florida, 1962), p. 204.

3. *Report of the Comptroller of the State of Florida for Year Ending 12/31/1911,* pp. 7–9.

4. Box no. 5, November, 1906, Napoleon Bonaparte Broward Papers, P. K. Yonge Library of Florida History, University of Florida, Gainesville; Nelson, "The Economic Development of Florida," p. 190.

5. Nelson, "The Economic Development of Florida," p. 223.

6. Ibid., p. 226.

7. Ibid., p. 264.

8. John F. Sly, "Tax Assets and Tax Policies in Florida: A Report to the Florida Council of 100," May 27, 1964, p. 2, copy in P.K. Yonge Library of Florida History.

9. Charlton W. Tebeau, *A History of Florida* (Coral Gables, Florida: University of Miami Press, 1971), pp. 377–79.

10. Ibid., p. 386.

11. Report of the Special Committee on Taxation and Public Debt, p. 149, Box no. 97, David Sholtz Papers, Florida State Archives, Tallahassee.

12. *Tampa Tribune,* April 5, 1923.

13. Florida Committee on Taxation and Bonded Indebtedness Report. Box no. 97, David Sholtz Papers, Florida State Archives, Tallahassee; Tebeau, *A History of Florida,* p. 394.

14. Jacksonville *Florida Times-Union,* May 25, 1929. D. B. Pinkston to Doyle Carlton, January 19, 1929, Box no. 7, Motor Vehicle Department—Re-Organization, Doyle Carlton Papers, Florida State Archives, Tallahassee.

15. Jacksonville *Florida Times-Union,* May 23, 1929.

16. Ibid., June 8, 1931; Tebeau, *A History of Florida,* p. 395.

17. Jacksonville *Florida Times-Union,* May 1, June 21, 1929; Tebeau, *A History of Florida,* p. 395.

18. Jacksonville *Florida Times-Union,* June 1, 24, 1931.

19. Ibid., June 24, 1931.

20. Ibid., July 26, 29, 1931.

21. Tebeau, *A History of Florida,* pp. 400–401.

22. Nelson, "The Economic Development of Florida," pp. 268–69.

23. *Tampa Tribune,* January 4, 1933.

24. Ibid., January 12, 14, 1933.

25. Jacksonville *Florida Times-Union,* January 6, 1935; *Tampa Tribune,* October 8, 1934. Cone, in fact, opposed all increases in taxation.

26. Tebeau, *A History of Florida,* p. 401.

27. *Tampa Tribune,* January 5, 1937; May 31, June 4, 1939. Cone did, however, like Roosevelt personally. He also sent a telegram to the president in March 1937, supporting the

court reorganization plan (Box 108, March 1937, Fred Cone Papers, Florida State Archives, Tallahassee).

28. *Report of the Comptroller* (Tallahassee, 1935).

29. Radio Address by Governor David Sholtz, October 29, 1935, in the P. K. Yonge Library of Florida History, Gainesville; *Tampa Tribune,* October 8, 1932

30. *Florida Statistical Abstract, 1967* (Gainesville: University of Florida Press, 1967), p. 118.

31. General Materials Con–G, Editorials, Spessard Holland Papers, 1941, P. K. Yonge Library of Florida History, Gainesville.

32. *Tampa Tribune,* January 9, February 27, 1946.

33. Clement H. Donovan, "Do We Need A Sales Tax in Florida?" *Economic Leaflets,* Bureau of Economic and Business Research, College of Business Administration, University of Florida, December 1948, pp. 1–4; "How to Balance Florida's Budget," *Economic Leaflets,* February 1949, pp. 1–4.

34. Fuller Warren's Message to the Legislature, April 5, 1949, pp. 8–11, uncatalogued Fuller Warren Papers, P. K. Yonge Library of Florida History, University of Florida, Gainesville.

35. Jacksonville *Florida Times-Union,* September 30, 1949; "What's Ahead for Florida Forests," *Florida Trend* (August 1973), p. 44.

36. *Tampa Tribune,* April 10, 1955.

37. Ibid., June 30, 1959.

38. *Orlando Sentinel,* March 3, 1961; Tebeau, *A History of Florida,* pp. 444, 445; *Tampa Tribune,* April 9, 1963.

39. *Tampa Tribune,* May 14, 27, November 3, 1965.

40. Ibid., January 17, 1967.

41. *Florida Statistical Abstract, 1972,* pp. 22, 154; *Tampa Tribune,* January 6, April 7, 1971.

42. *Tampa Tribune,* September 9, 1971.

43. Arch Fredric Blakey, *The Florida Phosphate Industry: A History of the Development and Use of a Vital Mineral* (Cambridge: Harvard University Press, 1973), pp. 127–28; *Tampa Tribune,* October 1, 1971.

44. *An Introduction to Florida Corporate Income Taxation* (Tallahassee: College of Law, Florida State University, 1972), p. 2. Clement H. Donovan, "Proposed Corporate Income Tax Amendment to the Constitution, 1971," University of Florida, Public Administration Clearing Service, 1971, Civic Information Series, No. 51, p. 8; *Miami Herald,* November 3, 1971.

45. *Report of the Comptroller for Fiscal Year Ending June 30, 1973,* pp. 8, 89.

46. *Gainesville Sun,* April 2, 1974.

47. *Tampa Tribune,* May 6, 1939.

48. Ibid., May 4, 1946.

49. Wayne Flynt, "Pensacola Labor Problems and Political Radicalism, 1908," *Florida Historical Quarterly* 42, no. 4 (April 1965): 326, 327.

50. *Tampa Morning Tribune,* December 1, 5, 1910; *El Internacional,* December 16, 1910.

51. General Materials, Gi–I, Box no. 185, File Frank Holland, Holland Papers, 1941, Gainesville.

52. George R. LaNoue and Marvin R. Pilo, "Teacher Unions and Educational Accountability," in *Unionization of Municipal Employees, Proceedings of the Academy of Political Science* (1970), 30: 146–58.

53. *Tampa Tribune,* February 8, March 2, April 28, May 24, 25, 1967; *St. Petersburg Times,* April 5, 1967; *Florida Times-Union,* April 15, June 4, 1967; *Miami Herald,* April 27, 1967; *Gainesville Sun,* April 30, May 13, 1967; *New York Times,* June 4, 7, 1967.

54. *New York Times,* September 6, 1967.

55. Ibid., February 19, 20, 21, 22, March 9, 1968.

56. Flynt, *Cracker Messiah,* pp. 221–22.

57. Ibid., p. 223.

58. Ibid., pp. 223–26.

59. Ibid., p. 226.

60. David R. Colburn and Richard K. Scher, "Florida Gubernatorial Politics: The Fuller Warren Years," *Florida Historical Quarterly* 53, no. 4 (April 1975): 403, 404; *Tampa Tribune,* June 2, 1974.

61. Allen Morris, *Florida Handbook, 1971–72* (Tallahassee: Peninsular Publishing Co., 1972), p. 420.

Year	Tourists	Expenditures ($)
1929	1,925,000	215,000,000
1939	2,600,000	291,000,000
1949	4,700,000	825,000,000
1959	11,300,000	1,767,562,843
1969	21,965,910	5,242,164,000
1975	27,260,000	8,843,714,000

62. Albert Waller Gilchrist Papers, 145c, microfilm P. K. Yonge Library of Florida History, University of Florida, Gainesville; *Gainesville Sun,* April 7, 1913.

63. *Florida Times-Union,* January 9, 1929

64. *Tampa Tribune,* June 30, 1926; August 17, 1934; general materials, P–Z, Box 166-45 Ro, Spessard Holland Papers, 1941, P. K. Yonge Library of Florida History, University of Florida, Gainesville.

65. Transcript of radio speech by Fuller Warren, April 25, 1950, in Fuller Warren, "Speeches, prepared for delivery over a statewide radio hook-up, December 26, 1949–February 26, 1952," p. 6, copy in P. K. Yonge Library of Florida History, University of Florida, Gainesville.

66. *Tampa Tribune,* May 11, 1935.

67. "Disney Impact Greater than Expected," *Florida Trend,* November 1972, pp. 45, 47.

68. Baynard Kendrick, *Florida Trails to Turnpikes, 1914–1964* (Gainesville: University of Florida Press, 1964), pp. 8–9; *Tampa Tribune,* May 18, 1923.

69. Jacksonville *Florida Times-Union,* July 18, 1925.

70. Kendrick, *Florida Trails to Turnpikes,* p. 187.

71. *Tampa Tribune,* May 5, 6, 21, 1965.

72. Ibid., May 2, June 2, 1965.

73. Ibid., September 5, 1965.

74. *Miami Herald,* November 3, 1965.

75. *Gainesville Sun,* April 6, 1976.

76. Samuel Proctor, *Napoleon Bonaparte Broward: Florida's Fighting Democrat* (Gainesville: University of Florida Press, 1950), p. 216.

77. Junius Elmore Dovell, "A History of the Everglades of Florida" (Ph.D. dissertation, University of North Carolina, 1947), pp. 100, 123, 124.

78. Proctor, *Broward,* p. 218.

79. *Message of William Sherman Jennings, Governor of Florida to the Legislature, Regular Session of 1903 with Accompanying Documents* (Tallahassee: I. B. Wilson State Printer, 1904), pp. 64–78.

80. Dovell, "Everglades," pp. 203–4.

81. *Message of Napoleon B. Broward, Governor of Florida to the Legislature, Regular Session, May 3, 1905* (Tallahassee: Capitol Publishing Company, 1905), p. 34; Proctor, *Broward,* pp. 222–23.

82. Proctor, *Broward,* pp. 245–46.

83. Ibid., p. 250.

84. Ibid., pp. 256–57.

85. Box no. 6, January, 1908, Napoleon B. Broward Papers, P. K. Yonge Library of Florida History, University of Florida, Gainesville.

86. *Tampa Tribune,* January 6, 1909.

87. *Jacksonville Evening Metropolis,* April 22, 1912.

88. Dovell, "Everglades," pp. 233, 234, 274, 379–80.

89. Ibid., pp. 485, 486.

90. Ibid., pp. 518–21.

91. In 1909 Governor Gilchrist urged the construction of such a canal (*Tampa Tribune,* May 9, 1909); Tebeau, *A History of Florida,* p. 405.

92. Box no. 422, Democratic Party, 1963, Farris Bryant Papers, Florida State Archives, Tallahassee.

93. *New York Times,* June 9, 1970.

94. "What's Ahead For Florida Forests," *Florida Trend,* August 1973, p. 44.

95. *St. Petersburg Times,* April 5, 1967; *New York Times,* November 26, 1967.

96. Robert B. Rackleff, *Close to Crisis: Florida's Environmental Problems* (Tallahassee: New Issues Press, 1972), p. 122.

97. *Tampa Tribune,* February 2, 1972; Interview with Reubin O'D. Askew, January 10, 1975, Tallahassee; Reubin Askew, "Five Bills Important to Florida's Future," *Florida Conservation News,* April 1972, pp. 2, 3.

98. *New York Times,* November 19, October 12, 1973; January 13, 1974. Askew unsuccessfully opposed Amoco's oil drilling in the Ocala National Forest.

99. Cambridge Survey Research, *Environment and Florida Voters: Their Concerns on Growth; Energy; Pollution; Land Use Control; Immigration Taxes; Politics and The Future of the State* (Cambridge, Mass.: Urban and Regional Development Center, 1974), p. iv.

CHAPTER 8

1. Charlton W. Tebeau, *A History of Florida* (Coral Gables, Florida: University of Miami Press, 1971) pp. 289–90.

2. Box no. 10, William Jennings Papers, P. K. Yonge Library of Florida History, University of Florida, Gainesville. "Race Problem," February 8, 1907, in Box no. 5, February, 1907, Napoleon B. Broward Papers, P. K. Yonge Library of Florida History, University of Florida, Gainesville. Also see Samuel Proctor, *Napoleon Bonaparte Broward: Florida's Fighting Democrat* (Gainesville: University of Florida Press, 1950), p. 252; Jerrell Shofner, "Custom, Law, and History: The Enduring Influence of Florida's 'Black Code,'" *Florida Historical Quarterly* 55, no. 3 (January 1977): 287–89.

3. *Tampa Morning Tribune,* April 20, May 23, 1905; Donald H. Bragan, "Status of Negroes in a Southern Port City in the Progressive Era: Pensacola, 1896–1920," *Florida Historical Quarterly* 51, no. 3 (January 1973): 299.

4. *Tampa Morning Tribune,* April 17, May 9, 1907; May 1, 1909.

5. Albert Waller Gilchrist Papers, 145c, microfilm, P. K. Yonge Library of Florida History, University of Florida, Gainesville; *Tampa Morning Tribune,* January 6, May 4, April 2, 1909.

6. *Tampa Morning Tribune,* July 25, 1913; January 13, 1914; January 29, 1916.

7. Ibid., May 2, 1917; *Tallahassee Democrat,* September 20, 1964.

8. Jerrell H. Shofner, "Florida and Black Migration," *The Florida Historical Quarterly* 57, no. 3 (January 1979): 267, 272–73, 280–81.

9. Doyle Carlton to Robert W. Bentley, chairman, Road Department, October 9, 1929, in Box no. 10, Road Department Chairman, Doyle Carlton Papers, Florida State Archives, Tallahassee.

10. *Tampa Morning Tribune,* October 8, 28, 1934; Box no. 100, Fred P. Cone Papers, Florida State Archives, Tallahassee.

11. *Tampa Morning Tribune,* May 17, 1923; June 18, 1929.

12. *The Tampa Lynching,* April 13, 1911, National Archives, Washington, State Decennial File, 1910–29, Box no. 3671; ibid., Albert W. Gilchrist to Secretary of State P. C. Knox, March 4, 1911, p. 2.

13. "Japanese in Florida," *The Florida Grower* 9, no. 3 (October 18, 1913): 14; Box no. 38, Doyle Carlton Papers, 1932, Florida State Archives, Tallahassee.

14. *The Congressional Quarterly,* May 21, 1954, p. 637; *Tampa Tribune,* May 19, 1954.

15. Florida's southern neighbors had a much larger black population in 1954. For instance, blacks made up 32 percent of the population in Alabama, 39 percent in South Carolina, 46 percent in Mississippi, and 31 percent in Georgia: *Census of Population: 1950. Characteristics*

of the Population (Washington, 1952), vol. 2, pt. 2, Alabama, p. 27; pt. 10, Florida, p. 27; pt. 11, Georgia, p. 35; pt. 24, Mississippi, p. 19; pt. 40, South Carolina, p. 23. See also V. O. Key, Jr., *Southern Politics in State and Nation* (New York: A. A. Knopf, 1949), p. 9.

16. Helen L. Jacobstein, *The Segregation Factor in the Florida Democratic Primary of 1956,* University of Florida Social Sciences Monograph Series, no. 47 (Gainesville: University of Florida Press, 1972), p. 8.

17. Inaugural Address, 1957, 10, 12, in Box no. 1 (Speeches, January 8–April 2, 1957), LeRoy Collins Papers, 1955 61, Florida Collection, Main Library, University of South Florida, Tampa, hereafter cited as LCP:USF.

18. Transcript of News Conference, May 20, 1960, in Box no. 4 (Speeches, April 20–June 20, 1960), LCP:USF.

19. Statement of LeRoy Collins to Conference on Segregation, March 21, 1956, in Box (8d)3, LCP:USF; *Tampa Tribune,* July 17, 1956.

20. Interview with LeRoy Collins, Tallahassee, February 11, 1975.

21. Message to the Legislature, January 8, 1957, 14, in Box no. 1 (Speeches, January 8–April 2, 1957), LCP:USF.

22. Typescript of Governor LeRoy Collins Statement, Accession 68–02, pt. 9, Box 336, Florida State Archives, Tallahassee; *Tampa Tribune,* April 19, June 4, 7, October 13, 1957.

23. *Tampa Tribune,* June 6, 1957.

24. Interview with LeRoy Collins, Tallahassee, February 11, 1975; *Tampa Tribune,* December 17, 19, 1958; February 19, 1959.

25. Statement of LeRoy Collins to Conference on Segregation, March 21, 1956, in Box (8d)3, LCP:USF; *Tampa Tribune,* March 13, 21, 1956, January 30, 31, 1959. Harrell R. Rodgers, Jr., in "The Supreme Court and School Desegregation: Twenty Years Later," *Political Science Quarterly* 89, no. 4 (Winter 1974–75): 751–76, points out that the federal government was not pressuring Florida to desegregate its schools during the Collins years. Collins' efforts were made strictly on his own initiative.

26. *Miami Herald, Tampa Tribune,* February 28, 1961.

27. Race Relations, 1962, in Box no. 412, Farris Bryant Papers, Florida State Archives, Tallahassee.

28. When Bryant became governor in January, 1961, only Dade County had integrated its schools. By the fall of 1964, Volusia, Broward, Palm Beach, Hillsborough, Monroe, Sarasota, Pinellas, Orange, Escambia, Charlotte, Duval, Leon, Okaloosa, St. Johns, Santa Rosa, Alachua, Bay, Brevard, Marion, and Lee counties had integrated their schools. At that time 6,652 black students were attending biracial classes in 170 schools (*Southern School News,* May, September, 1964); *Tampa Tribune,* April 7, 1965.

29. *Tampa Tribune,* July 18, 1967.

30. Ibid., January 6, 1971.

31. Jacksonville *Florida Times-Union,* September 5, 1971.

32. *St. Petersburg Times,* August 29, 1971.

33. *Gainesville Sun,* February 21, 1972.

34. Speech presented by Governor Reubin Askew at the Governor's Luncheon, Central Florida Fair, Orlando, Florida, February 21, 1972, Reubin O'D. Askew Papers, Office of the Governor, Capitol Building, Tallahassee. See also *Miami Herald,* February 22, 1972.

35. *Tampa Tribune,* March 15, 1972. Some scholars argue that the antibusing sentiment is not based solely on racial motivations. For instance, Jonathan Kelley declares that the public is much more concerned with the distance their children travel to school and the condition of the school they will be bused to than they are with the integration of the classrooms ("The Politics of School Busing," *Public Opinion Quarterly* 38 [Spring 1974]: 23–39).

36. Interview with Governor Reubin O'D. Askew, Tallahassee, January 10, 1975; memorandum, "Equality of Opportunity: Askew Administration in Motion," Reubin O'D. Askew Papers, Office of the Governor, Capitol Building, Tallahassee; "White Voices of the South," *Ebony,* August 1971, p. 164.

37. The 1975 black demonstrations in Pensacola against the shooting of a black youth by a deputy sheriff have been the notable exception; "White Voices of the South," p. 164.

38. *Tallahassee Democrat,* July 3, 1956; January 2, 1957.

39. *Tampa Tribune,* March 4, 18, 1960.

40. Jacksonville *Florida Times-Union,* April 29, 1958.

41. Transcript of statewide television-radio talk to the people of Florida on race relations, March 20, 1960, 5, in Box no. 4 (Speeches, March 17–April 13, 1960), LCP:USF.

42. *Tampa Tribune,* September 2, 1960.

43. Florida Legislature, Investigating Committee, *Racial Civil Disorders in St. Augustine, Report of the Legislative Investigative Committee* (Tallahassee, 1965), p. 33. Also see Robert Wayne Hartley, "A Long, Hot Summer: The St. Augustine Racial Disorders of 1964" (Master's thesis, Stetson University, 1972).

44. "Farris Bryant Scores with TV Speech," p. 1, in *Around the Clock with Bryant,* April 4, 1960, found in Bryant's "Platform and Campaign Literature," P. K. Yonge Library of Florida History, University of Florida, Gainesville; "Remarks of the Honorable Farris Bryant, Governor of Florida, before the Senate Commerce Committee, July 29, 1963," copy in the P. K. Yonge Collection.

45. *Miami Herald,* June 11, 1964.

46. David M. Chalmers, *Hooded Americanism: The First Century of the Ku Klux Klan, 1865–1965* (New York: Doubleday, 1965), pp. 377–79; *Tampa Tribune,* June 14, 27, 1964.

47. *Racial and Civil Disorders in St. Augustine,* p. 22.

48. *Tampa Tribune,* July 11, 1964.

49. *Racial and Civil Disorders in St. Augustine,* p. 23.

50. *Miami Herald,* July 12, 1964.

51. U.S. Riot Commission, *Report of the National Advisory Commission on Civil Disorders* (New York: Bantam Books, 1968), p. 158.

52. *Tampa Tribune,* June 14, 1967.

53. *New York Times,* July 27, 1967. See also Neal R. Peirce, *The Deep South States of America: People, Politics, and Power in the Seven Deep South States* (New York: W. W. Norton, 1974), p. 449.

54. *New York Times, Tampa Tribune,* April 6–13, 1970.

Chapter 9

1. *Florida Times-Union,* January 9, 1929; *Tampa Tribune,* April 3, 1907; remarks of Governor Reubin O'D. Askew to the Florida Education Association Convention, Jacksonville, Florida, March 29, 1973, Box 160, Item 4, p. 5, P. K. Yonge Library of Florida History, University of Florida, Gainesville.

2. Bureau of the Census, *Statistical Abstract of the United States, 1975* (Washington: Government Printing Office, 1975), p. 75; *Digest of Educational Statistics, 1974* (Washington: National Center of Educational Statistics, 1974), p. 116; *Chronicle of Higher Education,* October 25, 1977.

3. This chapter deals with only two areas of educational policymaking: finance and higher education. Other areas are important but will be left for more specialized studies. Race relations and education are treated in chap. 8.

4. See, for example, Frank DePalma, "The Governance of Education in Florida," mimeographed paper prepared for the Educational Governance Project (Columbus: Ohio State University, 1974).

5. See chaps. 4 and 5 for a detailed analysis of the structure and politics of the cabinet system.

6. The commissioners, and the year in which each assumed office, are: William M. Holloway, 1893; William N. Sheats, 1913; W. S. Cawthon, 1922; Colin English, 1937; Thomas D. Bailey, 1949; Floyd T. Christian, 1965; Ralph D. Turlington, 1974.

7. See Ronald F. Campbell, Luvern L. Cunningham, and Roderick F. McPhee, *The Organization and Control of American Schools* (Columbus, Ohio: Charles E. Merrill Books, 1965), pp. 47–79; Allen Morris, *The Florida Handbook 1975–1976* (Tallahassee: Peninsular Publishing Co., 1975), p. 306.

8. *Gainesville Sun,* June 16, 1972.

9. One of the best discussions of this issue can be found in Laurence Iannaccone, *Politics in Education* (New York: The Center for Applied Research in Education, 1967). See also Frederick M. Wirt and Michael W. Kirst, *The Political Web of American Schools* (Boston: Little, Brown and Company, 1972), p. 5.

10. Campbell, Cunningham, and McPhee, *The Organization and Control of American Schools,* pp. 47–79.

11. This percentage has remained relatively constant during the course of the twentieth century — see Morris, *The Florida Handbook, 1975–1976,* p. 307. Localism in Florida politics is admirably explained in V. O. Key, Jr., *Southern Politics in State and Nation* (New York: Vintage Books, 1949), pp. 82–105.

12. *Florida Times Union and Citizen,* January 9, April 3, 1901, April 8, 1903.

13. *Tampa Tribune,* March 10, 1915. Moreover, Florida's whole system of public finance has been weak throughout the century. For other instances of this, see Charlton W. Tebeau, *A History of Florida* (Coral Gables: University of Miami Press, 1971), pp. 413–14.

14. See, for example, Thomas R. Dye, *Politics, Economics and the Public: Policy Outcomes in American States* (Chicago: Rand McNally, 1966); Richard E. Dawson and James R. Robinson, "Interparty Competition, Economic Variables, and Welfare Policies in American States," *Journal of Politics* 25 (May 1963): 265–89; and Ira Sharkansky and Richard Hofferbert, "Dimensions of State Politics, Economics, and Public Policy," *American Political Science Review* 63 (February 1971): 112–32.

15. Tebeau, *A History of Florida,* pp. 382–83.

16. Ibid., pp. 393–94.

17. Ibid., pp. 395–98.

18. Ibid., pp. 398–99.

19. *Tampa Tribune,* April 12, May 5, 12, 20, 1933.

20. Ibid., May 30, 31, June 2, 1933.

21. Ibid., October 22, November 1, 2, 5, 15, 1933; speech by Governor David Sholtz, St. Petersburg, Florida, November 14, 1933, P. K. Yonge Library of Florida History, University of Florida, Gainesville; Box 70, 1934, "Florida School Affairs," Papers of Governor David Sholtz, Florida State Archives, Tallahassee; *Tampa Tribune,* May 31, 1935.

22. *Tampa Tribune,* April 3, 24, June 1, 1935, January 4, 1936.

23. Ibid., April 7, June 5, 15, 1937.

24. Ibid., April 2, 5, June 3, 4, 1939, December 31, 1940.

25. Ibid., February 17, 1944.

26. Ibid., February 17, 1944, January 3, 1945.

27. Ibid., February 25, March 15, 1945.

28. Ibid., April 4, 1945.

29. Ibid., April 5, 11, 1945.

30. Ibid., November 8, 13, December 4, 1946. Of all the reports issued by the committee the briefest and most accessible is Florida Citizens' Committee on Education, *Education and Florida's Future* (Tallahassee: Florida Citizens' Committee on Education, January 1947).

31. *Tampa Tribune,* April 17, 1947.

32. Ibid., April 20, 25, 1947.

33. Ibid., August 8, 1971.

34. Morris, *The Florida Handbook, 1975–1976,* pp. 307–10. The FEFP formula is very similar to those which have recently been developed in other states. Florida chose not to move in the direction which some states did following the *Serrano* v. *Priest* decision in California. In that case use of the property tax for raising school funds was held to be a violation of students' rights to equal educational opportunity and equal protection of the laws because it discriminated against poor students. Florida still employs the property tax as an important source of revenue for schools. Nevertheless the FEFP formula is flexible and comprehensive enough so that, given full funding (which so far it has not received, and, based on historical precedent, may never have), it can serve to help overcome some of the economic disparities in the state and to provide educationally disadvantaged students with greater equality of opportunity in education. See William N. Greenbaum, "Serrano v. Priest: Implications for Education Equality," *Harvard*

Educational Review 41 (November 1971): 501–34; DePalma, *The Governance of Education in Florida,* pp. 51–67.

35. *Tampa Tribune,* June 27, 1973.

36. See note 5.

37. See note 6.

38. See, for example, Caldwell's statement before the Senate Judiciary Committee, March 12, 1948, Box 1, "Regional Higher Education," Millard Caldwell Papers, P. K. Yonge Library of Florida History, University of Florida, Gainesville.

39. Ibid.; see especially the Miscellaneous Correspondence, 1948; ibid., telegram from NAACP to Caldwell, February 7, 1948. The text of the telegram reads: "As students of Florida Agricultural and Mechanical College and citizens of the state of Florida, we wish to go on record as being opposed to the establishment of Negro regional universities. We appreciate your sincere interest in Negro education. But we feel that the regional university system is a faulty approach in solving the problem. We feel that the plan will be harmful and injurious to the development and welfare of the Negroes and certainly contradictory to the best interest of education in the state of Florida." See also *New York Times,* June 4, 1950.

40. *Tampa Tribune,* March 13, 1955; December 9, 12, 19, 1956; November 23, 1957.

41. Morris, *Florida Handbook, 1975–1976,* pp. 312–14.

42. *Tampa Tribune,* April 26, 27, 29, 1959.

43. Interviews with LeRoy Collins, February 11, 1975, Tallahassee, and Manning J. Dauer, December 1, 1977, Gainesville.

44. Interviews with Farris Bryant, August 26, 1975, Jacksonville, and Manning J. Dauer, December 1, 1977, Gainesville.

45. *Tampa Tribune,* April 19, 1963; *Report of the Florida Legislative Investigation Committee* (Tallahassee: Florida Senate, February 1965).

46. Interview with Charley E. Johns, Starke, June 10, 1975.

47. *Tampa Tribune,* January 7, 15, February 12, 16, 1965. See also *Tampa Tribune,* June 9, 1954, for a similar episode in the Johns administration.

48. Interview with Haydon Burns, Jacksonville, July 21, 1975.

49. Ibid.

50. Ibid.

51. Interview with Manning J. Dauer, December 1, 1977, Gainesville.

CHAPTER 10

1. N. Gordon Carper, "The Convict Lease System in Florida" (Ph.D. dissertation, Florida State University, 1964), p. 14; Fletcher Green, ed., *Essays in Southern History,* vol. 30 of the James Sprunt Studies in History and Political Science (Chapel Hill: University of North Carolina Press, 1949), p. 115; *Senate Journal, 1899: Committee Report,* pp. 786–95.

2. Carper, "Convict Lease System," p. 186.

3. Kathleen Falconer Pratt, "The Development of the Florida Prison System" (Master's thesis, Florida State University, 1949), p. 67; *Report of the Commissioner of Agriculture of the State of Florida to the Governor,* 1903–4, pp. 303–7; Carper, "Convict Lease System" pp. 233–34.

4. Albert Waller Gilchrist Papers, 145c, microfilm, P. K. Yonge Library of Florida History, Gainesville; Pratt, "The Development of the Florida Prison System," p. 82.

5. D. D. Clark to Governor Albert Gilchrist, January 15, 1909, Official Papers of Albert Waller Gilchrist, Florida State University, Tallahassee; *Report of the Commissioner of Agriculture,* pp. 303–7.

6. *Tampa Morning Tribune,* January 7, 1909.

7. D. D. Clark to Governor Albert Gilchrist, January 15, 1909; Pratt, "The Development of the Florida Prison System," p. 76.

8. Pratt, "The Development of the Florida Prison System," pp. 89–90.

9. D. D. Clark to Governor Albert Gilchrist, January 15, 1909.

10. Pratt, "The Development of the Florida Prison System," pp. 78–81.

11. Ibid., pp. 84, 86; Carper, "Convict Lease System," p. 294.

12. Pratt, "The Development of the Florida Prison System," p. 102; Flynt, *Cracker Messiah*, pp. 137–38.

13. Flynt, *Cracker Messiah*, p. 332; *Tampa Morning Tribune*, April 18, May 9, 25, 1923; Carper, "Convict Lease System," p. 342.

14. Doyle Carlton to Robert W. Bentley, chairman, Road Department, October 9, 1929, Box no. 10, Road Department chairman, Doyle Carlton Papers, Florida State Archives, Tallahassee.

15. *Tampa Morning Tribune*, May 27, 1925.

16. Prison Industries Reorganization Administration, *The Prison Problem in Florida: A Survey*, (n.p., 1939), pp. i, ii, in P. K. Yonge Library of Florida History, Gainesville; Jacksonville *Florida Times-Union*, April 1, 1929; editorials, General Materials, Ed–H, Spessard Holland Papers, 1942, P. K. Yonge Library of Florida History, Gainesville.

17. *Tampa Morning Tribune*, November 26, 1958.

18. *Final Report of the Governor's Adult Corrections Reform Plan* (Tallahassee, March 1973), p. ii; *Journal of the House of Representatives*, April 6, 1971, p. 60.

19. *Journal of the House of Representatives*, April 8, 1975, p. 7.

20. *Tampa Morning Tribune*, April 12, 1909, April 7, 1935.

21. Ibid., September 1, 1963.

22. *Journal of the House of Representatives*, February 1, 1972, p. 9.

23. *New York Times*, December 9, 1972.

24. See chap. 5, this volume for additional information on the relationship between the governor and the attorney general.

25. *Tampa Morning Tribune*, July 25, 1913, January 13, 1914, January 29, 1916, October 8, 28, 1934.

26. Ibid., November 2, 1951; Jacksonville *Florida Times-Union*, May 12, 1951; *Miami Daily News*, April 9, 1951; *Jacksonville Journal*, July 27, 1950; *Tampa Times*, August 5, 1950, Fuller Warren Papers, P. K. Yonge Library of Florida History, Gainesville.

27. *Tampa Morning Tribune, Palm Beach Post*, March 23, 1951.

28. *Tampa Morning Tribune*, November 10, 1966.

29. *New York Times*, January 8, 1967.

30. *St. Petersburg Times*, April 5, 1967.

31. *New York Times*, April 7, 30, May 6, 1967; *Miami Herald*, July 19, 26, 1967.

32. *New York Times*, May 6, July 13, 1967.

CHAPTER 11

1. T. Harry Williams, *Huey Long* (New York: Alfred A. Knopf, 1969), p. 432.

2. *Southern Politics in State and Nation* (New York: A. A. Knopf, 1949), pp. 159–61.

3. William C. Havard and Loren P. Beth, *The Politics of Mis-Representation: Rural-Urban Conflict in the Florida Legislature* (Baton Rouge: Louisiana State University Press, 1962), p. 28.

4. David R. Colburn and Richard K. Scher, "Florida Gubernatorial Politics: The Fuller Warren Years," *Florida Historical Quarterly* 53, no. 4 (April 1975): 403, 404. Wayne Flynt, *Cracker Messiah: Governor Sidney J. Catts of Florida* (Baton Rouge: Louisiana State University Press, 1977), pp. 221–25.

5. Speech at Central Florida Fair, Orlando, February 21, 1972, Reubin O'D. Askew Papers, Office of the Governor, Capitol Building, Tallahassee. See also *Miami Herald*, February 22, 1972.

6. Fuller Warren Papers, Florida Collection, Robert Manning Strozier Library, Florida State University, Tallahassee.

7. Charley Johns Papers, Florida State Archives, Box 311, Road Department Miscellaneous, 1954, letter from Cecil Webb, chairman of Road Department, to C. K. Ireland, purchasing agent for Road Department, August 11, 1954. See also chap. 5, this volume, for futher discussion of problems within the Johns administration. For problems in Haydon Burns' administration, see, for example, *Tampa Morning Tribune*, January 10, March 7, 1965, April 1, 1966.

Bibliographic Essay

THIS essay is not an attempt to provide a list of all the sources on Florida gubernatorial politics. Rather it is intended to point out materials of particular significance for this study and, thereby, serve as a guide for scholars and students.

Manuscript Collections

The literature on Florida history and politics in the twentieth century is limited. As we noted in the introduction to this book, more research is necessary if Florida's past is to be understood. Studies of only seven of the twenty governors in this century have been presented in master's theses, dissertations, or scholarly publications. Because of the limited number of secondary works, one is forced to examine the manuscripts as much by necessity as by choice. Even here, however, the record is far from ideal. The governors' public records from William Jennings through Park Trammell are in the Florida State Library, Tallahassee, while the records of Doyle Carlton through Claude Kirk can be found in the Division of Archives, History and Records Management, Tallahassee. Unfortunately, these papers are often nothing more than office memoranda or public correspondence. The nearly 600 boxes of gubernatorial papers in the State Archives, for example, offer only a limited insight into the complexity of the governor's office. Contributions of the newspaper clipping service provided to each administration have been retained in these papers and offer the most informative and accessible source of information.

For a number of years, including the period during which we examined them, the gubernatorial papers in the State Archives were housed in the Leon

County Jail. Their location gives some indication of why Florida's historical record in the twentieth century remains circumscribed.

The private papers of the governors are much more informative. The Fuller Warren Collection in the Robert Manning Strozier Library at Florida State University, Tallahassee, provides a detailed picture of Warren and his administration and offers some interesting insights into the political nature of the governor's office. Less informative but helpful are the LeRoy Collins Papers in the Main Library at the University of South Florida, Tampa, and the Millard Caldwell Papers and the Napoleon Broward Papers in the P. K. Yonge Library of Florida History, University of Florida, Gainesville. The Spessard Holland Papers at the University of Florida appear to be complete for his senatorial career but are very superficial for his gubernatorial years. Other gubernatorial papers which aided our research include the William Jennings Papers, the Park Trammell Papers, and the Fuller Warren Papers at the University of Florida, and the Albert Gilchrist Papers at Florida State University.

The best manuscript collection dealing with Florida political history is in the P. K. Yonge Library of Florida History, University of Florida, Gainesville. The manuscripts in the Robert Manning Strozier Library at Florida State University, Tallahassee, are also worth noting. Both libraries have gubernatorial and legislative papers as well as a number of public and private documents. Of particular help for our study were the papers (all in the P. K. Yonge Library) of James B. Hodges, a prominent Democratic politician, Congressmen Donald Ray "Billy" Mathews, Robert Alexis "Lex" Green, and Claude L'Engle, and Virgil Newton, editor of the *Tampa Tribune*. One should also consult the papers (also in the P. K. Yonge Library) of senators Duncan Fletcher and Charles Andrews, state senators Verle Pope and Ernest Graham, Congressman Joseph Hendricks, Commissioner of Agriculture Nathan Mayo, and J. Broward Culpepper, member of the Board of Regents.

The authors also conducted interviews with former governors and legislators. Interviews with Millard Caldwell, LeRoy Collins, and Reubin Askew were very enlightening. The legislative interviews were very unsatisfactory. Only former legislators Collins, Askew, and Robert Saunders of Gainesville would describe the inner workings of gubernatorial-legislative relations. Former pork-chop legislators were the most reticent of all—when asked about former governors or legislators, they typically replied: "He was a good ole boy." Many of the most helpful insights came from those who have closely observed Florida politics over the years—professors Manning J. Dauer and Clement Donovan of Gainesville and reporters Malcolm Johnson and Allen Morris of Tallahassee.

The Oral History Collection at the University of Florida provided additional insights, particularly the interviews with state senators William A. Shands, congressmen "Lex" Green and "Billy" Mathews, and Commissioner of Agriculture Nathan Mayo.

GOVERNMENT PUBLICATIONS

Certainly one of the most important public documents for our needs was the *Florida Statistical Abstract* published annually by the Bureau of Economic and Business Research at the University of Florida since 1967. Serving as a supplement to the *Census of the United States*, it offers a wealth of information on Florida's socioeconomic and political conditions. While it has been published only since 1967, the information in the early volumes often goes back to 1900. The *Journal of the House of Representatives* and the *Journal of the Senate* from 1900 to the present were also invaluable. The following documents provided essential information as well: *The Report of the Secretary of State* (1901 to the present), *Report of the State Treasurer,* (1904 to the present), *Report of the Superintendent of Public Instruction* (1900–1968), *Report of the Commissioner of Education* (1968 to the present), *Florida School Bulletin* (1941 to the present), *Florida Conservation News* (1965 to the present), *Report of the Comptroller* (1901 to the present), and *Messages and Documents* (1901–7). One should also consult *Mass Transportation in Florida; Problems and Approaches* (Tallahassee, 1969), and *Education and the Future of Florida: A Report of the Comprehensive Study of Education in Florida* (Tallahassee, 1947).

NEWSPAPER FILES AND PERIODICALS

To supplement the primary and secondary sources on Florida gubernatorial politics, we relied heavily on newspaper coverage of state politics. While there is no shortage of Florida newspapers, we found only a few that provided substantial coverage of the governor's office and state politics generally.

Without question, the *Tampa Morning Tribune* consistently provided the most thorough coverage and offered the best behind-the-scenes reporting of gubernatorial politics from 1910 to 1960. From 1900 to 1910 no paper was really adequate, although generally we found the Jacksonville *Florida Times-Union* helpful. From 1960 to the present, several newspapers are quite useful, particularly the *Miami Herald, Tampa Tribune, Florida Times-Union,* and *St. Petersburg Times*.

The conservative, businessmen's point of view was best represented by the *Florida Times-Union*. The liberal position has been most consistently championed by the *Daytona Beach Evening News* and the *St. Petersburg*

Times. Since 1960 both the *Miami Herald* and the *Gainesville Sun* have also been exponents of a liberal political philosophy.

Three able political writers of recent years are Malcolm Johnson of the *Tallahassee Democrat,* Allen Morris who wrote a column "Cracker Politics" for the Associated Press in Florida, and Hank Drane of the *Florida Times-Union*.

There are only four scholarly journals of note which provide more than an occasional article on Florida. The two best are clearly the *Florida Historical Quarterly* and the *Journal of Politics. Tequesta,* a journal primarily concerned with events occurring in South Florida, and *Apalachee* are also worth examining. *Florida Trend,* a business journal, has several short but informative articles on the state government, tourism, and transportation.

SECONDARY SOURCES

A number of excellent studies on southern politics in the twentieth century have been published which will assist the student of Florida politics. Still the most incisive study of southern politics is V. O. Key, Jr., *Southern Politics in State and Nation* (New York, 1949). Key's chapter on "Florida: Every Man for Himself" should be the starting point for any analysis of Florida politics. For a more recent political survey, the reader should consult William C. Havard, editor, *The Changing Politics of the South* (Baton Rouge, 1972) and Manning Dauer's chapter on "Florida: The Different State" which offers a general survey of Florida politics and of the emergence of the black voter and the Republican party. An even newer study similar in scope to Havard's work is Jack Bass and Walter DeVries' *The Transformation of Southern Politics: Social Change and Political Consequence since 1945* (New York, 1976). Two important and informative accounts of southern life in the twentieth century are C. Vann Woodward's *Origins of the New South* (Baton Rouge, 1951) and George E. Tindall's *The Emergence of the New South* (Baton Rouge, 1967). For an introduction to southern political history see Dewey W. Grantham, *The Democratic South* (Athens, 1963). Neal Peirce offers a fairly recent and very informative journalistic study entitled *The Deep South States of America* (New York, 1974), a part of his regional study of American politics.

Two recent and very insightful studies of the South since the *Brown* decision are Numan Bartley and Hugh Davis Graham's *Southern Politics and the Second Reconstruction* (Baltimore, 1975), and Earl Black's *Southern Governors and Civil Rights: Racial Segregation as a Campaign Issue in the Second Reconstruction* (Cambridge, 1976). Both books make frequent reference to Florida's racial politics.

For an overview of the office of governor and gubernatorial politics, Thad Beyle and J. Oliver Williams have edited an excellent study, *The American*

Governor in Behavorial Perspective (New York, 1972). Although it has little to say about the southern governorship, the book offers a number of perceptive comments on the nature of the governor's office. For supplemental reading on the office of governor one should consult Coleman Ransone's *Office of Governor in the South* (University, Alabama, 1951) and *Office of Governor in the United States* (University, Alabama, 1956). Unfortunately, Ransone tends to examine the office often at the expense of the men who have held it. Information concerning the origins and backgrounds of governors is available in Joseph Schlesinger's *How They Became Governor* (East Lansing, Michigan, 1957).

For the state of Florida, the best general work is Charlton Tebeau's *A History of Florida* (Coral Gables, Florida, 1971). Although Tebeau has done considerable research, the book still reflects the absence of good secondary accounts of Florida's past. An older but thorough general history can be found in Kathryn Hanna's *Florida, Land of Change* (Chapel Hill, North Carolina, 1948). An excellent compendium of information on Florida politics and government can be found in Allen Morris' *Florida Handbook,* published annually since 1947.

There are few individual studies of Florida governors in the twentieth century. Napoleon Broward and Sidney Catts are the only two governors who have received book-length examination. Samuel Proctor's biography, *Napoleon Bonaparte Broward: Florida's Fighting Democrat* (Gainesville, 1950), is an informative account of Florida in the late nineteenth and early twentieth century and of the state's ablest governor to that time. Also see Samuel Proctor, "Napoleon B. Broward: The Years to the Governorship," *Florida Historical Quarterly* 26, no. 2 (October 1947): 117–34. Wayne Flynt has published an excellent study of Sidney J. Catts' life, *Cracker Messiah: Governor Sidney J. Catts of Florida* (Baton Rouge: Louisiana State University Press, 1977). He has sketched a part of this controversial governor's life in "Sidney J. Catts: The Road to Power," *Florida Historical Quarterly* 49, no. 12 (October 1970): 107–28. David Sholtz and John Martin have received similar treatment in Merlin Cox's "David Sholtz: New Deal Governor of Florida," *Florida Historical Quarterly* 43, no. 2 (October 1964): 142–52, and Victoria H. McDonnell's "Rise of the 'Businessman's Politician': The 1924 Florida Gubernatorial Race," *Florida Historical Quarterly* 52, no. 1 (July 1973): 39–50. For a critical assessment of Governor Fuller Warren's administration see David R. Colburn and Richard K. Scher, "Florida Gubernatorial Politics: The Fuller Warren Years," *Florida Historical Quarterly* 53, no. 4 (April 1975): 389–408. One should also consult John Richard Deal, "Sidney Johnston Catts, A Stormy Petrel of Florida Politics" (Master's thesis, University of Florida, 1949); Jean Carver Chance, "Sidney J. Catts and the Press: A Study of the Editorial Coverage of the 1916 Governor's Race by Florida's Newspapers" (Master's thesis, University of Florida,

1969); Daisy Parker, "The Inauguration of Albert Waller Gilchrist, Nineteenth Governor of the State of Florida," *Apalachee* 6 (1963–67): 20–32; Sister Mary Evangelista Staid, "Albert Waller Gilchrist, Florida's Middle of the Road Governor" (Master's thesis, University of Florida, 1950); Elvin Vernon Parnell, "Fuller Warren and Florida Politics at Mid-Century" (Master's thesis, University of Miami, 1967); Kathleen Falconer Pratt, "The Development of the Florida Prison System" (Master's thesis, Florida State University, 1949).

A very informative study of the Democratic party in Florida during its early years has been written by William T. Cash, *History of the Democratic Party in Florida* (Tallahassee, 1936). Also see Herbert J. Doherty, "Liberal and Conservative Voting Patterns in Florida," *Journal of Politics* 14 (August 1952): 403–17. Although we occasionally disagree with some of his conclusions, Doherty makes a number of important observations about state Democratic politics. For a description of Florida's two most controversial campaigns see Wayne Flynt's "William V. Knott and the Gubernatorial Campaign of 1916," *Florida Historical Quarterly* 51, no. 4 (April 1973): 423–30, and Terry L. Christie, "The Collins-Johns Election, 1954: A Turning Point," *Apalachee* 6 (1963–67): 5–19. Also see Helen L. Jacobstein, "The Segregation Factor in the Florida Democratic Gubernatorial Primary of 1956" (Master's thesis, University of Miami, 1964; published by the University of Florida Press, 1972). An invaluable resource tool for Florida politics is Annie Mary Hartsfield and Elston E. Roady, *Florida Votes, 1920–1962* (Tallahassee, 1963). Another is Numan V. Bartley and Hugh D. Graham, *Southern Elections: County and Precinct Data, 1950-1972* (Baton Rouge: LSU Press, 1978); unfortunately our manuscript was completed before we could make full use of this book.

Florida's constitutional development has been most successfully discussed by political scientist Manning J. Dauer in a number of monographs, the best of which are (with William Havard) *The Florida Constitution of 1885—A Critique* (Gainesville, 1955) and (with Clement Donovan and Gladys Kammerer) *Should Florida Adopt the Proposed Constitution?* (Gainesville, 1968). Jerrell Shofner in "The Constitution of 1868," *Florida Historical Quarterly* 41, no. 4 (April 1963): 356–74, has written a thoughtful historical assessment of this controversial constitution. Although William Havard and Loren Beth's *The Politics of Mis-Representation* (Baton Rouge, 1962) is chiefly concerned with the reapportionment issue, the authors have a number of interesting things to say about constitutional development in Florida.

Two informative dissertations have been written on the constitutional development of the office of the governor: Daisy Parker, "An Examination of the Florida Executive" (Ph.D. dissertation, University of Virginia, 1959), and Juanita Gibson, "The Office of Governor in Florida" (Ph.D. dissertation, University of Michigan, 1958).

While Florida's pattern of race relations has yet to receive adequate study, there have been a number of excellent examinations of southern race relations which give some indication of Florida's racial condition. The best overview of race relations in the South has been provided by Woodward, *Origins of the New South,* and Tindall, *The Emergence of the New South.* Gunnar Myrdal's *An American Dilemma: The Negro Problem and Modern Democracy,* 2 vols. (New York and London, 1944) still remains unsurpassed as a general statement. C. Vann Woodward outlines the history of segregation in *The Strange Career of Jim Crow* (New York, 1955). The southern response to the *Brown* decision is excellently recounted in Numan Bartley's *The Rise of Massive Resistance* (Baton Rouge, 1970). For an assessment of race relations and the political process, see V. O. Key, Earl Black, Numan Bartley and Hugh Davis Graham, and Donald R. Mathews and James W. Prothro, *Negroes and the New Southern Politics* (New York, 1966).

Certainly the best study of Florida race relations is Hugh D. Price's uncritical *The Negro and Southern Politics: A Chapter of Florida History* (New York, 1957). The impact of the *Brown* decision on Florida politics is discussed by Joseph Tomberlin in "Florida Whites and the *Brown* Decision," *Florida Historical Quarterly* 51, no. 1 (July 1972): 22–36; David R. Colburn and Richard K. Scher, "Race Relations and Florida Gubernatorial Politics," *Florida Historical Quarterly* 53, no. 4 (April 1975): 389–408; and Robert Howard Akerman, "The Triumph of Moderation in Florida Thought and Politics: A Study of the Race Issue From 1954 to 1960" (Ph.D. dissertation, American University, 1967). Also see William G. Carleton, "Negro Politics in Florida: Another Middle Class Revolution," *South Atlantic Quarterly* 57 (Autumn 1958): 419–32, and Jerrell H. Shofner, "Florida and Black Migration," *The Florida Historical Quarterly,* 57, no. 3 (January 1979): 267–88. Bartley and Graham, and Black also have a number of references to racial issues and Florida politics.

The St. Augustine racial disturbances of 1963 and 1964 during which civil rights forces were embattled by Klansmen and rebellious white youths is referred to by David Chalmers in *Hooded Americanism: The History of the Ku Klux Klan* (New York, 1965). A more detailed study is provided in *Racial and Civil Disorders in St. Augustine, Report of the Legislative Investigation Committee* (Tallahassee, 1965). For a broader evaluation of Florida's racial conditions in the early 1960s see the *United States Civil Rights Commission: Florida Advisory Committee Reports.*

Florida's educational development has yet to be fully described although there are a number of very informative doctoral dissertations and masters theses. For a general overview one should consult Arthur D. Pollock, "The

Evolution of the Organizational Structure of Local Public Education in Florida, 1845–1947" (Ph.D. dissertation, Florida State University, 1968), and Donald D. Chipman, "The Development of the Florida State System of Public Education, 1922–1948" (Ph.D. dissertation, Florida State University, 1968). Two studies of public school segregation worth examining are William L. Greer, "The Problem of Segregation in Florida Schools and Society" (Master's thesis, Stetson University, 1955), and Joseph Aaron Tomberlin, "The Negro and Florida's System of Education" (Ph.D. dissertation, Florida State University, 1967).

There are many gaps in literature on Florida politics and the state's environmental condition. The best study of the Everglades drainage program is Junius E. Dovell's "A History of the Everglades of Florida" (Ph.D. dissertation, University of North Carolina, 1947). On Florida's water problems, see Nelson Blake, *Land into Water—Water into Land: A History of Water Management in Florida* (Tallahassee, 1980). For an analysis of Florida's environmental condition since 1960 see Robert B. Rackleff, *Close to Crisis: Florida's Environmental Problems* (Tallahassee, 1972), Florida Defenders of the Environment, *Environmental Impact of the Cross-Florida Barge Canal* (Gainesville, 1970), and *Environment* (a journal published since 1973). For an assessment of the state's transportation program see Baynard Kendrick's *Florida Trails to Turnpikes* (Gainesville, 1964). Kendrick's book tends to be excessive in its praise of the State Road Department. For a more balanced view see Junius E. Dovell, *The State Road Department of Florida* (Gainesville, 1955).

There have been a number of useful studies made of Florida's labor-industrial scene and the political ramifications. Fred Blakey's *The Florida Phosphate Industry: A History of the Development and Use of a Vital Mineral* (Cambridge, 1973) is a very thorough account of that industry and its labor practices. For a useful study of working conditions in the South see F. Ray Marshall, *Labor in the South* (Cambridge, 1967). James Wayne Flynt has written on "Florida Labor and Political 'Radicalism', 1919–1920," *Labor History* 9, no. 1 (Winter 1968): 73–90.

The alliance between Tallahassee and the railroad industry has been explored by Kathryn T. Abbey in "Florida Versus the Principles of Populism, 1896–1911," *Journal of Southern History* 4, no. 4 (November 1938): 462–75, and Edward Akin, "Southern Reflection of the Gilded Age: Henry M. Flagler's System, 1885–1913" (Ph.D. dissertation, University of Florida, 1975). Durwood Long has looked at the state's important cigar industry in "The Open-Closed Shop Battle in Tampa's Cigar Industry, 1919–1921," *Florida Historical Quarterly* 47, no. 2 (October 1968): 101–21. For an assessment of Florida's immigrant labor see George Pozzetta, "Foreigners in Florida: A Study of Immigration Promotion, 1865–1910," *Florida Historical Quarterly* 53, no. 2 (October 1974): 164–80, and "Foreign Colonies in South Florida, 1865–1910," *Tequesta* 34 (December 1974): 45–56.

Historians and political scientists have paid little attention to law enforcement and prison policy in Florida with the exception of N. Gordon Carper's very thorough examination of "The Convict Lease System in Florida 1866–1923" (Ph.D. dissertation, Florida State University, 1964). Also see N. Gordon Carper, "Martin Tabert, Martyr of an Era," *Florida Historical Quarterly* 52, no. 2 (October 1973): 115–31. On the subject of prison reform, one should consult *The Final Report of the Governor's Adult Corrections Reform Plan* (Tallahassee, 1973).

The relationship between Florida's economic condition and its politics has been largely ignored. Clement Donovan, however, has written on state fiscal policy in "Do We Need a Sales Tax In Florida?" *Economic Leaflets,* Bureau of Economic and Business Research, December 1948, "How to Balance Florida's Budget," *Economic Leaflets,* February 1949, and "Sources of Florida Tax Revenues," *Economic Leaflets,* February 1947. One should also consult Junius E. Dovell's *History of Banking in Florida, 1828–1954* (Orlando, 1955). Of additional value is Wallace Nelson's "The Economic Development of Florida, 1890–1930" (Ph.D. dissertation, University of Florida, 1962). As yet, the impact of Florida's economic collapse of the late 1920s and the 1930s has not been studied. In addition, no assessment has been made of the economic boom of the post–World War II period despite the fact that Florida's politicians seem primarily concerned with economic prosperity in the private sector of the economy.

Florida's agricultural history in the twentieth century is largely the story of Commissioner of Agriculture Nathan Mayo who served in this post for thirty-seven years (1923–60). For an evaluation of Mayo's career see Martin M. LaGodna, "The Florida State Department of Agriculture during the Administration of Nathan Mayo" (Ph.D. dissertation, University of Florida, 1970). Also see Martin M. LaGodna, "Greens, Grist, and Guernseys: Development of the Florida State Agricultural Marketing System," *Florida Historical Quarterly* 53, no. 2 (October 1974): 146–63. For a further look at Florida agricultural policy one should also examine the reports of the Florida Citrus Commission (1935 to the present).

Only one other cabinet officer rivaled Mayo's tenure in office and that was Secretary of State R. A. Gray, who served in that office for thirty-two years (1929–61). He has told his story in *The Power and the Glory* (Tallahassee, 1965) and in *My Story: Fifty Years in the Shadow of the Near Great* (Tallahassee, 1958).

Index

Adams, Tom, 86, 87, 255, 269
Administration: and the governors, 103–7, 113–14, 115–54
Administration, Board of, 121
Advertising Commission, 120, 206
Advisory Council on Marine Sciences, 216
Aged, in Florida, 18, 289
Agricultural Marketing Board, 121
Agriculture: commissioner of, 5, 103, 105, 106, 123, 239, 260, 261; Department of, 260; in Florida, 5, 11, 19–20, 34, 69–70, 92
Ailes, Robert, 84
Air and Pollution Control, Department of, 216
Alabama, 12, 34, 75
Alexander, James E., 162, 166
Allen, John, 252
Alligator (University of Florida newspaper), 40
American Federation of Labor, 201
American Federation of Teachers, 201
American Prison Association, 260, 261
Anderson, Dr. Claude, 230
Apalachicola, Florida, 67
Appointments, gubernatorial, 105, 110, 119, 120, 127, 129, 132–47, 153
Arizona, 11, 15, 17
Arkansas, 206
Askew, Reubin O'D., 34; administration of, 117, 143, 154, 281; appeal of, 276; appointments by, 132, 143; Big Cypress Swamp, acquisition of, 163; birthplace of, 38; budget of, 152; and busing, 277, 281, 288; cabinet of, 106–7, 126, 296; cam-
paigns of, 84–87, 92–93; character of, 277; and corporate income tax, 168, 277; and economic reform, 15, 84–87, 196, 199–200, 202, 286; education of, 40–41; and educational issues, 85, 237, 247–48, 256–57, 289; and environment, 85, 216–18, 277; ethics of, 291, 293–95; family background, 36; and Government in Sunshine, 277; and higher education, 241, 256–57; labor policy of, 202, 204; and law enforcement, 85; leadership of, 114, 219, 277, 291; and legislative relations, 160, 162, 167–68, 180, 181, 183, 284, 293, 294; liberalism of, 292–93, 294; and Little Trade Commission Act, 163; military service of, 42–43; and media, 85; national prominence of, 1; neopopulism of, 293; organizational memberships of, 43; political career prior to governorship, 45, 48–49; post-gubernatorial career, 295; and prison reform, 265, 266, 270; progressive leadership of, 114, 292, and race relations, 86, 92, 132, 224, 228–30, 235–36, 288, 289, 293; residence of, 39; senatorial career of, 168; and state election code, 163; and state taxes, 85–86, 168, 286–87; and statewide grand jury, 163; style of, 281; tenure in office, 117–18; and tourism, 205, 219; urban constituency of, 24, 84–87; women's appointments by, 132 (picture, 112)
Attorney general, 103, 105, 124
Auditor, state, 120, 151
Ausley, Charles, 252

331

Bafalis, Skip, 84
Bailey, Thomas, 125
Baillet, William, 189
Baisden, Mrs. Fred, 138
Baker v. *Carr,* 178
Ball, Ed, 72, 131, 196, 198
Ballinger, J. Kenneth, 225
Baptists, 39, 71
Barber, James David, 275, 297n1
Barnett, Ross, 228
Barron, Dempsey, 256
Bartow, Florida, 37
Bay County, Florida, 175
Beall, Philip, 162
Beggs, James D., 62
Belk, William M., 216
Bentley, Robert W., 222
Beverage Commission, 120, 132, 139, 142
Biennial legislative session, 169–71
Big Cypress Swamp, acquisition of, 163, 218
Bilbo, Theodore, 280
Blacks: as voters in FLorida, 28–30, 73, 81, 82, 83, 90, 92; as convicts, 260, 261, 262, 263, 266, 302n54; in Florida politics, 13, 17, 28–30, 59, 64, 73, 76–93, 209; population, 224, 315n17
Blease, Cole, 280
Blitch, J. S., 262–63
Bloxham, William, 210
Bourbon politics, 13, 26, 64, 102, 220
Brackin, Newman, 174
Bradford County, Florida, 36
Brewton, Alabama, 222
Brookings Institution, 195
Broome, James, 210
Broward, Napoleon B.: administration of, 282–83; appeal of, 275, 293; birthplace of, 38; cabinet of, 127; campaign of, 59–60, 63–65; and convict lease system, 260; economics of, 286; education of, 40; and educational issues, 237, 289; and environment, 218; ethics of, 291; and Everglades drainage, 13, 64, 160, 164, 168, 210–15, 281, 284; family background of, 34, 36; and higher education, 248–49; labor policy of, 201; leadership of, 292; and legislative relations, 168, 169, 183, 284; military service of, 43; neopopulism of, 294; occupation, 41–42; political career prior to governorship, 45, 48; post-gubernatorial career, 53, 56, 295; progressive leadership of, 63–64, 277; and race relations, 221, 288; and railroads and

corporations, 63–64; residence of, 38; and state taxes, 188; suspensions by, 145 (picture, 117)
Broward County, Florida, 177, 178
Brown, C. M., 63, 64–65
Brown, Jerry, 1
Brown v. *Board of Education, Topeka, Kansas,* 76, 81, 123, 222, 223, 224, 235, 236, 288, 293
Bryan, William Jennings, 61
Bryant, Farris, 34; administration of, 143, 283; appeal of, 276; appointments by, 143; and big business, 283; birthplace of, 38; cabinet of, 124–25; campaign of, 78–80, 90; character of, 279; and citrus, 253; and contracts, 131; and Cross-Florida Barge Canal, 215; economics of, 90, 197; and educational issues, 79, 247; and higher education, 197, 253, 254, 255; and highways, 78–79, 131; and legislative relations, 164, 165, 182, 285; and media, 79, 165; and merit system, 124–25; military service of, 42; and National Governors' Conference, 60; political career prior to governorship, 45, 48–52; post-gubernatorial career, 53, 55, 56; and prisons, 264, 266, 269; and race relations, 78–80, 226, 227, 228, 232–33, 235, 289, 316n28; and reapportionment, 177–78; style of, 282; and tourism, 79 (picture, 80)
Buckman Act, 248–49
Budget: cabinet's, 150–51; director, 120, 151; executive, 149–52; governors', 104, 113, 119, 149–52; 153; legislature's, 151
Budget Commission (cabinet), 104, 113, 121, 150–51
Burns, Haydon: administration of, 122, 143, 284, 295; appeal of, 276; appointments by, 143; birthplace of, 38; cabinet of, 123; campaign of, 80, 81, 82, 90; character of, 279; economics of, 90; and educational issues, 247; ethics of, 291, 294, 295; and higher education, 254–56; and legislative relations, 161, 164, 182, 183, 285, 295; military service of, 42; National Governors' Conference, 60; and occupation, 41–42; organizational memberships of, 43; political career prior to governorship, 45, 49, 51, 52; and prisons, 264; and race relations, 80, 81–82, 228, 235, 236; and reapportionment, 178; residence of, 39; style of, 282; and tourism, 205 (picture, 179)
Busing. *See* Schools

Cabinet, 2, 26, 50, 112–13, 116, 118, 121, 150–52, 153, 239–40, 246; and relationship to governors, 103–7, 122–27

Caldwell, Millard, 34; administration of, 119, 120–22, 132, 135–36, 139, 143–45, 282; appointments by, 134, 135–36, 139, 143–45, 148; appeal of, 276; birthplace of, 38; budget of, 151; cabinet of, 122–24, 127; campaign of, 60, 73, 242; character of, 276–77; and Citrus Commission, 148; economics of, 195; education of, 40; and educational issues, 60, 244–47, 257 (see also Minimum Foundations Program); ethics of, 291, 294; and executive agencies, 148; and higher education, 55, 249–50; and legislative relations, 160, 162, 169, 183, 284, 294; and merit system, 136; military service of, 42; and patronage, 135–36, 148; political career prior to governorship, 48, 50; post-gubernatorial career, 55–56, 295; psychological fulfillment of, 279; and public school finance, 277; and reapportionment, 167, 170, 172–73, 176, 277; residence of, 39; and reorganization of the executive branch, 121–22, 306n16; style of, 282; suspensions by, 145; view of office, 306n9 (pictures, 217, 251)

California, 11, 15, 251, 285

Cambridge Research Survey, 218

Campaigns, gubernatorial, 3, 59–98 passim; costs of, 60, 75, 87–88

Carlton, Doyle: administration of, 284, 292, 295; appeal of, 276; birthplace of, 38; cabinet of, 107; campaign of, 60, 70, 90; character of, 279; and the Depression, 15, 70, 90, 170, 187, 190–93, 242, 292; education of, 40; and educational issues, 70, 237, 242; and legislative relations, 160–61, 182, 285, 295; occupation of, 42; political career prior to governorship, 48; post-gubernatorial career, 53, 55; and prisons, 263; and race relations, 222; and roads, 70; style of, 282; suspensions by, 144; and tourism, 205

Carlton, Doyle, Jr., 78, 79, 80, 92, 151

Carswell, G. Harrold, 93

Carter, Jerry, 67, 171, 262

Carter, Jimmy, 1, 7, 87, 155

Catholicism, as issue in Florida politics, 14, 66–67, 280

Cattle industry, 19, 73

Catts, Edward Douglas, 137

Catts, Rozier, 137

Catts, Ruth, 137

Catts, Sidney, Jr., 137

Catts, Sidney J.: administration of, 143, 284, 294; age at inauguration, 43; anti-Catholicism of, 66–67; appeal of, 275; appointments by, 136–37, 143, 148; birthplace of, 38; campaign of, 66–69, 70; character of, 277; convict lease system, 262–63; and corporations, 67, 286; as demogogue, 66–67, 280, 294, 295; and dental board, 137; economics of, 67, 189, 286; and educational issues, 67; ethics of, 291, 294, 295; family background of, 34; as ideologue, 26, 66–69; labor policy of, 202, 203, 204; and legislative relations, 161, 162, 166, 168, 169, 182–83, 285, 295; and medical board, 137; occupation of, 42, 66; and patronage, 127, 136–37, 143, 144, 148; political career prior to governorship, 45; post-gubernatorial career, 53; and prisons, 262, 270, 289; and race relations, 67, 222, 236, 288; and State Road Board, 137; and state taxes, 67; style of, 280; suspensions by, 145–46; and the underprivileged, 67 (pictures, 68, 133)

Centralized purchasing, 73, 128, 139

Chamber of Commerce, 205, 286

Chemist, state, 120

Chicago, 17

Chiefland, Florida, 12

Children's Commission of Florida, 138

Chiles, Lawton, 87, 168

Christian, Floyd, 202

Church of Christ, 39

Cigar industry, in Tampa, Florida, 13

Citizens' Constitutional Revision Commission, 32, 111

Citizens' Constitution Committee of Florida, 108

Citrus Commission, 120, 133, 138, 148, 149, 201

Citrus industry in Florida, 19, 34, 36, 73, 148, 149, 190, 253

Civil Rights Act of 1964, 80, 81, 228, 233

Civil Rights Commission, U.S., 228

Civil Service. See Merit system

Civil War, 12, 220, 260

Clara, Florida, 263

Clark, D. D., 261

Clark, Walter, sheriff, 146, 268

Clarke, S. Dilworth, 174, 178

Clearwater, Florida, race riot in, 234

Clendinen, James, 31

Cochran, H. G., 132

Cohen, Paul, 28

Collins, LeRoy, 34; administration of, 142, 143, 144, 154, 282; appeal of, 274–75; 293; appointments by, 132, 139, 142, 143, 144; birthplace of, 38; cabinet of, 107, 109–10, 124, 126, 127, 296; campaigns of, 60, 75–78, 92, 93, 142; and central purchasing, 128; character of, 275, 276; and community colleges, 250–51; Community Relations Service Director, 233; and contracts, 129, 130; and constitutional reform, 109–11, 124, 161; and crime, 268–69; economics of, 77, 197; and educational issues, 77, 246, 257, 289; ethics of, 291; family background of, 36; and higher education, 197, 250–53, 254, 289; and highways, 130–31; and Johns, Charley, relations with, 142–43; and legislative relations, 161, 162, 164, 169, 173–77, 181, 183, 284; leadership of, 292, 293, 295; and media, 77–78, 92, 165; and migrant labor, 290; military service of, 42; political career prior to governorship, 45, 48, 49; post-gubernatorial career, 53, 55, 56, 295; and prisons, 264; and race relations, 76–78, 79, 80–81, 92, 132, 223, 224–27, 230–32, 233, 235, 236, 277, 288; and reapportionment, 77, 132, 161, 167, 173–77, 293; residence of, 39; and school desegregation, 288; suspensions by, 145, 146–47; and urban areas, 24, 77–78
Colorado, 83
Communism, 254, 269
Community College Advisory Board, 250
Community College Council, 250
Community colleges, 250–51
Community Relations Service, 233
Compton, Loyal, 138
Comptroller, 103, 105, 106, 123, 151, 239
Cone, Fred: administration of, 121, 132, 143, 148–49, 283; age at inauguration, 43; appeal of, 276; appointments by, 134, 135, 143, 166; birthplace of, 38; and Budget Commission, 148; cabinet of, 121, 122; campaign of, 71–72; character of, 279; and Citrus Commission, 134, 149; and depression, 292; economics of, 15, 71–72, 194; and educational issues, 243; and gambling, 148–49, 308n87; and item veto, 148, 194; and legislative relations, 164, 181, 285, 295; occupation of, 41, 42; and organized crime, 148–49; political career prior to governorship, 45, 48, 51; post-gubernatorial career, 53; and prisons, 264; and race relations, 222; and Racing Commission, 148–49; style of, 281; sus-

pensions by, 145; vetoes by, 167 (picture, 75)
Cone Brothers Construction Company, 130
Confederacy, 12
Congregationalists, 39
Connally, John, 1
Connor, Doyle, 125 (picture, 112)
Conservation: Board of, 104, 121; Department of, 124
Conservation 70s, 216
Conservatism, 238–39, 285
Constitution: and the governor, 3–4, 31–32, 101–14, 304n1
—of 1885, 102–4, 105, 156, 171, 180, 184, 188, 304n1
—of 1968, 111–14, 151, 180, 184, 188
Constitutional revision, 108–14, 124, 126, 161; Commission, 126
Contracts: and the governor, 119, 127–31, 140, 142, 143, 153
Control, State Board of (later Board of Regents), 120, 132, 147, 240, 248, 249, 252, 254
Convict lease system, 259–63
Coolidge, Calvin, 7
Corporate income tax, 198–200
Council for the Blind, 120
County debt, 190
Cramer, William, 93
Crary, Evans, 173
Crime prevention, 266–70
Criminal justice: and the governors, 259–71
Crippled Children's Commission, 120
Cross, J. Emory, 199
Cross-Florida Barge Canal, 215–16
Cuba, 42, 223
Cubans, in Florida, 17, 298n11
Culpepper, Broward, 256
Culver, Richard, 132

Dade County, Florida, 18, 177, 178, 227; Zoning Board of Adjustment, 138
Dauer, Manning, 17, 105, 171, 297n1
David, Ted, 175
Davidson, Jack L., 234
Davis, L. O., sheriff, 232
Davis, Robert W., 63, 64
Davis, W. Turner, 174, 176
Davis brothers, 199
Daytona Beach, Florida, 12, 18, 71, 231
Death penalty, 263–66
Death row population, 266, 271
Deerfield Beach, Florida, race riot in, 234
DeFuniak Springs, Florida, 262
DeLand, Florida, 72

Democratic convention, state of Florida, 61–62 (picture, 14)
Democratic Executive Committee, 215
Democratic party, 12, 22–27, 28, 29, 59–61, 72, 91–93, 119
Demogoguery, 66–69, 280–81
Demography, 15–19, 30
Depression, 12, 15, 22, 70–72, 90, 242–43, 277, 279, 285
Detroit, race riot in, 234
Development Commission. *See* Advertising Commission
Dickinson, Charles H., 63
Dickinson, Fred, 78 (picture, 112)
Direct primary system, 62–63
Disney World, 206
Disston, Hamilton, 210–11
Dixiecrats, 75
Doherty, Herbert J., 92
Donovan, Clement, 195
Drainage Commissioners, Board of, 121, 211, 213
Drainage tax, 213
Du Pont interests, 72, 196
Du Pont, Mrs. Jessie Ball, 132, 138
Duval County, Florida, 34
Dyson, Clifton, 82, 228

Eckerd, Jack, 84, 87, 88, 90
Economic development, 5, 13–15, 19–22, 187–19
Education: and the governors, 5, 92, 237–58; commissioner of (Superintendent of Public Instruction), 103, 105–6, 125, 239, 244, 257–58; Department of, 239; governing structures of, 239–40, 257–58; public school finance, 238, 240–48, 257–58, 318*n*34; State Board of, 104, 121, 239–40, 246, 249
Edwards, L. K., Jr., 176
Eisenhower, Dwight D., 75, 78, 235
Election results, gubernatorial, 94–98, 303*n*79
Elliott, Charles G., 211
Elliston, Florida, 260
English, Colin, 244
Environment, 15, 210–18. *See also* Conservation
Enzor, H. Isle, sheriff, 146, 268
Episcopalians, 39, 71
Ervin, Richard, 110, 125
Everglades: drainage of, 13–14, 64, 127, 195, 210–15, 294; Drainage District, 214
Executive agencies: and the governors, 147–49

Executive powers of governor. *See* Administration

Fabisinski Committee, 225
Factions in Florida politics, 22–26
Faircloth, Earl, 34, 84, 85, 86
Farm Bureau, 106
Farmer Labor Party in Minnesota, 286
Farris, Ion, 37, 45, 66
Federal Aid Road Act (1916), 206–7
Federal Emergency Relief Administration, 242
Federal aid, to Florida, 21–23, 194
Federal-state highway program, 207
Ferguson, Chester, 256
Filipinos, 223
Flagler County, Florida, 178
Fletcher, Duncan, 214–15
Florida: elderly citizens of, 289; debt in, 189–90, 192–93; employment, 21; fragmented political system in, 102–3, 105–7, 113, 115, 118–27, 135, 152–53, 155, 239–40, 296; frontier characteristics of, 12–13, 187–88, 286; highway program in, 204–10; per capita income in, 19–20, 190; political machines in, 53, 55, 63, 72; politics, twentieth-century characteristics of, 11–15, 22–32; population of, 15–19; prosperity, in the 1920s, 189–90; public welfare in, 288–90; retirees in, 18; socioeconomic setting of, 3, 11–32, 291–96; as a southern state, 11–12; suburban growth in, 18; as a Sunbelt state, 11; urban centers in, 17–18, 24, 77–78, 91
Florida Agricultural and Mechanical College for Negroes (now Florida A&M University), 227, 249, 319*n*39
Florida Bankers Association, 42
Florida Bar Association, 108
Florida Citizens' Committee on Education, 244, 249
Florida Constitutional Advisory Commission, 111
Florida East Coast Railroad, 15, 213
Florida Educational Association, 201, 202
Florida Education Finance Program (FEFP), 244–48, 318*n*34
Florida Pine Company, 261
Florida State University (formerly Florida Female College and Florida State College for Women), 4, 227, 249, 255
Florida Technological University, 256
"Force Bill," 221
Ford, Gerald, 7
Forestry and Parks, Board of, 120

Fort Lauderdale, Florida, 18
Fort Myers, Florida, 18
Fowler, Cody, 227
France, 43
Franklin, Mrs., in Tabert case, 263
Free Speech Movement, 269
Frey, Lou, 87, 88
Fruit fly, 70, 190
Furman v. *Georgia*, 266

Gainesville, Florida, 249, 252
Game and Fresh Water Fish Commission,
    120, 129, 133, 140, 142
Gardener, James, 230
Gasoline tax, 192, 207
Georgia, 13, 75
Ghiotto, Robert, 130
Gibbons, James, Cardinal, 67
Gilchrist, Albert W.: administration of, 122,
    283; appeal of, 276; appointments by,
    134; birthplace of, 38; campaign of, 65,
    66; and capital punishment, 265; charac-
    ter of, 279; convict lease system, 260–61;
    and Everglades Drainage, 214; family
    background of, 34, 37; labor policy of,
    201; and legislative relations, 160, 162,
    181, 183, 284–85; military service of, 43;
    occupation of, 42; political career prior to
    governorship, 45, 48; post-gubernatorial
    career, 56, 295; and primary system,
    302n29; and race relations, 221, 223,
    288; and reapportionment, 172; religion
    of, 39; style of, 282; and tourism, 205
    (picture, 203)
Glisson, Floyd, 84
Gold Coast, 24
Gomez, Arthur, 162, 166
Goodman, C. C., mayor, 201
Goodrich, Warren M., 215
Governor's Citizens' Committee on Educa-
    tion, 247
Governor's Committee on Quality Educa-
    tion, 247
Governor's Conference on Education, 247
Governors: addresses to legislature, 160–61;
    administrations of, 102–7, 115–54 passim;
    ages upon assuming office, 43–45;
    agenda setting by, 1–2, 158–65; appoint-
    ments by, 132–44; background and re-
    cruitment of, 3, 33–52; birthplaces of,
    37–38; budgets of, 149–52; and bureau-
    cracy, 116–17, 153; and business, 41, 90,
    219; campaigns of, 59–98 passim; and
    Chamber of Commerce, 41–42, 90;
    characters of, 7; characteristics of leader-
    ship of, 2–8, 275–96; criteria for ranking
    of, 7–8; and economic conservatism, 219;
    education of, 39–41; and elections,
    94–98, 303n79; ethics of, 8, 283–84,
    294, 295; and executive branch, 119–22;
    family backgrounds of, 34–37; future
    prospects of, 8, 295–96; ideologies of,
    5–7, 25; and intervention into executive
    agencies, 147–49; legislative conferences
    of, 160–61; legislative relations (*see*
    Legislature); liberalism of, 285; lobbying
    of legislature by, 161–66; military service
    of, 42–43; moral leadership of, 8; occu-
    pations of, 41–42; organizational mem-
    berships of, 43; personal characteristics
    of, 6–7, 118; political careers prior to
    governorship, 45–52; policy initiatives
    by, 5; post-gubernatorial careers, 52–56;
    and prisons, 259–71; as problem solvers,
    1–2; psychological satisfaction of, 7; rea-
    sons for running for office, 33–34; reli-
    gions of, 39; residences of, 38–39; and
    school finance, 240–48; and special ses-
    sions of legislature, 166–69; state offices
    as springboard to governorship, 45,
    48–52; styles of (defined and
    categorized), 6–7; suspensions by, 113,
    119, 139–47, 153; vetoes by, 159, 166–69
Graham, Robert: birthplace of, 38; and
    budget aide, 152; campaign of, 87–90;
    and death penalty, 266; economics of,
    187; education of, 41; family background
    of, 36, 37; organizational memberships
    of, 43; political career prior to govern-
    orship, 45, 48, 49; residence of, 39; and
    tax reform, 88; urban constituency of, 24,
    87–88 (picture, 89)
Gray, R. H., 106, 110
Greater Miami Crime Commission, 268
Greek immigrants, 17
Green, Alexis (Lex), 34, 73, 173
Green, Fletcher, 260
Griffin, Ben Hill, 199
Griffin, Charles V., 130, 137
Guardians of Liberty Clubs, 66
Gurney, Edward, 55, 88
Guernsey, S. Kendrick, 244

Hall, Chuck, 84, 85
Hammer, John, 131
Hardee, Cary: administration of, 90, 283,
    292; appeal of, 276; appointments by,
    144; birthplace of, 38; campaign of, 69,
    71, 90; character of, 279; and convict
    lease system, 263; economics of, 90, 189,

190, 292; education of, 40; family background of, 36; and legislative relations, 161, 181, 285; occupation of, 41, 42; political career prior to governorship, 45, 48; post-gubernatorial career, 53; style of, 282; and Tabert case, 263 (picture, 120)
Harding, Warren, 7
Hatchett, Joseph, 132, 230
Hawkins, Virgil, 227
Hayling, Robert, Dr., 232
Health, State Board of, 120, 136
Heflin, Tom, 280
Hendrix, Bill, 81
Hickel, Walter J., 216
High, Robert King, 80, 81, 83, 92, 269
Higher education, 78, 248–58
Hillsborough County, Florida, 18, 145, 177
Hodges, James B., 68
Hodges, W. Randolph, 125, 174
Hodges, William C., 71
Holden, Harry, 129
Holland, Spessard: administration of, 143, 282; appeal of, 276; appointments by, 134, 135, 143; birthplace of, 38; cabinet of, 124, 125; campaign of, 59, 72–73, 90; character of, 279; and contracts, 129; economics of, 15, 90; education of, 40; and educational issues, 244; ethics of, 291; and Everglades drainage, 215; family background of, 36, 37; and legislative relations, 160, 162, 166, 183, 284; labor policy of, 201; military service of, 43; organizational memberships of, 43; and Pardon Board, 264; and Parole and Probation Board system, 264; political career prior to governorship, 45, 48, 49; post-gubernatorial career, 53, 55, 295; psychological fulfillment of, 279; and race relations, 223; and road debts, 195; style of, 282; suspensions by, 144 (pictures, 75, 217)
Holland, Mrs. Spessard, 205 (picture, 75)
Holley, Charles, 83
Homestead exemption, 195, 289
Hoover, Herbert, 7
Hoover, Mrs. Herbert, 223
Hotels and motels, in Florida, 20
Hotel and Restaurant Commission, 120, 133, 137, 140, 254–56
House of Representatives, Florida, reapportionment of, 171–79
Hudson, F. M., 162
Humphrey, Jack, 142
Humphries, Joseph, 162
Hurricanes, of 1926 and 1928, 72, 190, 214

Ideology, in Florida politics, 5–7, 25
Immigration, into Florida, 17–18, 23, 189
Improvements Commission, 120
Income, per capita, in Florida, 19–20, 190
Industrial Commission, 120, 136, 139
Industrial development, 71
Ingraham, J. E., 213
Internal Improvement Fund, Trustees of, 120, 125, 218
Interposition resolution, 78, 226, 303n63. See also Schools
Irvin, Walter Lee, 123
Italian immigrants, 17
Item veto, 151

Jackson, Robert, sheriff, 145
Jacksonville, Florida, 38–39, 42, 45, 49, 52, 55, 57, 63, 66, 67, 71, 74, 81–83, 85, 88, 137, 202, 244; firemen's strike in, 286; racial troubles in, 231
Japanese, 223
Jefferson County, Florida, 175
Jennings, Frank E., 71
Jennings, William Sherman: administration of, 282; appeal of, 276; appointments by, 134; birthplace of, 38; cabinet of, 127; campaign of, 61–64; character of, 276; and control of railroads and corporations, 65; and convict lease sytem, 61, 290; economics of, 286, 292; education of, 40; and educational issues, 241; and environment, 218; ethics of, 294–95; and Everglades drainage, 14, 211, 213, 284, 286; family background of, 35–36; and legislative relations, 183, 284, 294; political career prior to governorship, 45–46, 49; post-gubernatorial career, 55, 295; progressivism of, 61, 65, 284; and race relations, 220; and State Railroad Regulatory Commission, 286 (pictures, 117, 212)
Jessup, Thomas S., 210
Jews, in Florida, 17, 72
Jim Crow, 220–22
Johns, Charley, 34; as acting governor, 76–77, 108, 140–43; administration of, 76–77, 122, 132, 139–43, 284, 294; appeal of, 276; birthplace of, 38; campaign of, 77–78, 109, 142; character of, 277, 279; and conflict with LeRoy Collins, 142–43; and contracts, 129–31, 135, 142, 147–48; ethics of, 291, 294; and executive agencies, 147–48; family background of, 36; and Game and Fresh Water Fish

Commission, 140, 142; and higher education, 254; and Hotel Commission, 141; and Industrial Commission, 140; and Johns Committee, 253–55; and limousine, 142; occupation of, 41–42; and patronage, 136, 139–43, 147–48; political career prior to governorship, 45–49; post-gubernatorial political career, 295; and prison camps, 142–43; and race relations, 223; and Racing Commission, 140; and reapportionment, 177; removal of McCarty appointees from office by, 76–77, 140–43; and roads, 130, 140–43; as senator, 132, 151; spoils system politics, 277, 279; style of, 281; suspensions by, 140–43; and Tag Department, 142; and Turnpike Commission, 140 (picture, 141)
Johns, Mackley, 36
Johnson, Lyndon B., 7, 55, 83, 215, 233
Johnson, Malcolm, 124
Johnston, William, 37

Kefauver, Estes, Senator, 268, 269, 285
Kefauver Crime Commission, 146
Kelly, Scott, 83
Kennedy, John, 6, 215
Kennedy family, 84
Key, V. O., Jr., 11, 224, 281
Key West, Florida, 17
King, Martin Luther, Jr., 232, 233
Kirk, Claude: administration of, 122, 131, 143–44, 284; appeal of, 275–76; appointments by, 143; birthplace of, 38; cabinet of, 107, 125–26; campaign of, 84–85, 87, 97; character of, 277; and constitutional reform, 111, 284; and contracts, 131; and crime, 269–70; Cross-Florida Barge Canal, 216; and demogoguery, 294; economics of, 187, 197–98; education of, 84, 247, 256, 289; and environment, 84, 216, 217, 280, 284; ethics of, 291, 294; family background of, 37; and Florida Highway Patrol, 216; and Governor's Club, 131; and higher education, 253, 256; and legislative relations, 163–64, 167, 182, 183, 284, 295; military service of, 42, 45; occupation of, 41–42; political career prior to governorship, 45; post-gubernatorial career, 53; and prisons, 264–65; and race relations, 84, 228–29, 234; and reapportionment, 284; and reorganization, 122; residence of, 39; and roads, 84, 131; style of, 280; and teacher strike, 201–2; and tenure, 117; and tourism, 205 (picture, 267)

Kiwanis, 286
Knabb, Ida M., 138
Knobb, T. J., senator, 263
Knott, William V., 67–70 (picture, 104)
Korean War, 43, 44
Krentzman, Ben, Judge, 234–35
Ku Klux Klan, 77, 82, 170, 223, 254, 288

Labor: Florida Department of, 200; in Florida, 259–60; strikes, 201–4; unions, 200–204
Labor Business Agents Licensing Board, 120
La Follette, Robert, 286
Lake City, Florida, 262
Lakeland, Florida, 36, 45; race riot in, 234
Lake Okeechobee, 210–11
Lamb Chop Gang, 176
Land boom, of 1920s, 15, 71, 241
Landon, Alf, 155
Langford, J. M., 203
League of Women Voters, 108
Lee, Robert Erwin, 84
Legislative committees, functioning of, 157
Legislative Reorganization Act of 1969, 32
Legislature: ad hoc factions in, 157–58; biennial sessions of, 122, 159; and conflict between personality groups and governors, 157–58; and differing perspectives from governor, 156–57; policy development of (with governor), 156–59; and prelegislative conference with governor, 160–61; and relations with governor (general), 2, 122, 181–82; representativeness of, 159; sessions of, 156; and sharing of power with governor, 156; strengthening of, 180–82
Liberal politics, in Florida, 74, 76–98
Liberty County, Florida, 175
Library Board, State, 120
Lieutenant governor, 50, 102, 110, 113, 152
Limerock. See Mining
Little Cabinet, 119, 120, 132–49 passim
Littlefield, Alex, sheriff, 146, 268
Little Rock, Arkansas, 235
Live Oak, Florida, 42
Livestock Sanitary Board, 120
Localism, in Florida politics, 22–26, 144–47
Logan, Sheriff, 203–4
Long, Huey, 155, 179
Lowry, Sumter, 26, 78, 82
Lumber industry, 13, 259, 261, 263
Lynchings, in Florida, 13, 221–23, 267

McArthur, James A., 268
McCall, Wayne, 256
McCarty, Dan: administration of, 139, 143–44, 282; appeal of, 276; appointments by, 135, 139–44; birthplace of, 38; campaign of, 60, 75–76, 95; and budget, 151; and central purchasing, 307n34; character of, 277; and contracts, 129, 139; and constitutional crisis, 108; death in office of, 56, 76, 78, 108, 139; education of, 40; ethics of, 291; and executive agencies, 148; and highways, 139; family background of, 34, 36; and legislative relations, 183, 284; military service of, 43, 45; occupation of, 42; organizational memberships of, 43; and patronage, 135, 148; political career prior to governorship, 45, 48, 49; post-gubernatorial career, 295; predecessor of Collins, 34; psychological fulfillment of, 279; and reorganization, 139; style of, 282 (picture, 109)
McCarty, John, 142 (picture, 109)
MacClenny Camp, 263
Mack, Connie, 40
McKenney, Everette, 142
McKethan, Alfred, 137
Manatee County, Florida, 175; school crisis in, 234–35, 280
Manucy, Halstead R. ("Hoss"), 232
Manufacturing, in Florida, 13, 20, 286
Map, Calvin, 230
Marchant, Jephtha, 162
Marianna, Florida, 90, 142, 222
Marketing Bureau, State, 120
Martin, John W.: administration of, 283; appeal of, 276; appointments by, 144; birthplace of, 38; campaign of, 71, 72, 91; character of, 277; and depression, 292; education of, 40; and educational issues, 241–42; family background of, 36, 37; and highways, 161, 205; and legislative relations, 284, 295; occupation of, 41–42; organizational memberships of, 43; political career prior to governorship, 45; post-gubernatorial career, 53, 56; and prisons, 264; psychological rewards to, 279; residence of, 38; and tourism, 205; and women's vote, 302n41 (picture, 191)
Massachusetts, 215
Mathews, Jack, 85–86
Mathews, John E., 37, 138, 170, 192, 304n89, 308n62
Matthews, D. R. "Billy," 166
Mayo, Nathan, 106
Mays, Dannette H., 63, 64

Media, 156; and campaigns, 76–93 passim
Merit system, 117, 124, 125, 133, 135, 136
Merit System Council, 125, 136
Messer, A. L., 171
Methodists, 39, 71
Miami, Florida, 12, 17, 18, 24, 76, 80, 84, 87, 88, 91, 137, 138, 146
Miami Lakes, Florida, 87
Migrants, 194
Milk Commission, 120
Miller, J. Hillis, 252
Milton, William Hall, 62
Minimum Foundation Program (MFP), 195, 244–47, 251, 277, 294
Mining, 12, 13, 20, 259–60, 263
Miscegenation, 220–21
Mississippi, 75
Mixson, Wayne, 88
Moderates, on race relations, 77–81
Monroe County, Florida, 175
Morphet, Edgar, 245
Morris, Mick, 221
Motor Vehicle Commission, 120
Myers, Frederick, 62
Myrdahl, Gunnar, 13

National Advisory Commission on Civil Disorders, 234
National Association for the Advancement of Colored People (NAACP), 77, 80, 82, 222, 231, 233, 254, 288
National Education Association, 201–2
National Guard, 222, 234
Nativism, 66
Natural Resources, Department of, 218
Naval stores, 13, 260–61, 263
Naval Stores and Commission Company, 260
Neal, Claude, 222, 267
Neo-populism, in Florida, 92
Nevada, 15, 17, 206
Newark, New Jersey, race riot in, 234
New Deal, 34, 193
Newfoundland, 36
New Mexico, 11
New York, 285
Nixon, Richard M., 7, 84, 86, 93, 216, 229, 265, 284, 304n86
Non-Partisan League in North Dakota, 286
North Dakota. See Tabert, Martin
North Florida, 91, 173–75

Ocala, Florida, 77, 91
O'Connell, Stephen C., 256
Odham, Braily, 109, 142

Ohio, 199
Olustee, Florida, 260
One-party politics, 157
Organized crime, 76, 268–70
Orientals in Florida, 17, 223
Orlando, Florida, 12, 18, 24, 87, 256

Palatka, Florida, 12
Palm Beach, Florida, 12, 24
Panhandle, 24
Pardon and Parole Board, 104, 113, 121,
    123, 264
Pari-mutuel gambling, 192
Party politics, in Florida, 12–15, 52, 59–61
Patronage: effects on administrations,
    127–49, 153; gubernatorial, 105, 118–19,
    121, 127–47, 153, 169; and merit system,
    spoils system, 128, 129, 131, 135–36,
    139, 143–44, 147, 153
Peabody, Mrs. George Endicott, 232
Pearson, Rutledge, 233
Pensacola, Florida, 17, 256
Pensions, Board of, 121
Per capita income, 19–20
Perlmutter, Julius Jay, 138
Petteway, Raleigh, 72
Philadelphia Athletics, 37, 40
Phosphate mining. See Mining
Pinellas County, Florida, 177, 178
Planning director, state, 25–26
Polish immigrants, 17
Political parties, 157
Polk County, Florida, 72, 178
Pope, Verle, 175
Population. See Demography
Populism, 12–13, 26
Pork Chop Gang, 31, 77, 140, 157, 167,
    170, 175–78, 196, 216, 281, 284
Powers, Earl, 140 (picture, 109)
Powers of governor (1885 constitution),
    102–3
Presbyterians, 39
Presidency, compared to governorship, 115
Price, Ed, 207, 255, 266
Primaries, gubernatorial, 2, 13, 59–93
    passim
Prison Industries Reorganization Adminis-
    tration, 264
Prisons, 259–66, 270–71
Proctor, Samuel, 63
Progressivism, in Florida politics, 13, 61,
    64, 66
Prohibition party, 67, 136
Protestants in Florida, 17, 66–67, 70
Pruitt, Prentice, 225

Pupil Placement Law, 225–27
Public school segregation proposals, 224–30
Putnam Lumber Company, 263

Quality Education, Commission for, 202,
    247

Race relations: and governors, 6, 13–15,
    76–93, 234, 247, 259–63
Racing Commission, 120, 133, 138, 140,
    149
Raiford Prison, 262, 264
Range, Athalie, 230
Reagan, Ronald, 1
Real Estate Commission, 138
Reapportionment, in Florida, 31, 77, 111,
    127
Recession of 1973, 218
Reconstruction, 12–13, 59, 62, 102, 220–21,
    260, 280
Reconstruction Finance Corporation, 215
Referendum, use of, 159, 167–68
Regents, State Board of (formerly Board of
    Control), 82, 134, 240, 252–56
Reitz, J. Wayne, 252, 255–56
Reorganization, and governors, 102–14, 119,
    121–22, 139, 153
Republican party, 13, 18, 26–27, 75, 78,
    82–84, 86–90, 92–93, 107, 111, 125, 184,
    291, 296
Reynolds v. Sims, 178
Rich, A. F., 130
Riviera Beach, Florida, race riot in, 234
Road Board, State, 103, 120, 137
Road Department (DOT), 103, 120, 129,
    130, 131, 137, 138, 140, 142, 143, 147
Roads: as campaign issue, 24, 70, 78, 130;
    construction of, and prisons, 262–64
Robineau, S. P., 166
Rockefeller, Nelson A., 1, 118, 155, 179
Roebuck, W. J., 162, 166
Roosevelt, Franklin D., 6, 7, 73, 168, 193
    (picture, 198)
Roosevelt, Theodore, 220, 293
Rose, Walter W., 173
Rotary Club, 286
Rothman, Robert, 88
Rural-urban cleavage, 12, 24, 64, 75–77,
    81, 85–88, 91–93, 132

St. Augustine, racial crisis in, 232–33
St. Johns County, Florida, 178
St. Johns River, 36
St. Petersburg, Florida, 24, 91, 231, 242;
    race riot in, 234

Sales tax, 196–97, 199–200, 241–43, 295
Sanford, Florida, 12
Sarasota, Florida, 231
Sarasota County, Florida, 175
Schools: busing, 228–30, 234–35, 316n35;
    as campaign issue, 24, 76–78, 80–81, 83,
    85, 92; integration, 228–30, 234–35,
    316n28. See also Education; Segregation
Seaboard Railroad, 15
Secretary of state (of Florida), 105–6
Sectionalism, 24, 26, 75–93 passim, 132
Segregation, 220–22. See also Race rela-
    tions
Seminole tribes, 211
Senate, Florida: and reapportionment,
    172–79; as stepping stone to govern-
    orship, 45, 48–52
Serrano v. Priest, 318n34
Service economy, Florida as a, 19–22
Severance tax, on phosphates, 199
Sheats, William D., 136–37 (picture, 104)
Sheldon, Raymond, 162
Sherman, William Tecumseh, 62
Shevin, Robert, 87–88, 270
Shivens, Olin, 137
Sholtz, David, 15; administration of, 134,
    143; appointments by, 134, 143; appeal of,
    276; birthplace of, 38; cabinet of, 107;
    campaign of, 71–72, 90–91; character of,
    277; and Citrus Commission, 149; and
    depression, 15, 90–91, 193, 242–43, 292;
    and educational issues, 242–43, 257,
    288–89; ethics of, 291, 294; and legisla-
    tive relations, 284, 295; and lobbying,
    163; and lynching, 222–23, 267; and
    media, 164–66; military service of, 42;
    organizational memberships of, 43; politi-
    cal career prior to governorship, 48;
    post-gubernatorial career, 53; and reap-
    portionment, 172; religion of, 39; style of,
    282 (picture, 198)
Simpson, Bryan, Judge, 233
Simpson, Richard, 140
Sims, Arthur, 130
Sinclair, Henry, 162
Sit-ins, 230–31
Smathers, Bruce, 87
Smathers, Frank, 131
Smathers, George, 87, 131
Smith, Alfred E., 70, 150, 155
Smith, Buckingham, 210
Smith, David, 131
Smith v. Allwright, 73
Social services, 219
Social Welfare, State Board of, 138

Southern California, 34, 75
Southern Christian Leadership Conference
    (SCLC), 232–33
Southern Governors' Conference, 225,
    249–50
Southern Regional Education Board, 55,
    250
South Florida, 173–79
Spain, 155
Spanish-American War, 42
Special session, legislative, 159
Spenkelink, John, 266
Sports Fisheries and Wildlife, Bureau of,
    217
Squires, Robert, 87
Speaker, Florida House of Representatives,
    45, 48
Standard Accident Insurance Company, 129
Starke, Florida, 42
State Biracial Advisory Committee, 227
State Industrial Commission, 201
State Institutions, Board of Commerce of,
    104, 121
State National Guard, 201, 203
Stetson University, 40
Stevenson, Adlai, 7, 75
Stockton, John, 65
Stoner, Jesse B., 232
Sturkie Resolution, 66–67
Sullivan, Daniel, 268
Sullivan, James A., sheriff, 146, 268
Sutton, Ruth Linda, 138
Swan, Harry, 60, 75, 78
Swann v. Adams, 31, 111, 178
Swearingen, Van, 69, 203
Sweat Turpentine Company, 261–62

Tabert, Martin, 263
Taft, William Howard, 7
Tallahassee, Florida, 38, 39, 142, 231, 248
Talmadge, Eugene, 280
Tampa, Florida, 12, 18, 24, 36, 48, 76, 91,
    201, 203, 231; race riot in, 234
Tanzler, Hans, 87
Taxation, 5, 20, 187–200; revenues from,
    21–22
Teachers' strike (1968), 280
Tenure, for governors, 112, 117–18
Texas, 11, 73, 199
Thomas, J. H., 263
Thomas, Jerry, 86
Tillman, Ben, 280
Tomasello, Peter, Jr., 71
Tourism, 5, 11–12, 19, 21, 70, 73, 92, 196,
    200, 268, 314n61 (picture, 208)

Trafficante, Henry, 76

Trammell, Park: appeal of, 276; age at inauguration, 44; birthplace of, 38; campaign of, 65–66; character of, 279; and convict lease system, 262; economics of, 188–89; and educational issues, 241; and Everglades drainage, 210–15; family background of, 36; and highways, 206; and legislative relations, 162–63, 285; and lynchings, 221–22, 267; military service of, 42; occupation, 42; political career prior to governorship, 45, 48, 50, 52; post-gubernatorial careeer, 53, 55, 295; and prisons, 262; and progressives, 65–66; and race relations, 221–22 (picture, 104)

Trammell, Worth W., 70

Treasurer, of Florida, 103, 105, 106

Truman, Harry, 7, 55 (picture, 217)

Trustees of the Internal Improvement Trust Fund, 121, 210, 218

Tuberculosis Board, 120

Turlington, Ralph, 163

Turnpike Authority, 131, 140

Turpentine industry. *See* Naval stores

U.S. Army Corps of Engineers, 215

U.S. Crime Commission, 268

U.S. crime study, 269

U.S. House of Representatives, 48

U.S. Senate Commerce Committee, 232

U.S. Supreme Court, 178, 223–24, 227, 266

University of California, Berkeley, 269

University of Central Florida, 256

University of Florida, 40, 41, 138, 227, 249, 252–53, 255–56

University of South Florida, 251–52, 254

University of West Florida, 256

Urban-rural cleavage. *See* Rural-urban cleavage

Urban centers, in Florida, 17–18, 24, 77–78, 91

Vardaman, C. J., 280

Vietnam War, 180

Vietnamese immigrants, 17

Vocelle, James, 140

Volusia County, Florida, 72–73

Voter registration, 25–29, 31, 81, 304*n*79

Voting Rights Act of 1965, 73, 81, 228

Wackenhut, George R., 269–70 (picture, 267)

Wakulla County, Florida, 175

Walker, Mrs. Mary, 147

Wallace, George, 1, 7, 224, 228–29

War Labor Board, 202

Warren, Earl, 155

Warren, Fuller: administration of, 122, 130, 132, 134–39, 143, 154, 284, 294; ambition of, 34; appeal of, 275; appointments by, 132, 134–39, 143; birthplace of, 38; campaign of, 73–75, 77, 90–92; character of, 277; and contracts, 130–32, 134–35; and crime, 268; economics of, 90, 195–96, 295; education of, 40; ethics of, 291, 294; and executive agencies, 147–49; family background of, 37; and gambling laws, 146; labor policy of, 202, 204; and Ku Klux Klan, 170, 223; and legislative relations, 164, 169–70, 181–83, 285, 295; military service of, 42; as neopopulist, 92; organizational memberships of, 43; and patronage, 137–39, 148; political career prior to governorship, 45, 48, 52; post-gubernatorial career, 53; psychological fulfillment of, 279; and race relations, 77, 223; residence of, 38–39; and roads, 137–38; and sales tax, 196 (*see also* Sales tax); style of, 281; suspensions by, 145; tourism, 205–6. (picture, 165)

Washburne, William, 78

Washington, Booker T., 220

Water and Land Management in South Florida, Conference on, 217

Watergate, 180

Watson, J. Tom, representative, 192

Watson, Tom, attorney-general, 124–25

Watson, Thomas E., magazine editor, 66, 280

Welfare, 288–90, 296*n*4

Welfare Board, State, 136

Wesberry v. *Sanders,* 178

West, Thomas F., 162 (picture, 104)

West Palm Beach, Florida, 82, 84; race riot in, 234

White, Paul, 263

Whitehair, Francis, 72–73

Williams, Frank M., 146, 268

Williams, G. Mennan, 118

Williams, Jim, 50, 87, 152

Williams, T. Harry, 280

Wilson, Woodrow, 160, 188

Winn-Dixie Stores, 199

Wisconsin, 286

Wolfson, Louis, 137–38, 291

World War I, 42, 282

World War II, 15, 36, 44, 73, 108, 132, 195, 244, 248, 257, 264, 266, 279, 282

Wright, Frank, 138